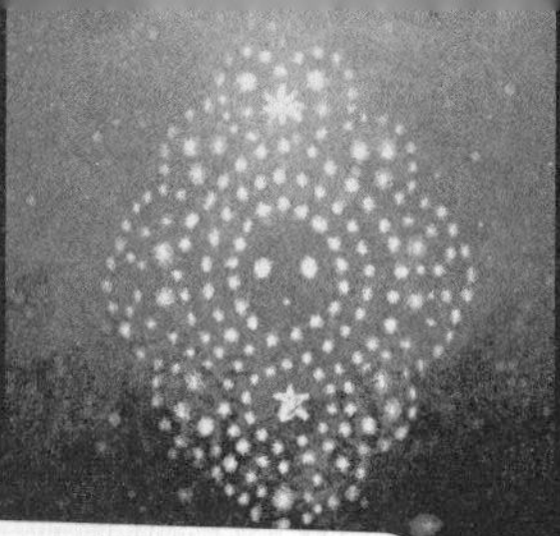

I loved the anime series *World Masterpiece Theater* from my childhood.* Beautiful scenery, life in faraway countries, tenderhearted people, upright heroes…

I used to dream of piloting a robot to defeat the bad guys, but I wanted just as much to stand firmly on the grassy hills of those worlds.

And always, before I knew it, I was spinning my own tales.

—Hiroyuki Asada, 2011

*The TV series *World Masterpiece Theater* presents anime adaptations of classic literature. —Ed.

Hiroyuki Asada made his debut in *Monthly Shonen Jump* in 1986. He's best known for his basketball manga *I'll*. He's a contributor to artist Range Murata's quarterly manga anthology *Robot*. *Tegami Bachi: Letter Bee* is his most recent series.

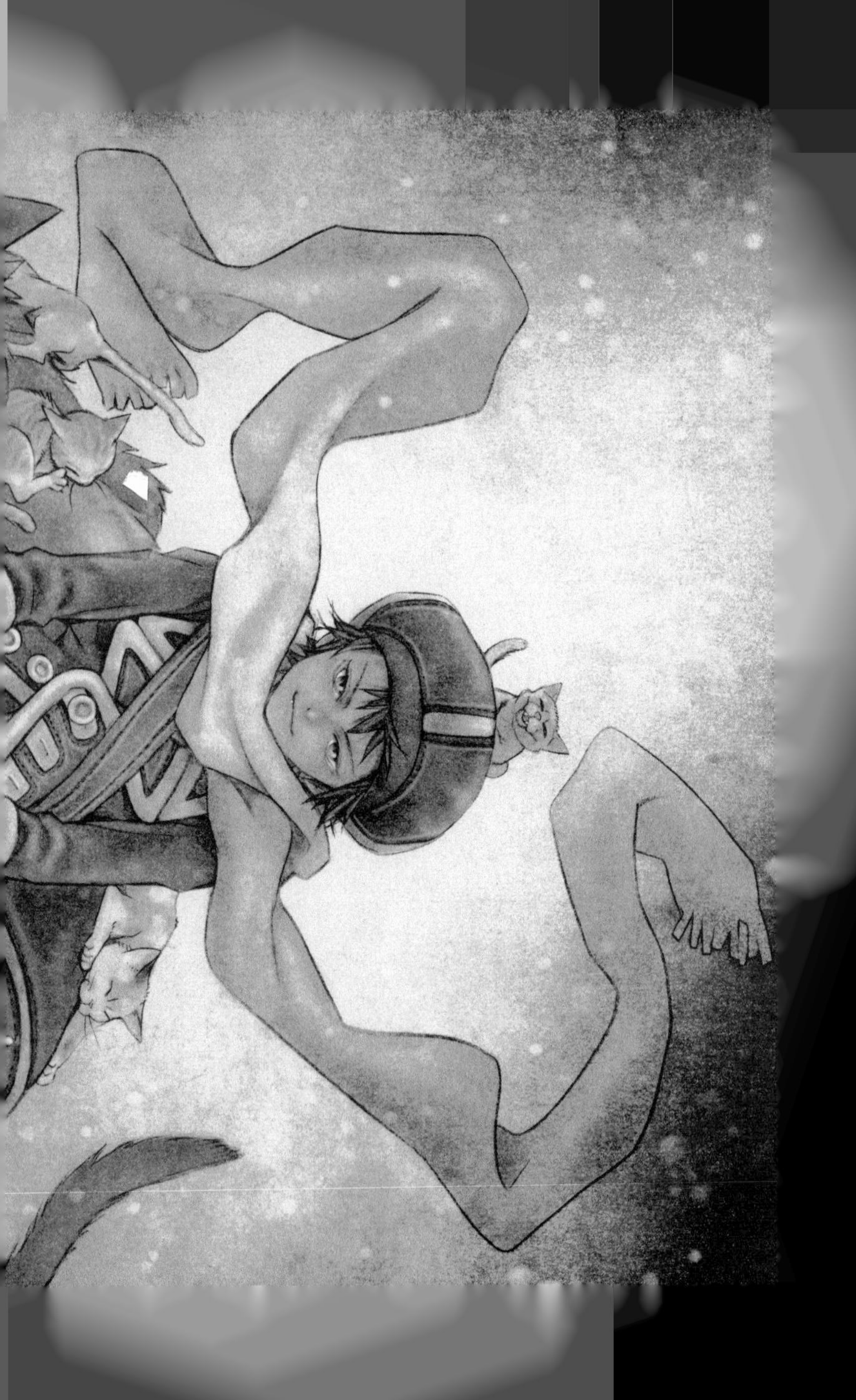

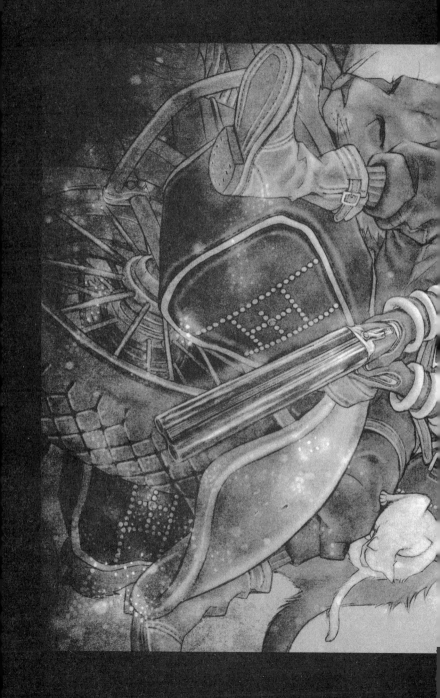

Tegami Bachi
LETTER · BEE

Volume 13

SHONEN JUMP Manga Edition

Story and Art by Hiroyuki Asada

English Adaptation/Rich Amtower
Translation/JN Productions
Touch-up & Lettering/Annaliese Christman
Design/Amy Martin
Editor/Shaenon K. Garrity

TEGAMIBACHI © 2006 by Hiroyuki Asada. All rights reserved.
First published in Japan in 2006 by SHUEISHA Inc., Tokyo. English
translation rights arranged by SHUEISHA Inc.

The rights of the author(s) of the work(s) in this publication to be so
identified have been asserted in accordance with the Copyright, Designs
and Patents Act 1988. A CIP catalogue record for this book is available
from the British Library.

Printed in the U.S.A.

Published by VIZ Media, LLC
P.O. Box 77010
San Francisco, CA 94107

10 9 8 7 6 5 4 3 2 1
First printing, May 2013

Tegami Bachi
LETTER · BEE

VOLUME 13

A District Called Kagerou

STORY AND ART BY
HIROYUKI ASADA

This is a country known as Amberground, where night never ends.

Its capital, Akatsuki, is illuminated by a man-made sun. The farther one strays from the capital, the weaker the light. The Yuusari region is cast in twilight; the Yodaka region survives only on pale moonlight.

Letter Bee Gauche Suede and young Lag Seeing meet in the Yodaka region—a postal worker and the "letter" he must deliver. In their short time together, they form a fast friendship, but when the journey ends, each departs down his own path. Gauche longs to become Head Bee, while Lag himself wants to be a Letter Bee, like Gauche.

In time, Lag becomes a Letter Bee. But Gauche has lost his *heart* and become a marauder named Noir, working for the rebel organization Reverse.

Largo Lloyd, former head of the Beehive, meets with Lawrence, the ringleader of Reverse, claiming to seek "revolution." He hands over a book containing the secret history of the Amberground government. What is his intention? Meanwhile, the Bees are dispatched to fight off a massively powerful Gaichuu called Cabernet. Lag manages to shoot Cabernet down, but in the process his teammate, Lily, loses her *heart*.

As the Bees watch in horror, Cabernet rises again with an ominous laugh...

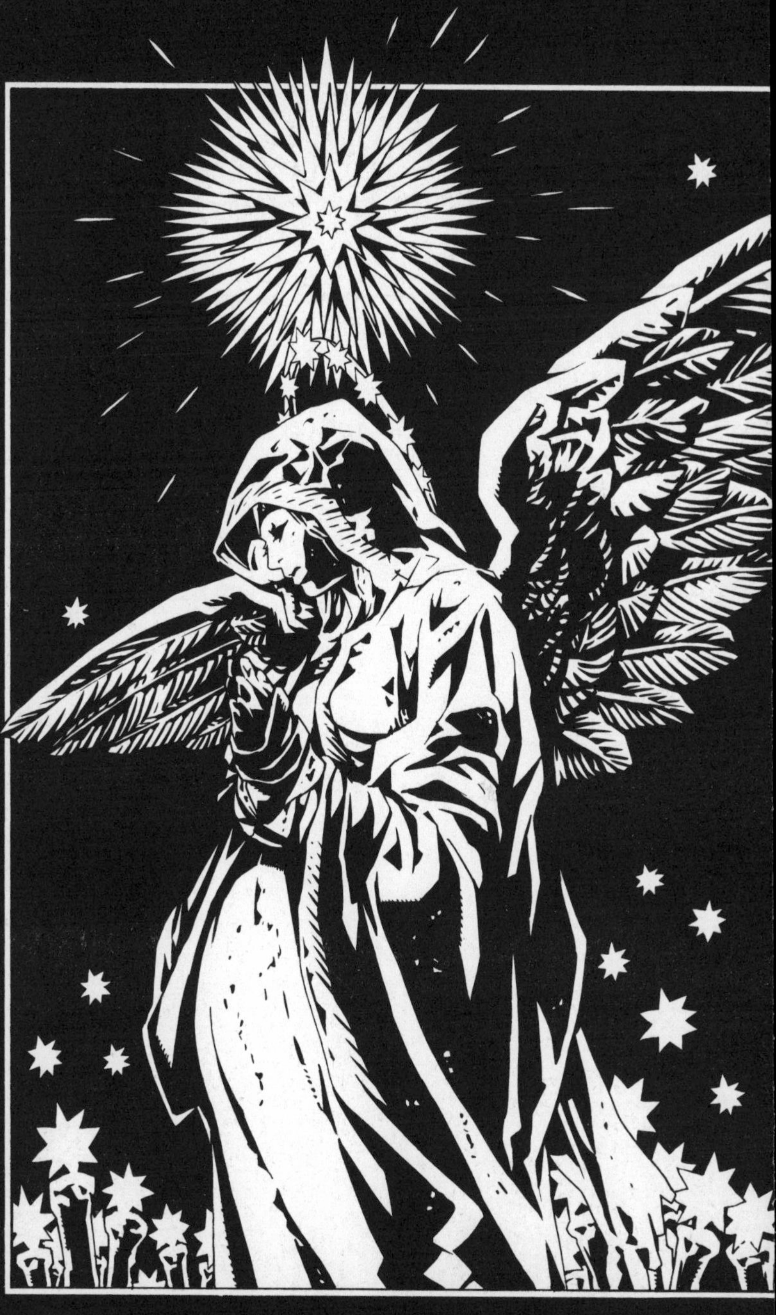

LARGO LLOYD
Ex-Beehive Director

ARIA LINK
Section Chief of the
Dead Letter Office

STEAK
Niche's...
live bait?

LAG SEEING
Letter Bee

NICHE
Lag's
Dingo

DR. THUNDERLAND, JR.
Member of the AG
Biological Science
Advisory Board,
Third Division and
head doctor at the
Beehive

CONNOR KLUFF
Letter Bee

GUS
Connor's Dingo

ZAZIE
Letter Bee

WASIOLKA
Zazie's Dingo

JIGGY PEPPER
Express Delivery
Letter Bee

HARRY
Jiggy's Dingo

MOC SULLIVAN
Letter Bee

CHALYBS GARRARD
Inspector and
ex-Letter Bee

HAZEL VALENTINE
Inspector and
Garrard's ex-Dingo

LAWRENCE
The ringleader of
Reverse

ZEAL
Marauder for
Reverse

NOIR (FORMERLY
GAUCHE SUEDE)
Marauder for
Reverse and an
ex–Letter Bee

RODA
Noir's Dingo

SYLVETTE SUEDE
Gauche's Sister

ANNE SEEING
Lag's Mother
(Missing)

Tegami Bachi
LETTER · BEE

VOLUME 13
A District Called Kagerou

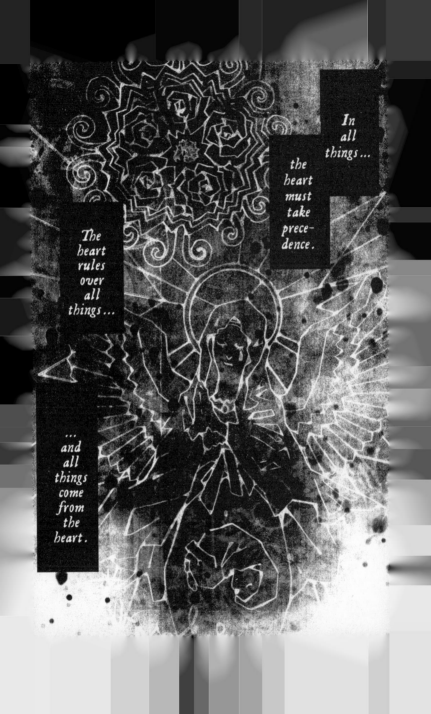

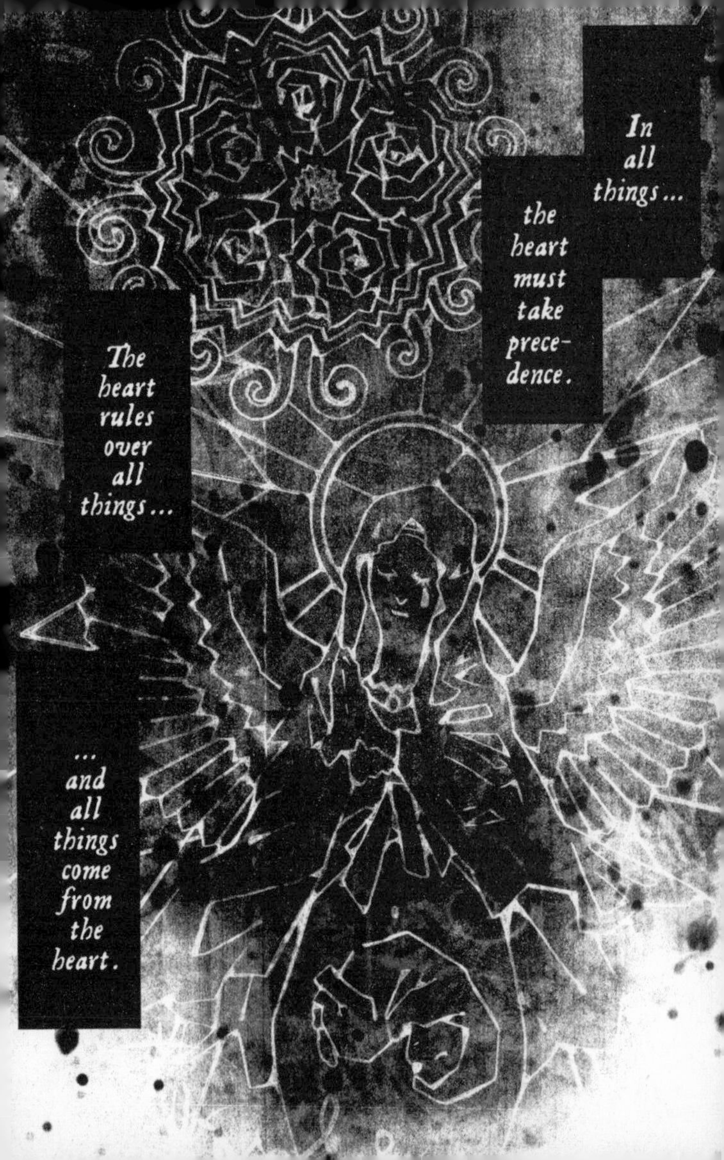
In all things...
the heart must take precedence.
The heart rules over all things...
... and all things come from the heart.

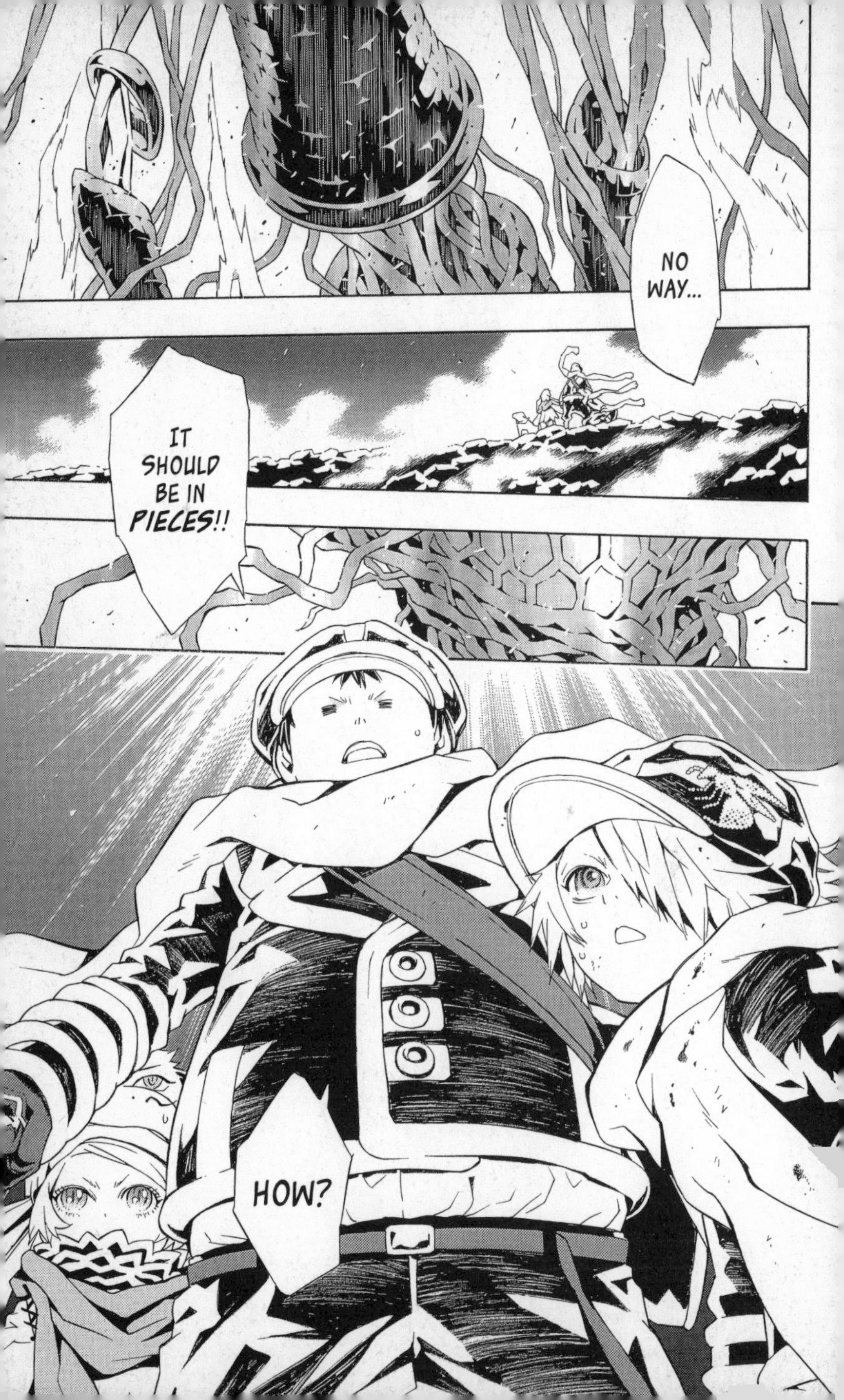
NO WAY...
IT SHOULD BE IN PIECES!!
HOW?

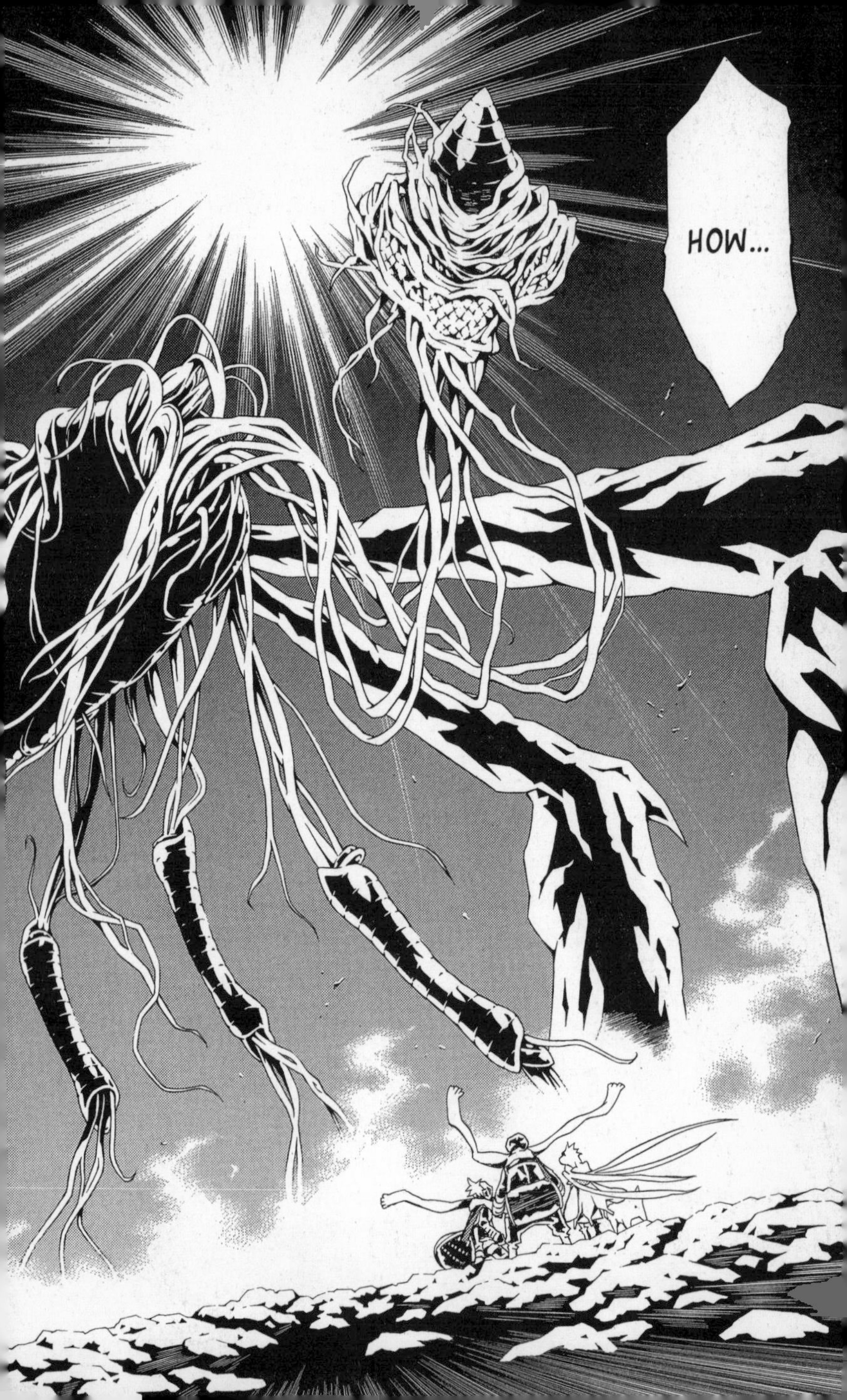
HOW...

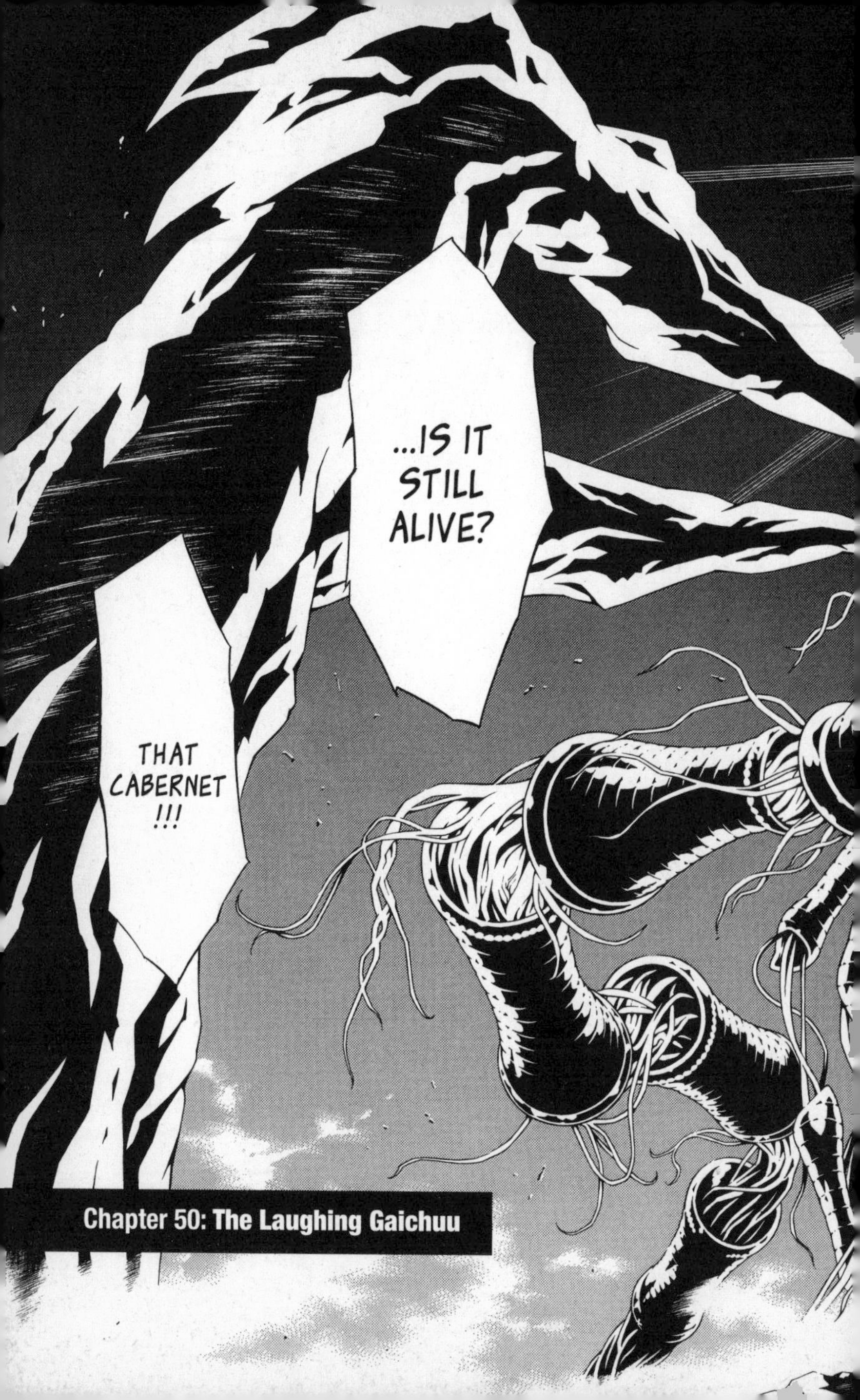
...IS IT STILL ALIVE?
THAT CABERNET !!!

Chapter 50: The Laughing Gaichuu

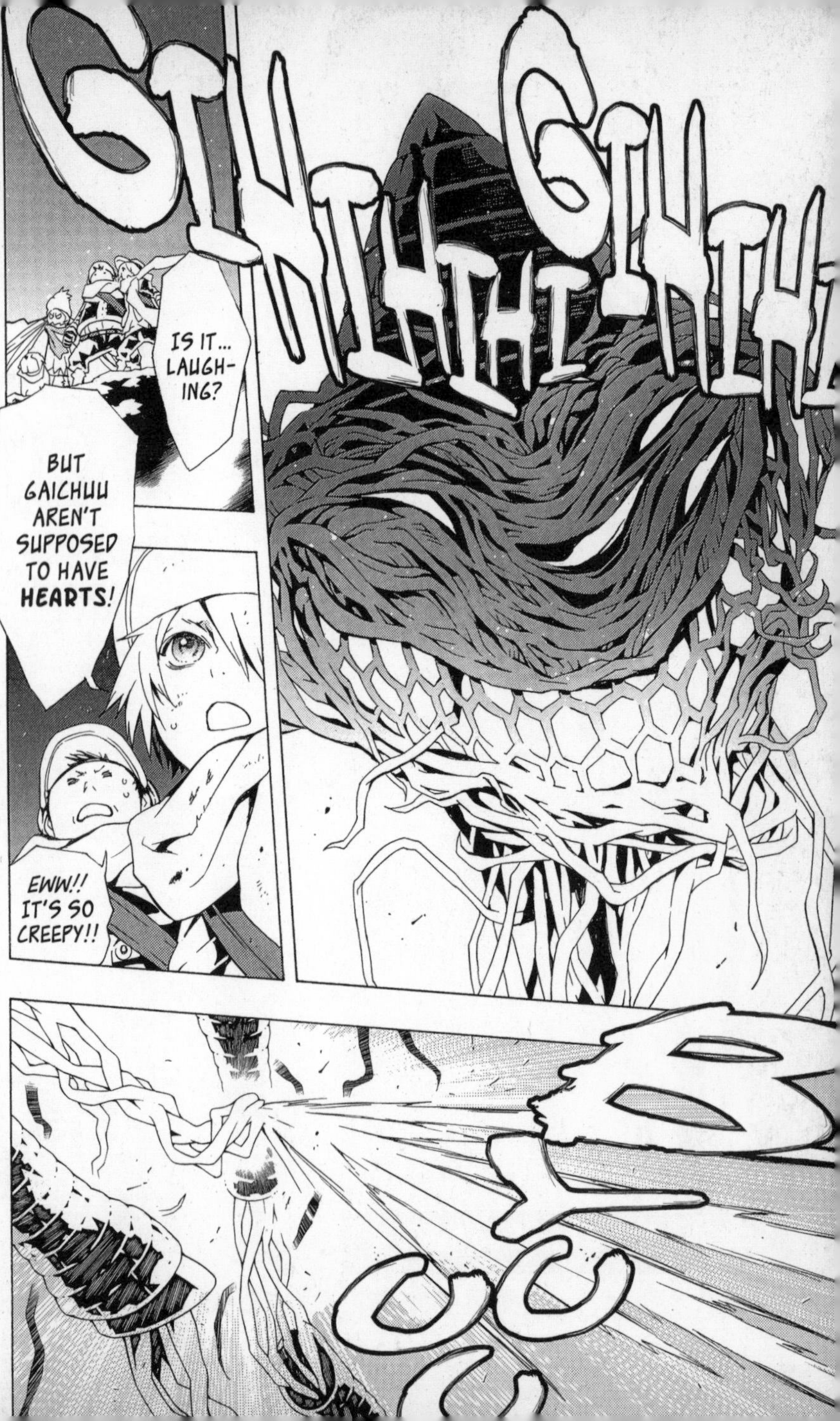
GIHIHI-GIHIHI
IS IT... LAUGHING?
BUT GAICHUU AREN'T SUPPOSED TO HAVE HEARTS!
EWW!! IT'S SO CREEPY!!

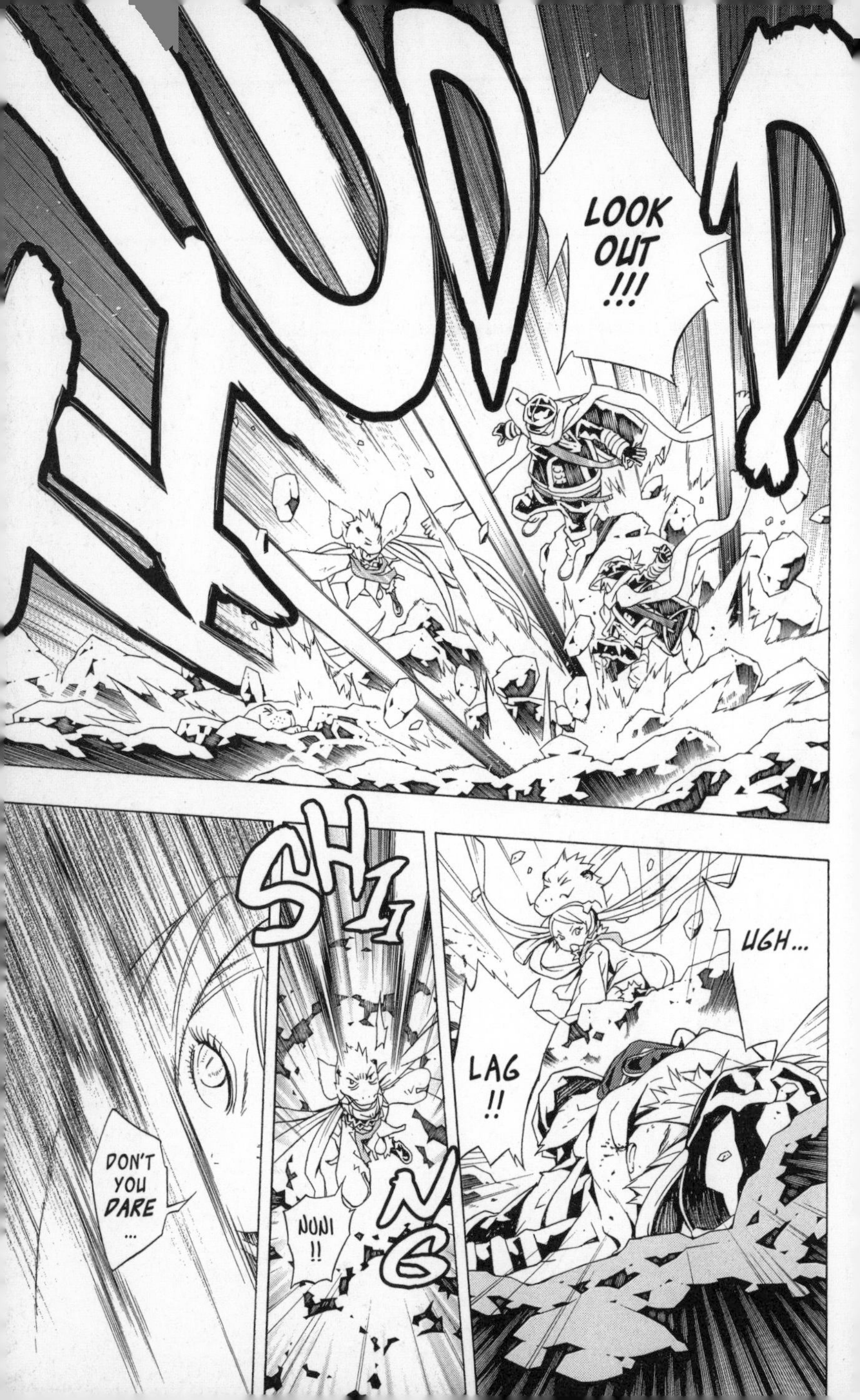
LOOK OUT !!!
UGH...
LAG !!
NUNI !!
DON'T YOU DARE ...

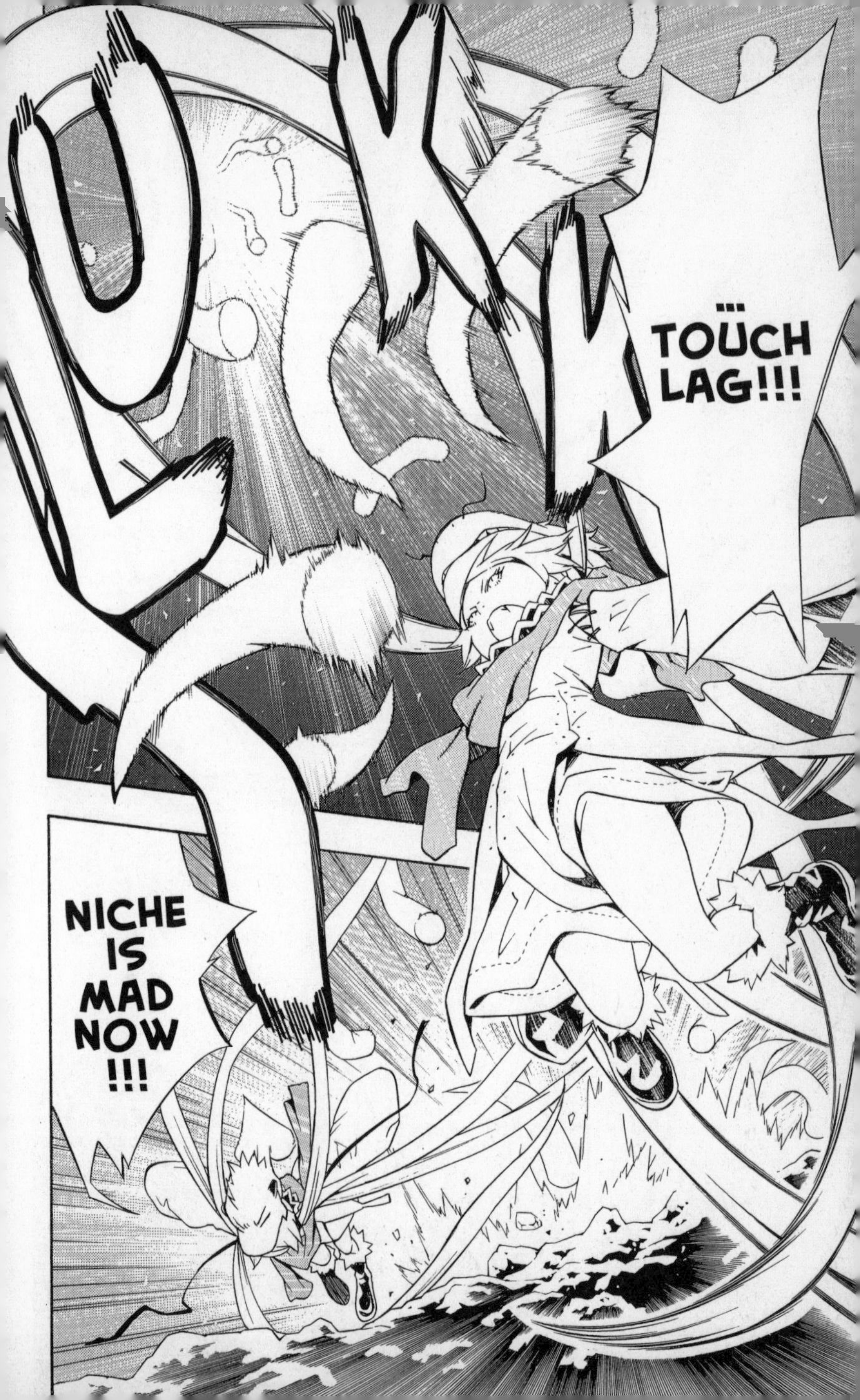
...TOUCH LAG!!!
NICHE IS MAD NOW!!!

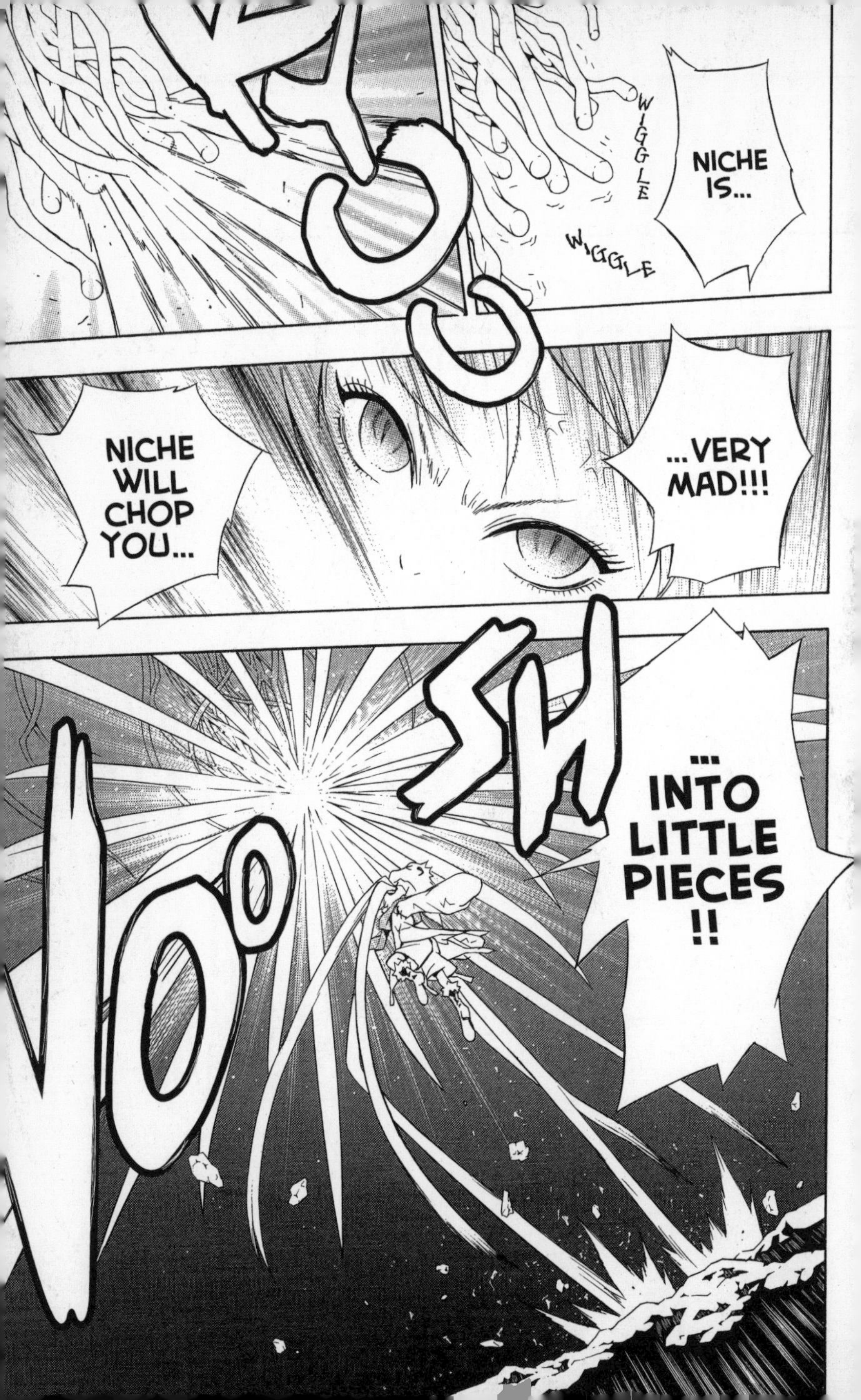
NICHE IS...
WIGGLE
WIGGLE
...VERY MAD!!!
NICHE WILL CHOP YOU...
...INTO LITTLE PIECES!!

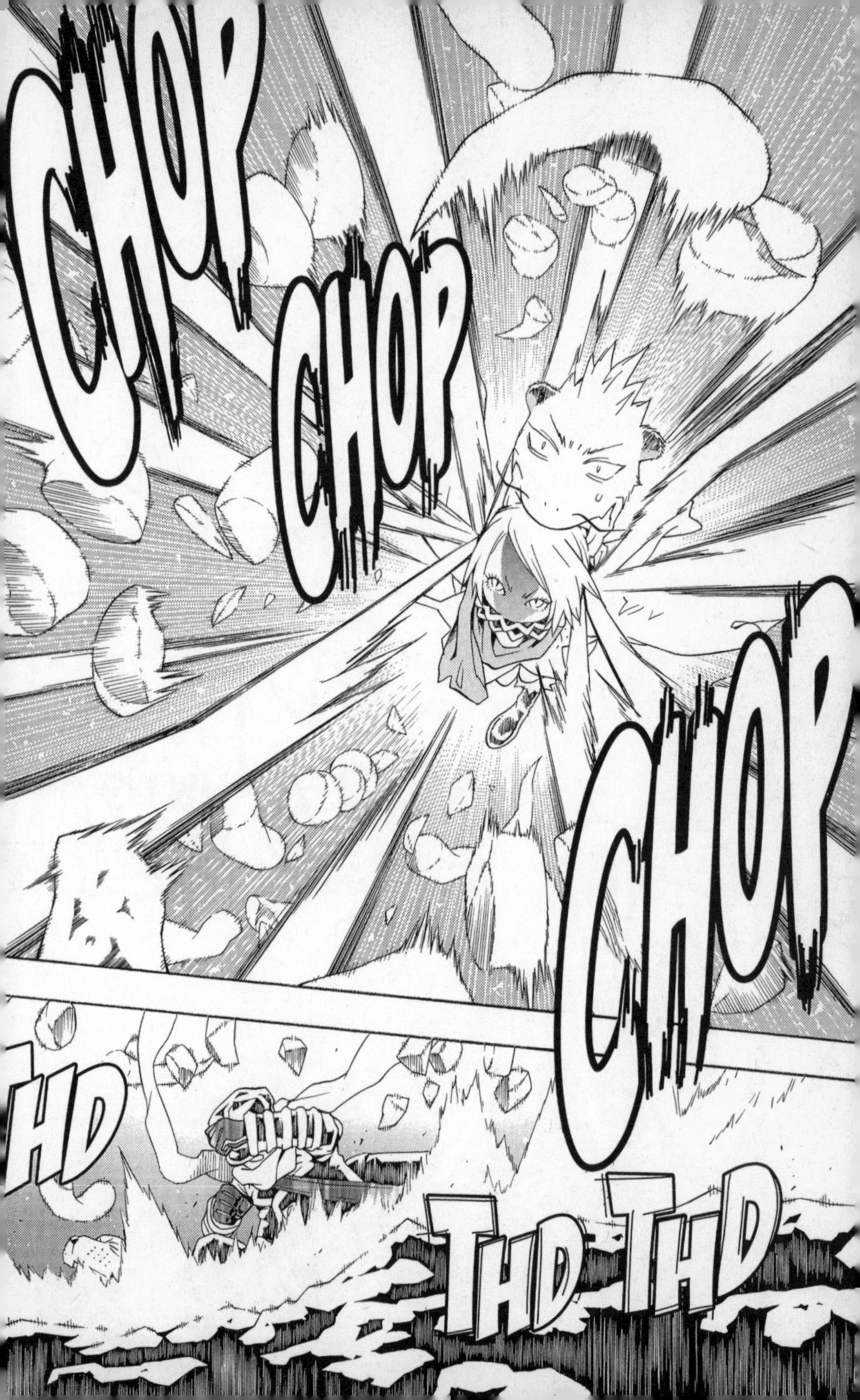
CHOP
CHOP
CHOP
THD THD
HD

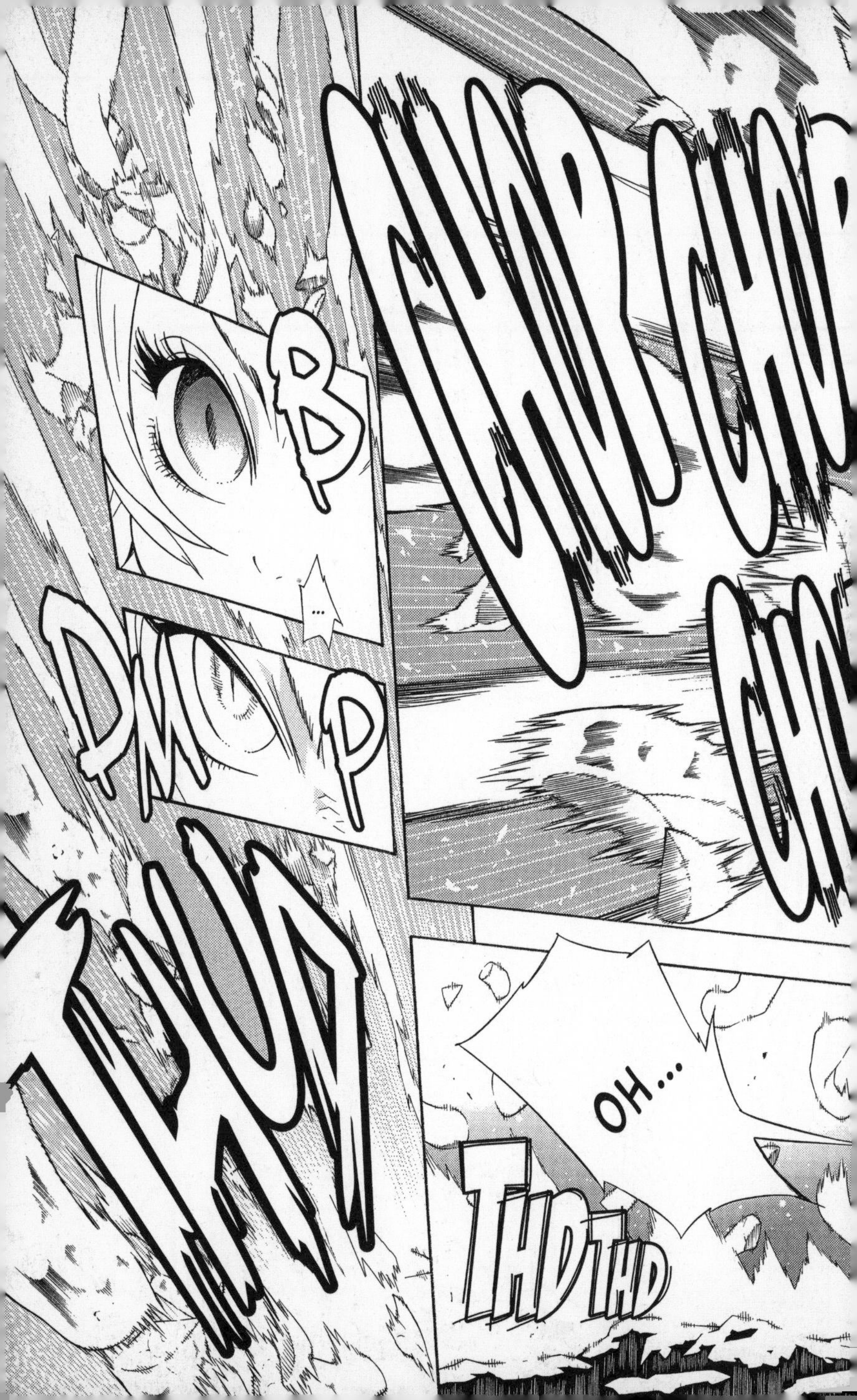
CHOP CHOP
CHOP
...
DMP
THUD
OH...
THD THD

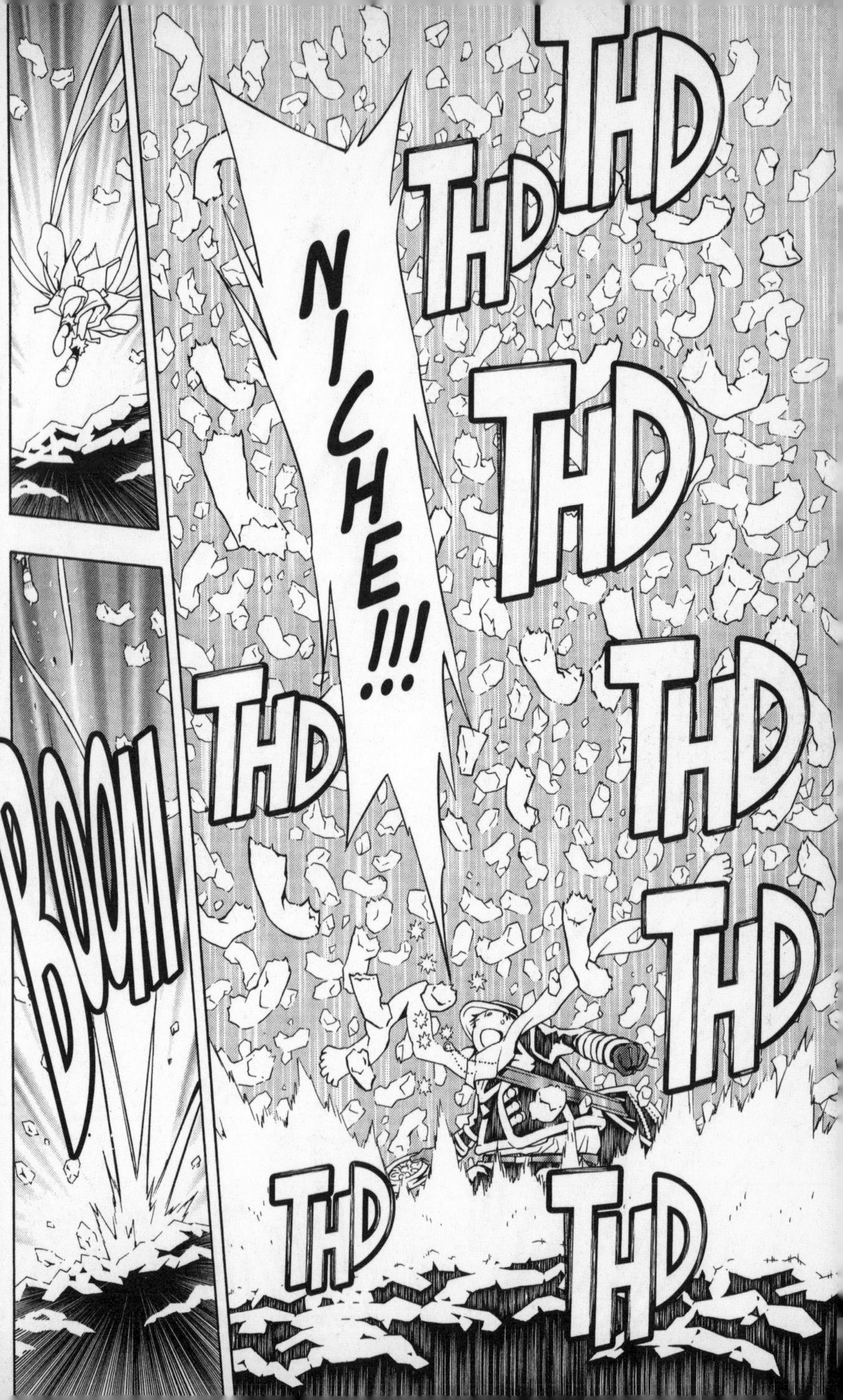

THD
THD
NICHE!!!
THD
THD
THD
THD
THD
THD
BOOM

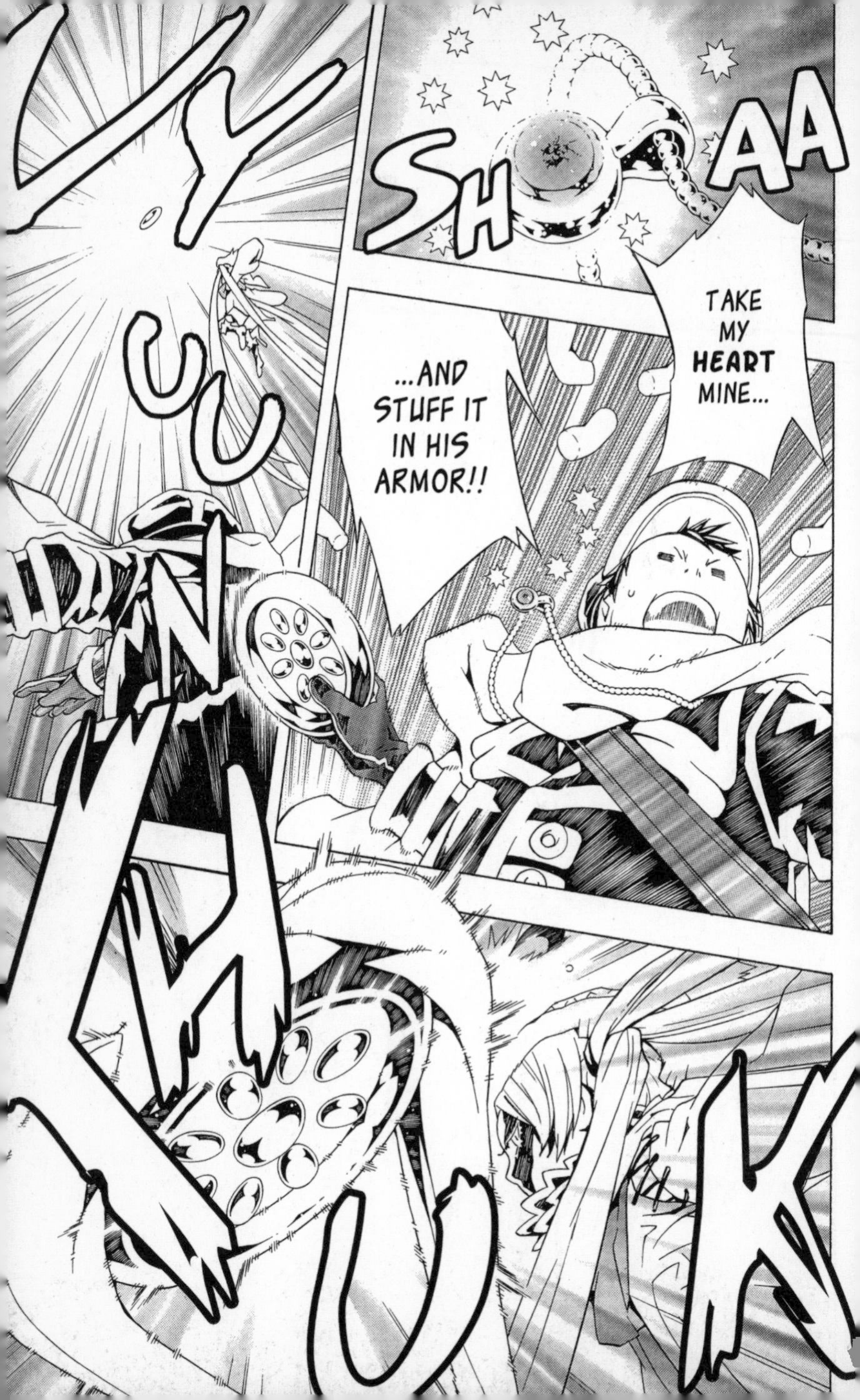
SHAA
TAKE MY HEART MINE...
...AND STUFF IT IN HIS ARMOR!!

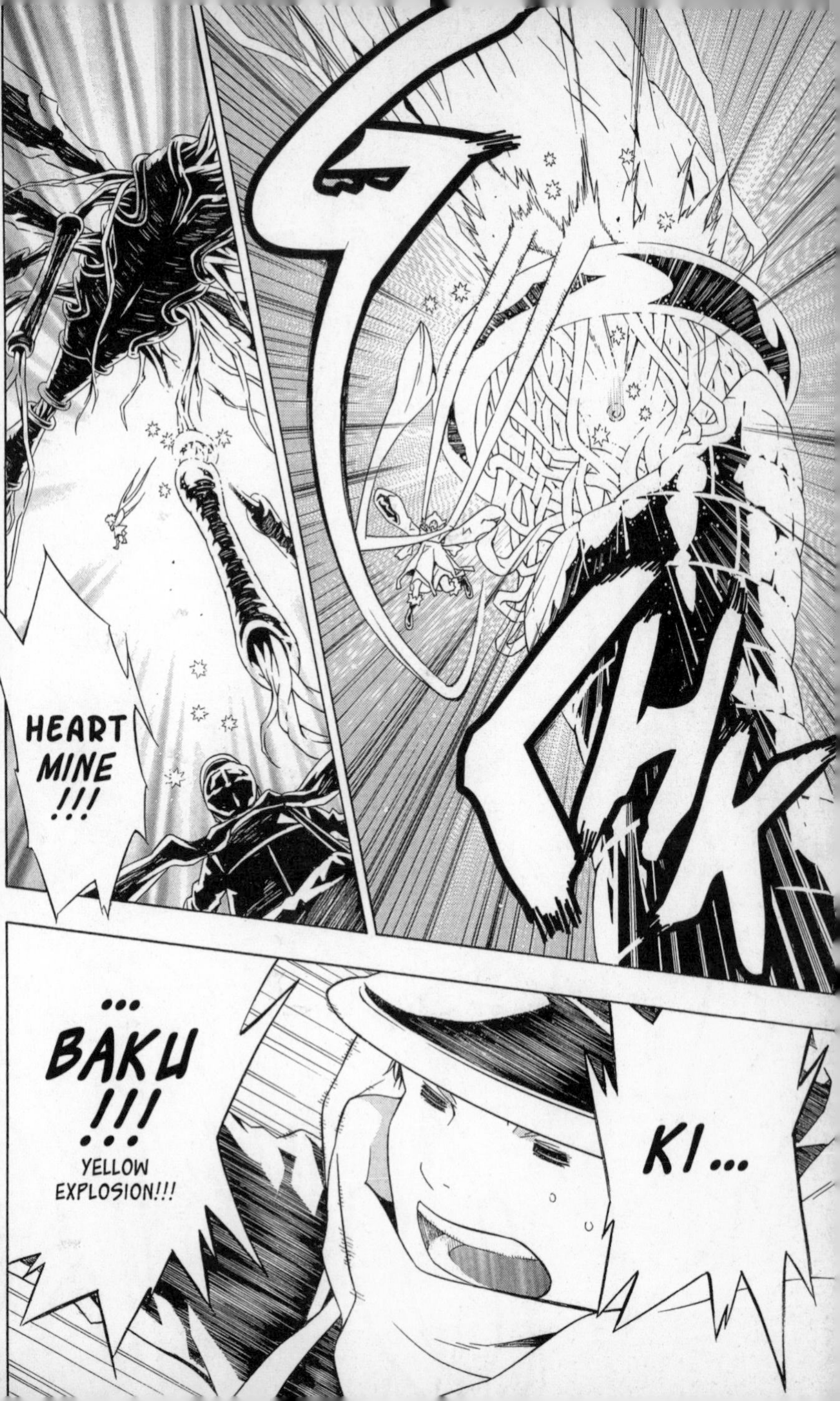
HEART MINE !!!
KI...
...BAKU !!! ...
YELLOW EXPLOSION!!!

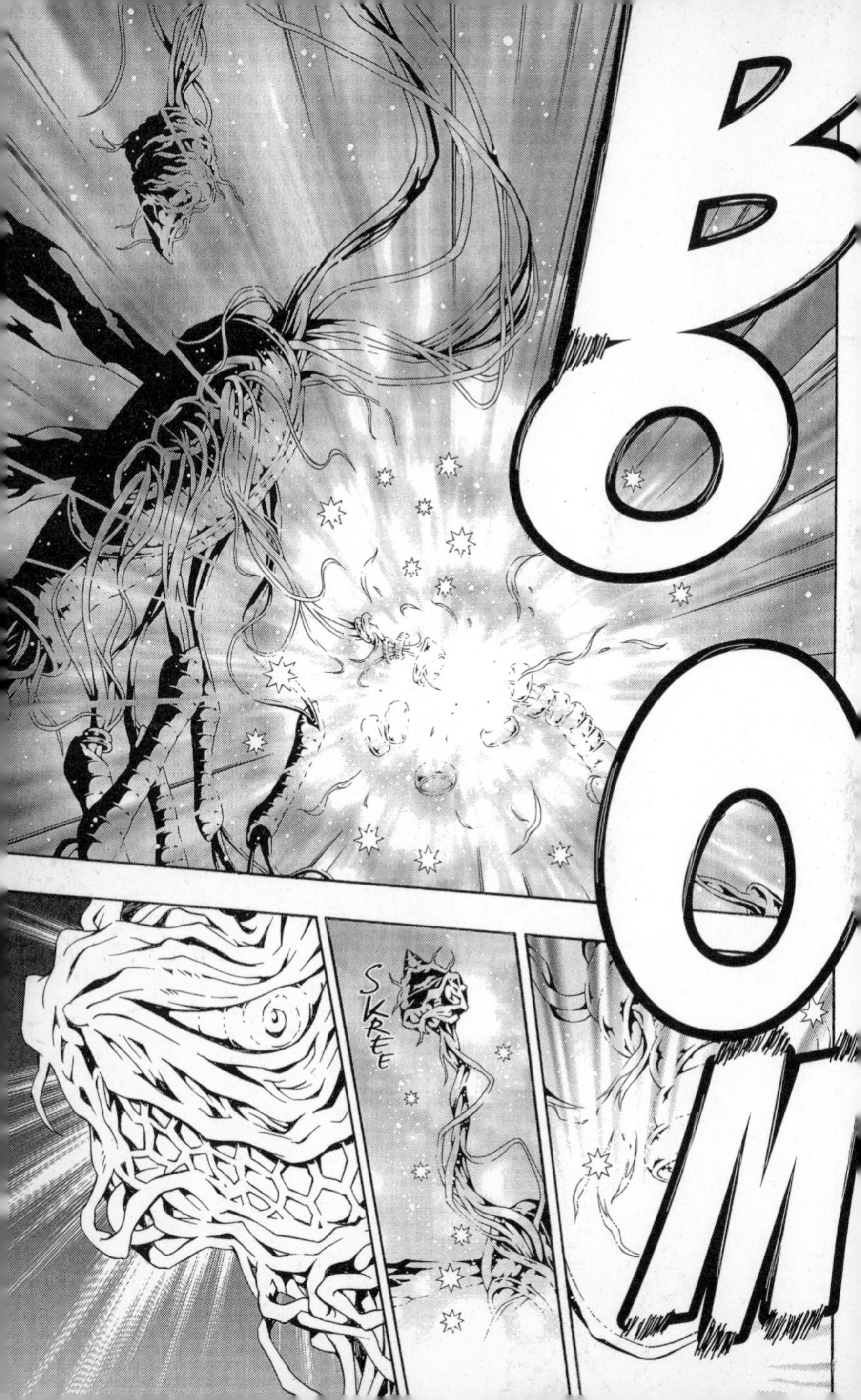
SKREE

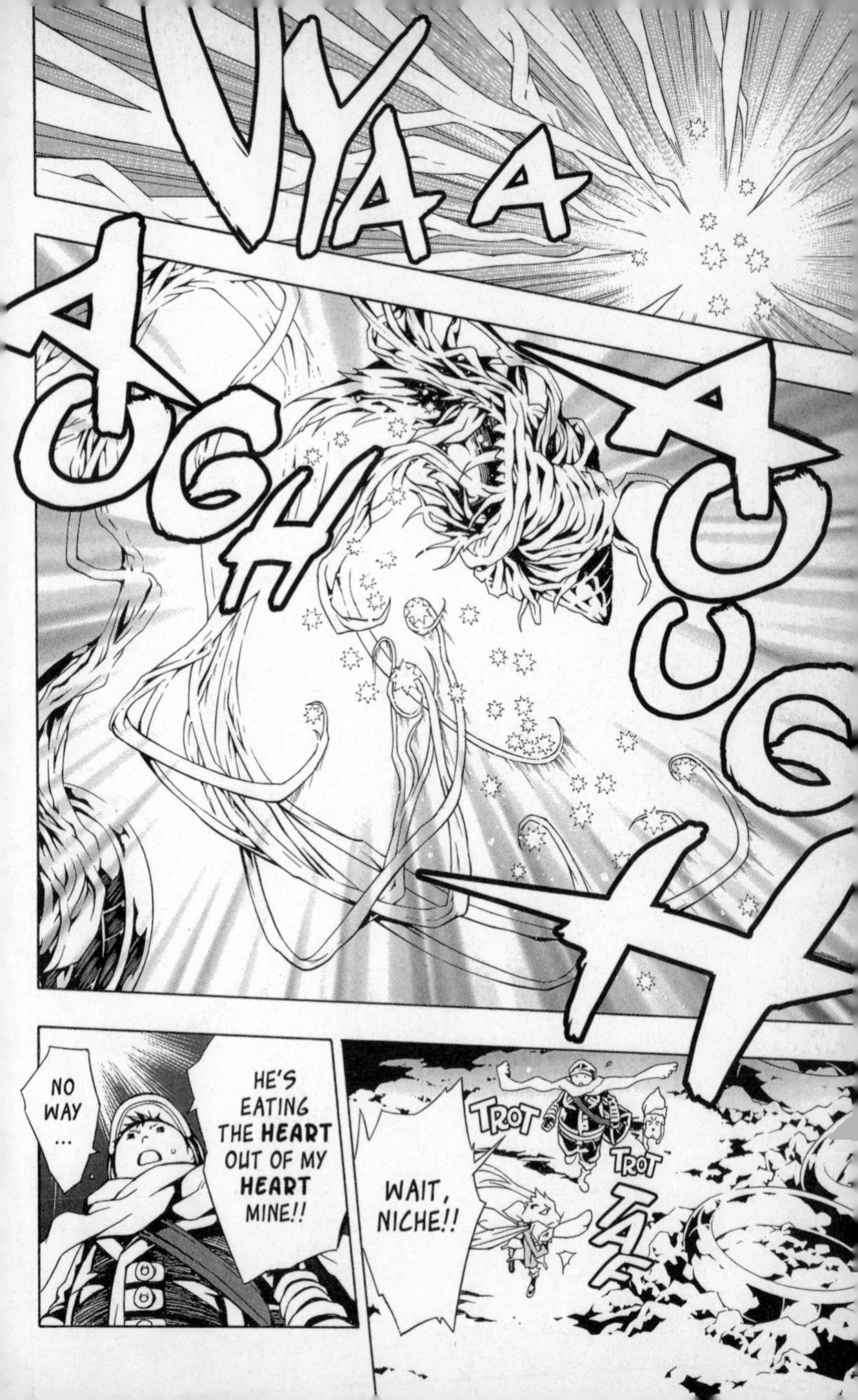
VYAA A
AUGH
AUUG
WAIT, NICHE!!
TROT
TROT
TAF
HE'S EATING THE **HEART** OUT OF MY **HEART MINE**!!
NO WAY ...

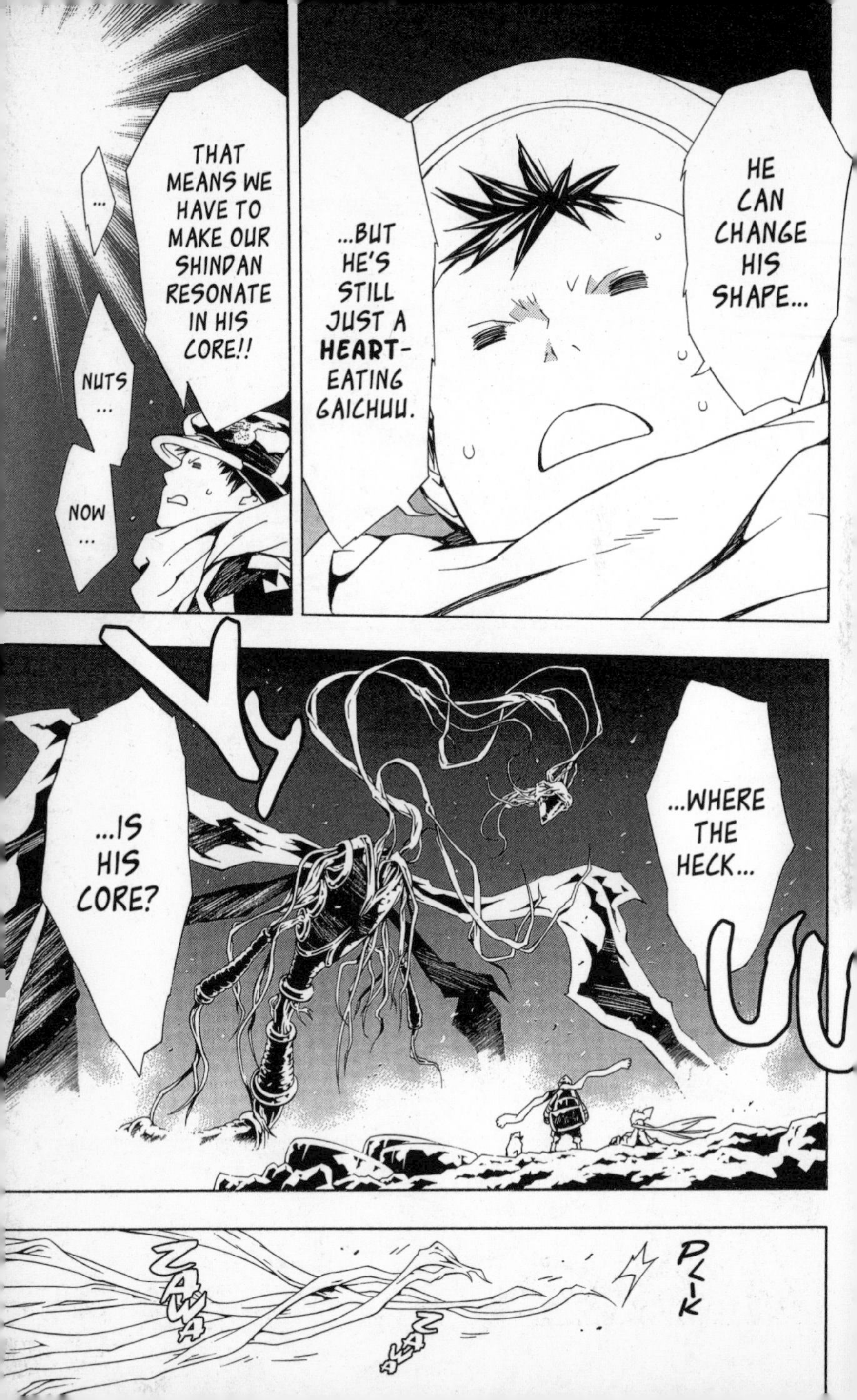
HE CAN CHANGE HIS SHAPE...
...BUT HE'S STILL JUST A HEART-EATING GAICHUU.
THAT MEANS WE HAVE TO MAKE OUR SHINDAN RESONATE IN HIS CORE!!
...
NUTS...
NOW...
...WHERE THE HECK...
...IS HIS CORE?
PLIK
ZAWA
ZAWA

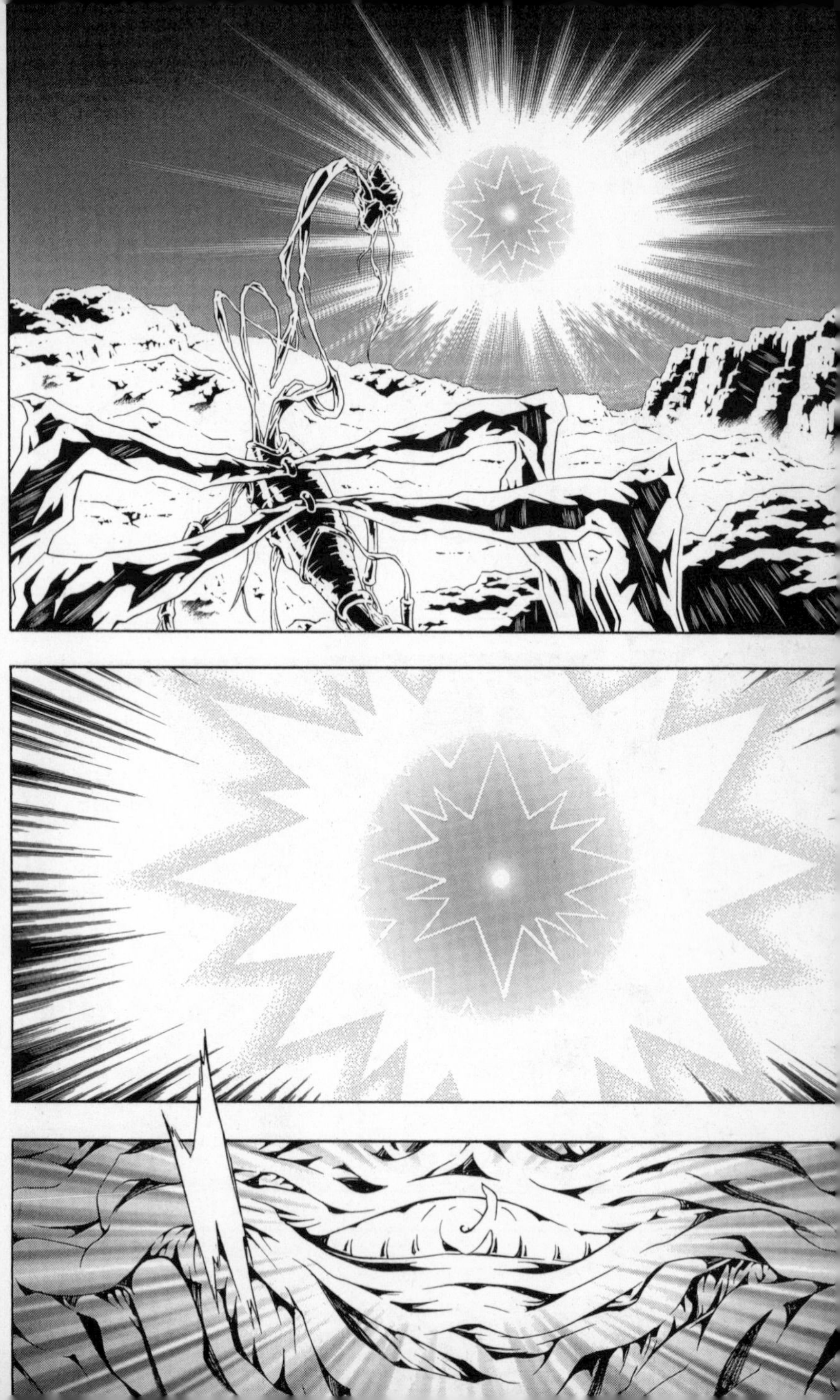

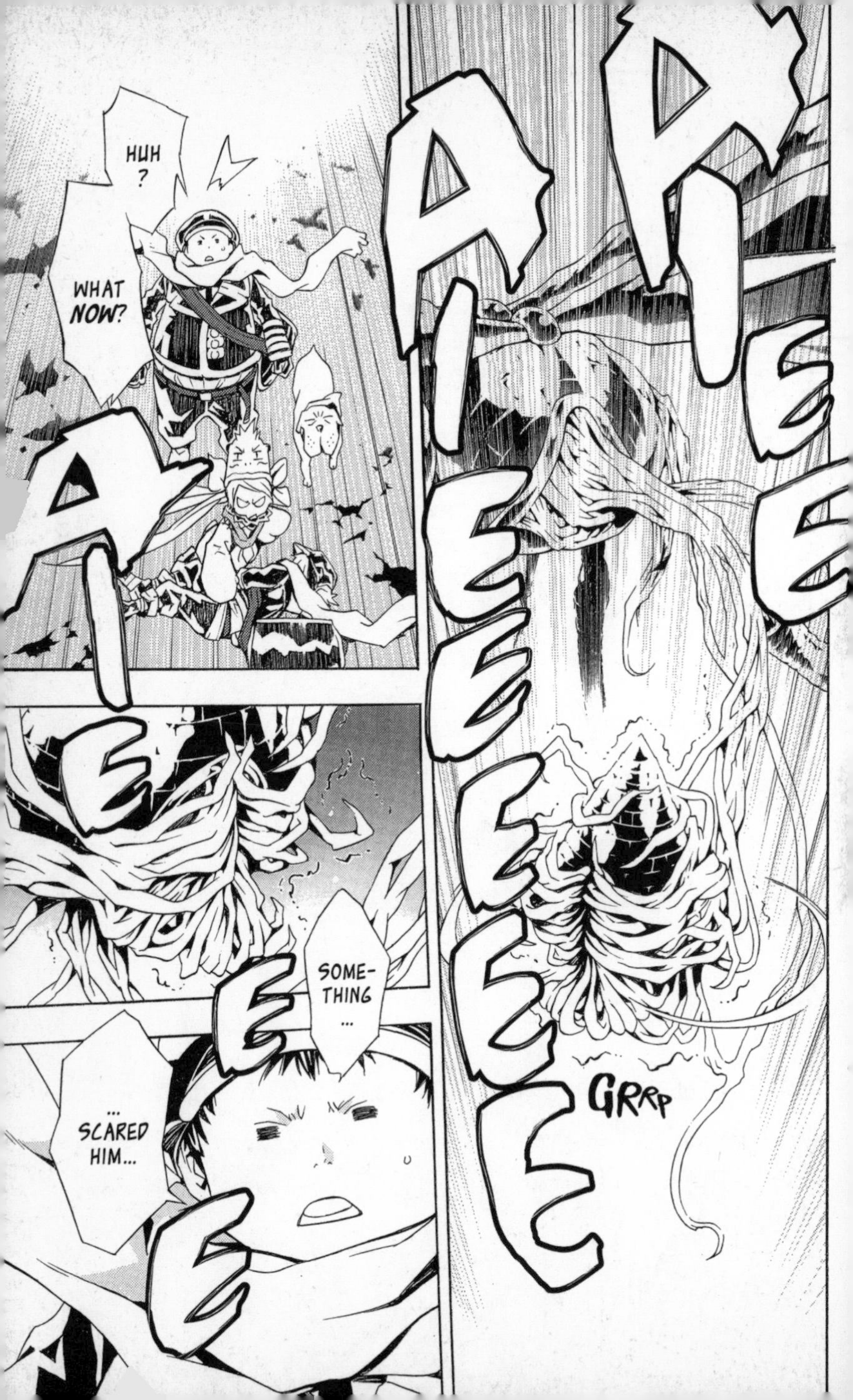
GRRP
HUH?
WHAT NOW?
SOME-THING...
...SCARED HIM...

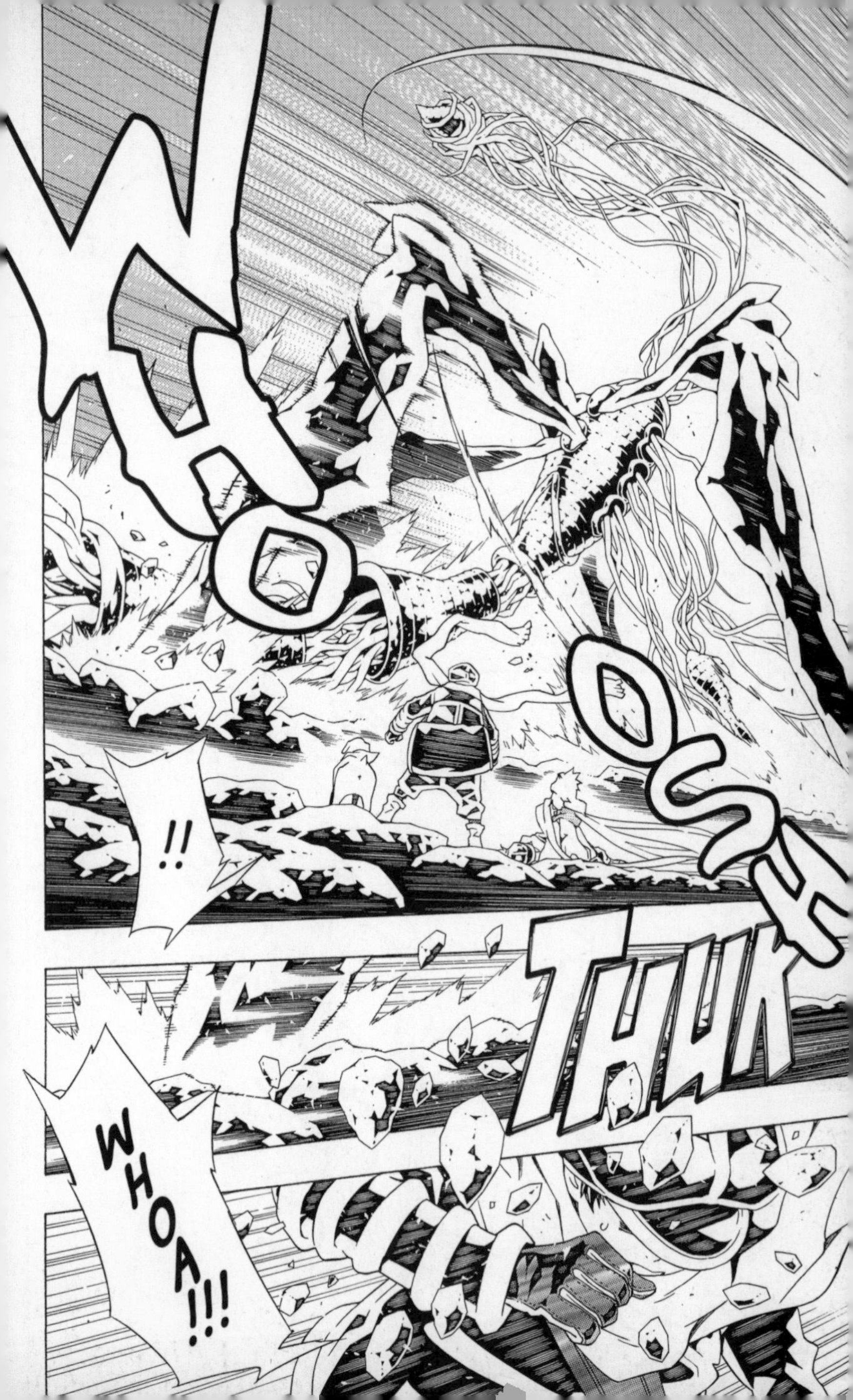
WHOOSH
!!
THUK
WHOA!!!

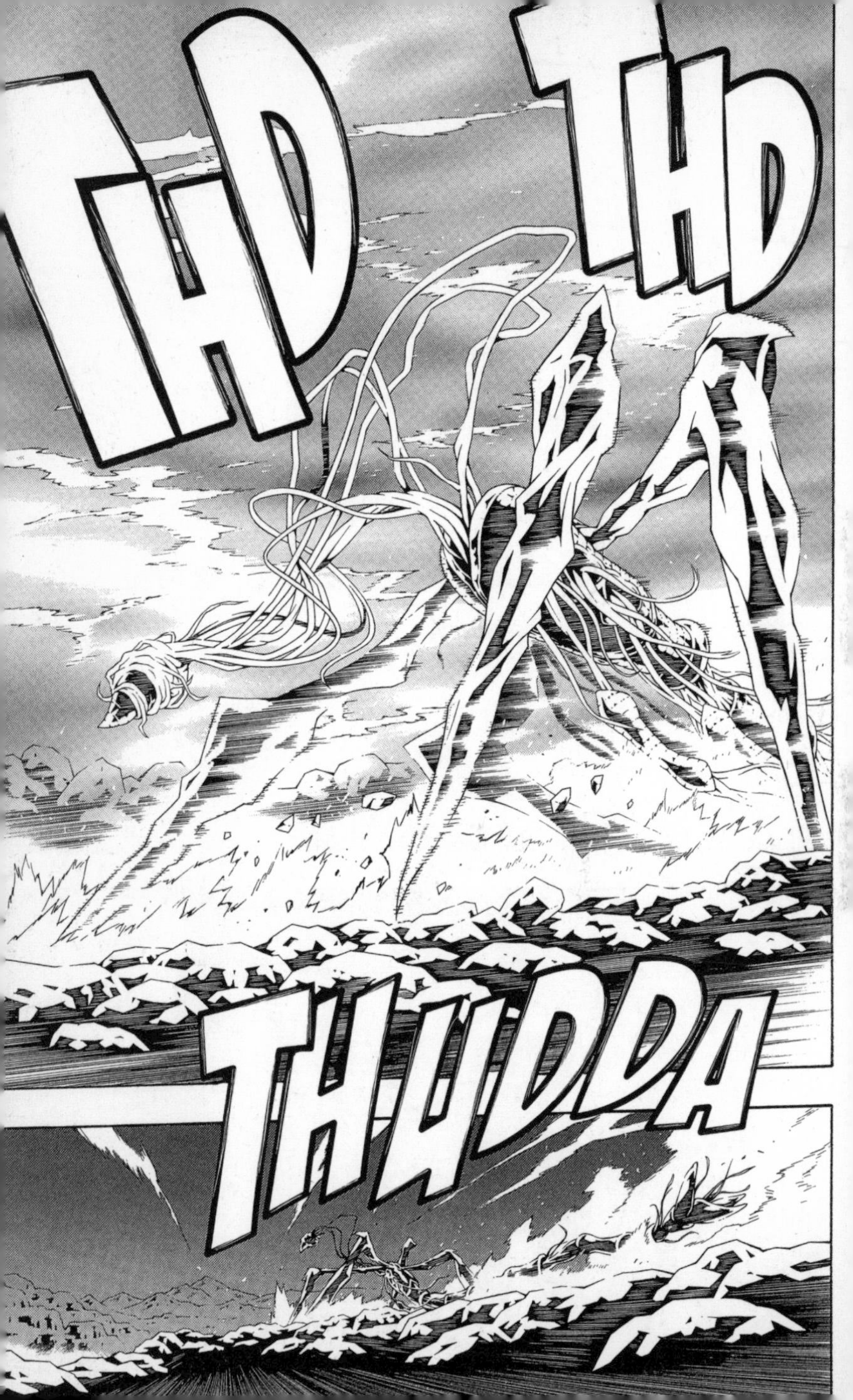
THD
THD
THUDDA

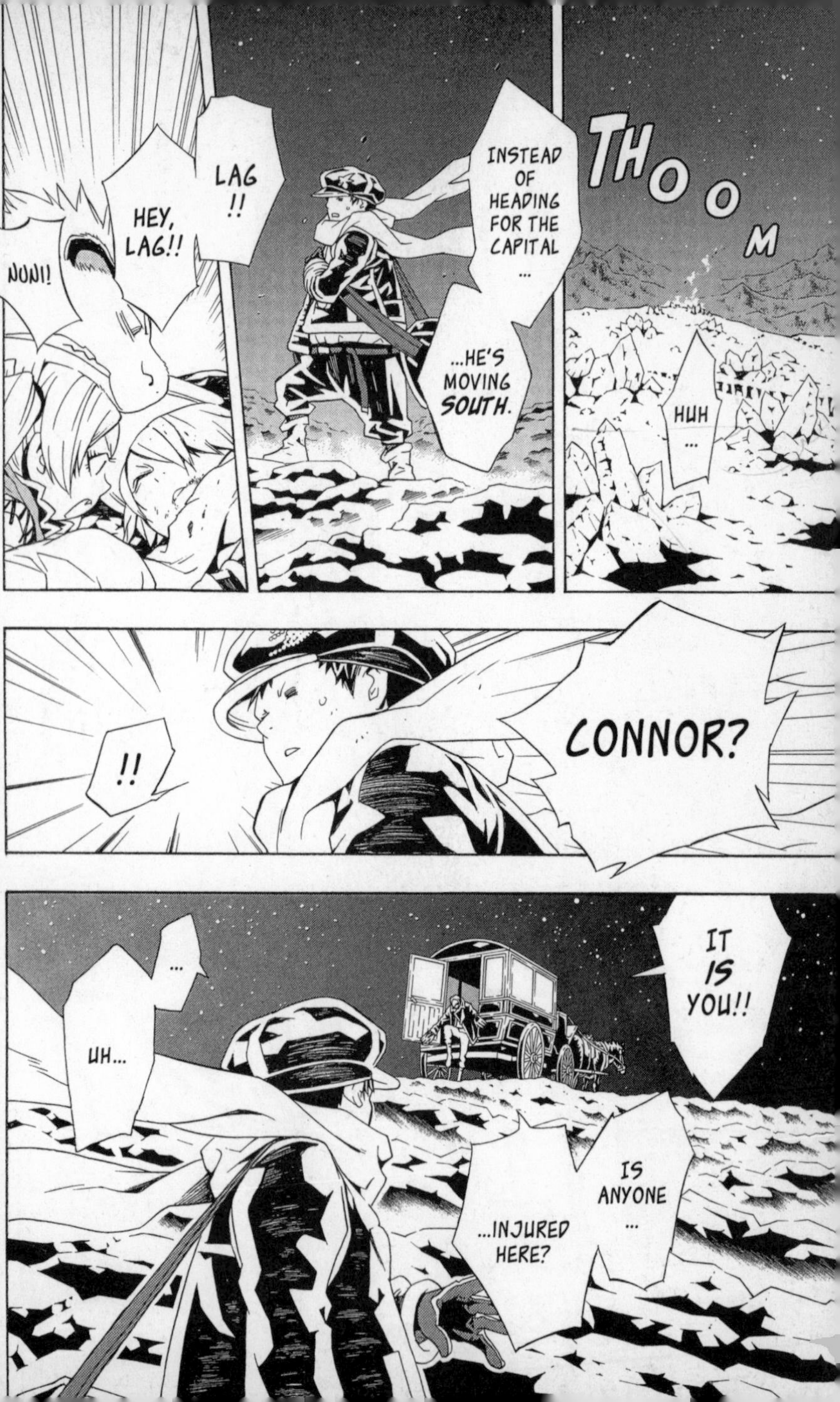
THOOOM
HUH...
INSTEAD OF HEADING FOR THE CAPITAL...
...HE'S MOVING SOUTH.
LAG!!
HEY, LAG!!
NUNI!
CONNOR?
!!
IT IS YOU!!
IS ANYONE...
...INJURED HERE?
...
UH...

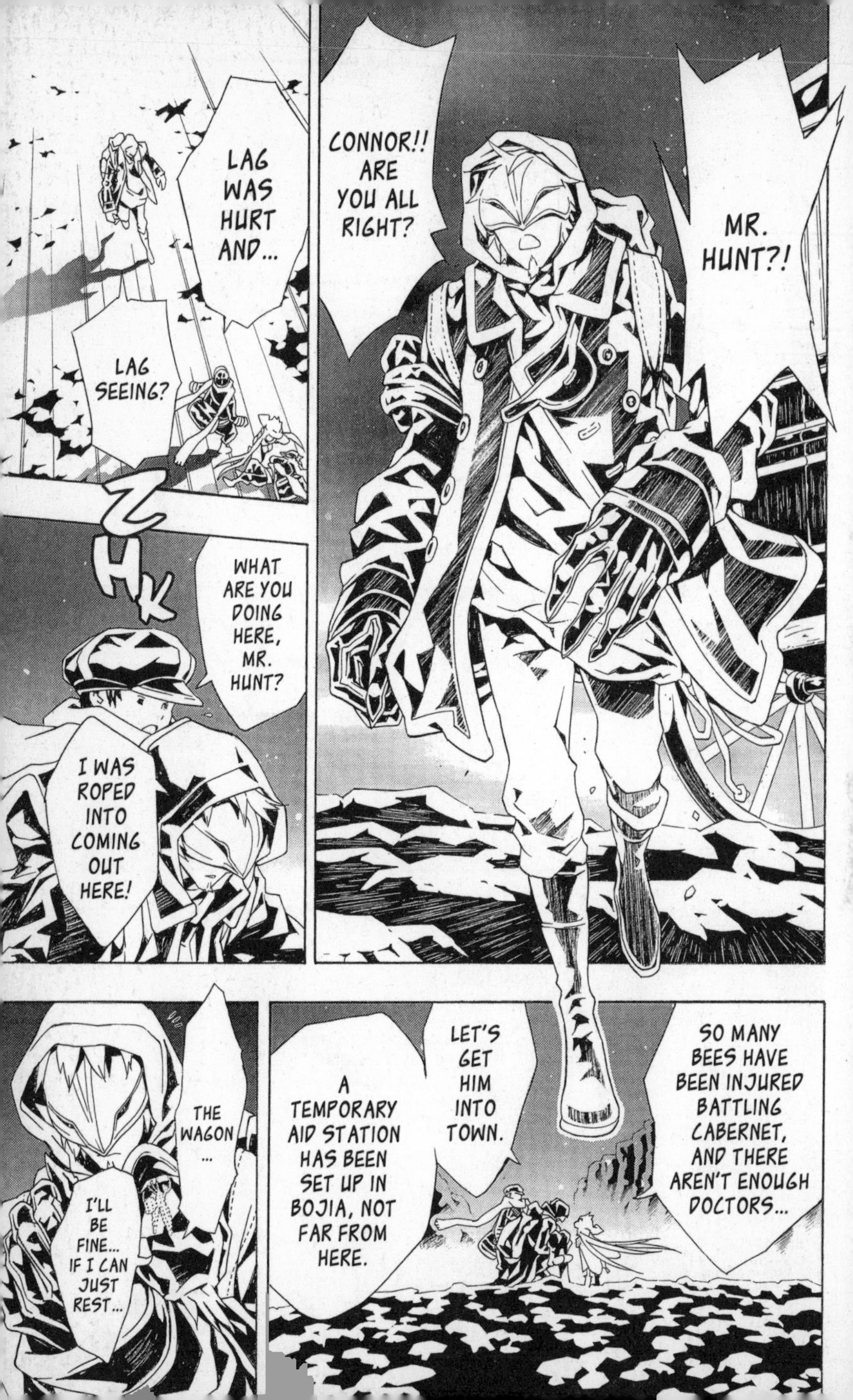
MR. HUNT?!
CONNOR!! ARE YOU ALL RIGHT?
LAG WAS HURT AND...
LAG SEEING?
ZHK
WHAT ARE YOU DOING HERE, MR. HUNT?
I WAS ROPED INTO COMING OUT HERE!
SO MANY BEES HAVE BEEN INJURED BATTLING CABERNET, AND THERE AREN'T ENOUGH DOCTORS...
LET'S GET HIM INTO TOWN.
A TEMPORARY AID STATION HAS BEEN SET UP IN BOJIA, NOT FAR FROM HERE.
THE WAGON...
I'LL BE FINE... IF I CAN JUST REST...

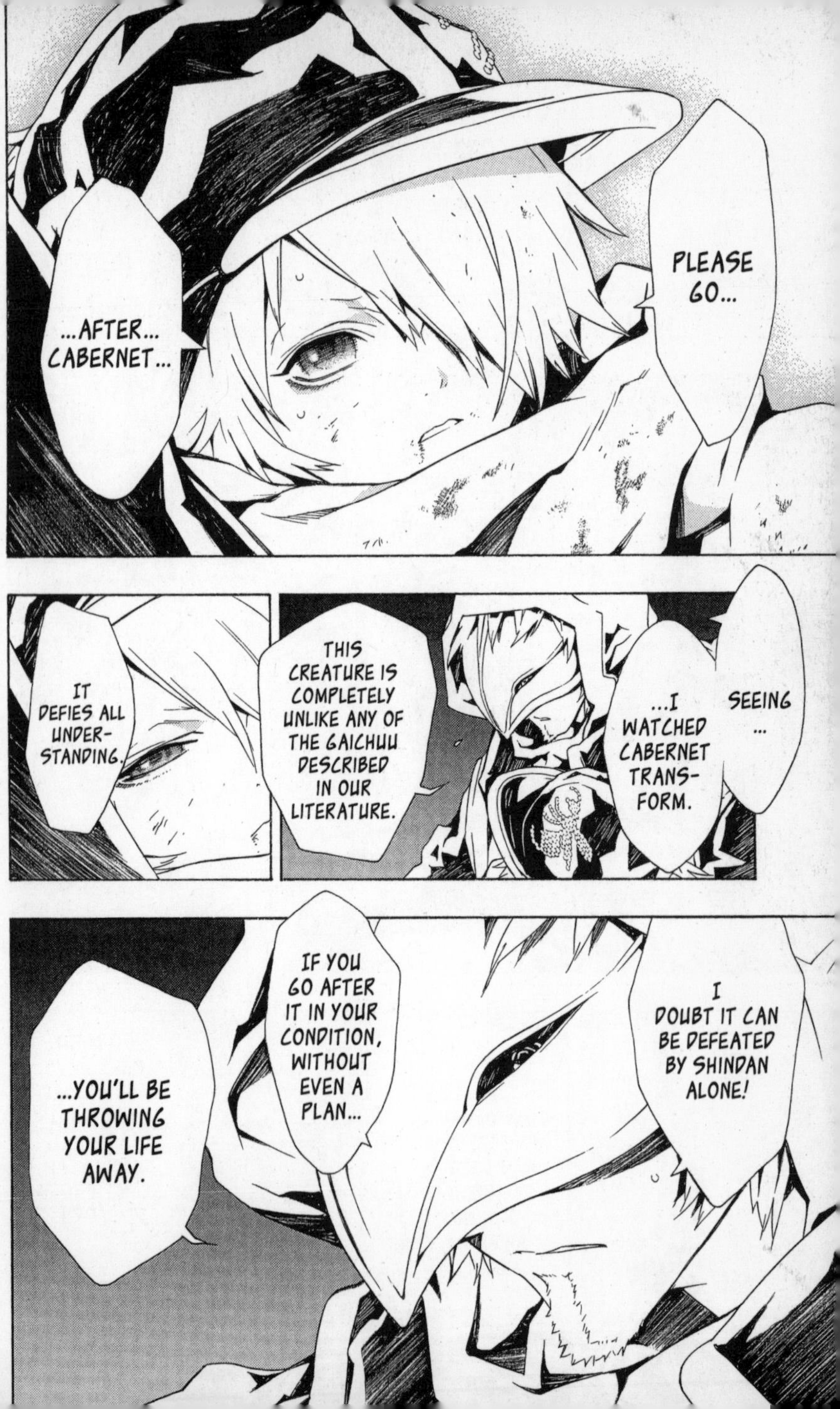
PLEASE GO...
...AFTER... CABERNET...
SEEING ...
...I WATCHED CABERNET TRANS-FORM.
THIS CREATURE IS COMPLETELY UNLIKE ANY OF THE GAICHUU DESCRIBED IN OUR LITERATURE.
IT DEFIES ALL UNDER-STANDING.
I DOUBT IT CAN BE DEFEATED BY SHINDAN ALONE!
IF YOU GO AFTER IT IN YOUR CONDITION, WITHOUT EVEN A PLAN...
...YOU'LL BE THROWING YOUR LIFE AWAY.

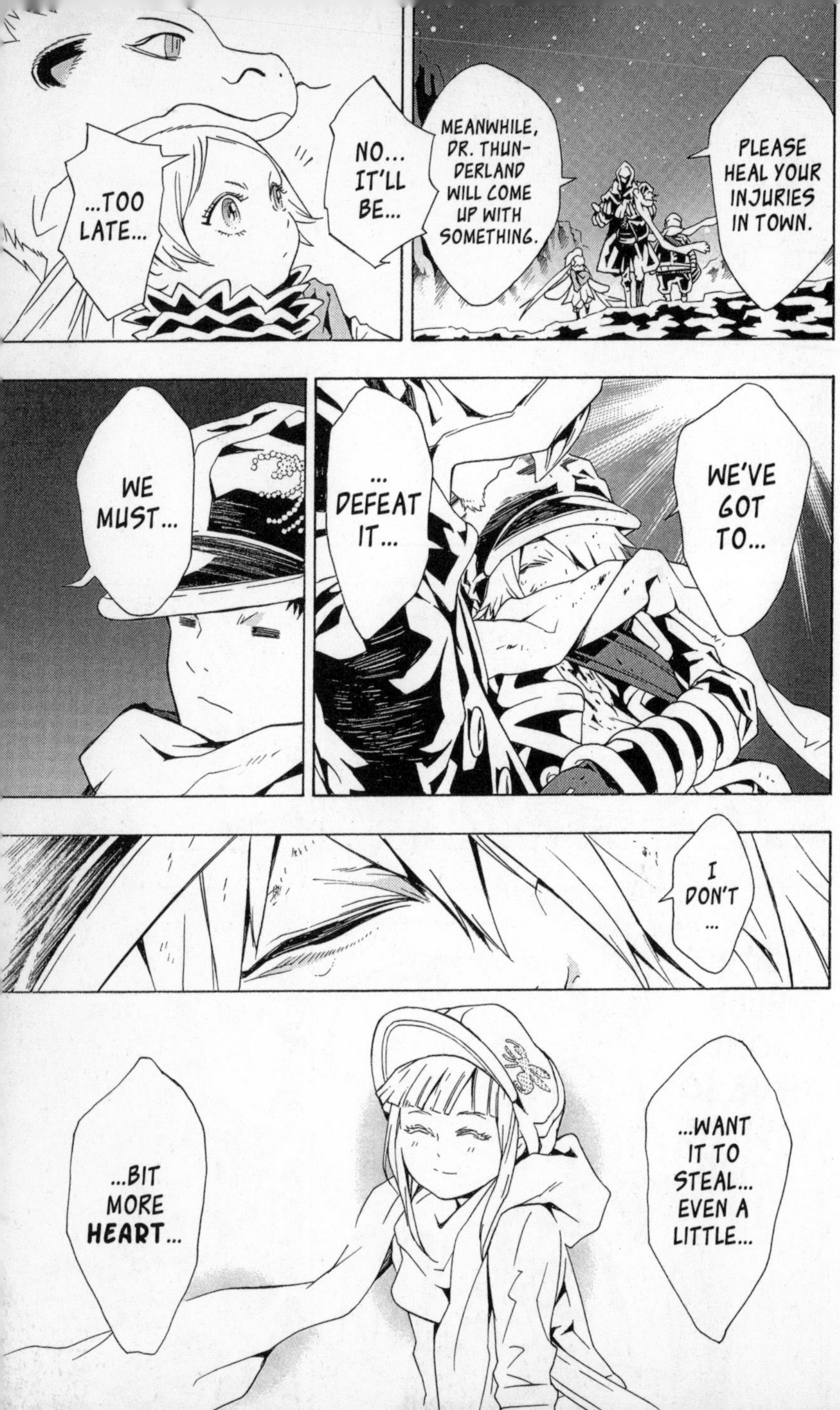
PLEASE HEAL YOUR INJURIES IN TOWN.
MEANWHILE, DR. THUNDERLAND WILL COME UP WITH SOMETHING.
NO... IT'LL BE...
...TOO LATE...
WE'VE GOT TO...
... DEFEAT IT...
WE MUST...
I DON'T ...
...WANT IT TO STEAL... EVEN A LITTLE...
...BIT MORE **HEART**...

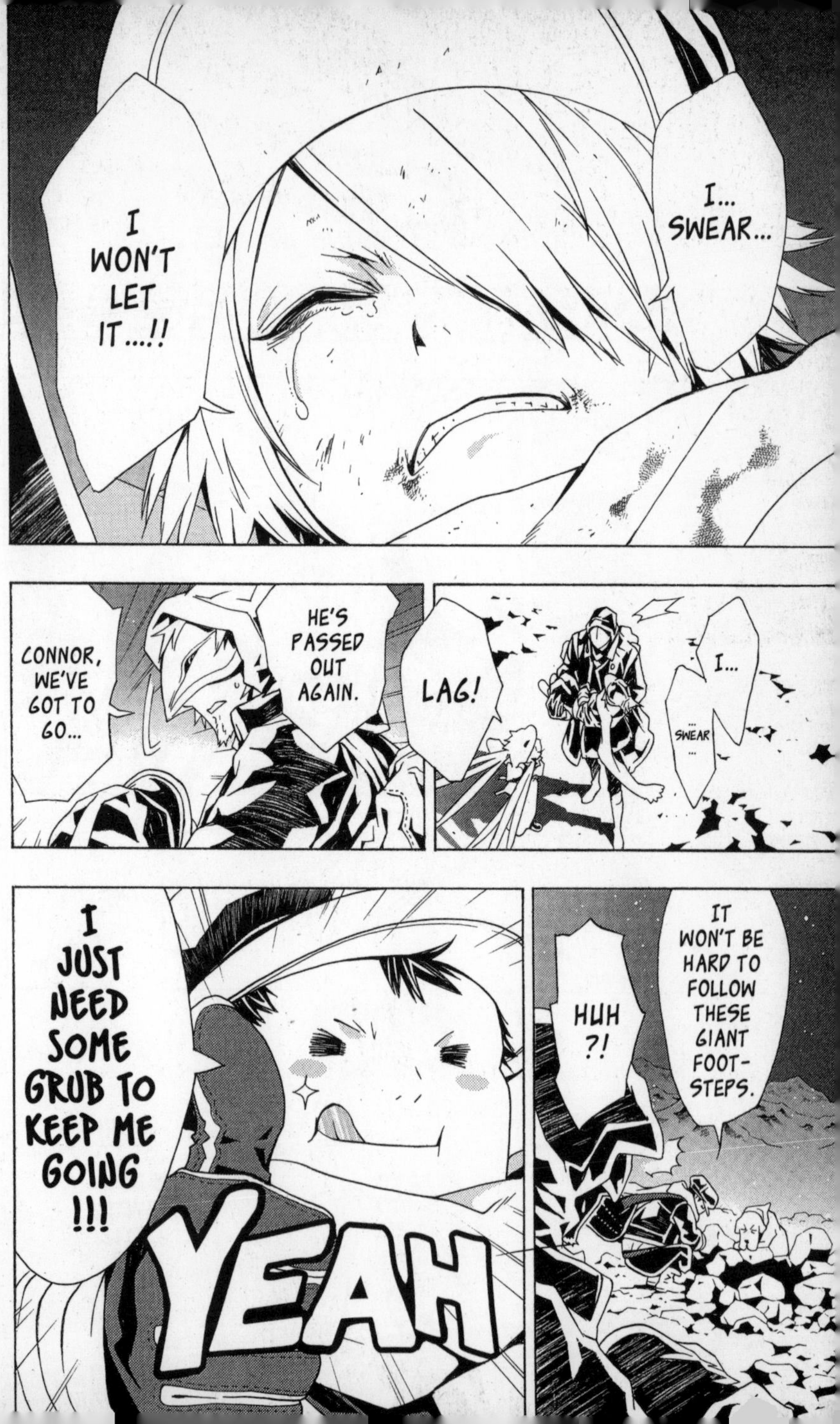
I... SWEAR...
I WON'T LET IT...!!
I... ...SWEAR...
LAG!
HE'S PASSED OUT AGAIN.
CONNOR, WE'VE GOT TO GO...
IT WON'T BE HARD TO FOLLOW THESE GIANT FOOT-STEPS.
HUH?!
I JUST NEED SOME GRUB TO KEEP ME GOING!!!
YEAH

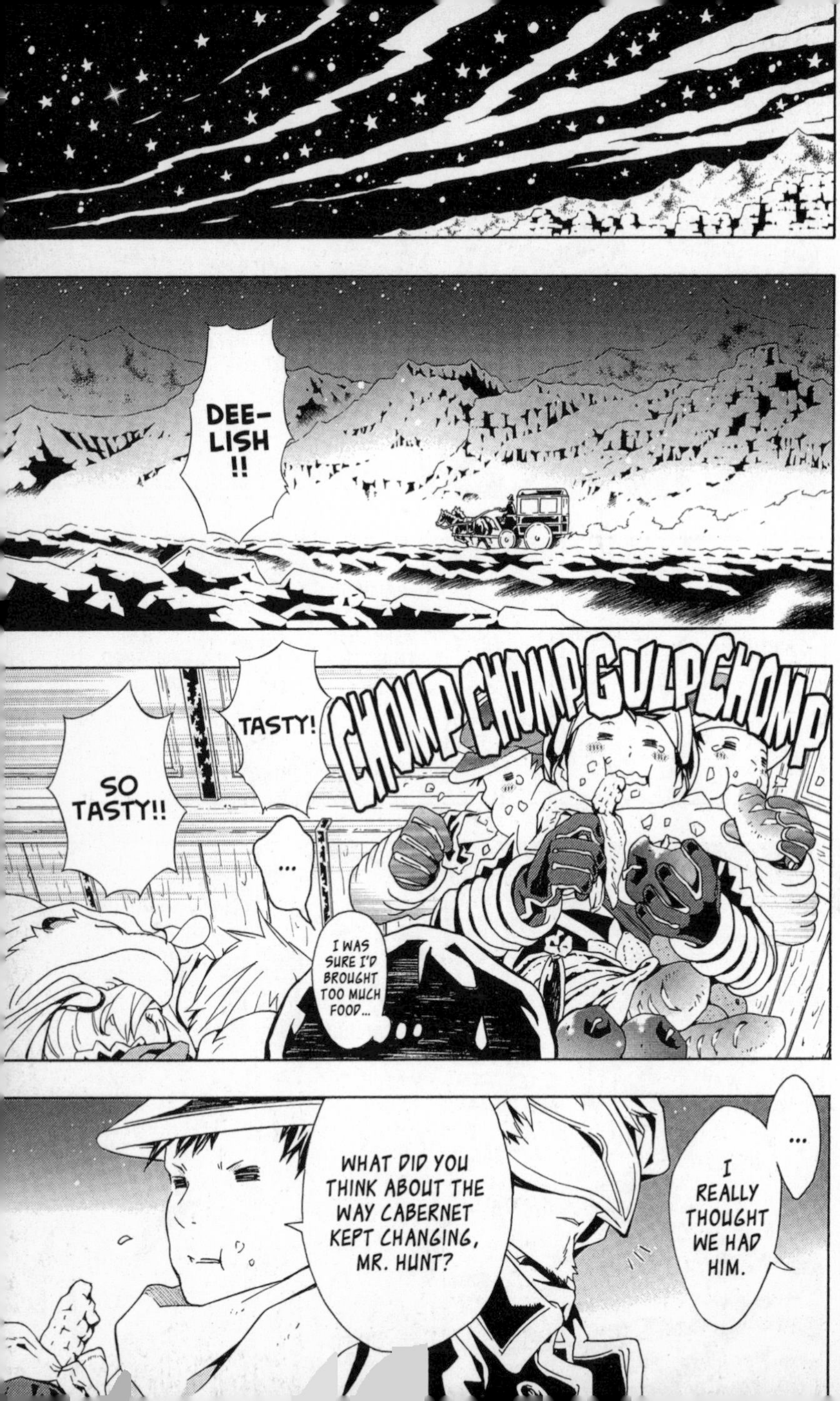
DEE-LISH!!
CHOMP CHOMP GULP CHOMP
TASTY!
SO TASTY!!
...
I WAS SURE I'D BROUGHT TOO MUCH FOOD...
...
...
I REALLY THOUGHT WE HAD HIM.
WHAT DID YOU THINK ABOUT THE WAY CABERNET KEPT CHANGING, MR. HUNT?

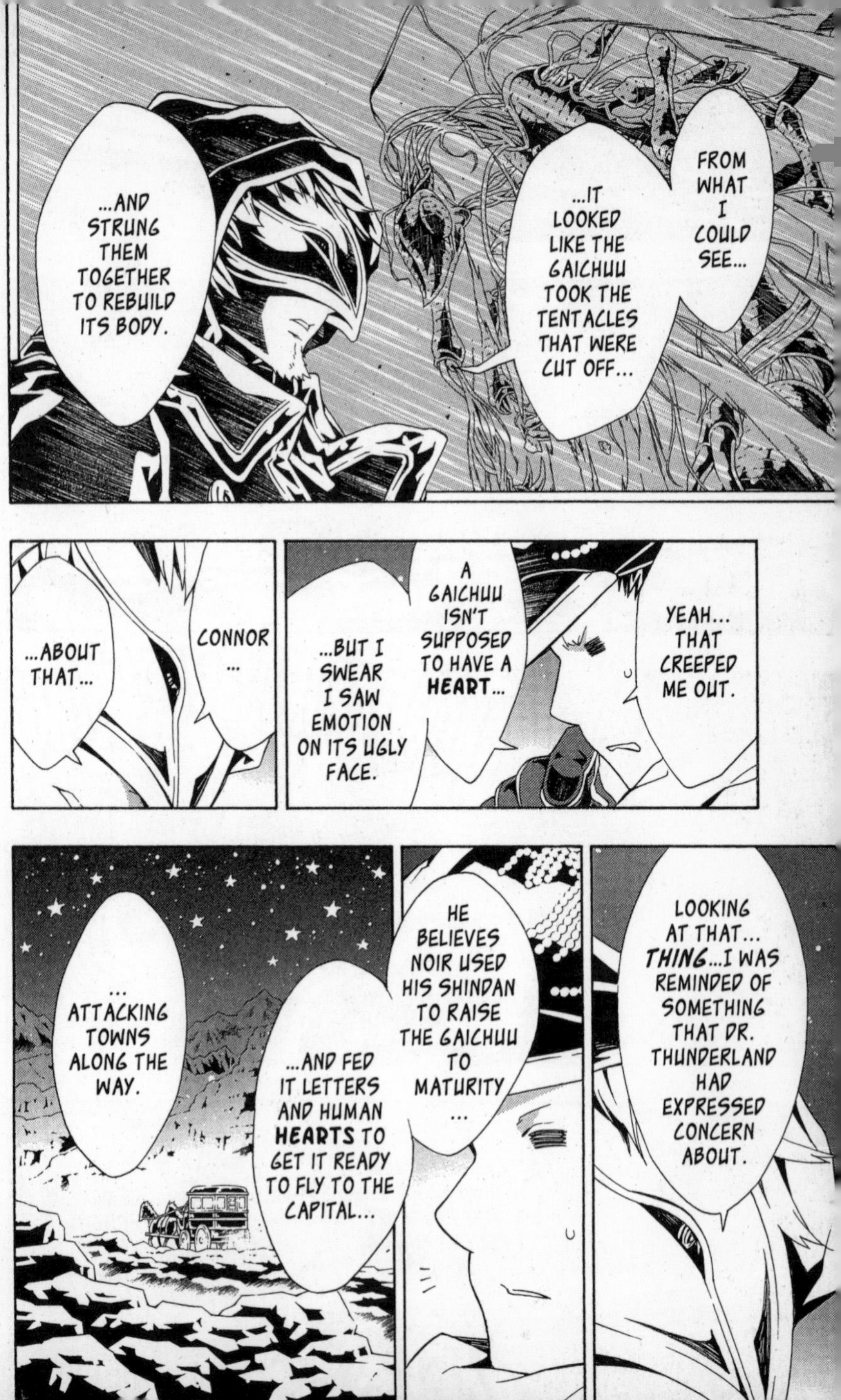
FROM WHAT I COULD SEE...
...IT LOOKED LIKE THE GAICHUU TOOK THE TENTACLES THAT WERE CUT OFF...
...AND STRUNG THEM TOGETHER TO REBUILD ITS BODY.
YEAH... THAT CREEPED ME OUT.
A GAICHUU ISN'T SUPPOSED TO HAVE A **HEART**...
...BUT I SWEAR I SAW EMOTION ON ITS UGLY FACE.
CONNOR ...
...ABOUT THAT...
LOOKING AT THAT... *THING*...I WAS REMINDED OF SOMETHING THAT DR. THUNDERLAND HAD EXPRESSED CONCERN ABOUT.
HE BELIEVES NOIR USED HIS SHINDAN TO RAISE THE GAICHUU TO MATURITY ...
...AND FED IT LETTERS AND HUMAN **HEARTS** TO GET IT READY TO FLY TO THE CAPITAL...
... ATTACKING TOWNS ALONG THE WAY.

HUH ?...

WHOA!

NO WAY!!

I DON'T KNOW OF ANY OTHER GAICHUU THAT HAS DEVOURED AS MANY **HEARTS** AS CABERNET.

IT COULD VERY WELL HAVE UNPREDICTABLE SIDE EFFECTS...

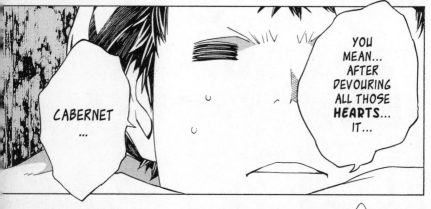

YOU MEAN... AFTER DEVOURING ALL THOSE **HEARTS**... IT...

CABERNET ...

...NO...

...NO...

IT CAN'T BE...

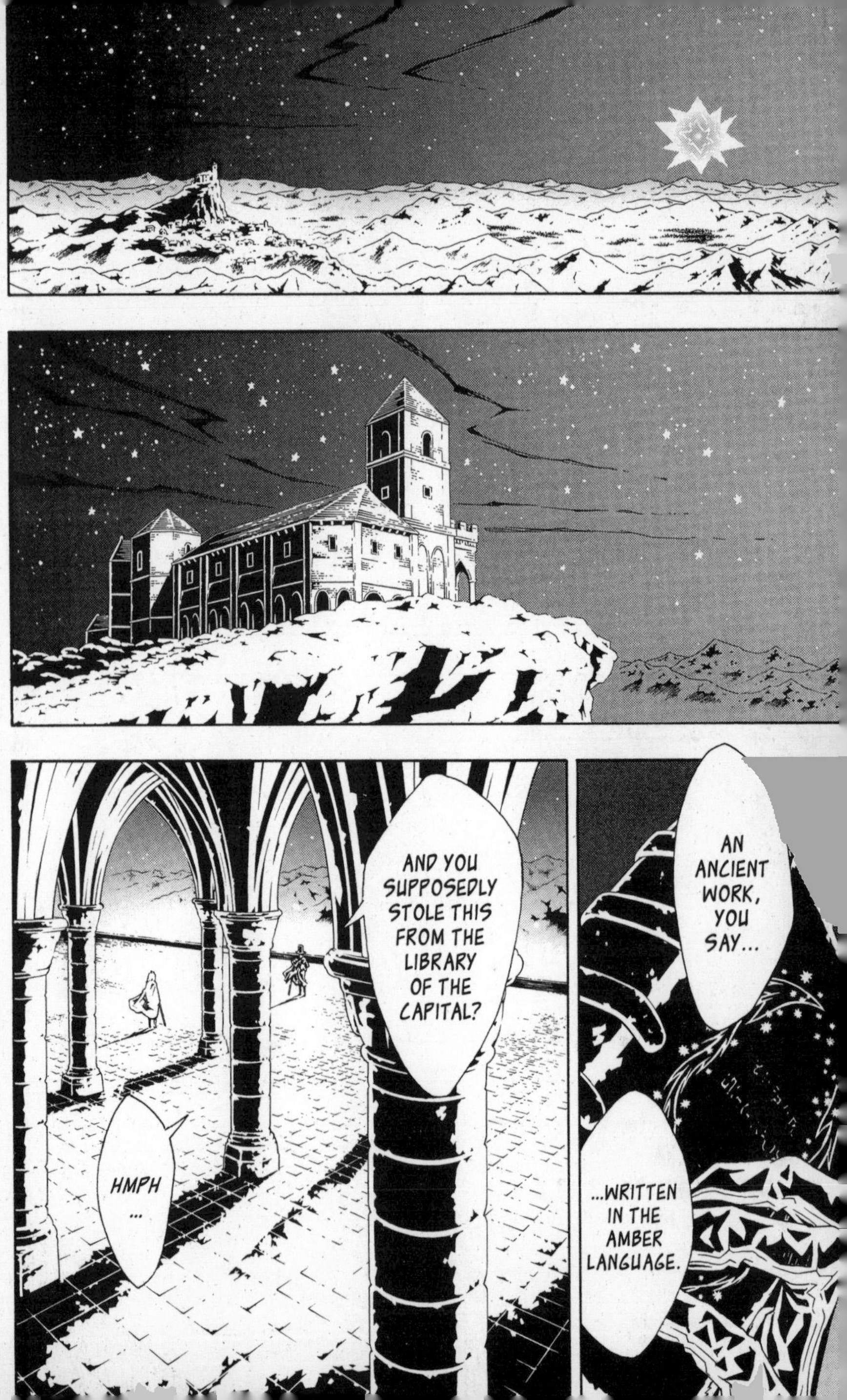
AN ANCIENT WORK, YOU SAY...
...WRITTEN IN THE AMBER LANGUAGE.
AND YOU SUPPOSEDLY STOLE THIS FROM THE LIBRARY OF THE CAPITAL?
HMPH ...

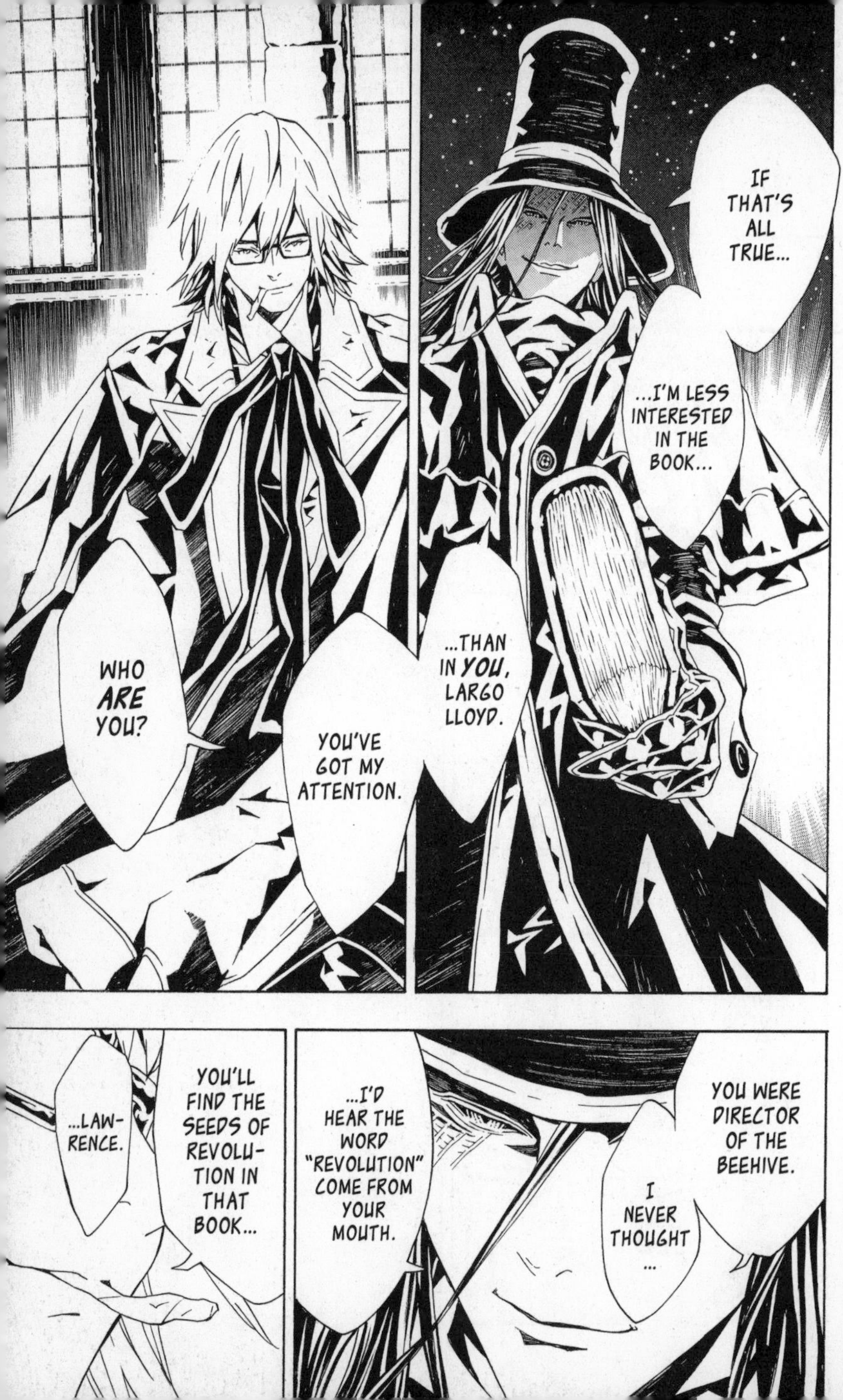
IF THAT'S ALL TRUE...
...I'M LESS INTERESTED IN THE BOOK...
...THAN IN *YOU*, LARGO LLOYD.
YOU'VE GOT MY ATTENTION.
WHO *ARE* YOU?
YOU WERE DIRECTOR OF THE BEEHIVE.
I NEVER THOUGHT ...
...I'D HEAR THE WORD "REVOLUTION" COME FROM YOUR MOUTH.
YOU'LL FIND THE SEEDS OF REVOLUTION IN THAT BOOK...
...LAWRENCE.

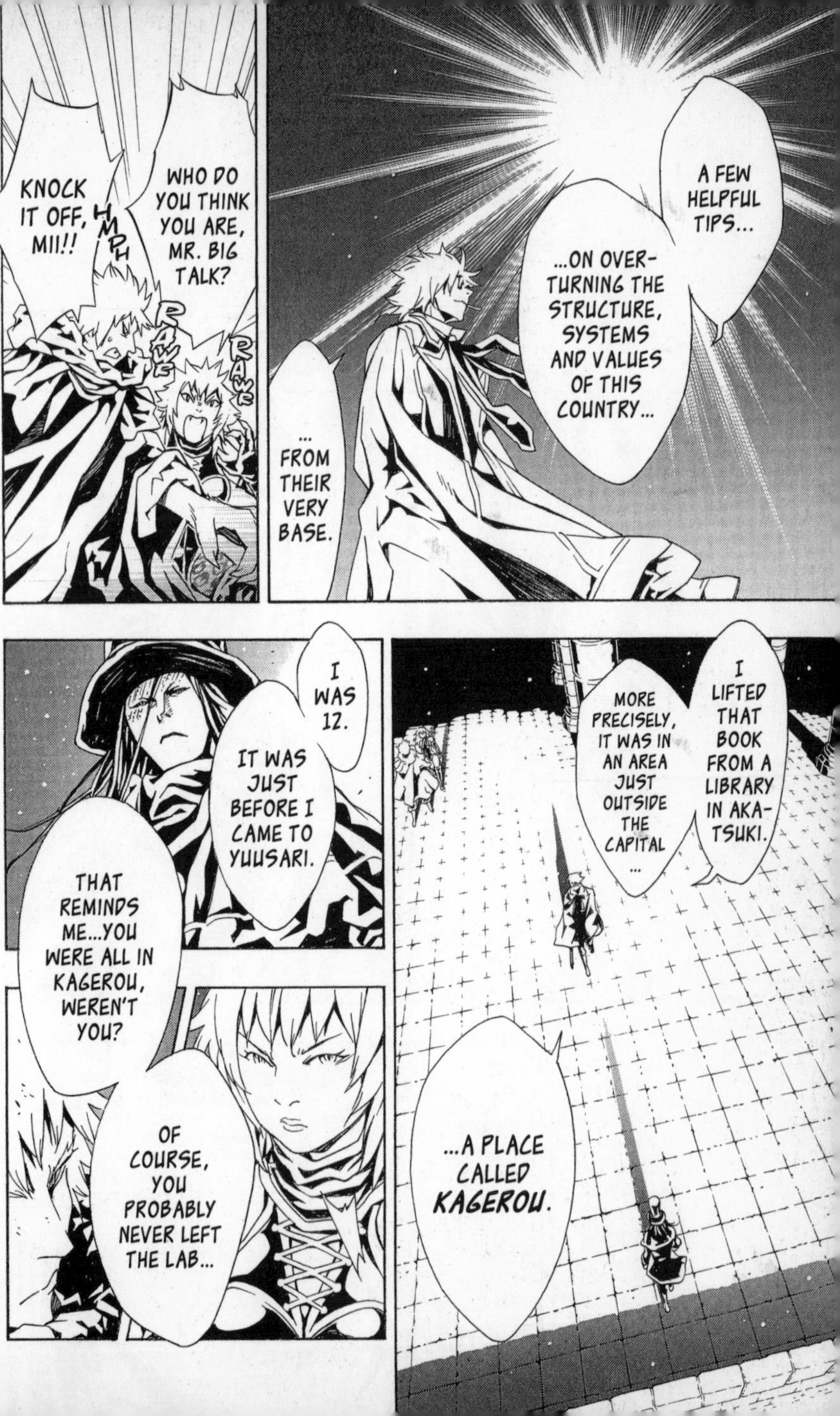
A FEW HELPFUL TIPS...
...ON OVER-TURNING THE STRUCTURE, SYSTEMS AND VALUES OF THIS COUNTRY...
...FROM THEIR VERY BASE.
WHO DO YOU THINK YOU ARE, MR. BIG TALK?
RAWR
HMPH
KNOCK IT OFF, MII!!
RAWR
I LIFTED THAT BOOK FROM A LIBRARY IN AKA-TSUKI.
MORE PRECISELY, IT WAS IN AN AREA JUST OUTSIDE THE CAPITAL...
...A PLACE CALLED **KAGEROU**.
I WAS 12.
IT WAS JUST BEFORE I CAME TO YUUSARI.
THAT REMINDS ME...YOU WERE ALL IN KAGEROU, WEREN'T YOU?
OF COURSE, YOU PROBABLY NEVER LEFT THE LAB...

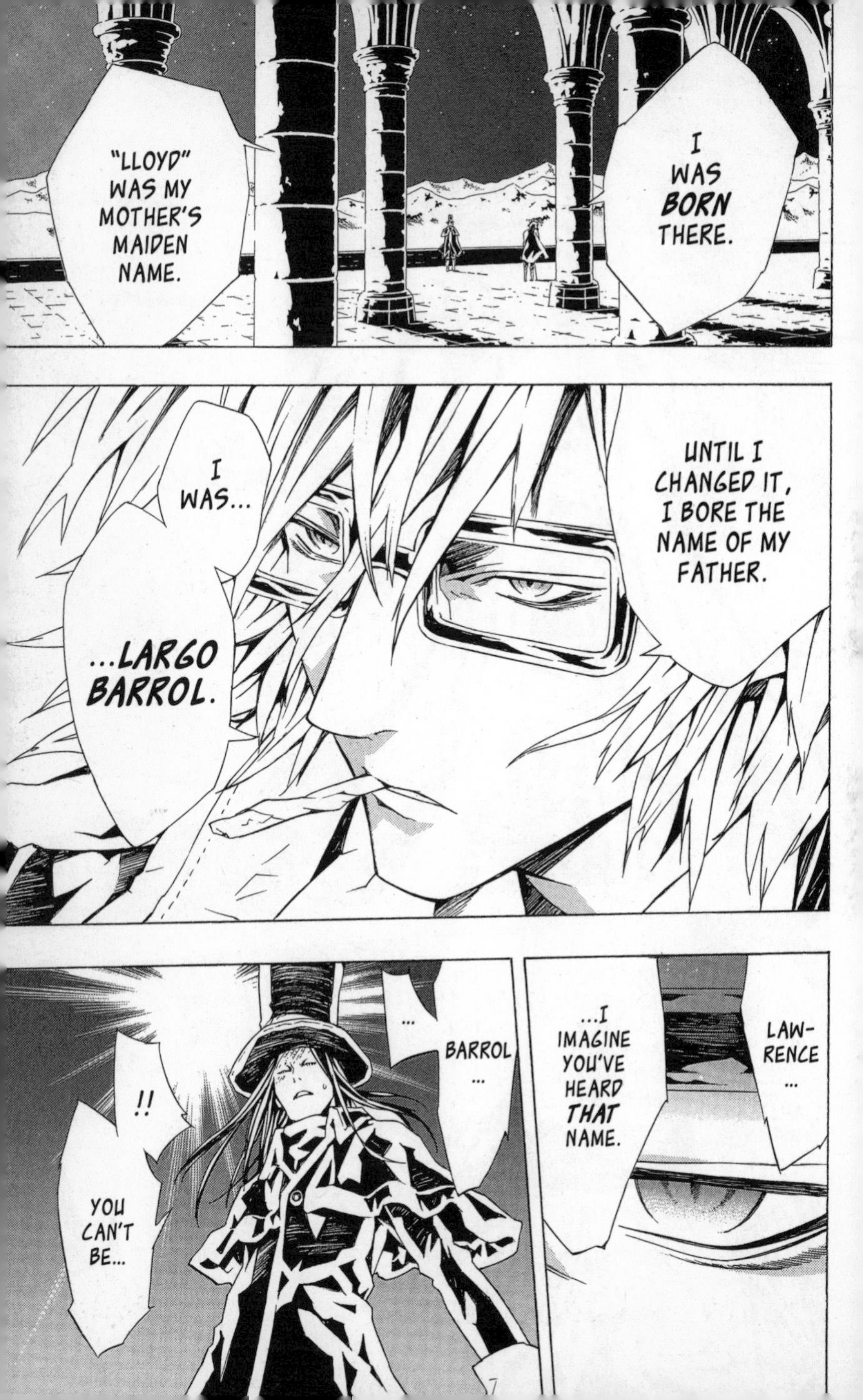
I WAS BORN THERE.
"LLOYD" WAS MY MOTHER'S MAIDEN NAME.
UNTIL I CHANGED IT, I BORE THE NAME OF MY FATHER.
I WAS...
...LARGO BARROL.
LAW-RENCE...
...I IMAGINE YOU'VE HEARD THAT NAME.
BARROL...
...
!!
YOU CAN'T BE...

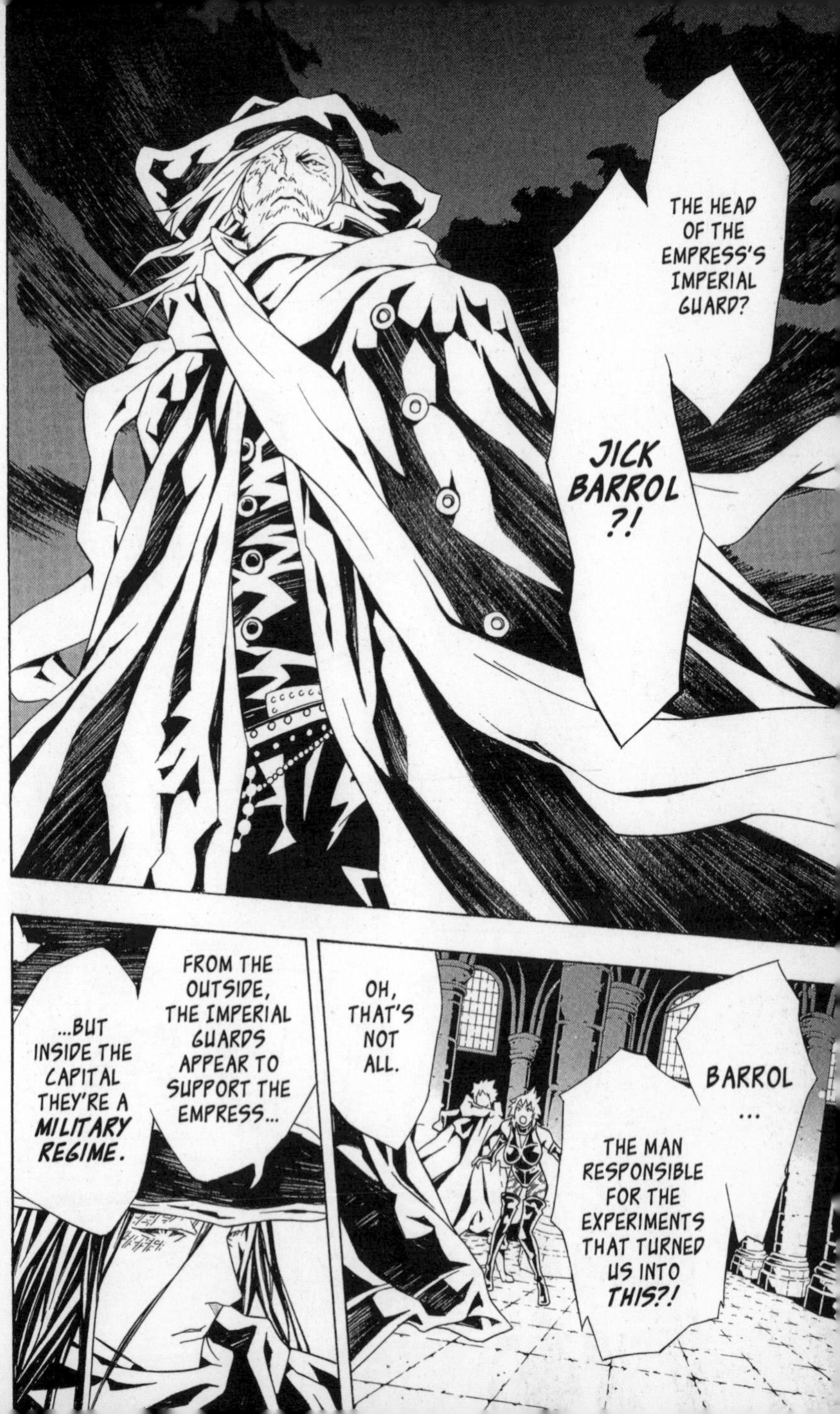
THE HEAD OF THE EMPRESS'S IMPERIAL GUARD?
JICK BARROL ?!
BARROL ...
THE MAN RESPONSIBLE FOR THE EXPERIMENTS THAT TURNED US INTO *THIS?!*
OH, THAT'S NOT ALL.
FROM THE OUTSIDE, THE IMPERIAL GUARDS APPEAR TO SUPPORT THE EMPRESS...
...BUT INSIDE THE CAPITAL THEY'RE A *MILITARY REGIME*.

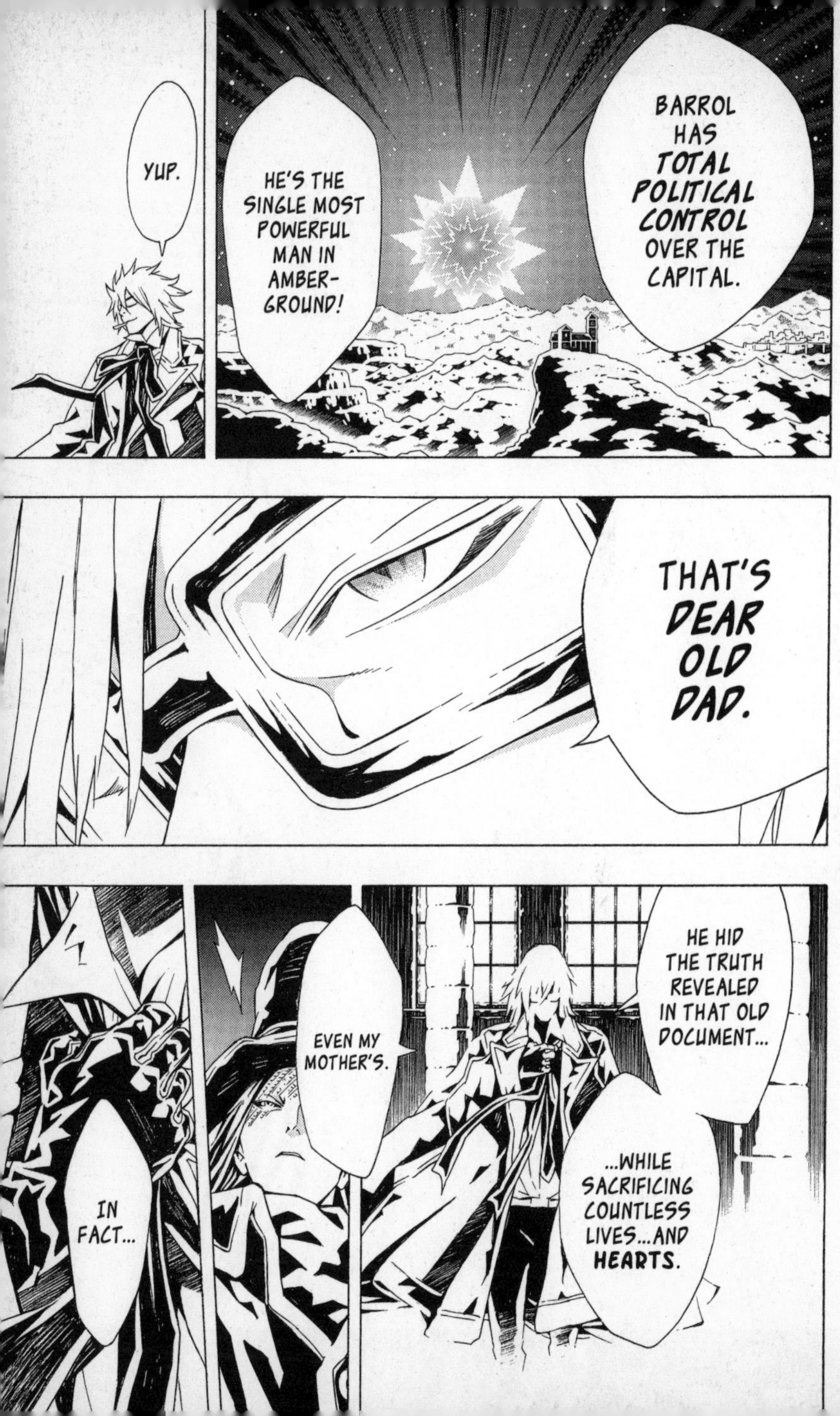
BARROL HAS TOTAL POLITICAL CONTROL OVER THE CAPITAL.
HE'S THE SINGLE MOST POWERFUL MAN IN AMBER-GROUND!
YUP.
THAT'S DEAR OLD DAD.
HE HID THE TRUTH REVEALED IN THAT OLD DOCUMENT...
...WHILE SACRIFICING COUNTLESS LIVES...AND HEARTS.
EVEN MY MOTHER'S.
IN FACT...

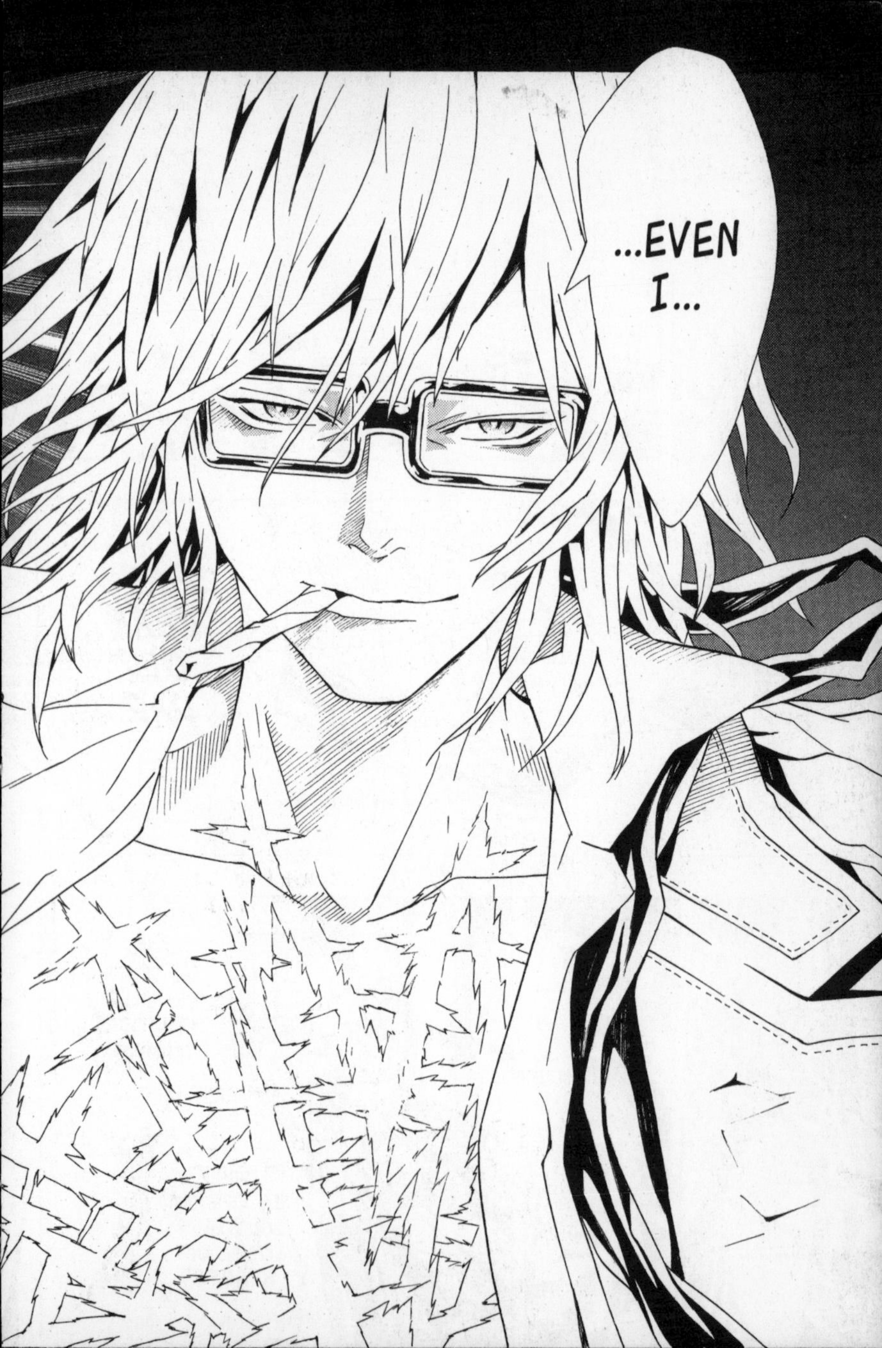
...EVEN I...

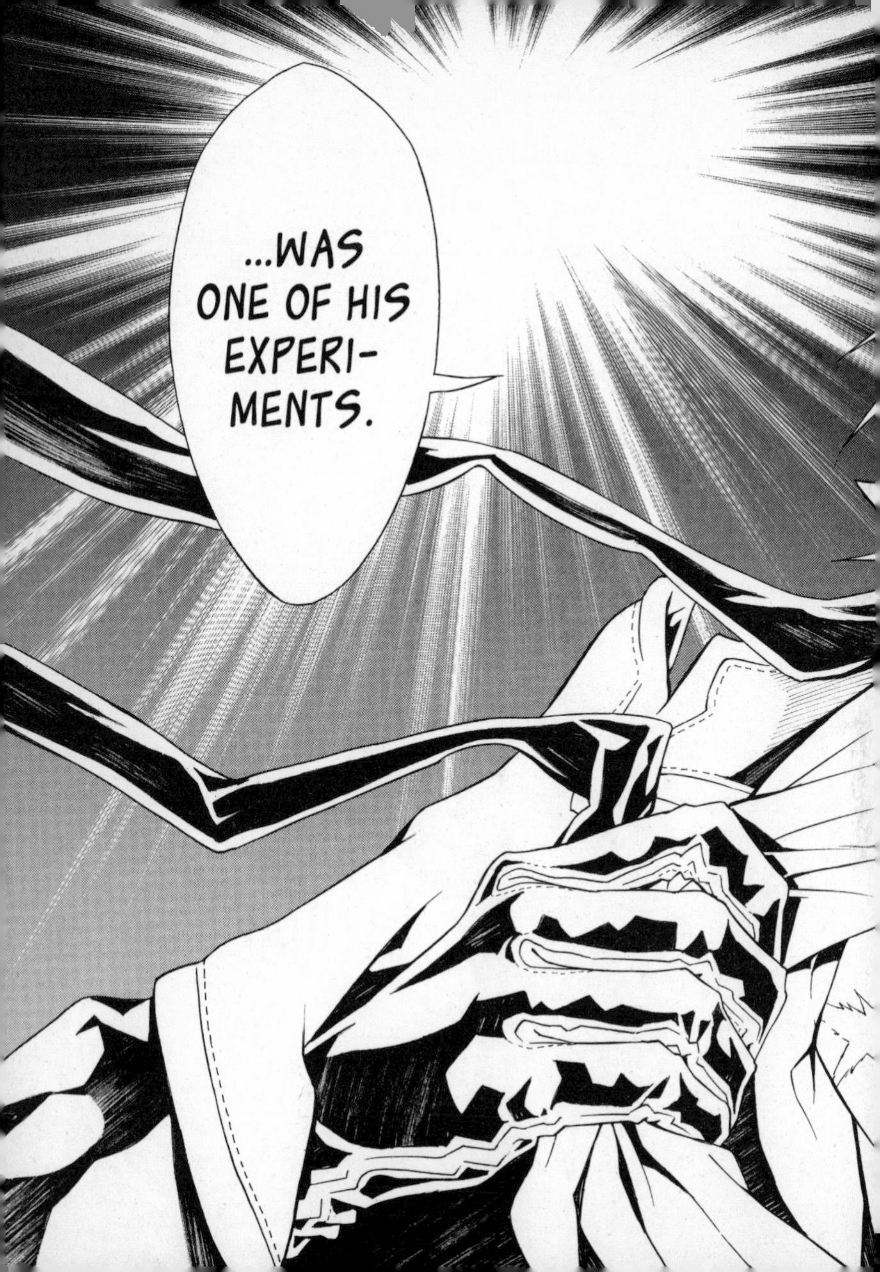
...WAS ONE OF HIS EXPERI- MENTS.

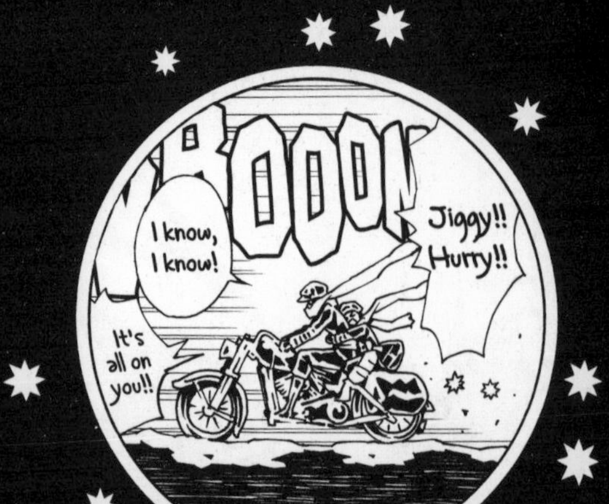
Jiggy!! Hurry!!
I know, I know!
It's all on you!!

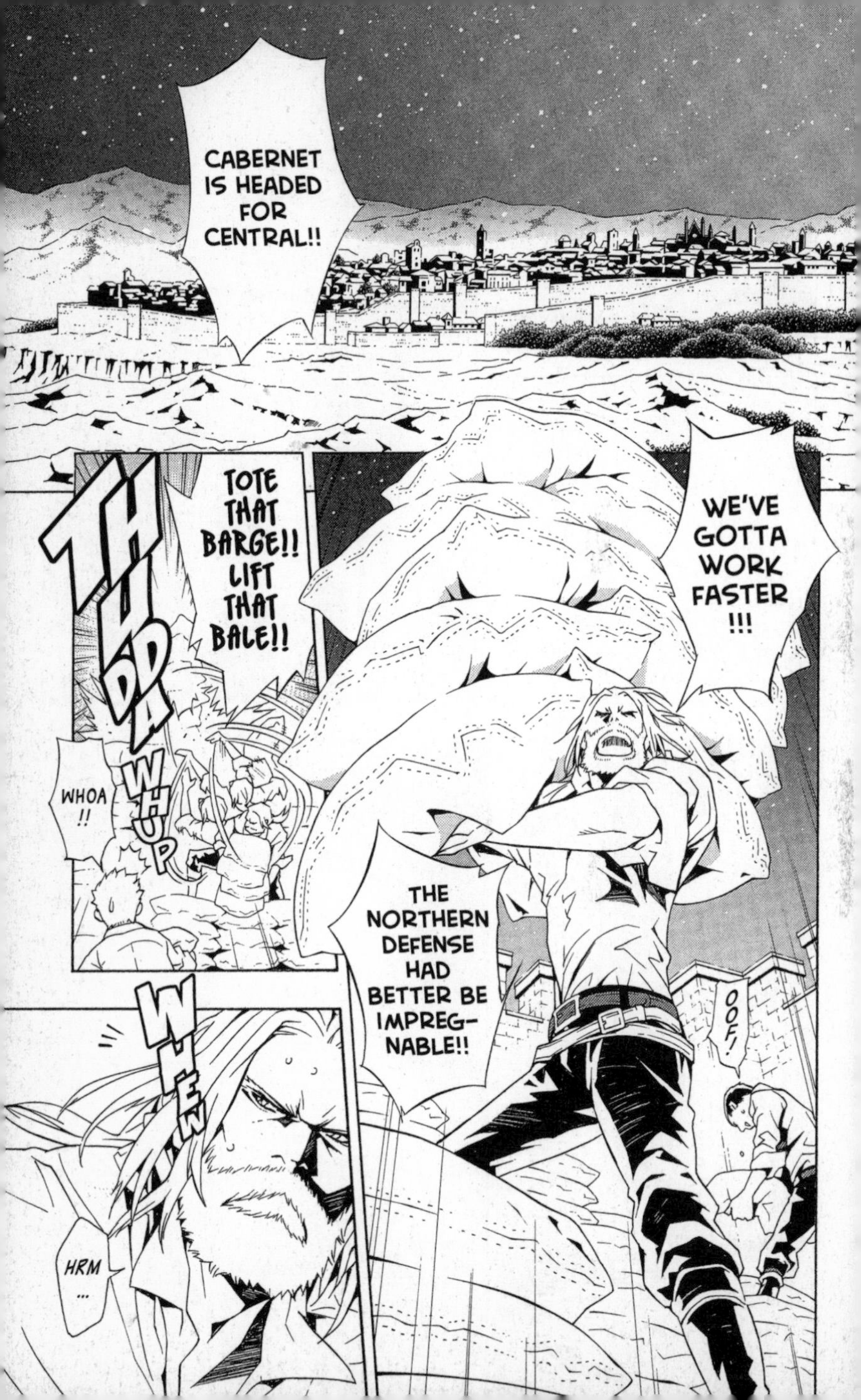
CABERNET IS HEADED FOR CENTRAL!!
WE'VE GOTTA WORK FASTER!!!
THE NORTHERN DEFENSE HAD BETTER BE IMPREG-NABLE!!
OOF!
TOTE THAT BARGE!! LIFT THAT BALE!!
THUDDA
WHUP
WHOA!!
WHEW
HRM...

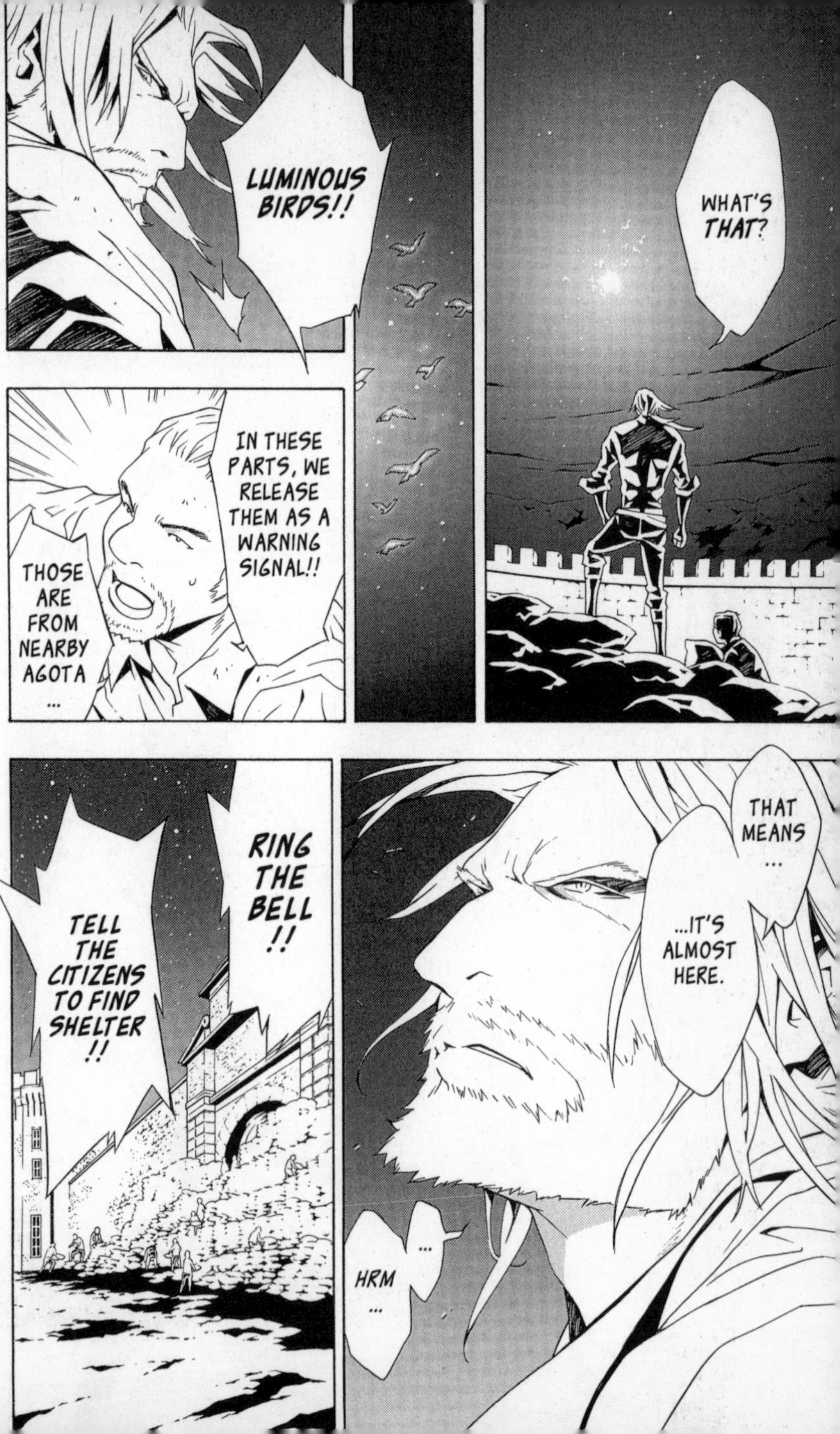
WHAT'S THAT?
LUMINOUS BIRDS!!
IN THESE PARTS, WE RELEASE THEM AS A WARNING SIGNAL!!
THOSE ARE FROM NEARBY AGOTA...
THAT MEANS...
...IT'S ALMOST HERE.
...
HRM...
RING THE BELL!!
TELL THE CITIZENS TO FIND SHELTER!!

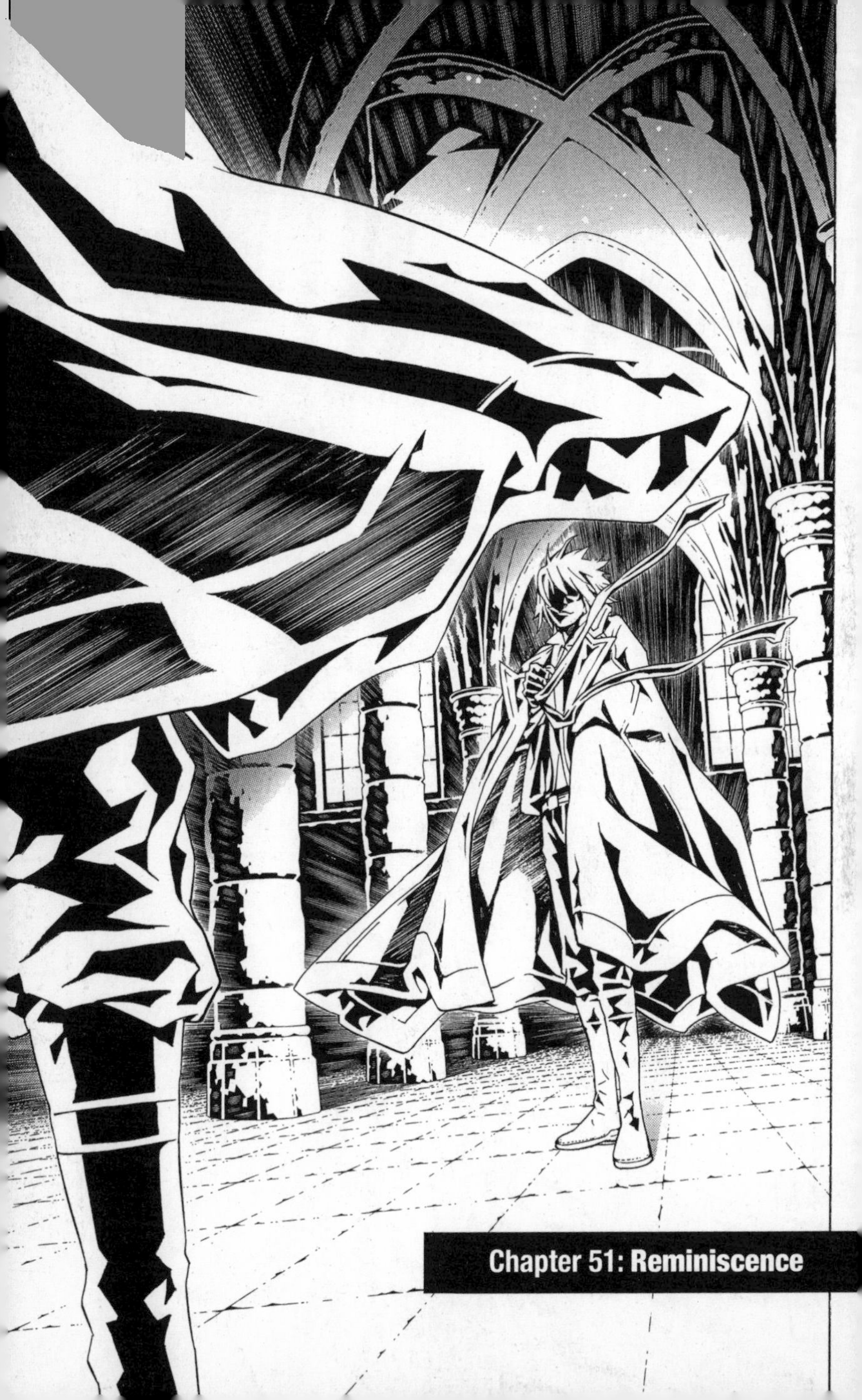
Chapter 51: Reminiscence

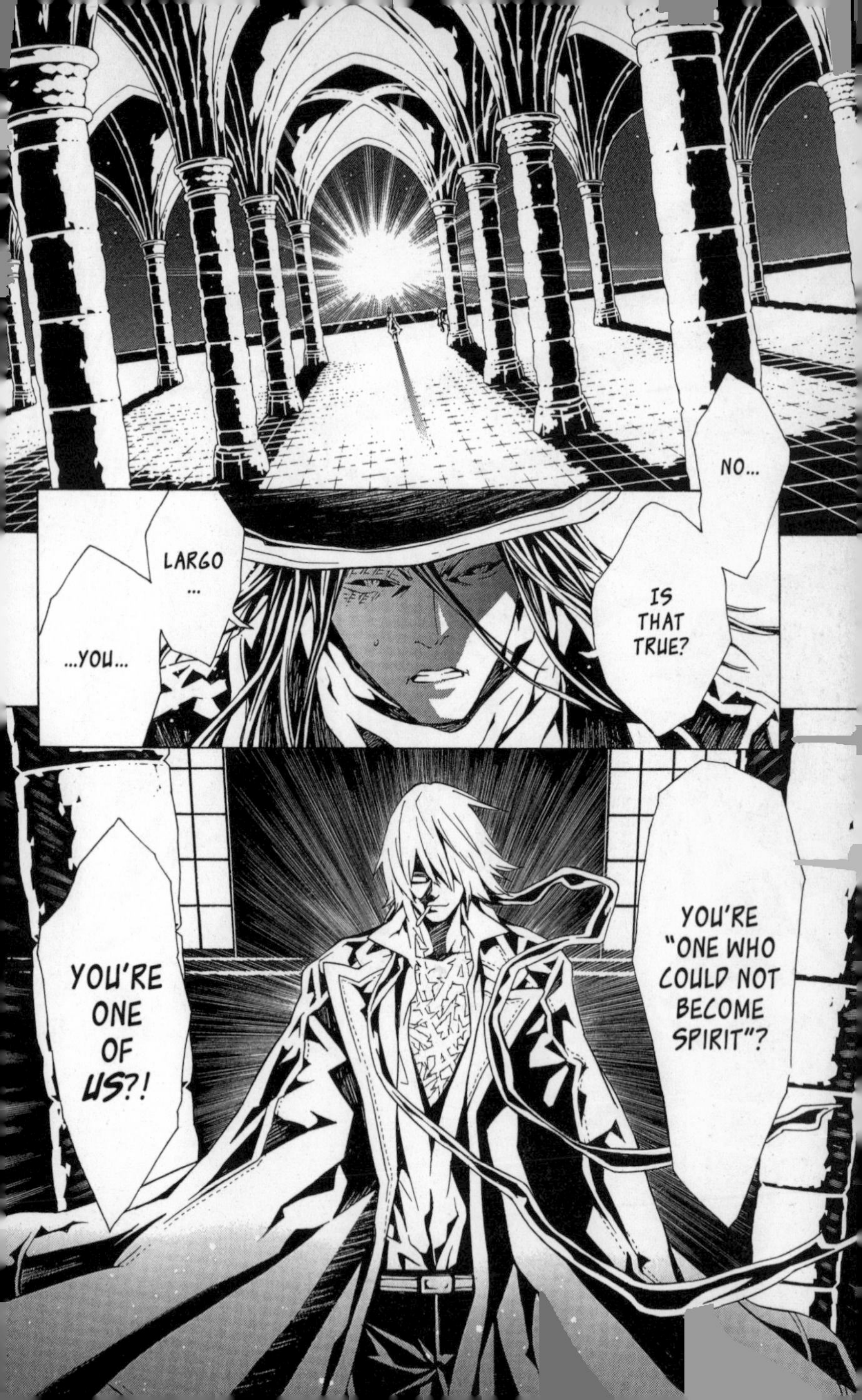
NO...
IS THAT TRUE?
LARGO ...
...YOU...
YOU'RE "ONE WHO COULD NOT BECOME SPIRIT"?
YOU'RE ONE OF US?!

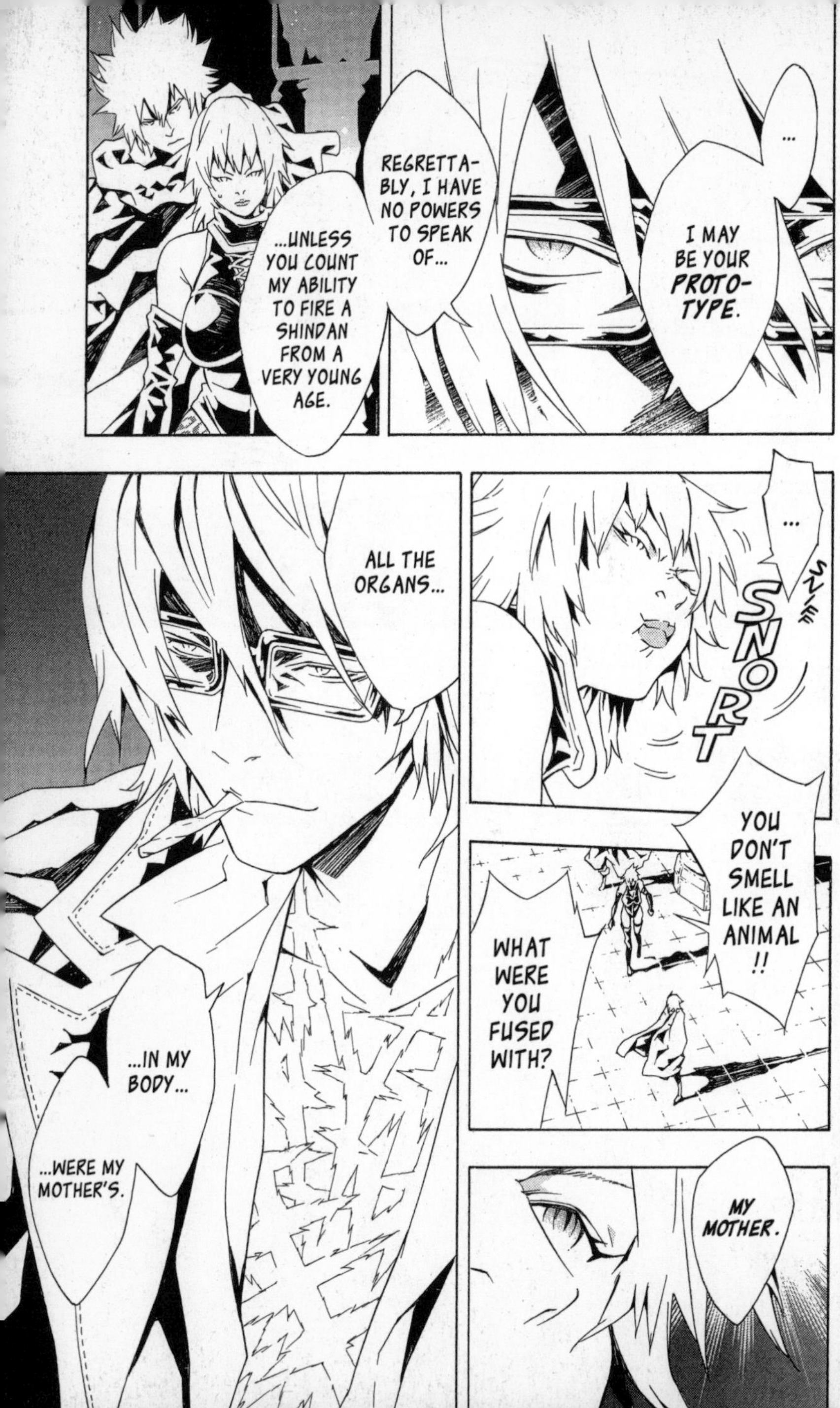
...
I MAY BE YOUR PROTOTYPE.
REGRETTABLY, I HAVE NO POWERS TO SPEAK OF...
...UNLESS YOU COUNT MY ABILITY TO FIRE A SHINDAN FROM A VERY YOUNG AGE.
...
SNIFF
SNORT
YOU DON'T SMELL LIKE AN ANIMAL!!
WHAT WERE YOU FUSED WITH?
MY MOTHER.
ALL THE ORGANS...
...IN MY BODY...
...WERE MY MOTHER'S.

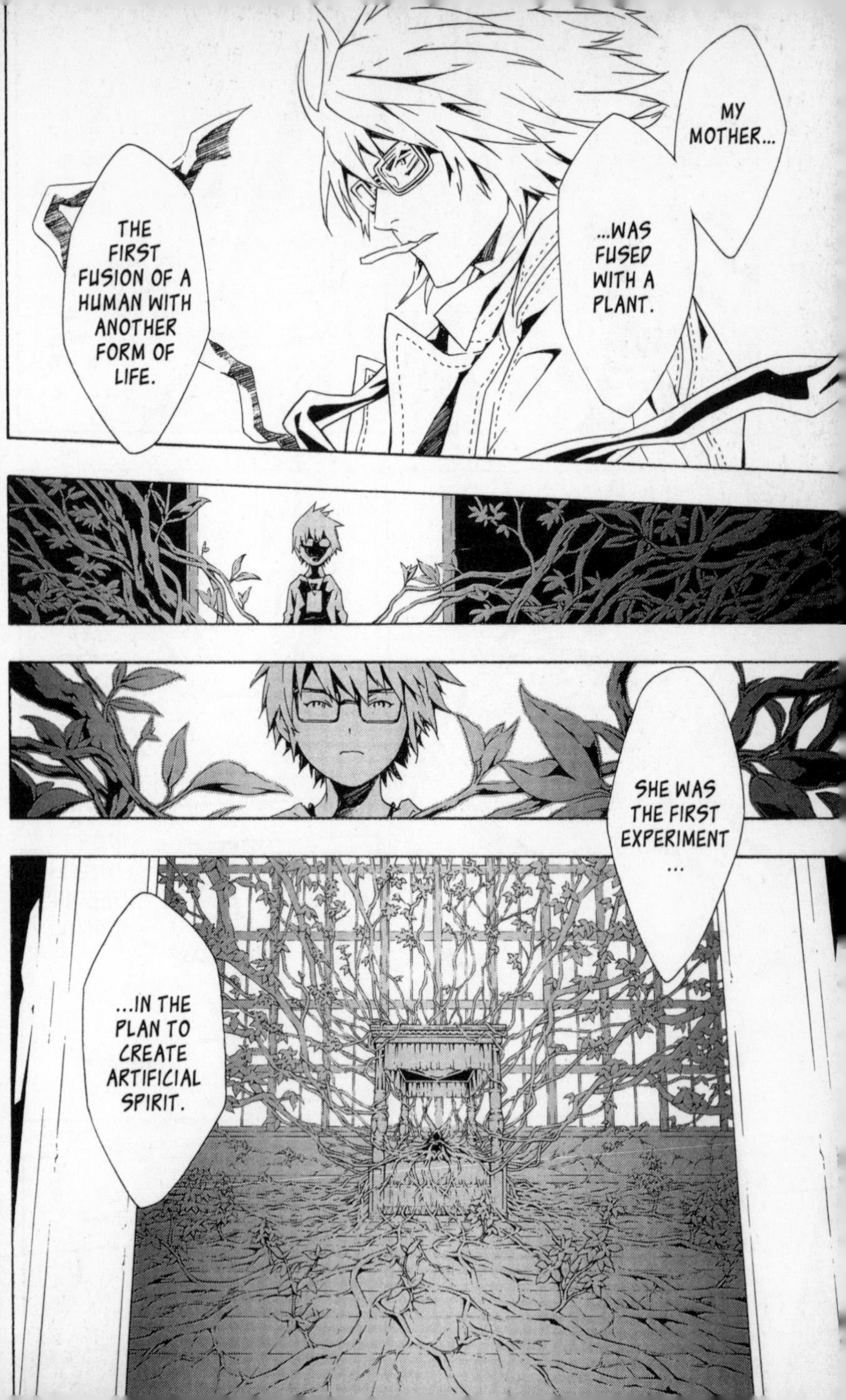
MY MOTHER...
...WAS FUSED WITH A PLANT.
THE FIRST FUSION OF A HUMAN WITH ANOTHER FORM OF LIFE.
SHE WAS THE FIRST EXPERIMENT ...
...IN THE PLAN TO CREATE ARTIFICIAL SPIRIT.

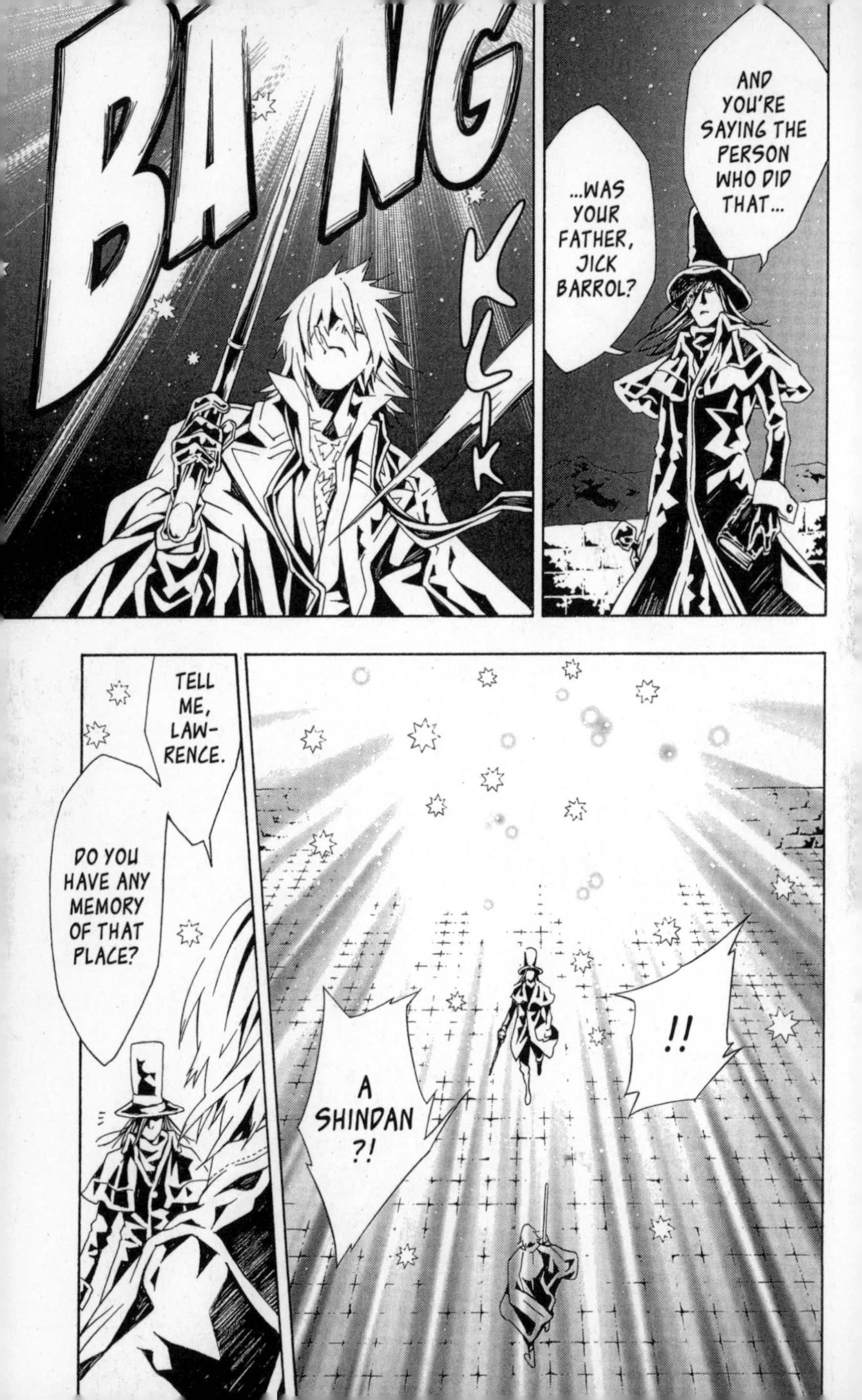
AND YOU'RE SAYING THE PERSON WHO DID THAT...
...WAS YOUR FATHER, JICK BARROL?
BANG
!!
A SHINDAN ?!
TELL ME, LAW-RENCE.
DO YOU HAVE ANY MEMORY OF THAT PLACE?

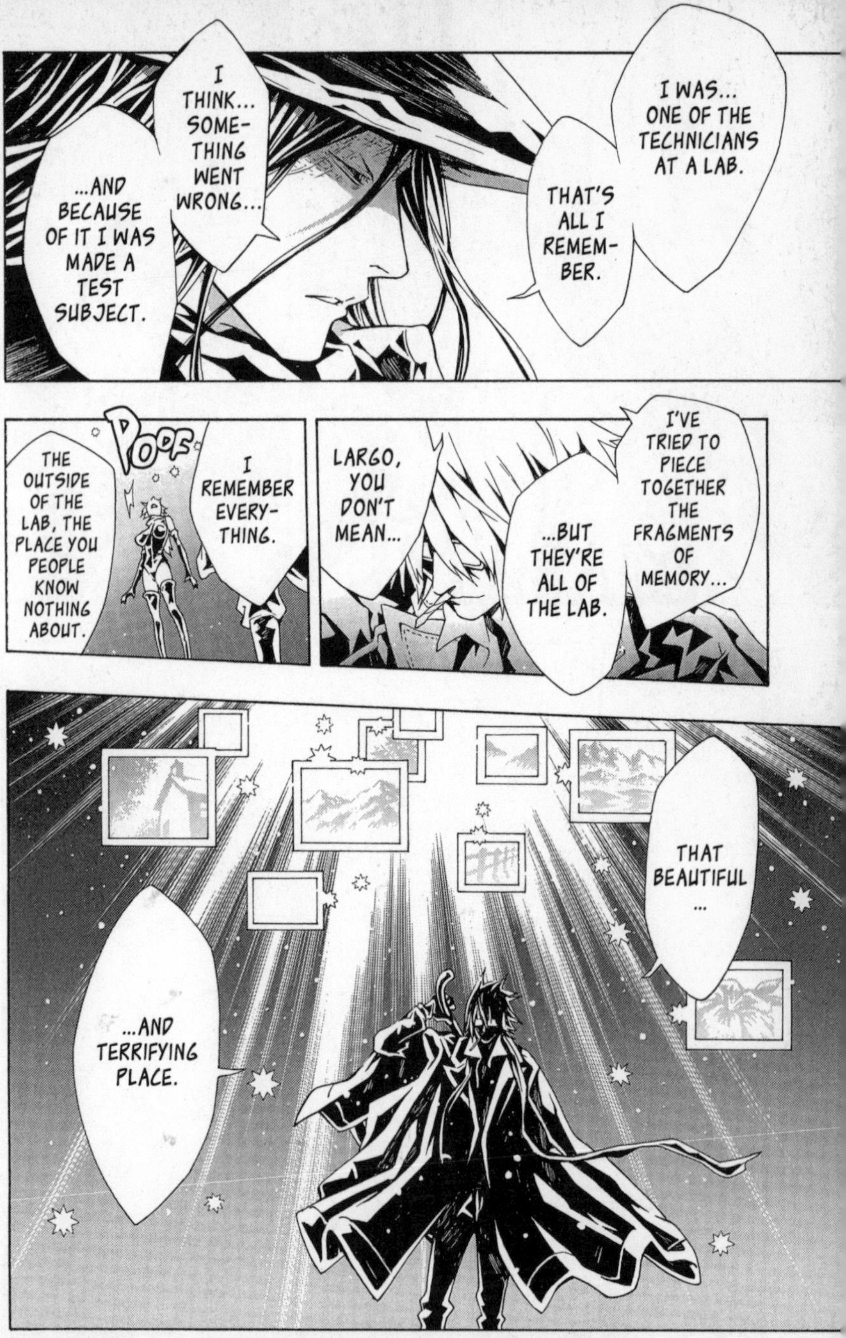
I WAS... ONE OF THE TECHNICIANS AT A LAB.
THAT'S ALL I REMEMBER.
I THINK... SOMETHING WENT WRONG...
...AND BECAUSE OF IT I WAS MADE A TEST SUBJECT.
I'VE TRIED TO PIECE TOGETHER THE FRAGMENTS OF MEMORY...
...BUT THEY'RE ALL OF THE LAB.
LARGO, YOU DON'T MEAN...
POOF
I REMEMBER EVERYTHING.
THE OUTSIDE OF THE LAB, THE PLACE YOU PEOPLE KNOW NOTHING ABOUT.
THAT BEAUTIFUL ...
...AND TERRIFYING PLACE.

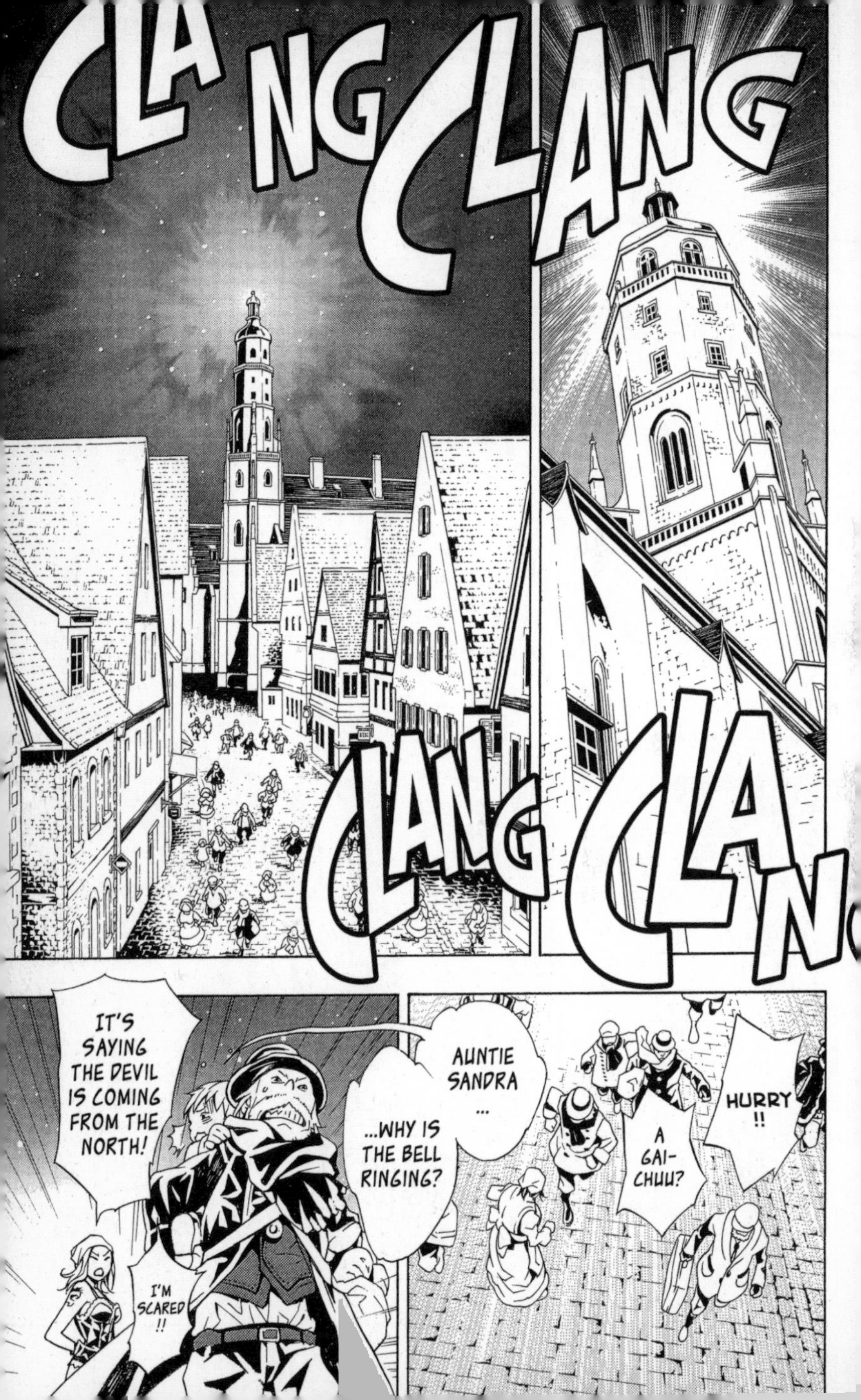
CLANG
CLAN
CLANG
CLANG
HURRY !!
A GAI-CHUU?
AUNTIE SANDRA ...
...WHY IS THE BELL RINGING?
IT'S SAYING THE DEVIL IS COMING FROM THE NORTH!
I'M SCARED !!

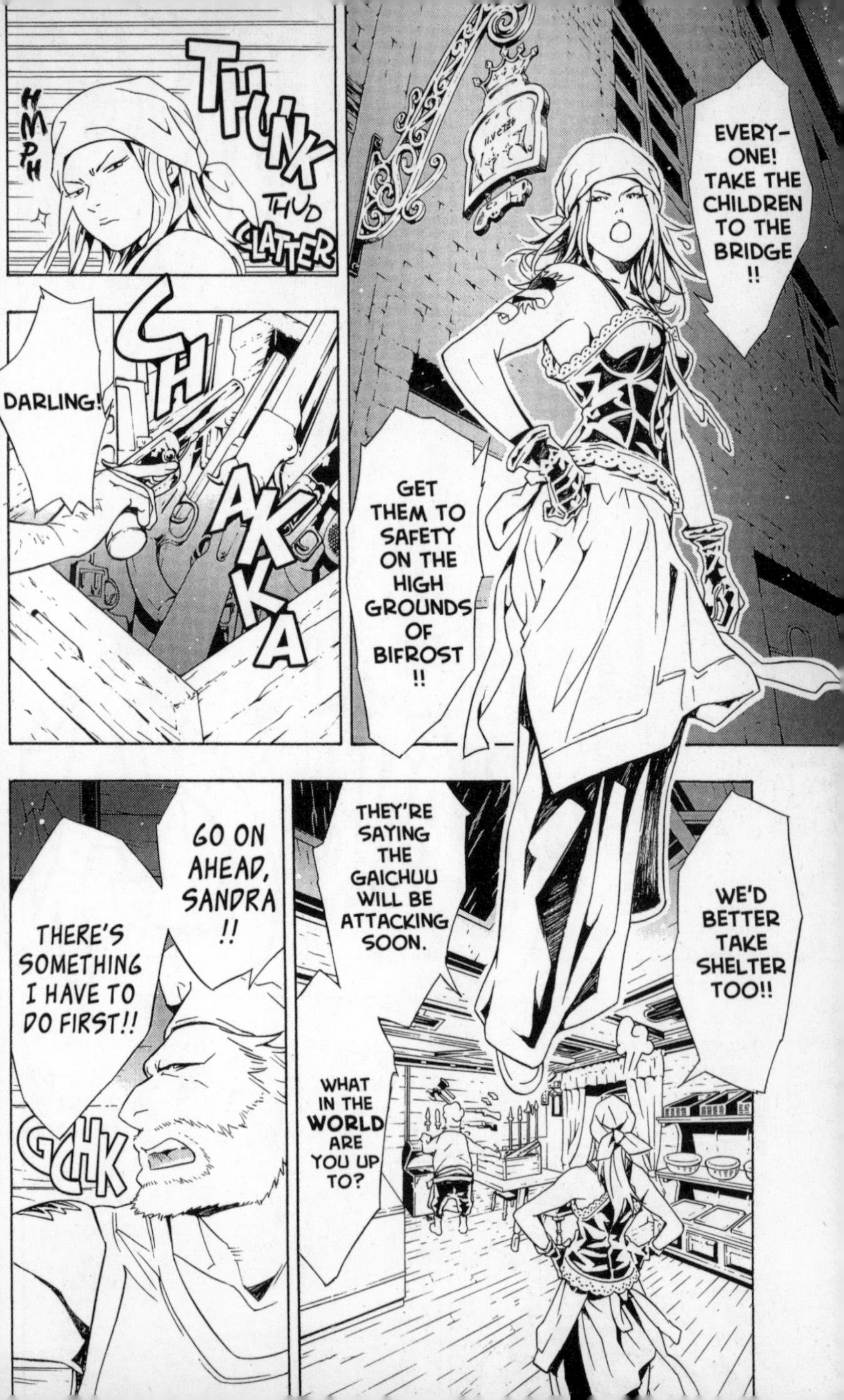
EVERY-ONE! TAKE THE CHILDREN TO THE BRIDGE !!
GET THEM TO SAFETY ON THE HIGH GROUNDS OF BIFROST !!
THUNK
THUD
CLATTER
HMPH
CHAKKA
DARLING!
WE'D BETTER TAKE SHELTER TOO!!
THEY'RE SAYING THE GAICHUU WILL BE ATTACKING SOON.
WHAT IN THE WORLD ARE YOU UP TO?
GO ON AHEAD, SANDRA !!
THERE'S SOMETHING I HAVE TO DO FIRST!!
GCHK

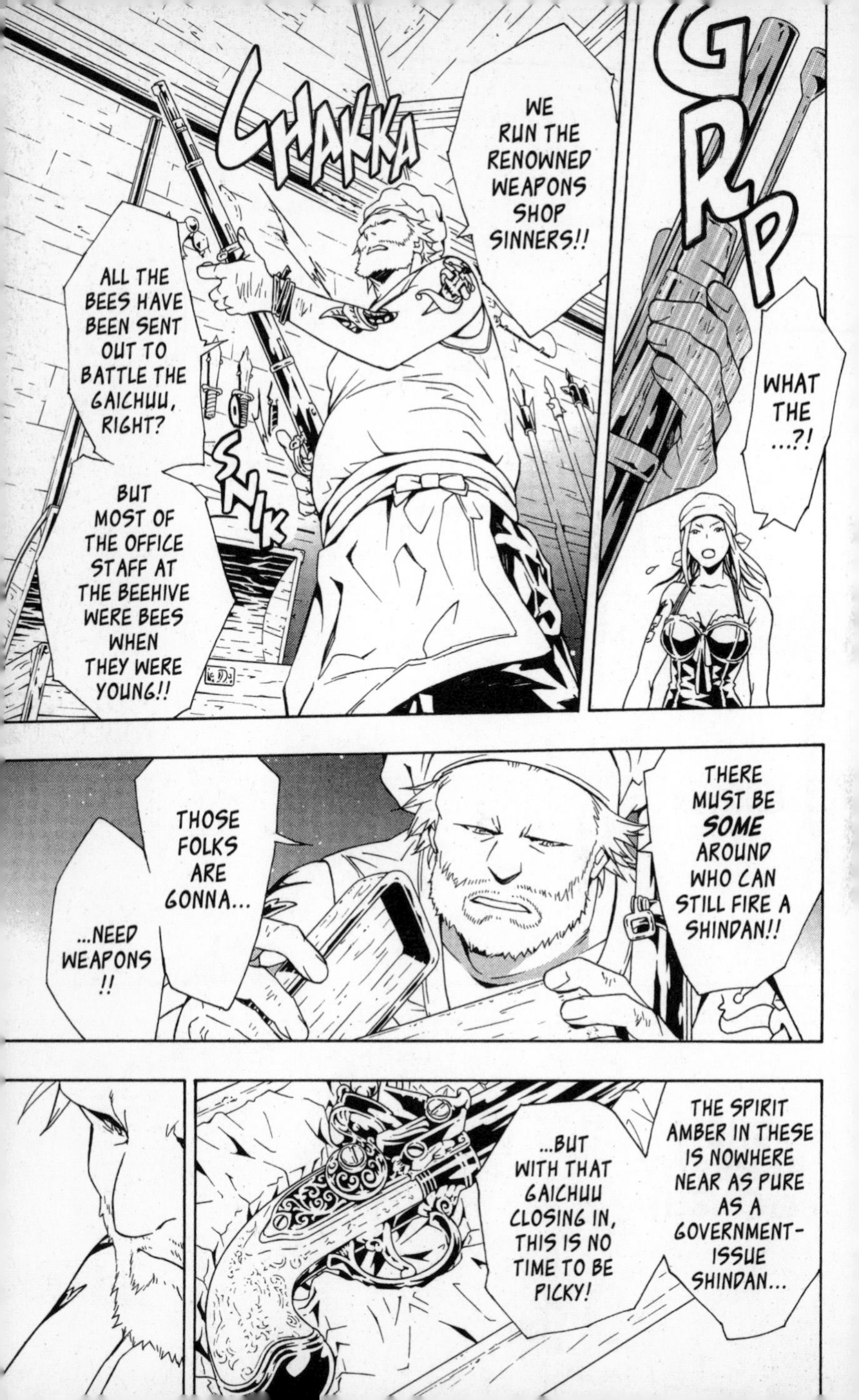
GRP
WHAT THE ...?!
WE RUN THE RENOWNED WEAPONS SHOP SINNERS!!
CHAKKA
ALL THE BEES HAVE BEEN SENT OUT TO BATTLE THE GAICHUU, RIGHT?
SNIK
BUT MOST OF THE OFFICE STAFF AT THE BEEHIVE WERE BEES WHEN THEY WERE YOUNG!!
THERE MUST BE **SOME** AROUND WHO CAN STILL FIRE A SHINDAN!!
THOSE FOLKS ARE GONNA...
...NEED WEAPONS!!
THE SPIRIT AMBER IN THESE IS NOWHERE NEAR AS PURE AS A GOVERNMENT-ISSUE SHINDAN...
...BUT WITH THAT GAICHUU CLOSING IN, THIS IS NO TIME TO BE PICKY!

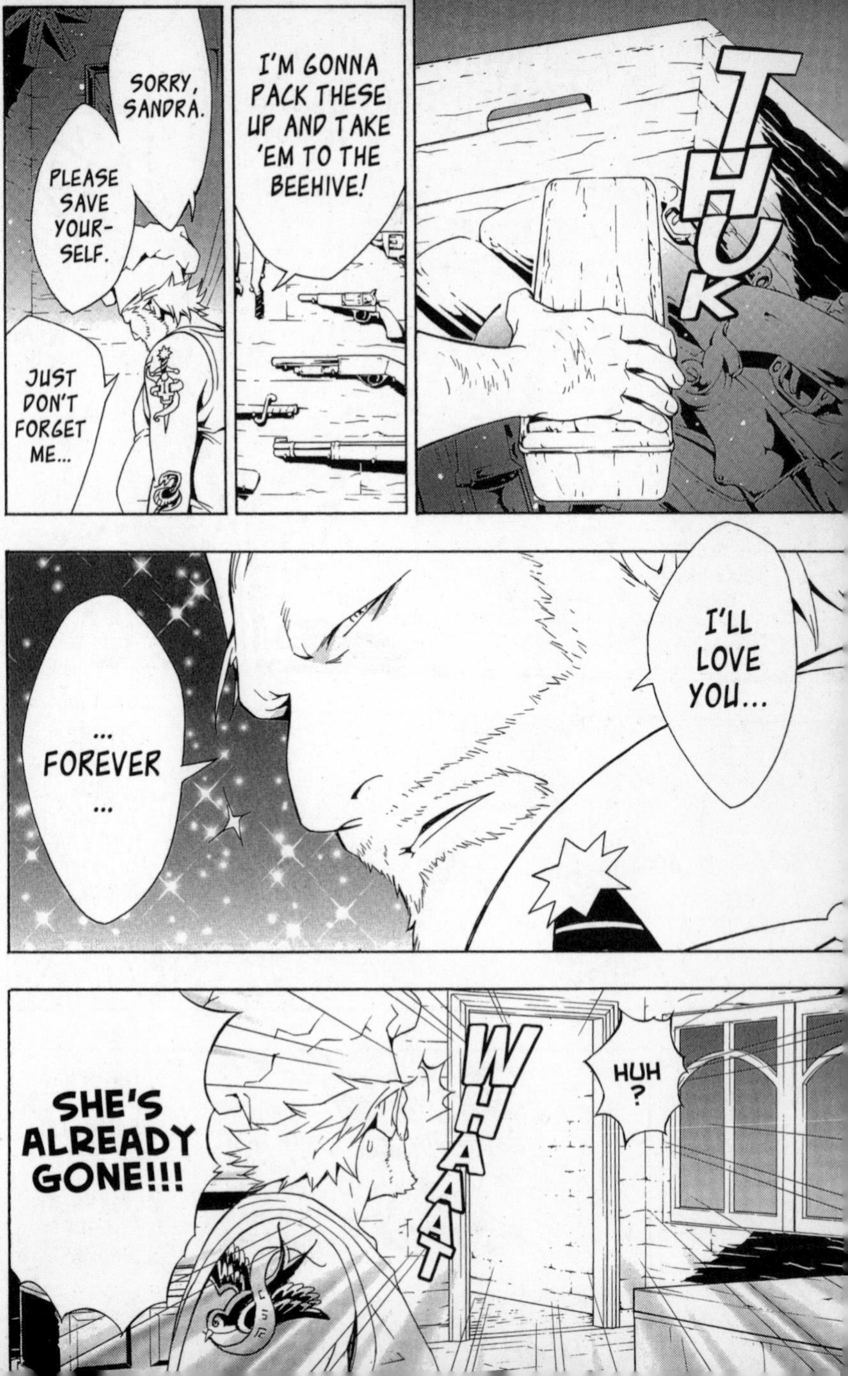
THUK
I'M GONNA PACK THESE UP AND TAKE 'EM TO THE BEEHIVE!
SORRY, SANDRA.
PLEASE SAVE YOUR-SELF.
JUST DON'T FORGET ME...
I'LL LOVE YOU...
... FOREVER ...
HUH ?
WHAAAT
SHE'S ALREADY GONE!!!

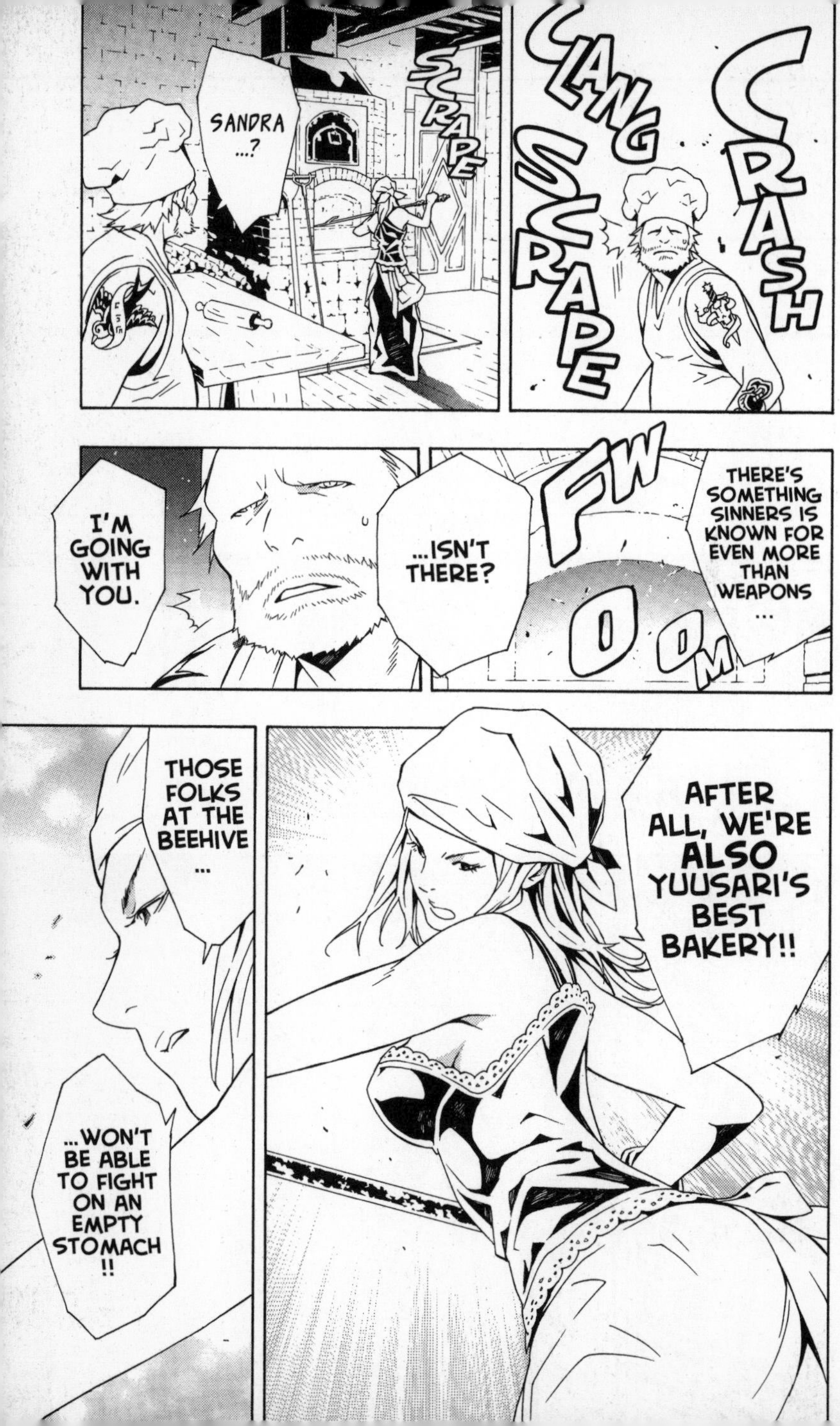
CRASH
CLANG
SCRAPE
SCRAPE
SANDRA ...?
THERE'S SOMETHING SINNERS IS KNOWN FOR EVEN MORE THAN WEAPONS ...
FWOOOM
...ISN'T THERE?
I'M GOING WITH YOU.
AFTER ALL, WE'RE ALSO YUUSARI'S BEST BAKERY!!
THOSE FOLKS AT THE BEEHIVE ...
...WON'T BE ABLE TO FIGHT ON AN EMPTY STOMACH !!

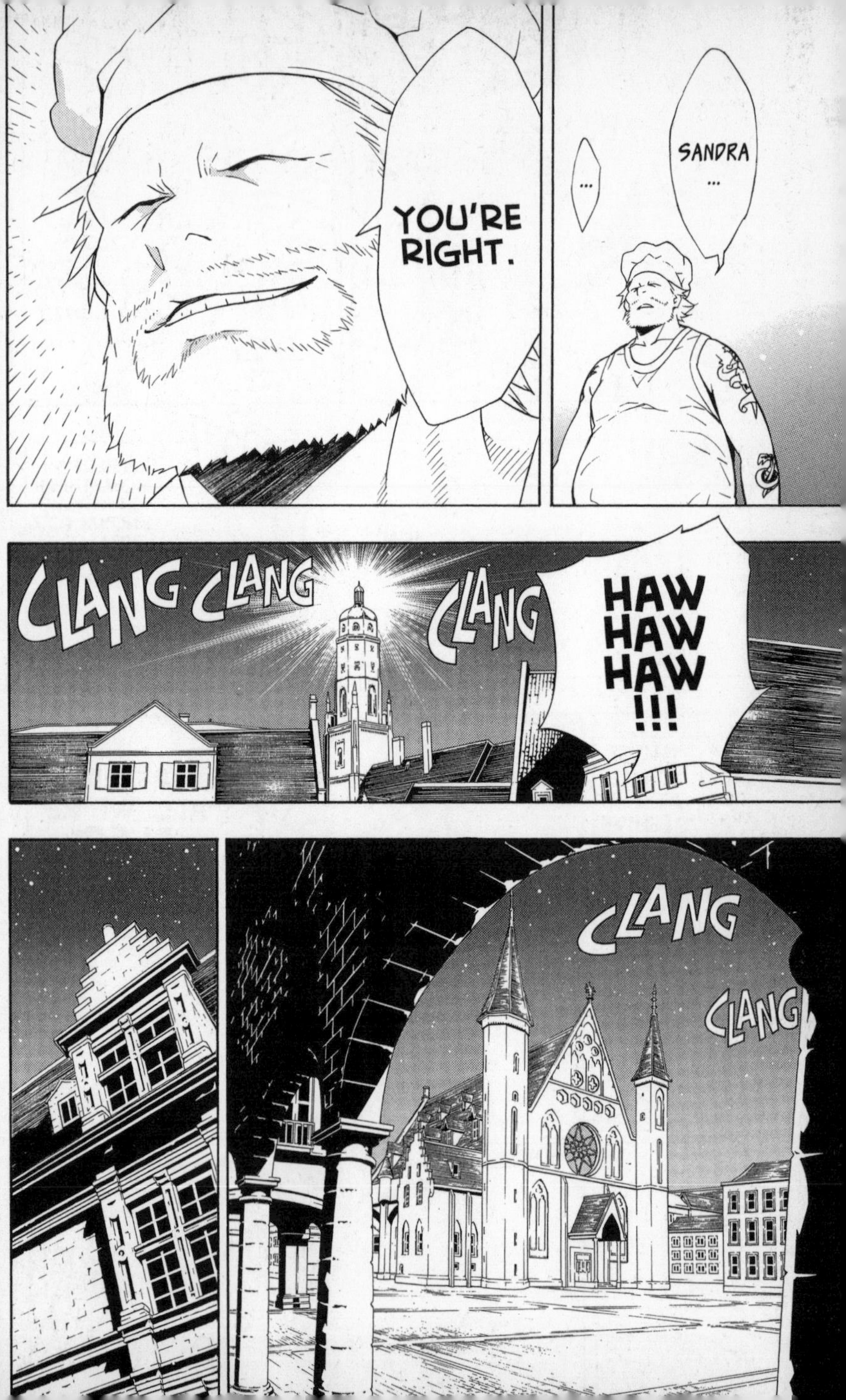
SANDRA ...
...
YOU'RE RIGHT.
HAW HAW HAW !!!
CLANG
CLANG CLANG
CLANG
CLANG

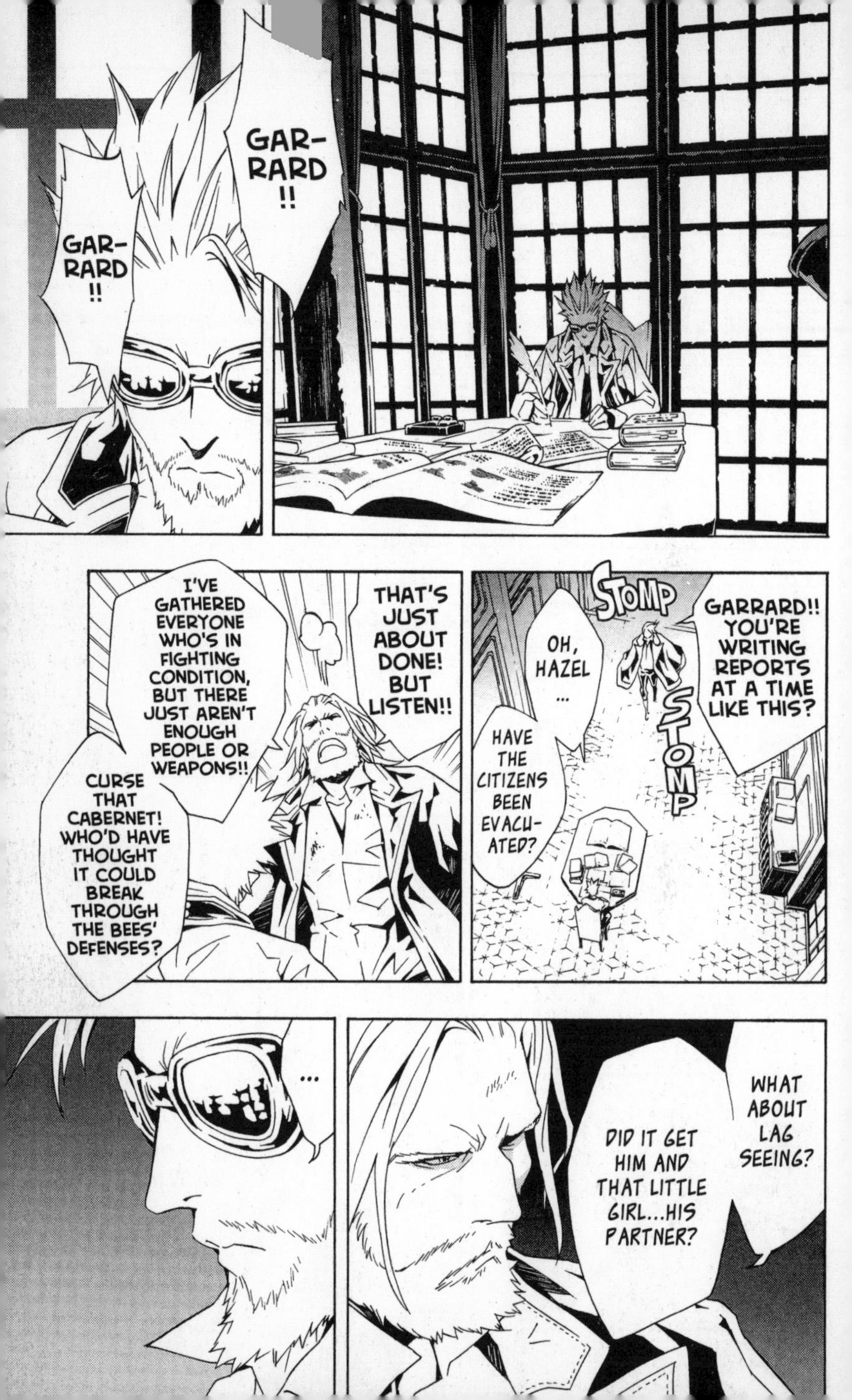
GAR-RARD!!
GAR-RARD!!
STOMP
GARRARD!! YOU'RE WRITING REPORTS AT A TIME LIKE THIS?
STOMP
OH, HAZEL...
HAVE THE CITIZENS BEEN EVACUATED?
THAT'S JUST ABOUT DONE! BUT LISTEN!!
I'VE GATHERED EVERYONE WHO'S IN FIGHTING CONDITION, BUT THERE JUST AREN'T ENOUGH PEOPLE OR WEAPONS!!
CURSE THAT CABERNET! WHO'D HAVE THOUGHT IT COULD BREAK THROUGH THE BEES' DEFENSES?
WHAT ABOUT LAG SEEING?
DID IT GET HIM AND THAT LITTLE GIRL...HIS PARTNER?
...

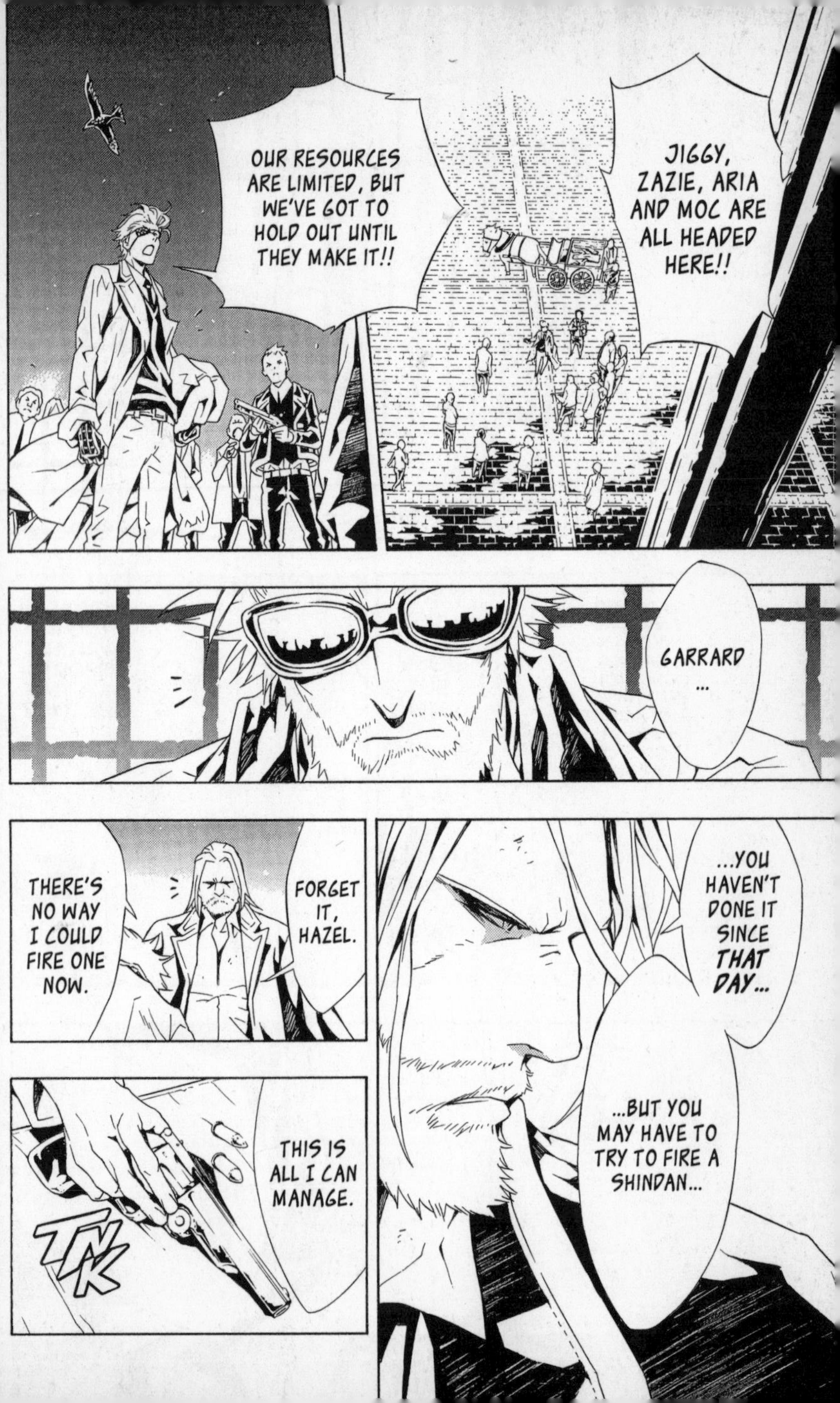
JIGGY, ZAZIE, ARIA AND MOC ARE ALL HEADED HERE!!
OUR RESOURCES ARE LIMITED, BUT WE'VE GOT TO HOLD OUT UNTIL THEY MAKE IT!!
GARRARD ...
...YOU HAVEN'T DONE IT SINCE *THAT DAY*...
...BUT YOU MAY HAVE TO TRY TO FIRE A SHINDAN...
FORGET IT, HAZEL.
THERE'S NO WAY I COULD FIRE ONE NOW.
THIS IS ALL I CAN MANAGE.
TNK

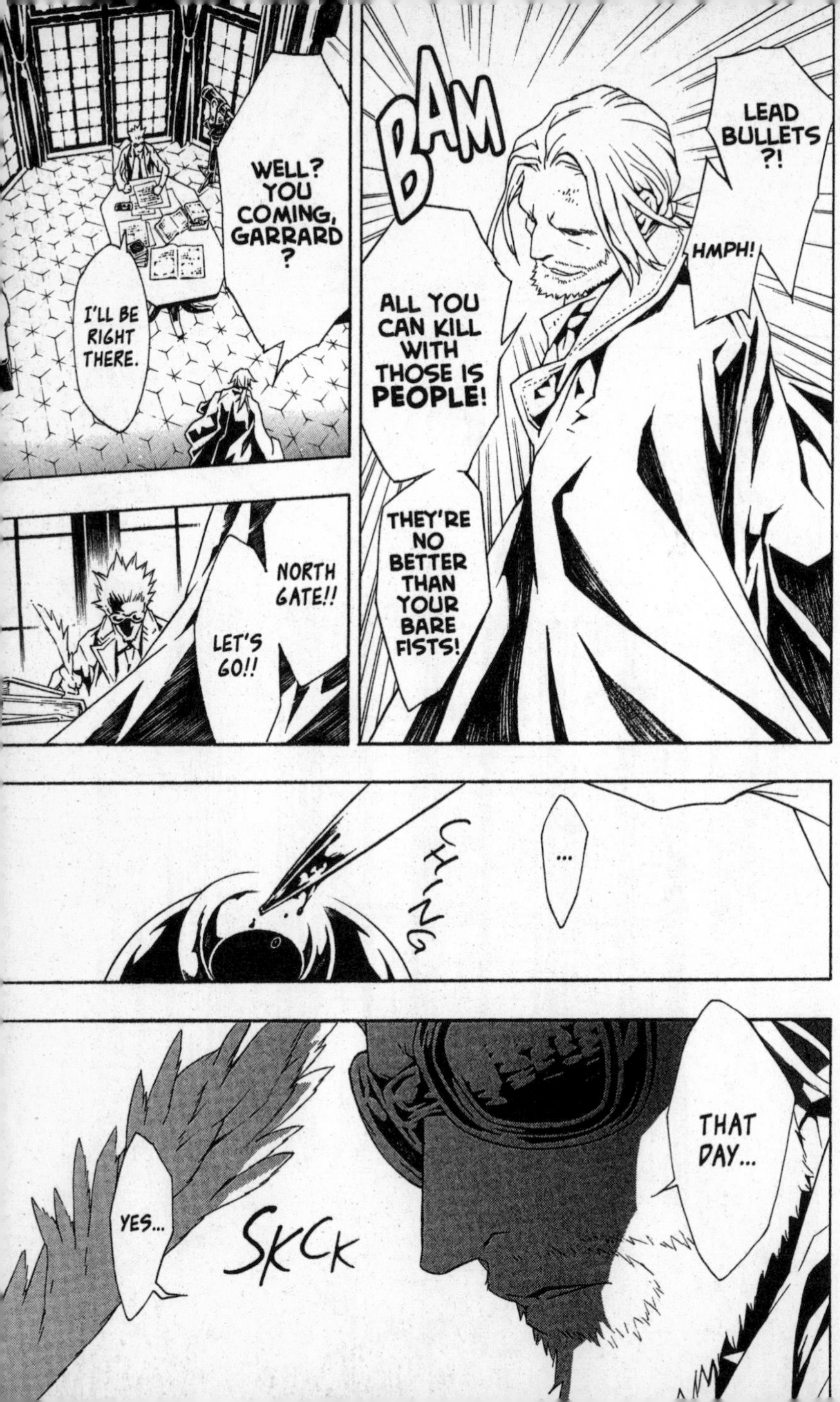
LEAD BULLETS?!
BAM
HMPH!
ALL YOU CAN KILL WITH THOSE IS **PEOPLE**!
THEY'RE NO BETTER THAN YOUR BARE FISTS!
WELL? YOU COMING, GARRARD?
I'LL BE RIGHT THERE.
NORTH GATE!!
LET'S GO!!
...
CHING
THAT DAY...
SKCK
YES...

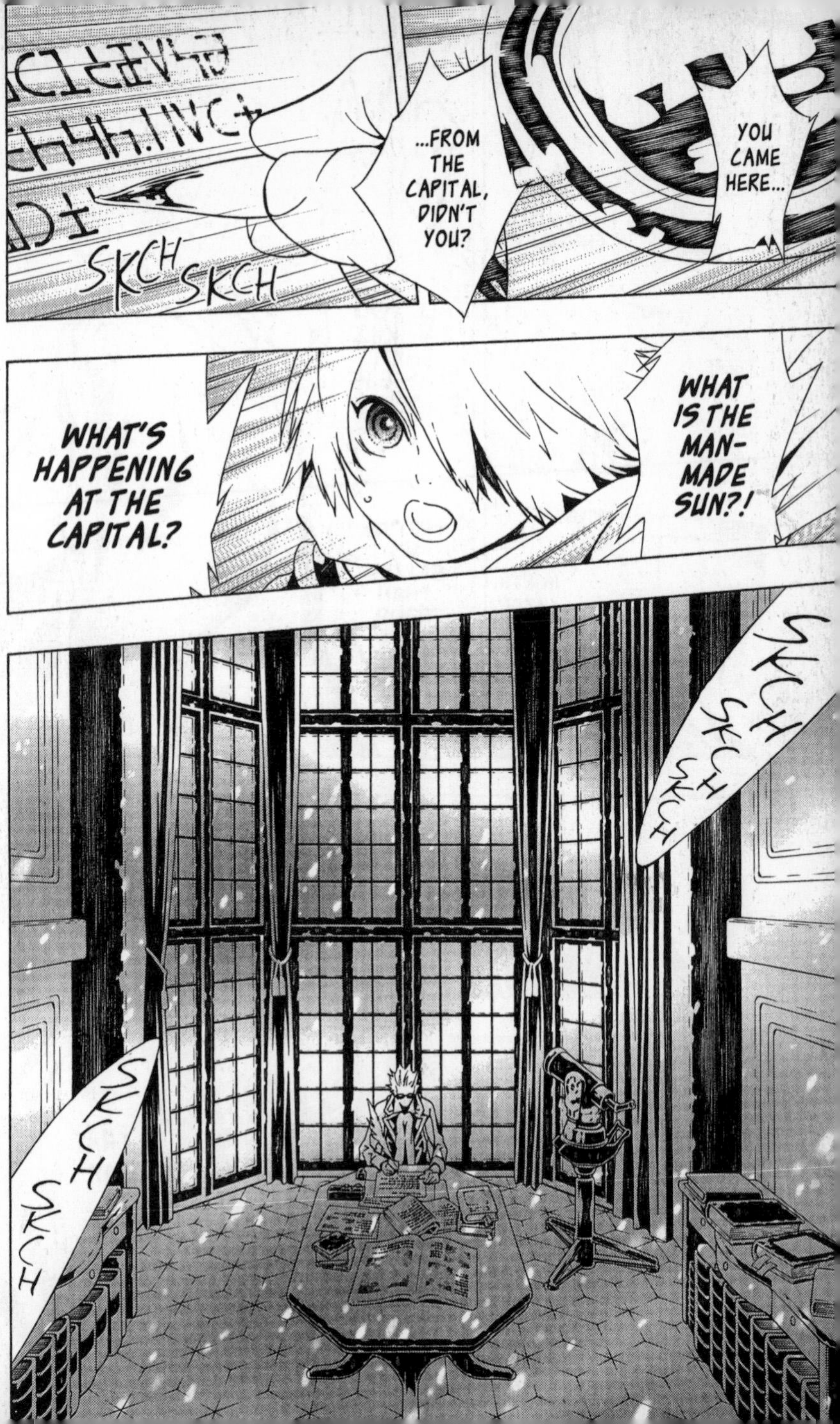
YOU CAME HERE...
...FROM THE CAPITAL, DIDN'T YOU?
SKCH SKCH
WHAT IS THE MAN-MADE SUN?!
WHAT'S HAPPENING AT THE CAPITAL?
SKCH SKCH SKCH
SKCH SKCH

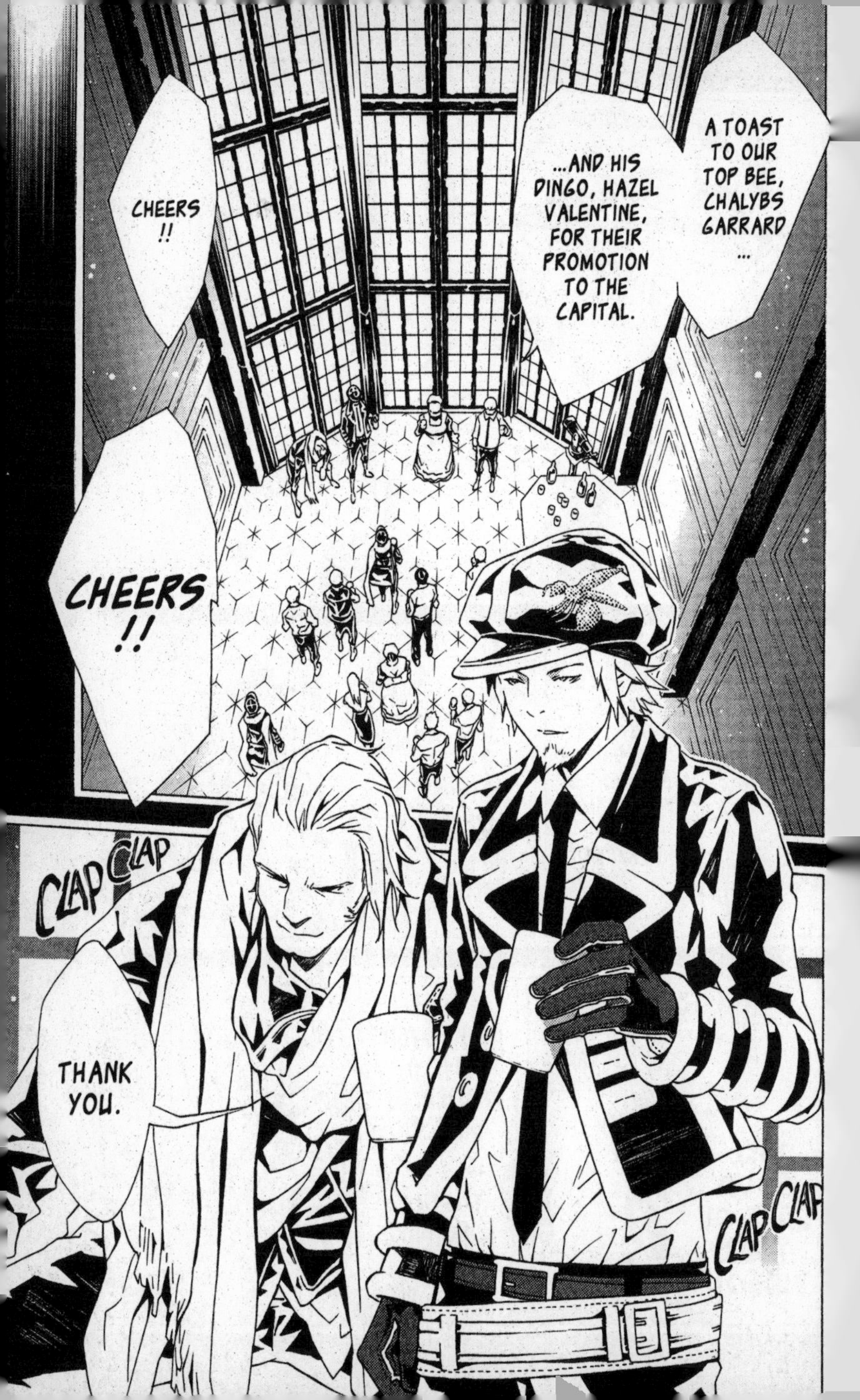
A TOAST TO OUR TOP BEE, CHALYBS GARRARD ...
...AND HIS DINGO, HAZEL VALENTINE, FOR THEIR PROMOTION TO THE CAPITAL.
CHEERS !!
CHEERS !!
CLAP CLAP
THANK YOU.
CLAP CLAP

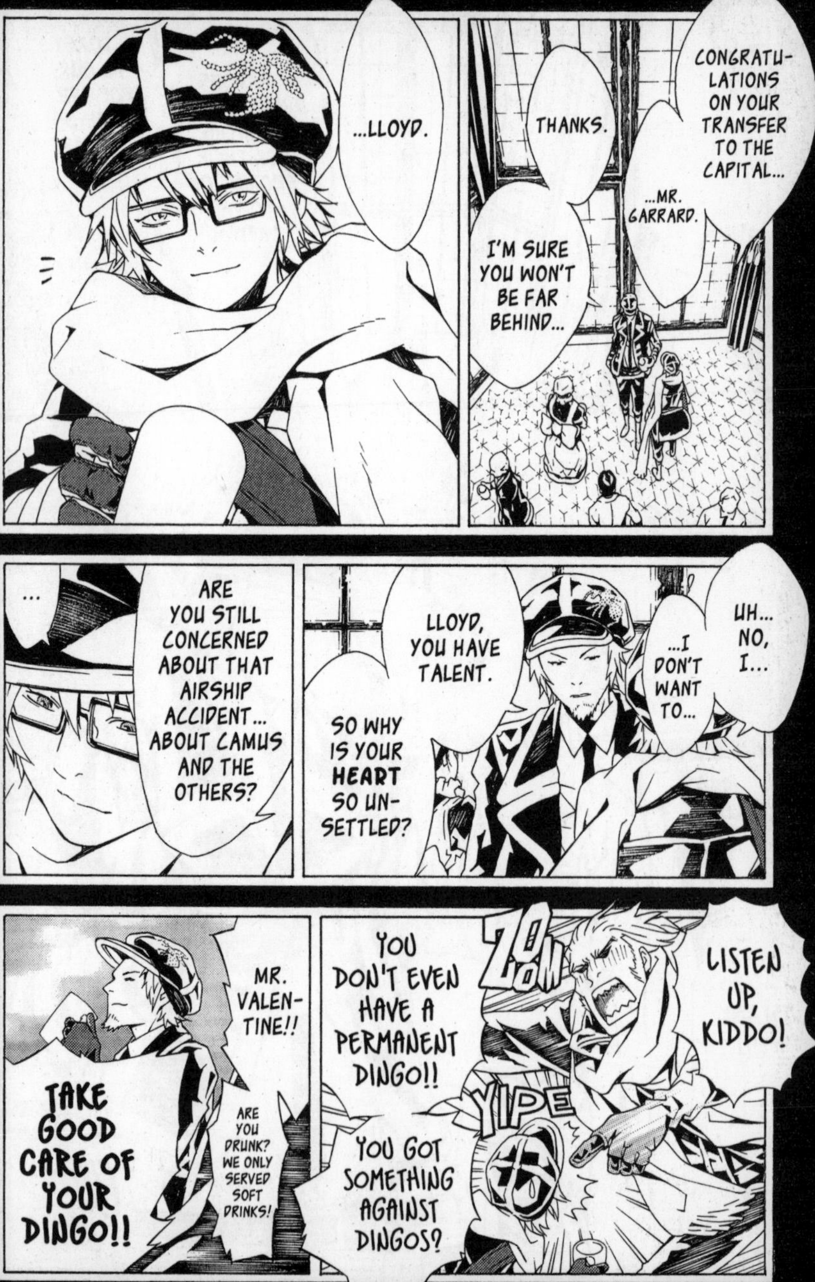
CONGRATULATIONS ON YOUR TRANSFER TO THE CAPITAL...
...MR. GARRARD.
THANKS.
I'M SURE YOU WON'T BE FAR BEHIND...
...LLOYD.
UH... NO, I...
...I DON'T WANT TO...
LLOYD, YOU HAVE TALENT.
SO WHY IS YOUR HEART SO UNSETTLED?
...
ARE YOU STILL CONCERNED ABOUT THAT AIRSHIP ACCIDENT... ABOUT CAMUS AND THE OTHERS?
LISTEN UP, KIDDO!
ZOOM
YOU DON'T EVEN HAVE A PERMANENT DINGO!!
YIPE
YOU GOT SOMETHING AGAINST DINGOS?
MR. VALENTINE!!
ARE YOU DRUNK? WE ONLY SERVED SOFT DRINKS!
TAKE GOOD CARE OF YOUR DINGO!!

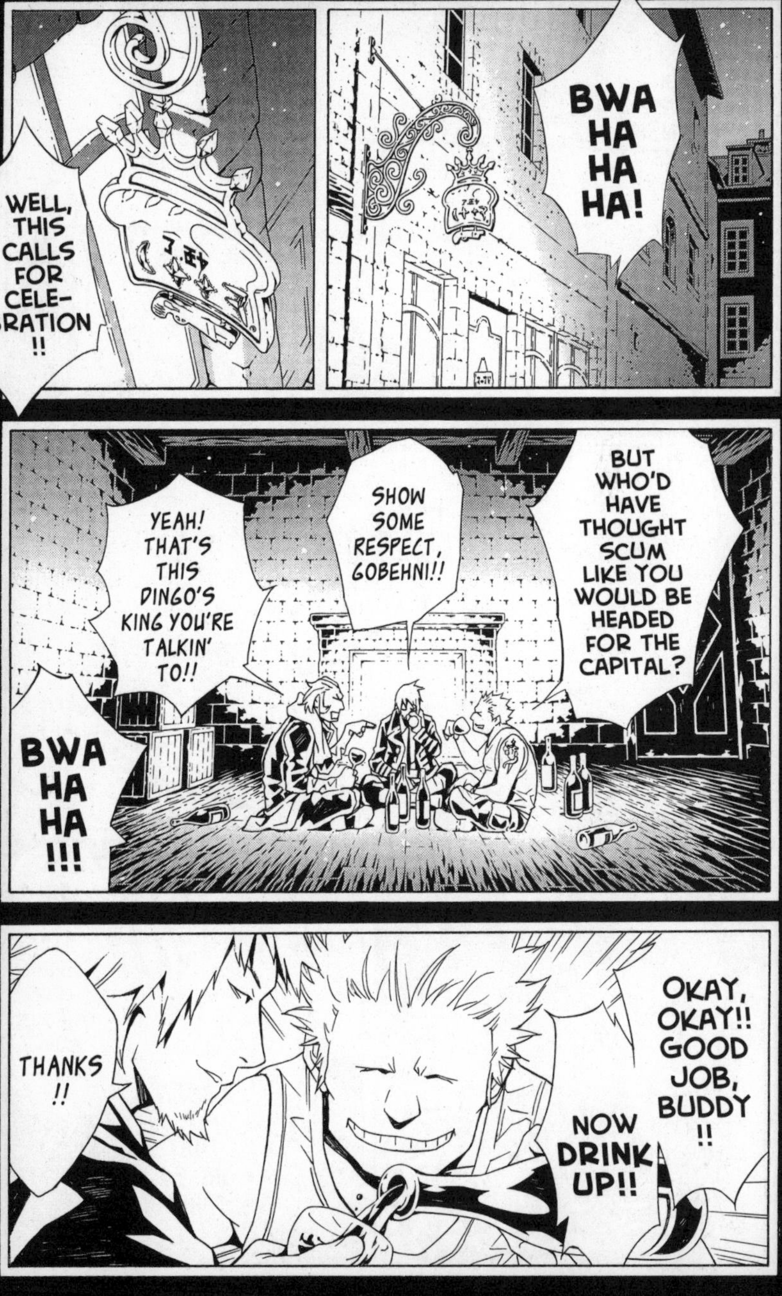
BWA HA HA HA!
WELL, THIS CALLS FOR CELE-BRATION!!
BUT WHO'D HAVE THOUGHT SCUM LIKE YOU WOULD BE HEADED FOR THE CAPITAL?
SHOW SOME RESPECT, GOBEHNI!!
YEAH! THAT'S THIS DINGO'S KING YOU'RE TALKIN' TO!!
BWA HA HA!!!
OKAY, OKAY!! GOOD JOB, BUDDY!!
NOW DRINK UP!!
THANKS!!

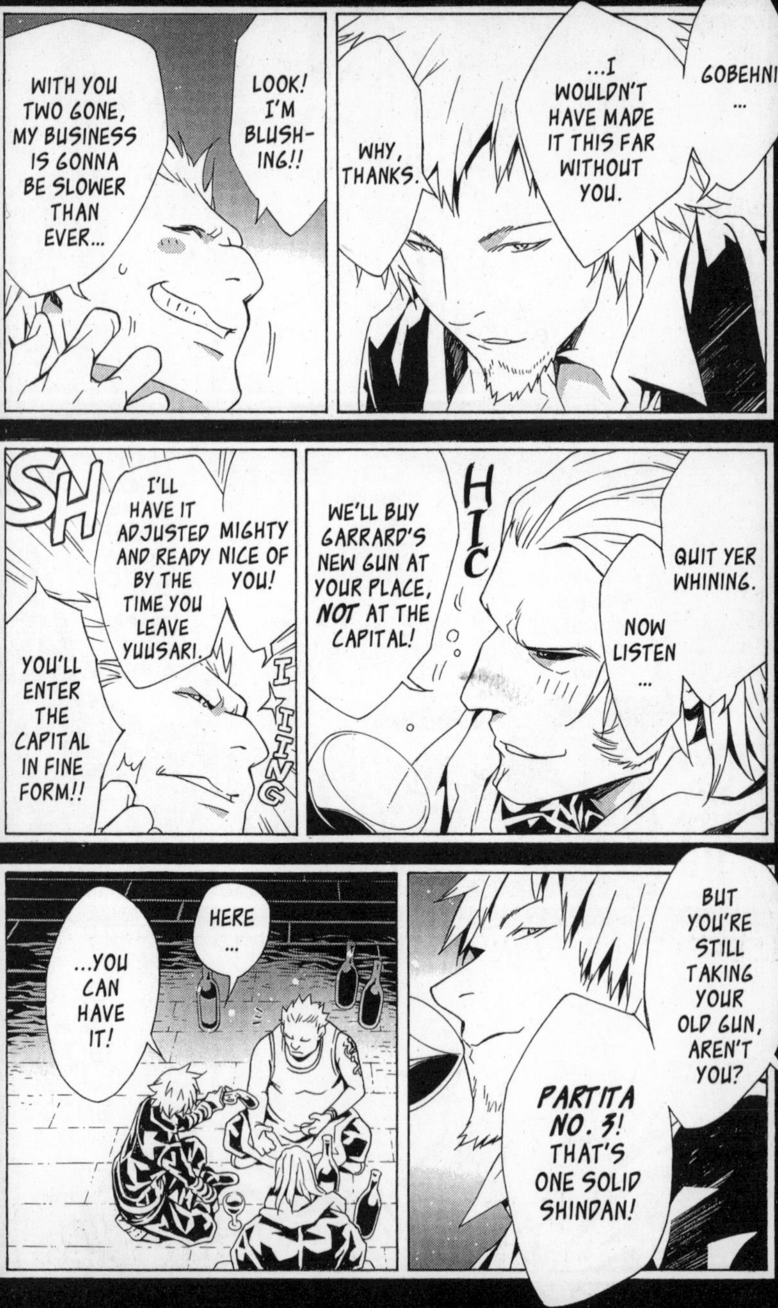
GOBEHNI ...
...I WOULDN'T HAVE MADE IT THIS FAR WITHOUT YOU.
WHY, THANKS.
LOOK! I'M BLUSH-ING!!
WITH YOU TWO GONE, MY BUSINESS IS GONNA BE SLOWER THAN EVER...
QUIT YER WHINING.
NOW LISTEN ...
HIC
WE'LL BUY GARRARD'S NEW GUN AT YOUR PLACE, *NOT* AT THE CAPITAL!
MIGHTY NICE OF YOU!
I'LL HAVE IT ADJUSTED AND READY BY THE TIME YOU LEAVE YUUSARI.
SH
IIIING
YOU'LL ENTER THE CAPITAL IN FINE FORM!!
BUT YOU'RE STILL TAKING YOUR OLD GUN, AREN'T YOU?
PARTITA NO. 3! THAT'S ONE SOLID SHINDAN!
HERE ...
...YOU CAN HAVE IT!

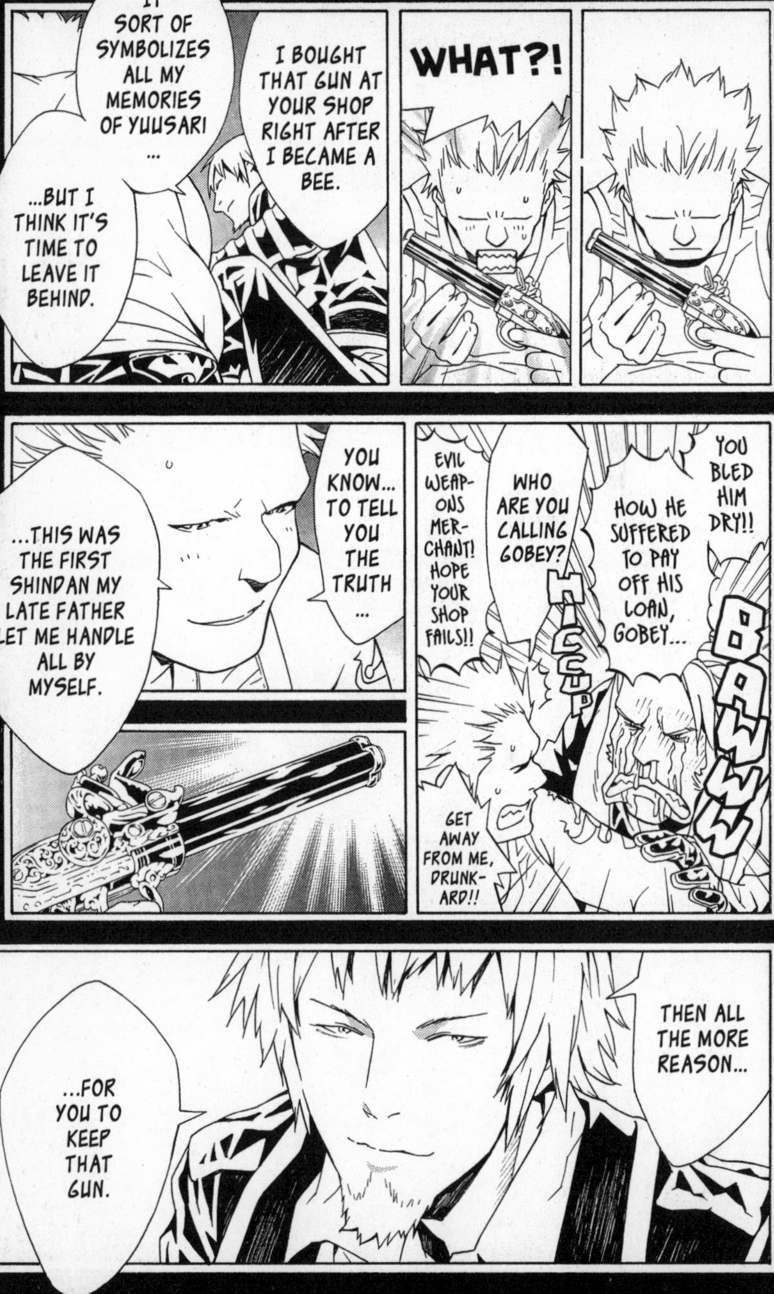
WHAT?!
I BOUGHT THAT GUN AT YOUR SHOP RIGHT AFTER I BECAME A BEE.
IT SORT OF SYMBOLIZES ALL MY MEMORIES OF YUUSARI ...
...BUT I THINK IT'S TIME TO LEAVE IT BEHIND.
YOU BLED HIM DRY!!
HOW HE SUFFERED TO PAY OFF HIS LOAN, GOBEY...
BAWWW
WHO ARE YOU CALLING GOBEY?
HICCUP
EVIL WEAPONS MERCHANT! HOPE YOUR SHOP FAILS!!
GET AWAY FROM ME, DRUNKARD!!
YOU KNOW... TO TELL YOU THE TRUTH ...
...THIS WAS THE FIRST SHINDAN MY LATE FATHER LET ME HANDLE ALL BY MYSELF.
THEN ALL THE MORE REASON...
...FOR YOU TO KEEP THAT GUN.

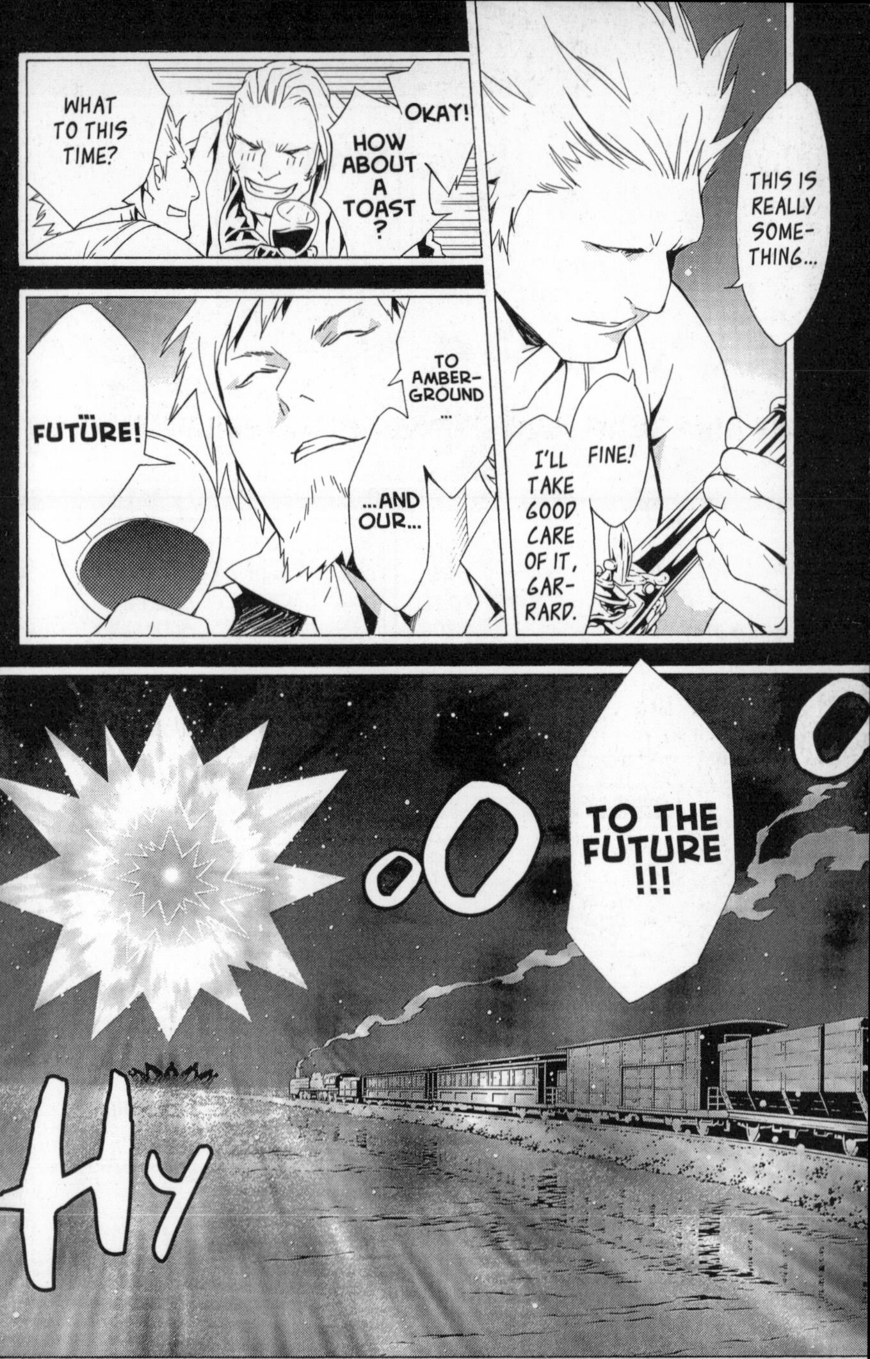
THIS IS REALLY SOME-THING...
FINE!
I'LL TAKE GOOD CARE OF IT, GAR-RARD.
OKAY!
HOW ABOUT A TOAST?
WHAT TO THIS TIME?
TO AMBER-GROUND...
...AND OUR...
FUTÜRE!
TO THE FUTURE!!!

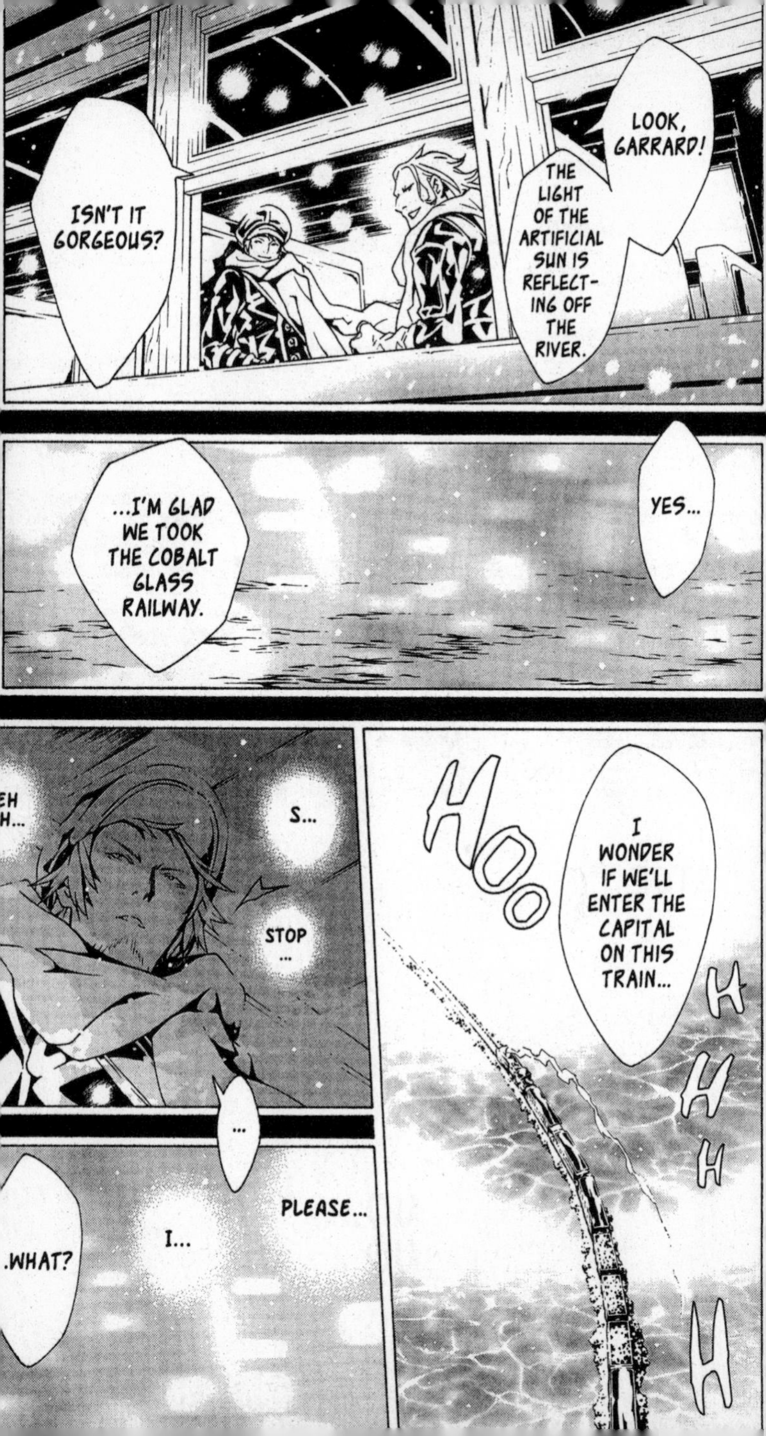
LOOK, GARRARD!
THE LIGHT OF THE ARTIFICIAL SUN IS REFLECTING OFF THE RIVER.
ISN'T IT GORGEOUS?
YES...
...I'M GLAD WE TOOK THE COBALT GLASS RAILWAY.
HOOHHHH
I WONDER IF WE'LL ENTER THE CAPITAL ON THIS TRAIN...
S...
STOP ...
...
PLEASE...
I...
.WHAT?

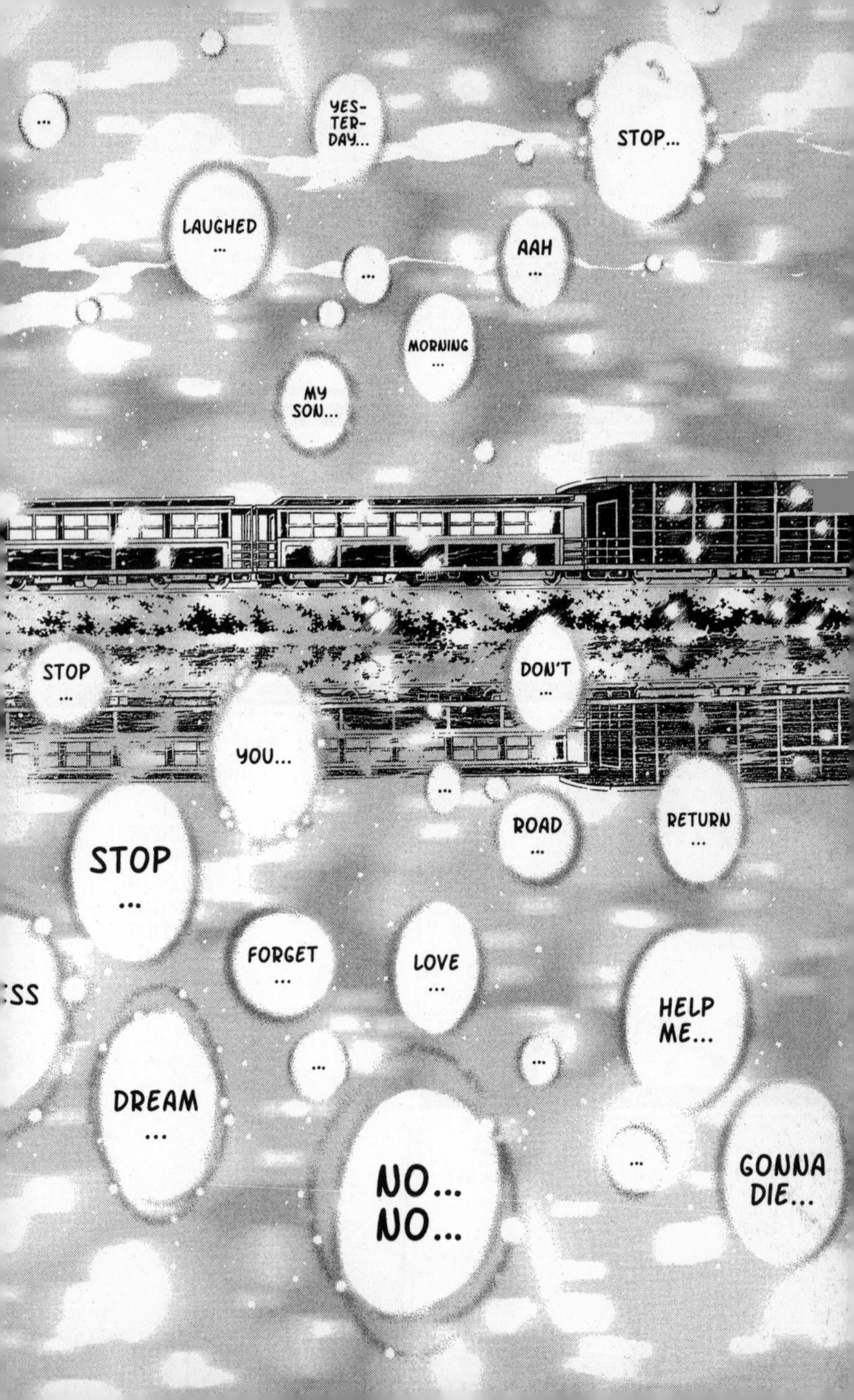
STOP...
YES-TER-DAY...
...
AAH ...
...
LAUGHED ...
MORNING ...
MY SON...
DON'T ...
STOP ...
RETURN ...
ROAD ...
...
YOU...
HELP ME...
LOVE ...
FORGET ...
STOP ...
...
...
DREAM ...
GONNA DIE...
...
NO... NO...

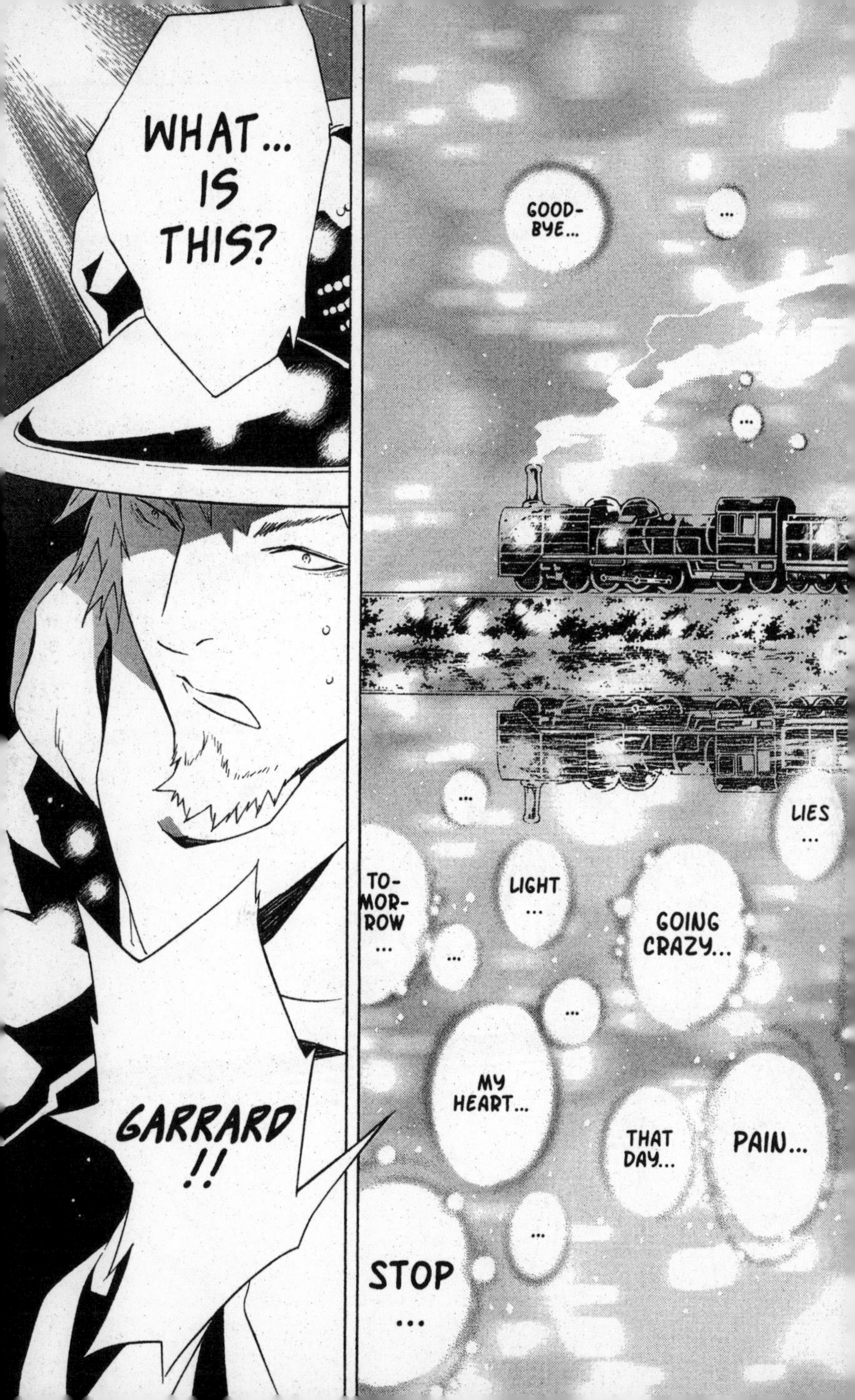
...
GOOD-BYE...
...
LIES...
...
GOING CRAZY...
LIGHT...
TO-MOR-ROW...
...
...
PAIN...
THAT DAY...
MY HEART...
...
STOP...
WHAT... IS THIS?
GARRARD!!

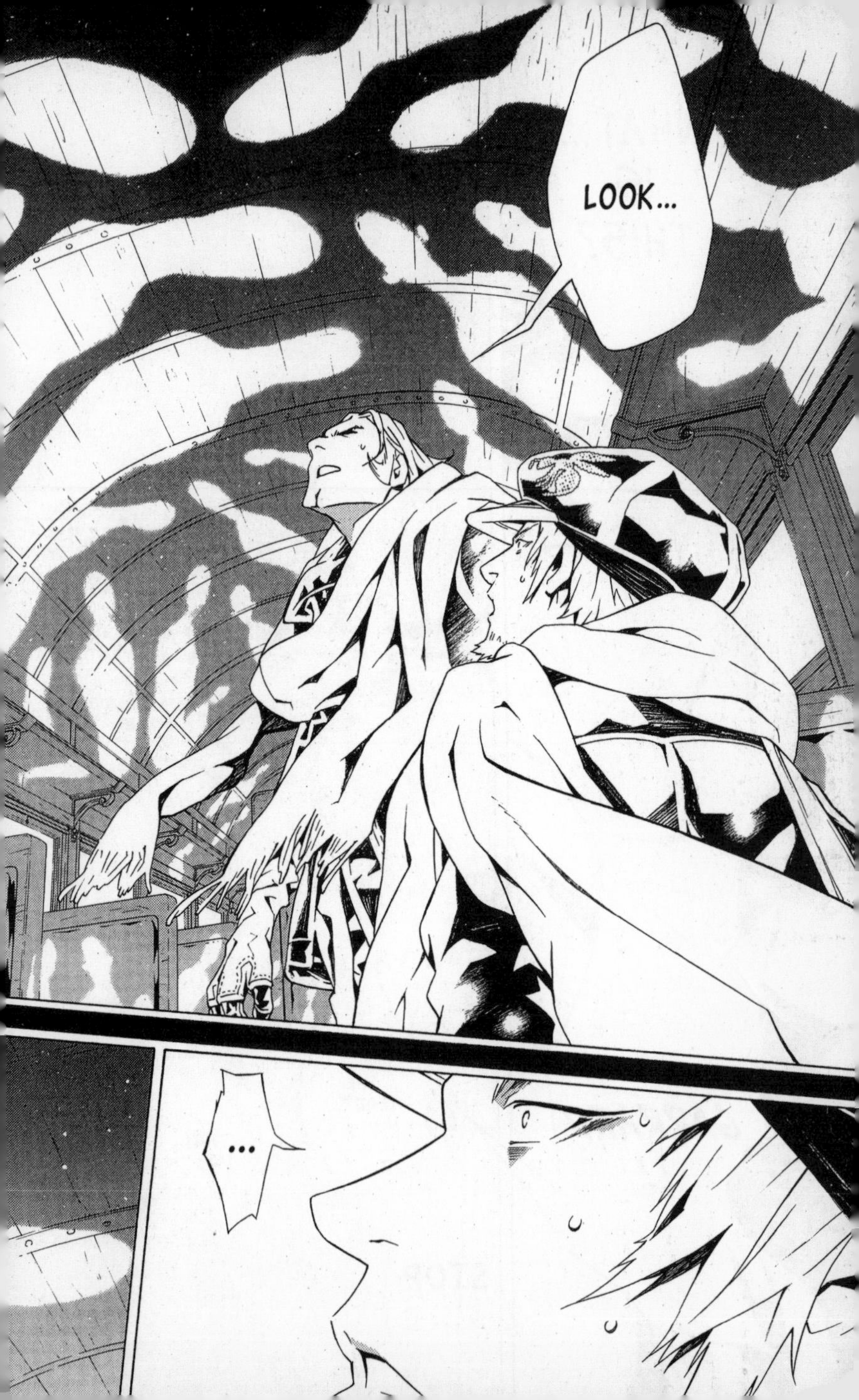
LOOK...
...

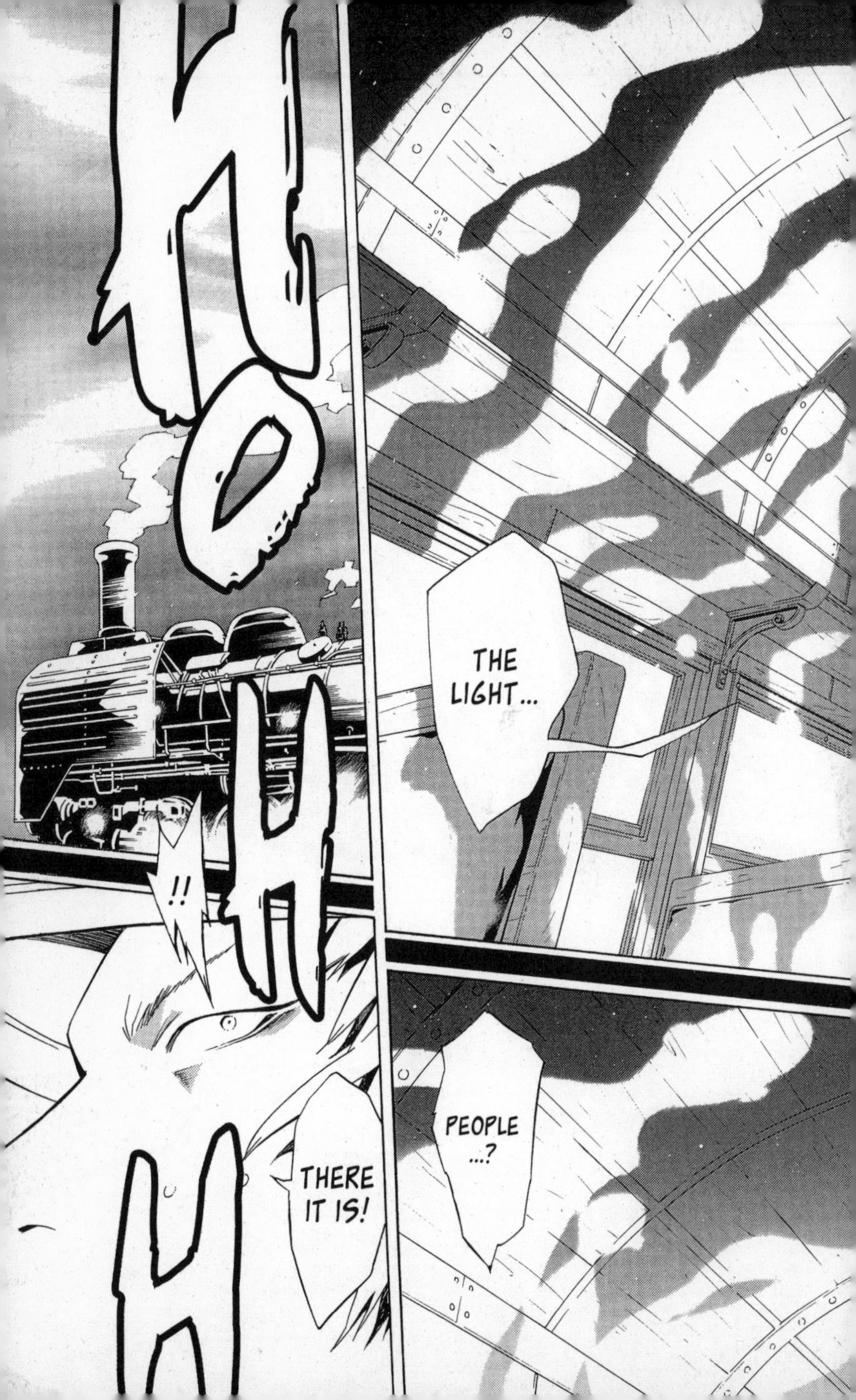
THE LIGHT...
PEOPLE ...?
!!
THERE IT IS!

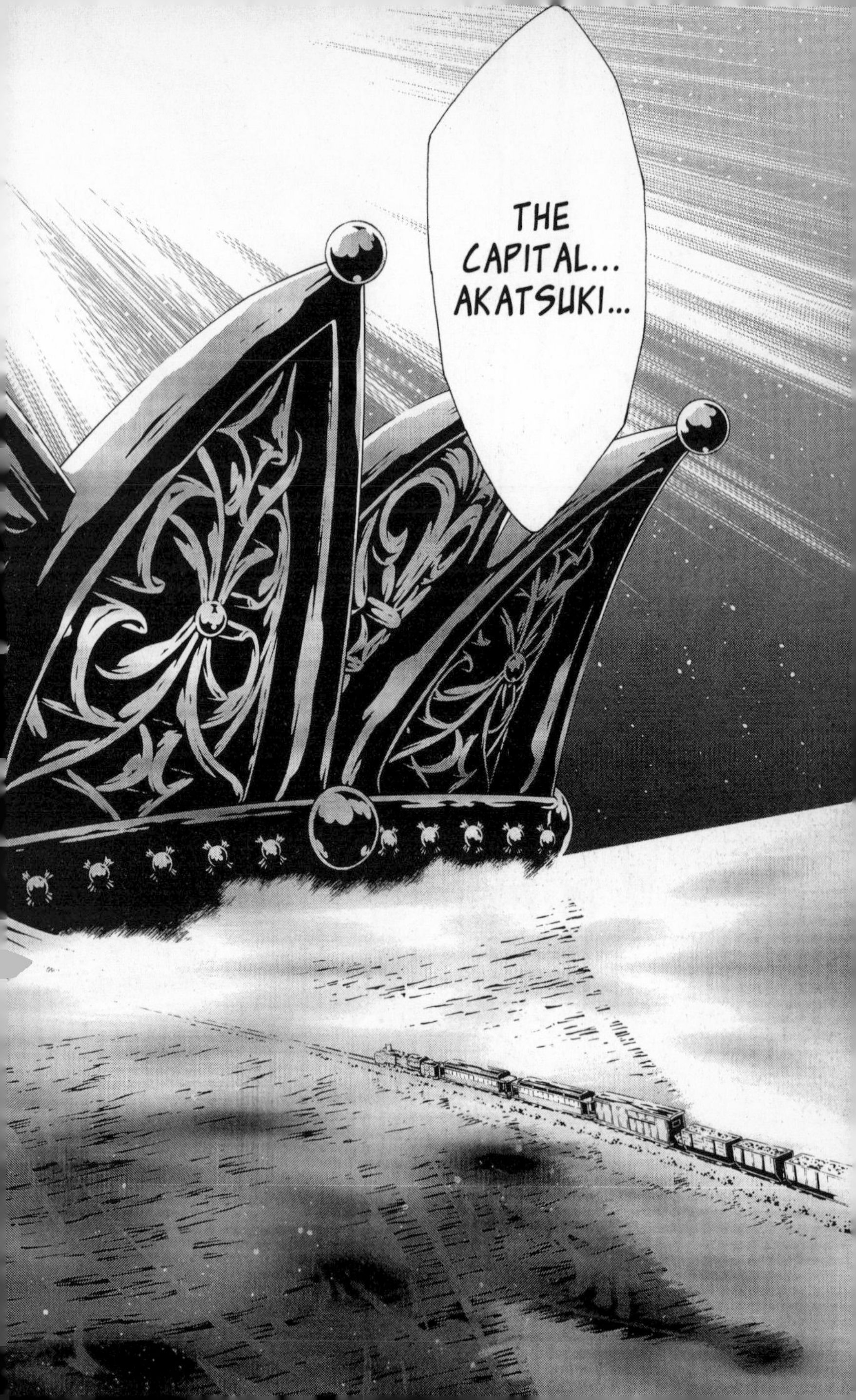
THE CAPITAL... AKATSUKI...

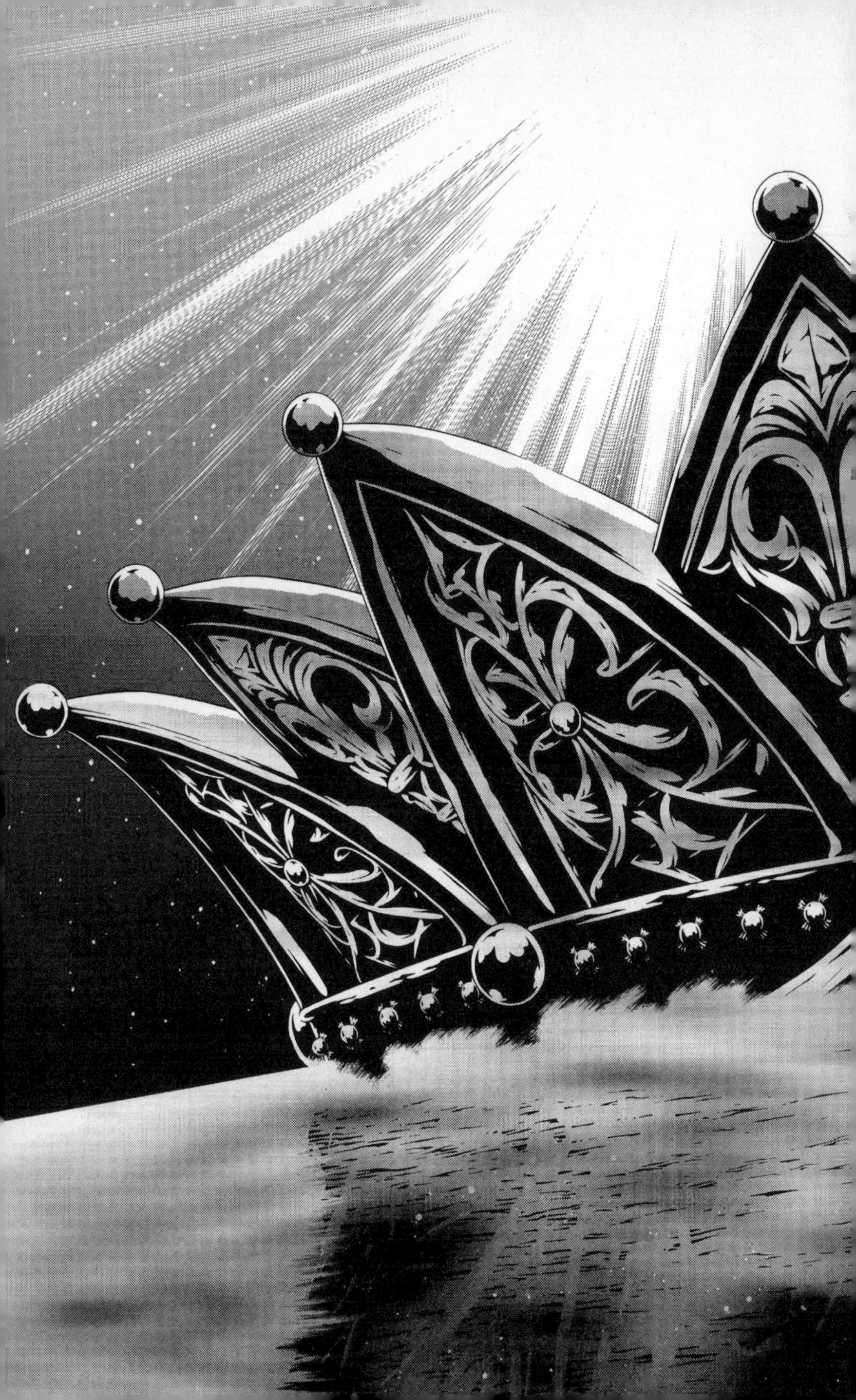

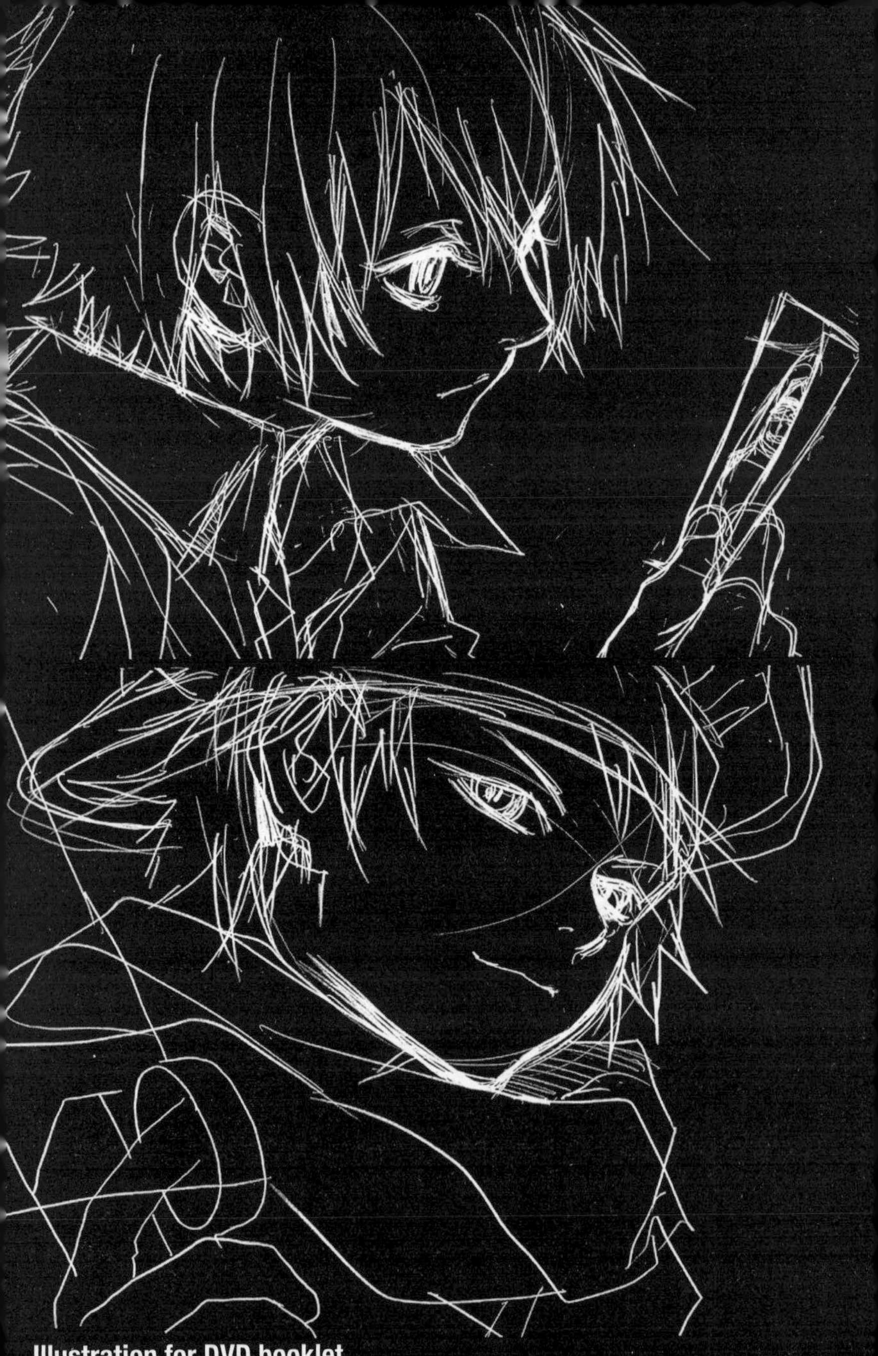

Illustration for DVD booklet.

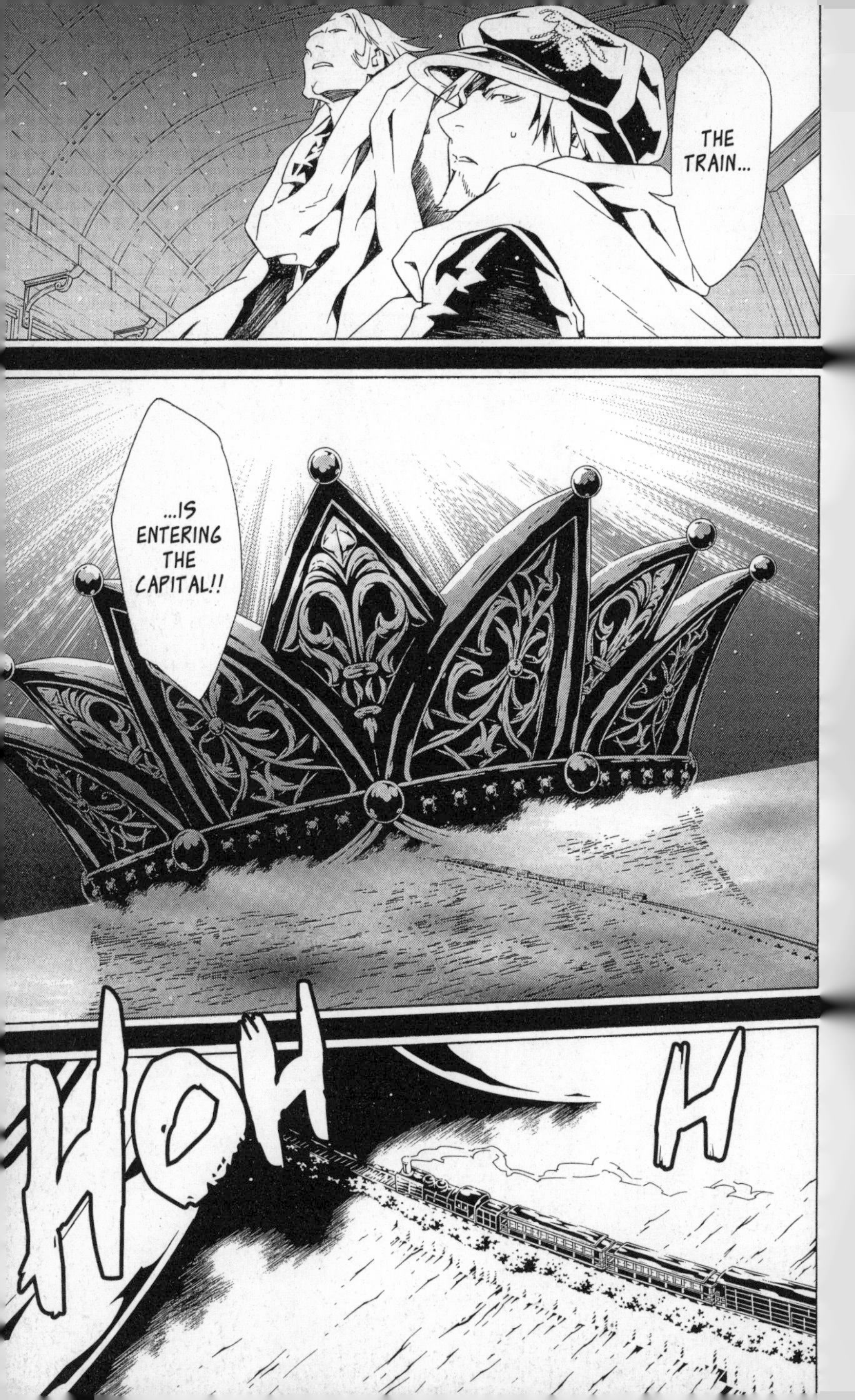
THE TRAIN...
...IS ENTERING THE CAPITAL!!

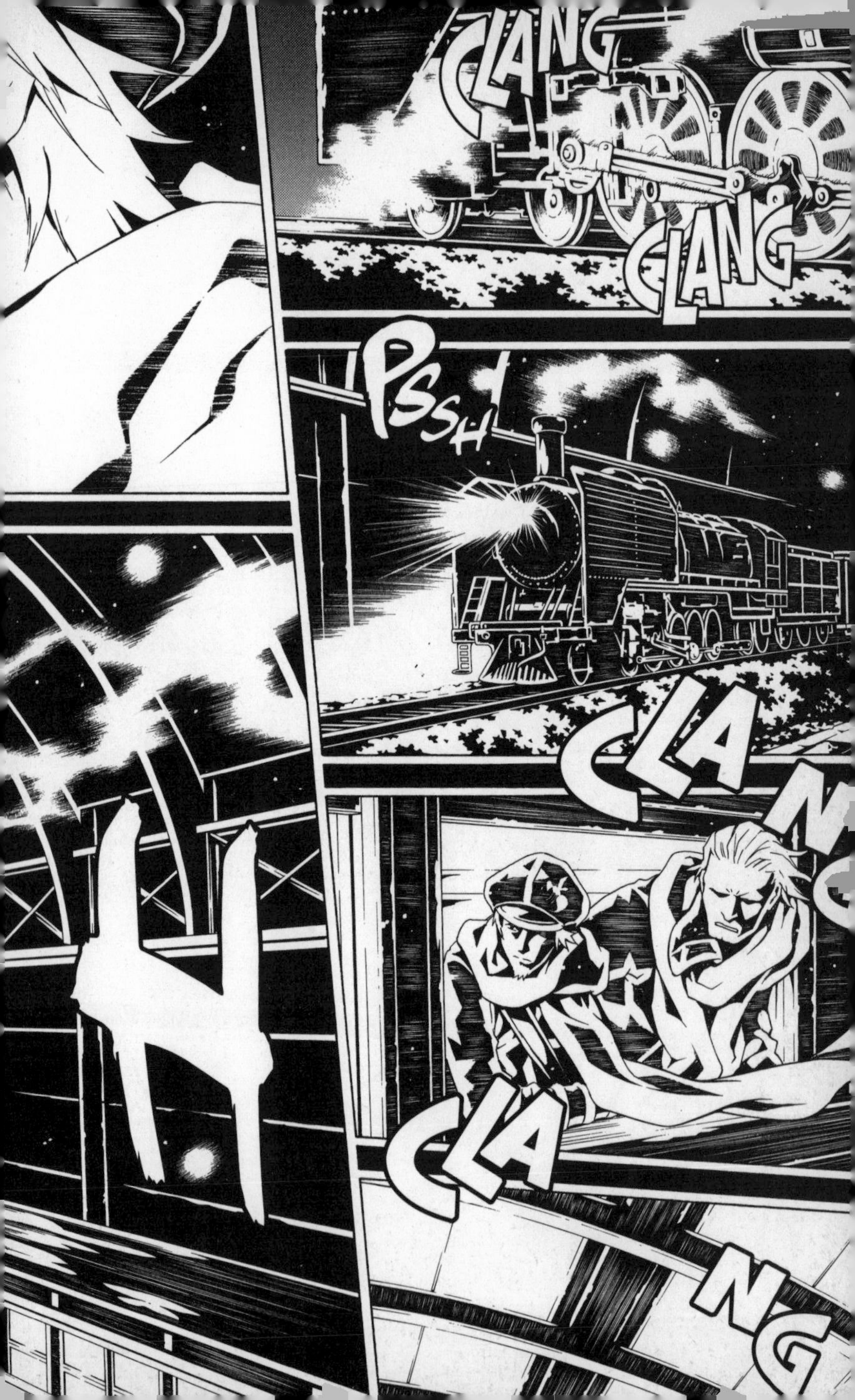
CLANG
CLANG
PSSH
CLANG
CLANG

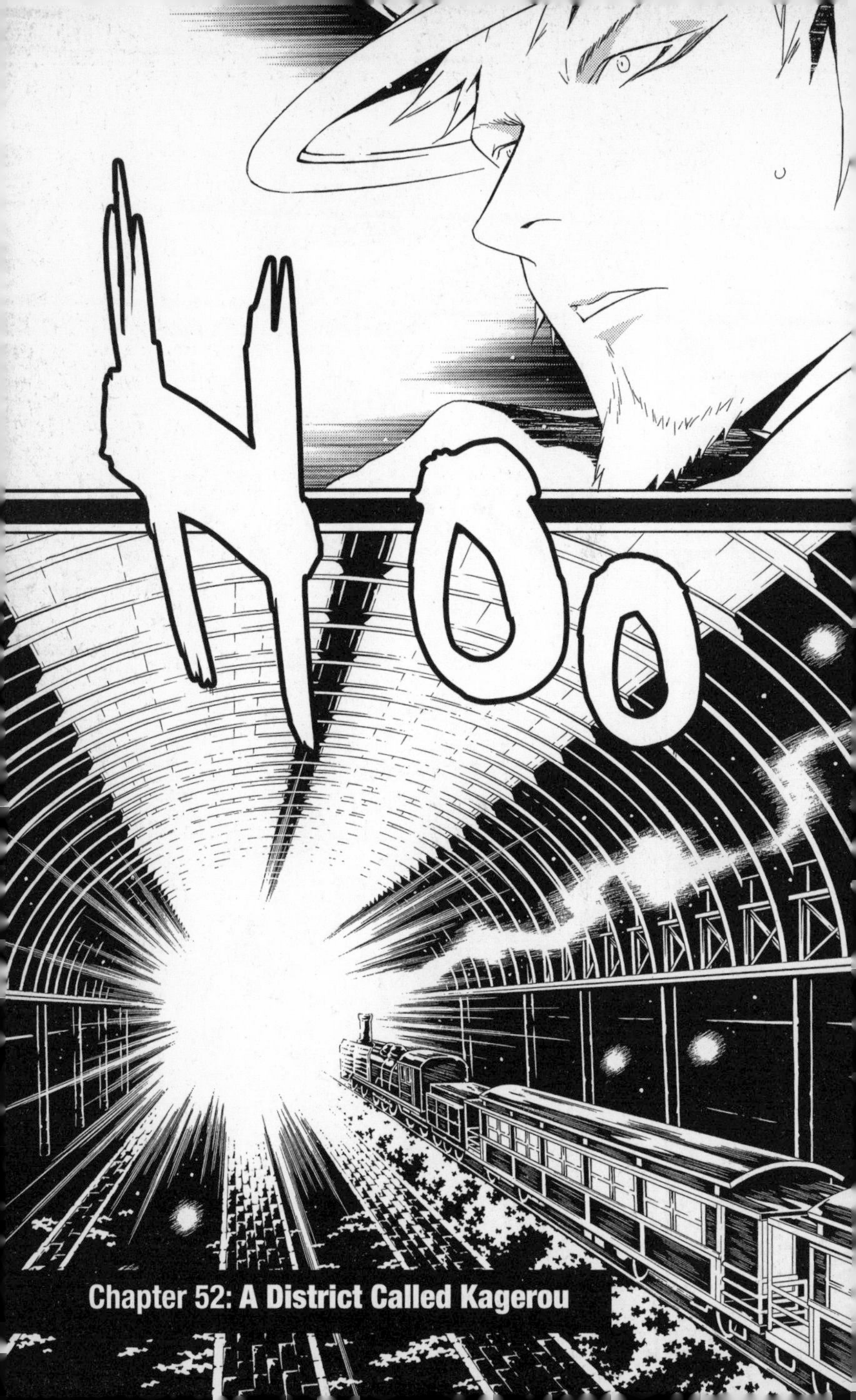
HOO
Chapter 52: A District Called Kagerou

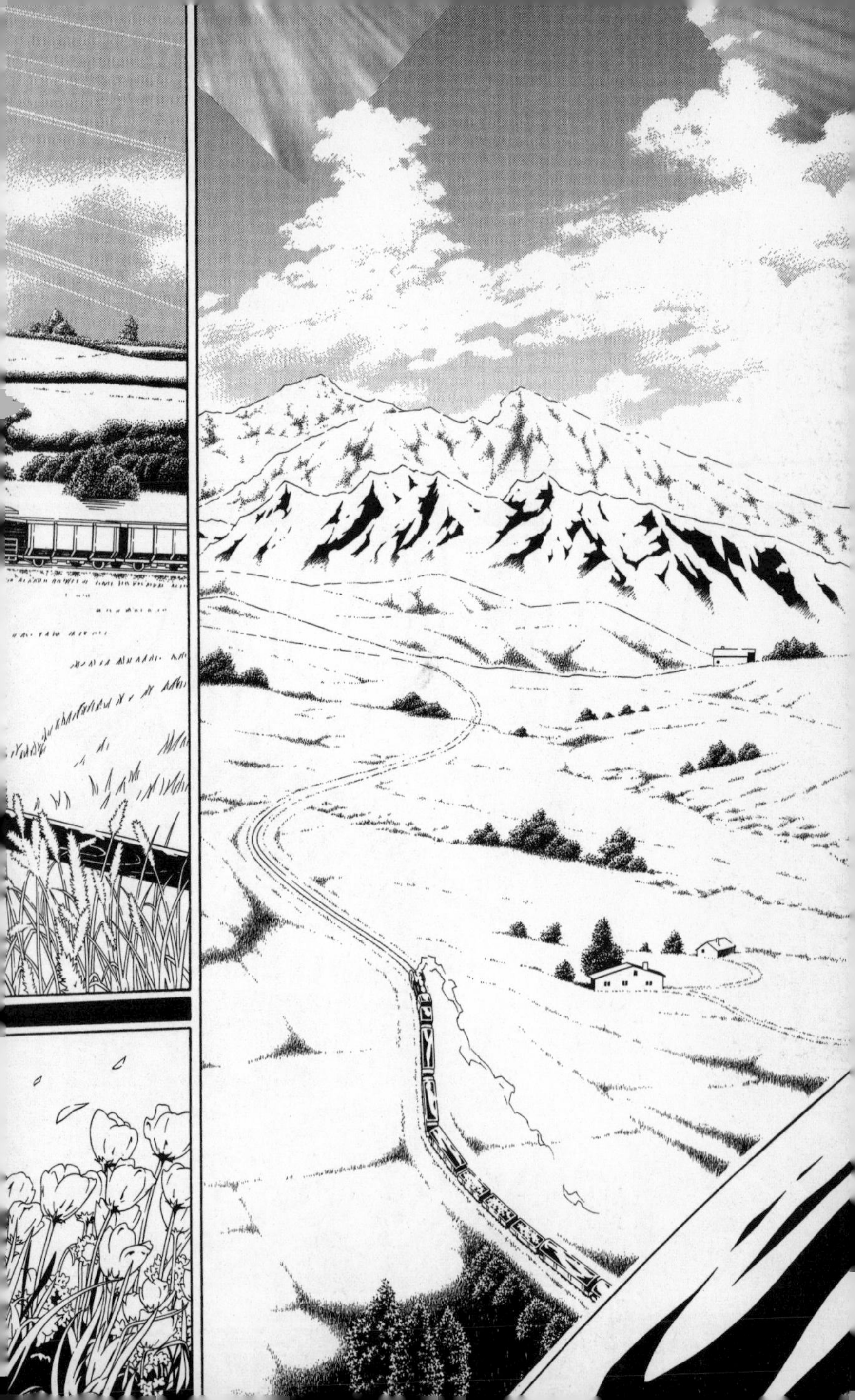

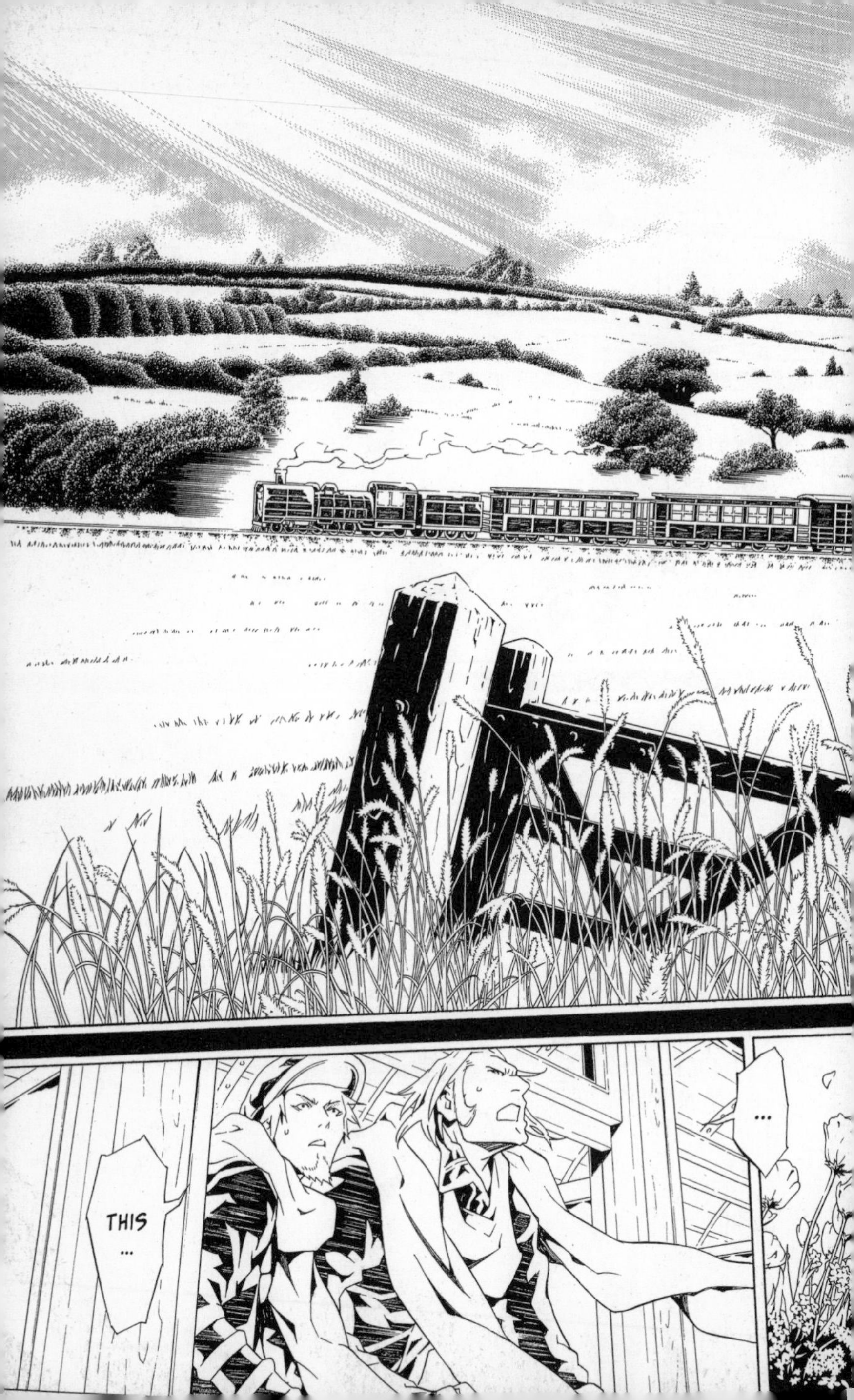
...
THIS ...

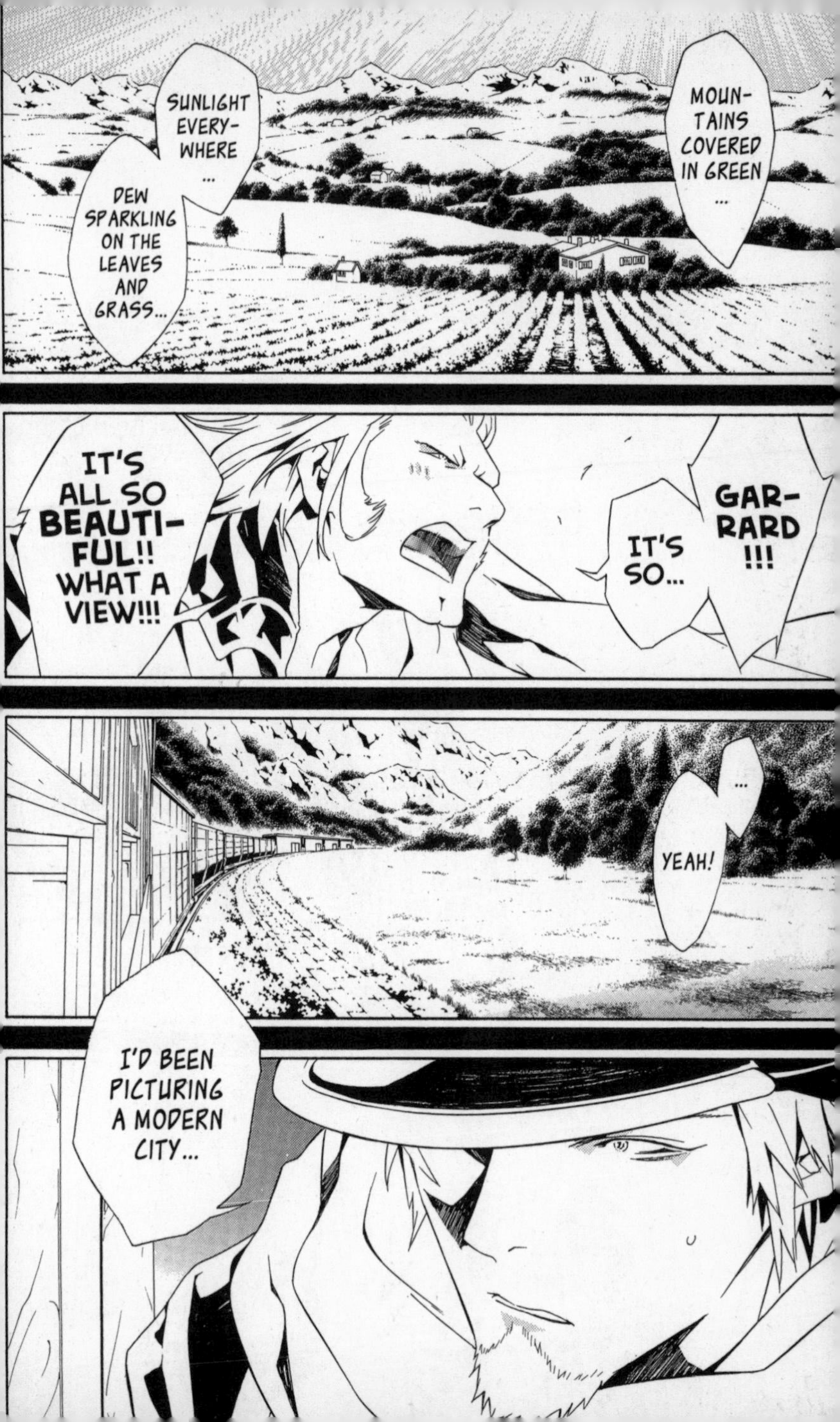
MOUN-TAINS COVERED IN GREEN ...
SUNLIGHT EVERY-WHERE ...
DEW SPARKLING ON THE LEAVES AND GRASS...
GAR-RARD !!!
IT'S SO...
IT'S ALL SO BEAUTI-FUL!! WHAT A VIEW!!!
...
YEAH!
I'D BEEN PICTURING A MODERN CITY...

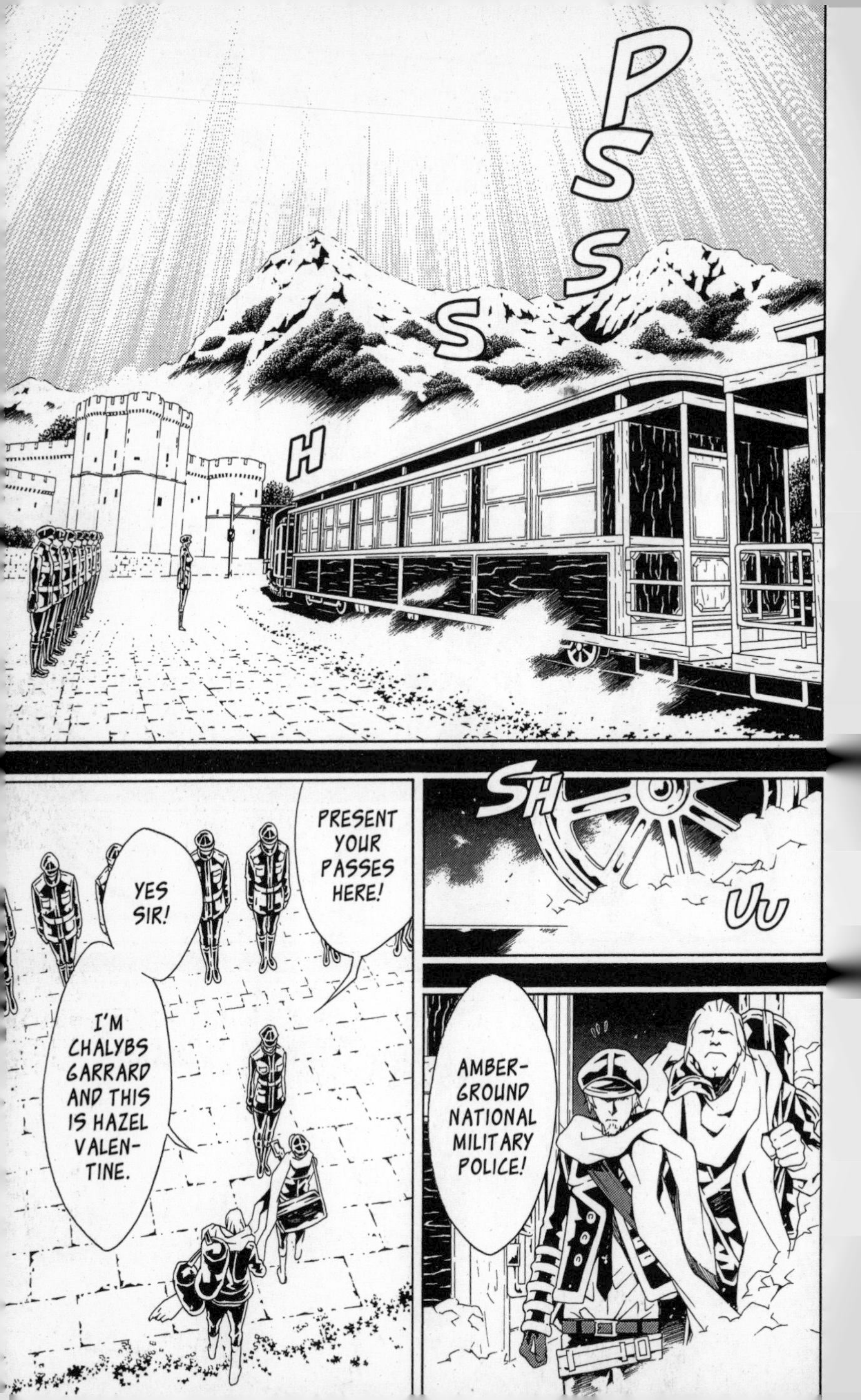
PSSS
H
SH
UU
AMBERGROUND NATIONAL MILITARY POLICE!
PRESENT YOUR PASSES HERE!
YES SIR!
I'M CHALYBS GARRARD AND THIS IS HAZEL VALENTINE.

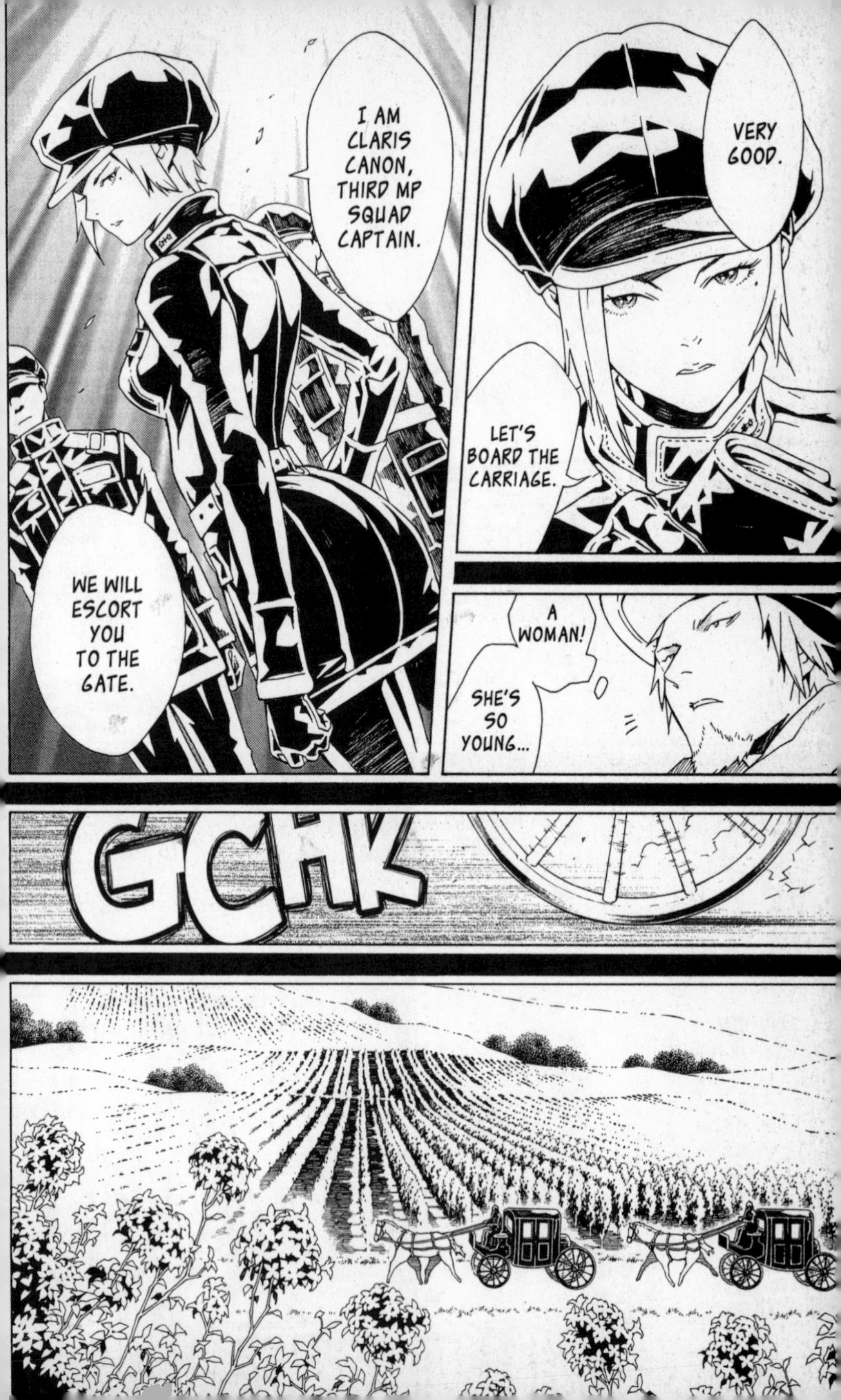
VERY GOOD.
LET'S BOARD THE CARRIAGE.
A WOMAN!
SHE'S SO YOUNG...
I AM CLARIS CANON, THIRD MP SQUAD CAPTAIN.
WE WILL ESCORT YOU TO THE GATE.
GCHK

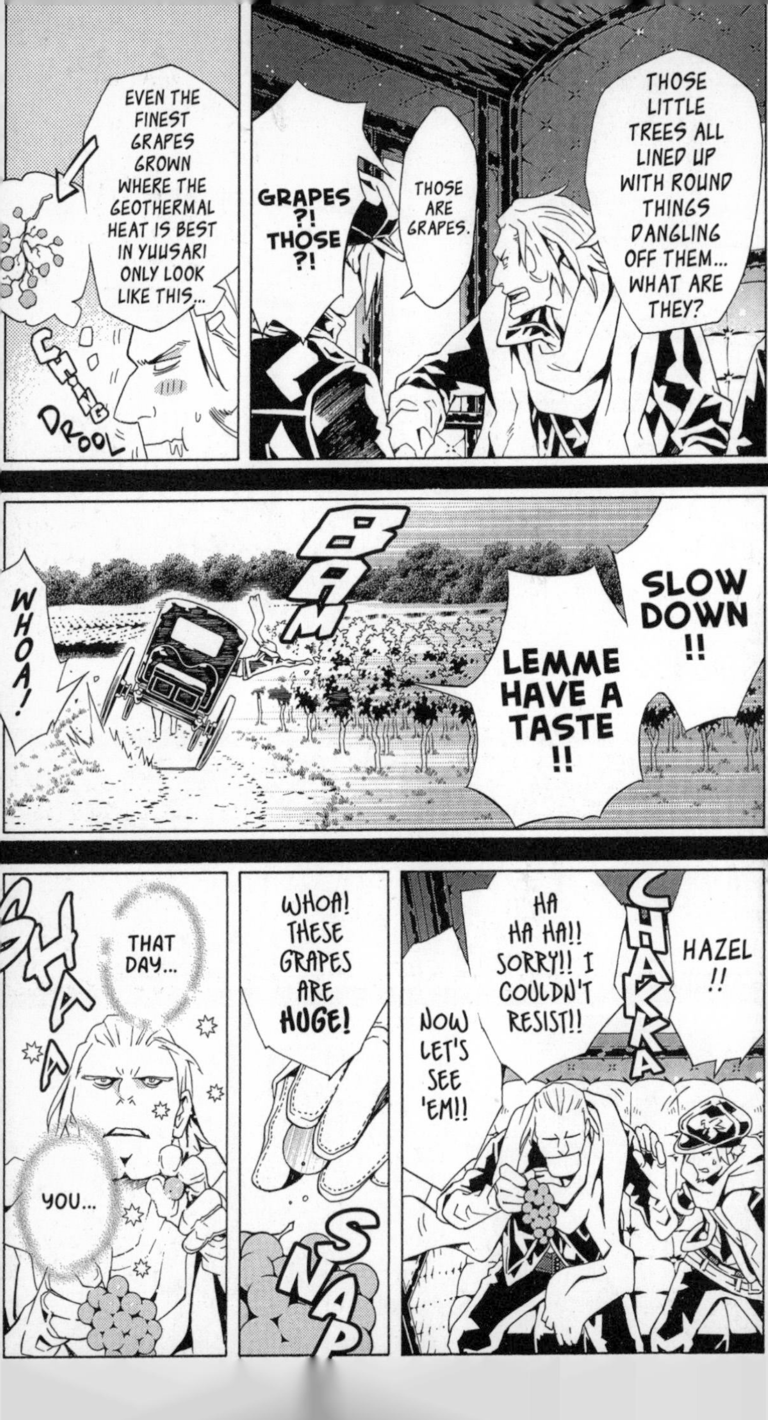
THOSE LITTLE TREES ALL LINED UP WITH ROUND THINGS DANGLING OFF THEM... WHAT ARE THEY?
THOSE ARE GRAPES.
GRAPES?! THOSE?!
EVEN THE FINEST GRAPES GROWN WHERE THE GEOTHERMAL HEAT IS BEST IN YUUSARI ONLY LOOK LIKE THIS...
CHING
DROOL
SLOW DOWN!!
LEMME HAVE A TASTE!!
BAM
WHOA!
HAZEL!!
CHAKA
HA HA HA!! SORRY!! I COULDN'T RESIST!!
NOW LET'S SEE 'EM!!
WHOA! THESE GRAPES ARE HUGE!
SNAP
THAT DAY...
SHAA
YOU...

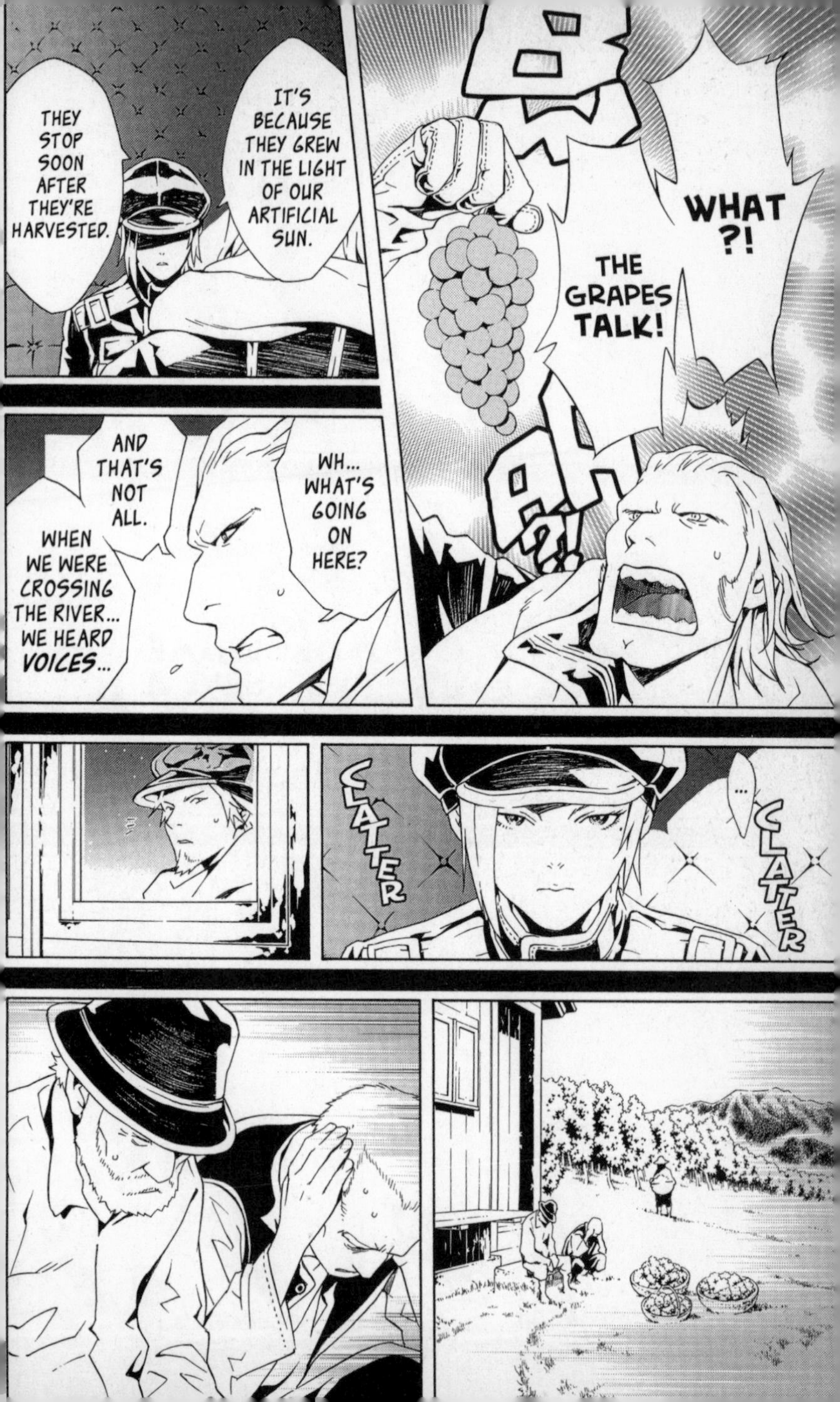

WHAT?!
THE GRAPES TALK!
IT'S BECAUSE THEY GREW IN THE LIGHT OF OUR ARTIFICIAL SUN.
THEY STOP SOON AFTER THEY'RE HARVESTED.
WH... WHAT'S GOING ON HERE?
AND THAT'S NOT ALL.
WHEN WE WERE CROSSING THE RIVER... WE HEARD VOICES...
...
CLATTER
CLATTER

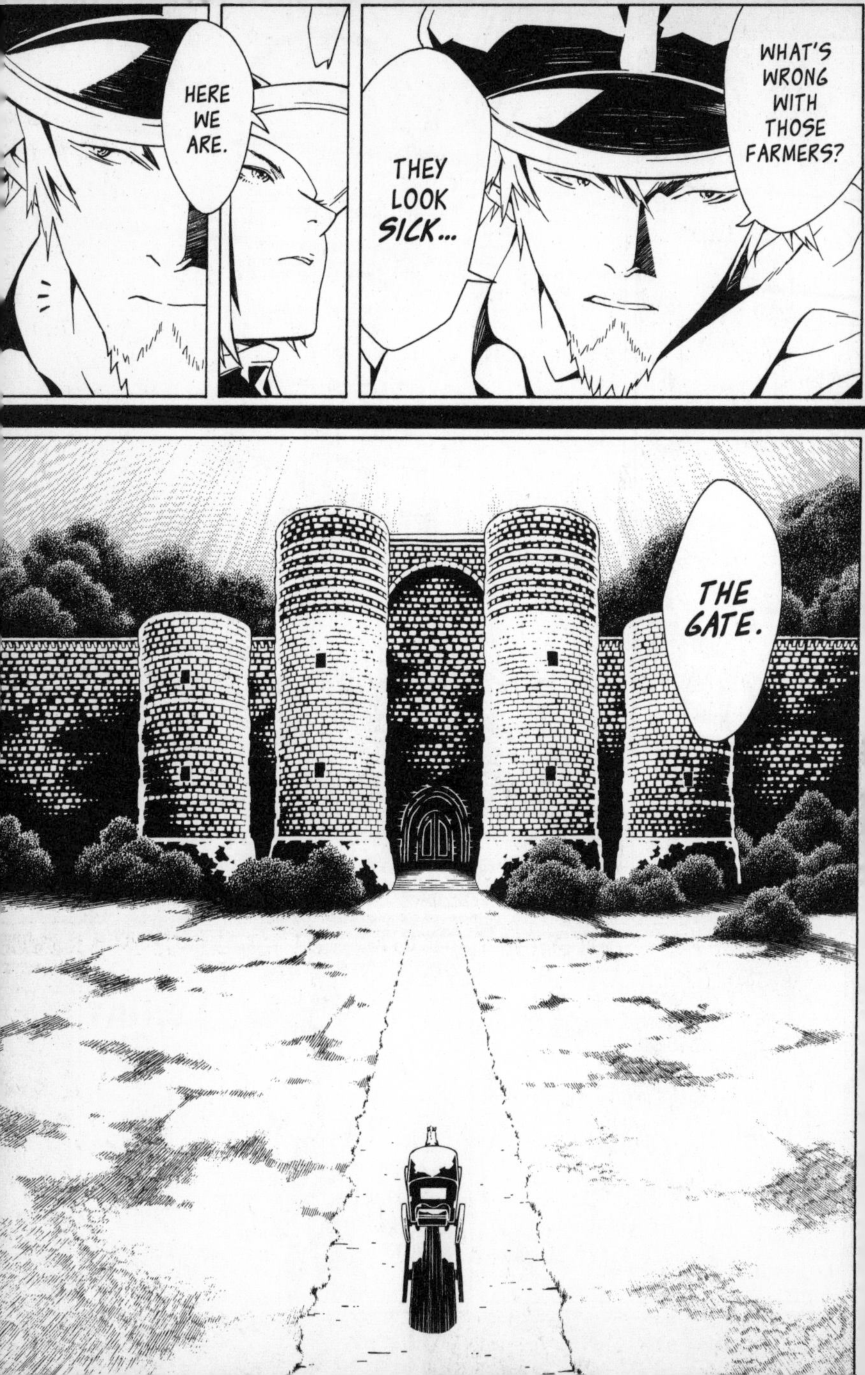
WHAT'S WRONG WITH THOSE FARMERS?
THEY LOOK SICK...
HERE WE ARE.
THE GATE.

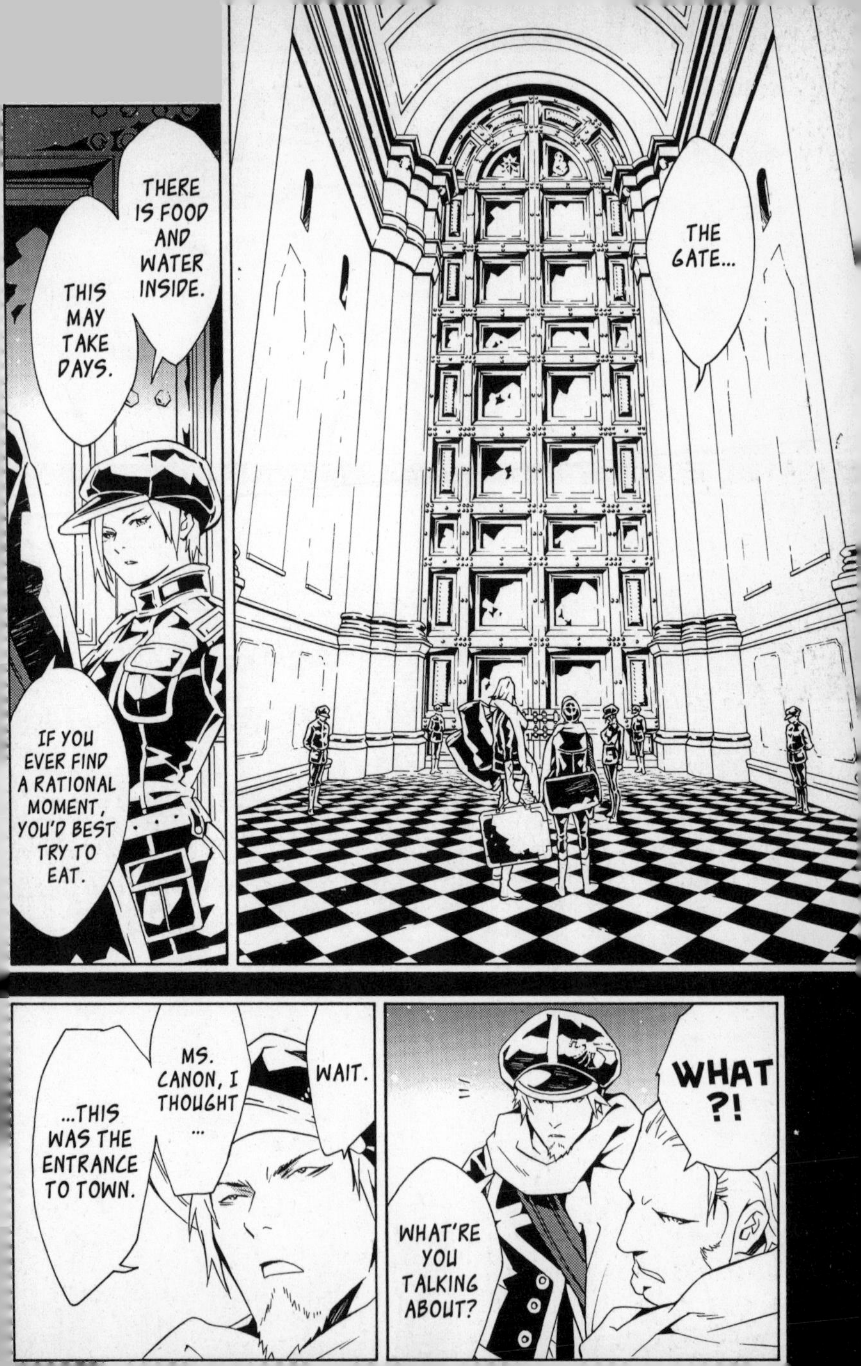
THE GATE...
THERE IS FOOD AND WATER INSIDE.
THIS MAY TAKE DAYS.
IF YOU EVER FIND A RATIONAL MOMENT, YOU'D BEST TRY TO EAT.
WHAT?!
WHAT'RE YOU TALKING ABOUT?
WAIT.
MS. CANON, I THOUGHT...
...THIS WAS THE ENTRANCE TO TOWN.

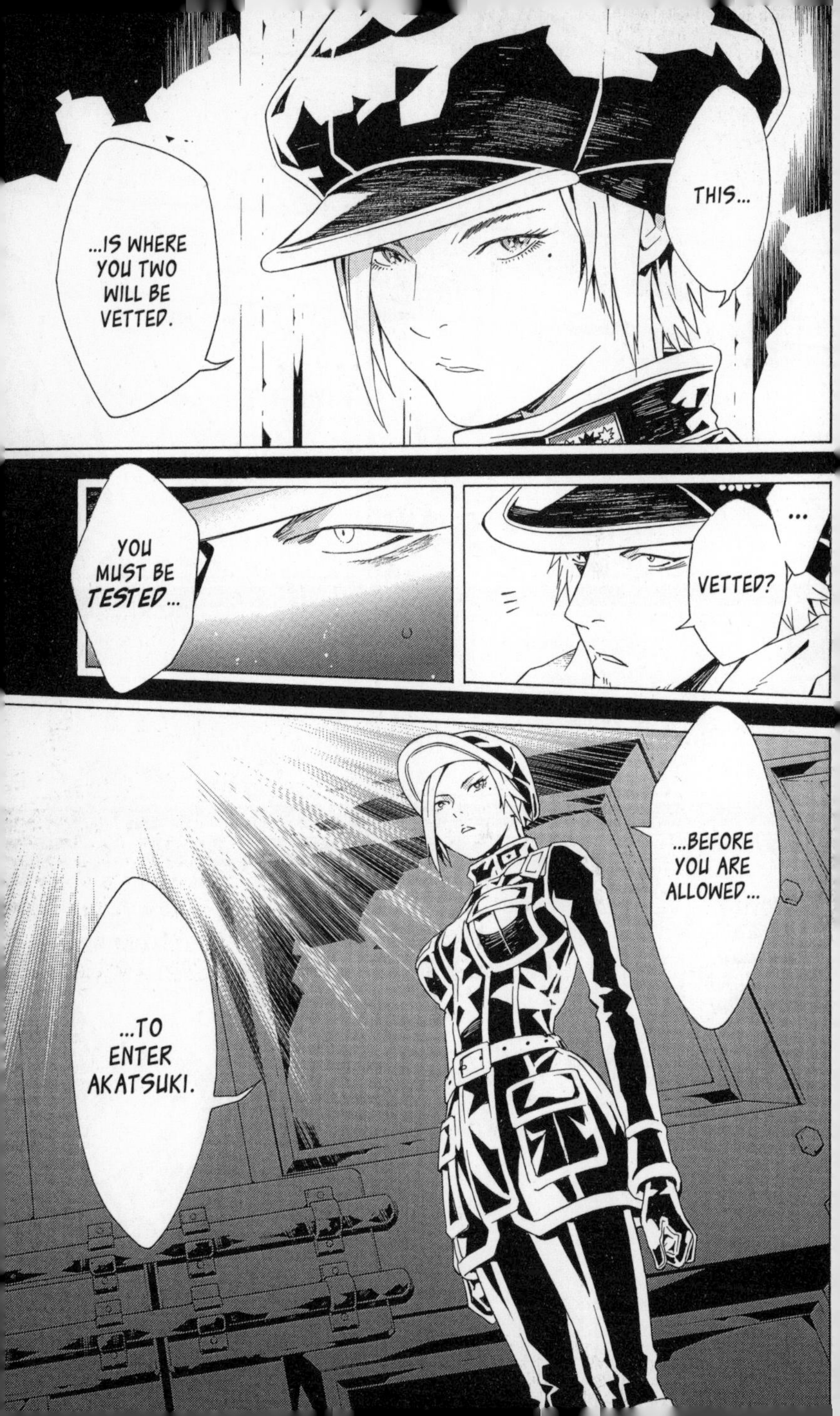
THIS...
...IS WHERE YOU TWO WILL BE VETTED.
...
VETTED?
YOU MUST BE *TESTED*...
...BEFORE YOU ARE ALLOWED...
...TO ENTER AKATSUKI.

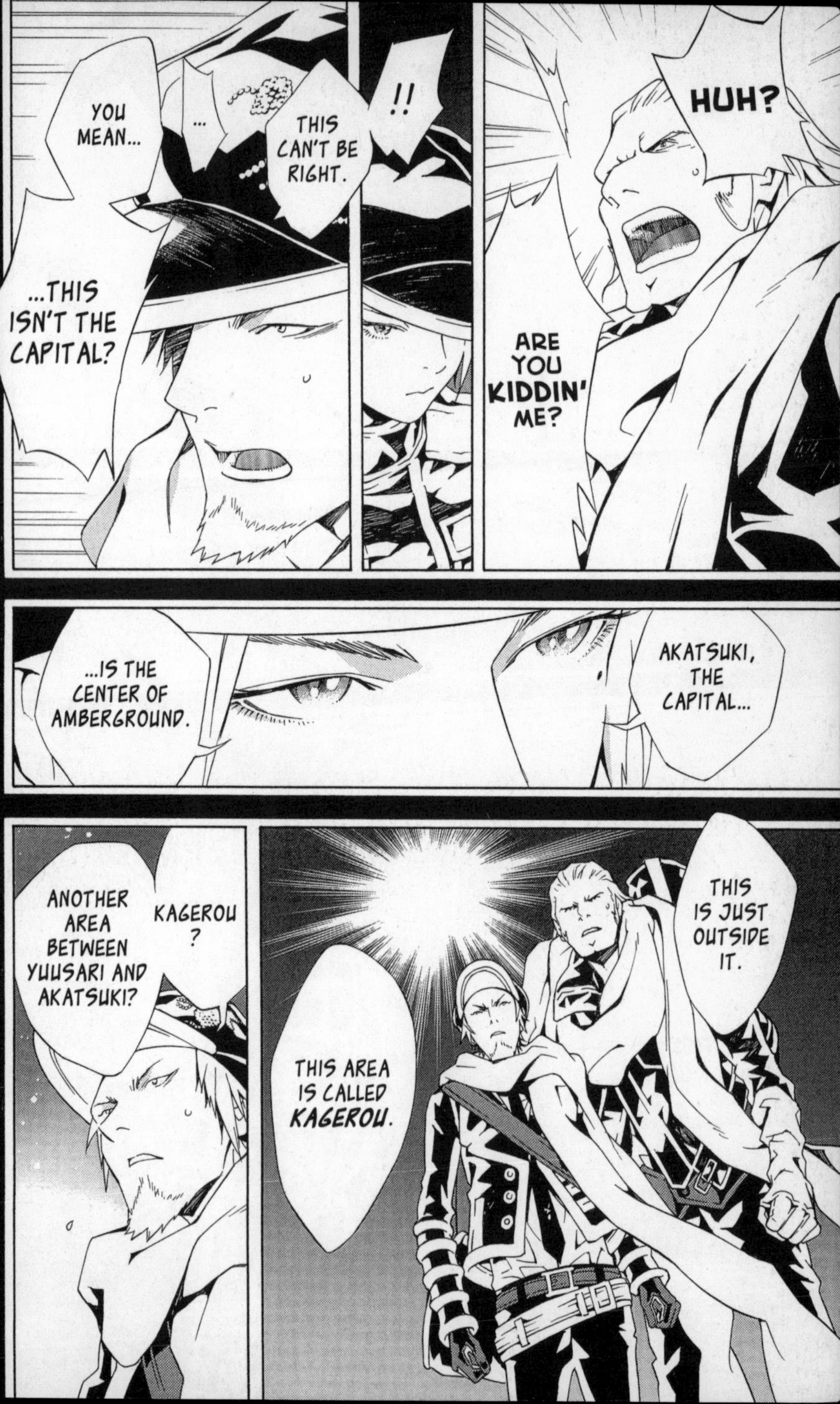
HUH?
ARE YOU KIDDIN' ME?
!!
THIS CAN'T BE RIGHT.
...
YOU MEAN...
...THIS ISN'T THE CAPITAL?
AKATSUKI, THE CAPITAL...
...IS THE CENTER OF AMBERGROUND.
THIS IS JUST OUTSIDE IT.
THIS AREA IS CALLED KAGEROU.
KAGEROU?
ANOTHER AREA BETWEEN YUUSARI AND AKATSUKI?

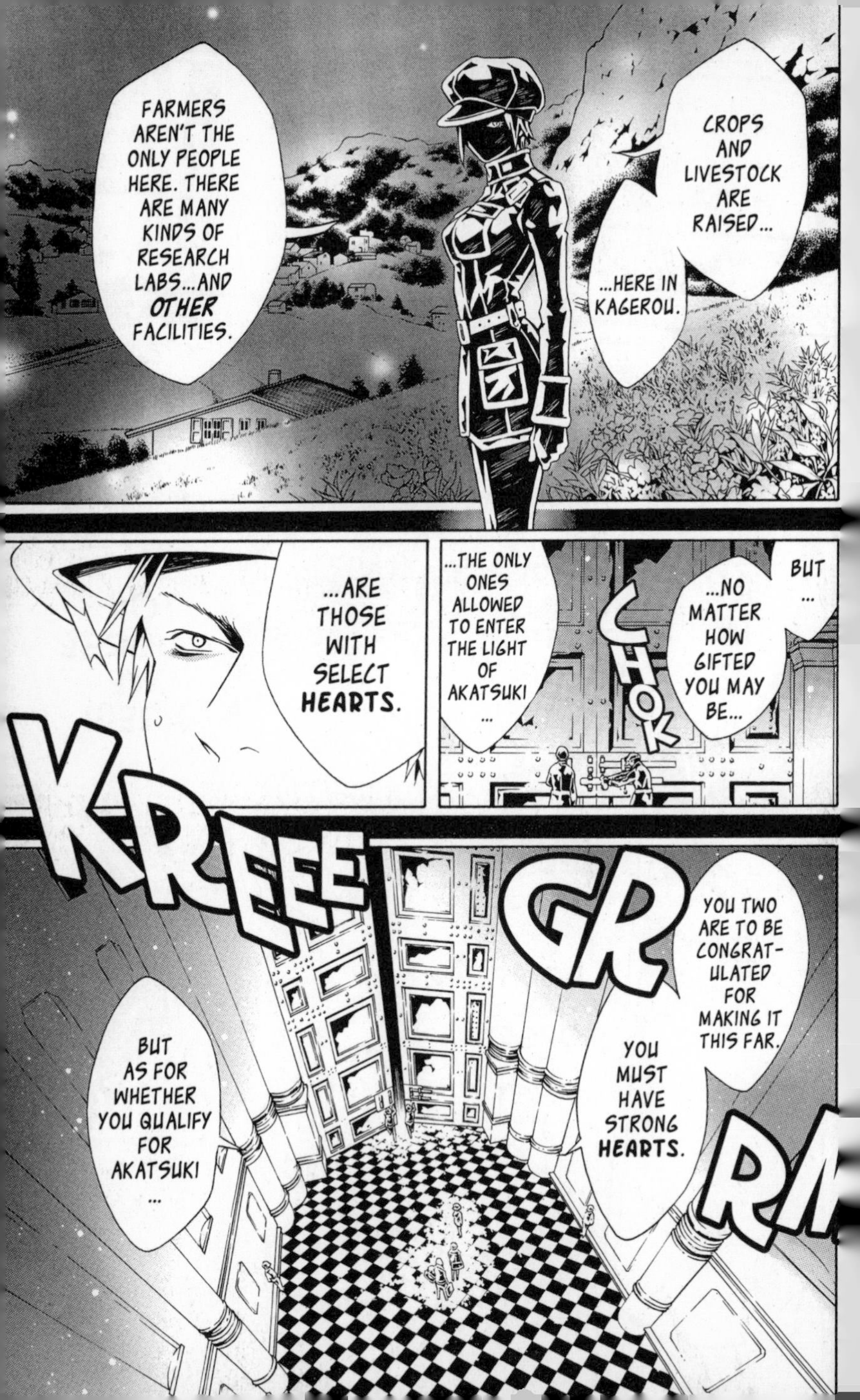
CROPS AND LIVESTOCK ARE RAISED...
...HERE IN KAGEROU.
FARMERS AREN'T THE ONLY PEOPLE HERE. THERE ARE MANY KINDS OF RESEARCH LABS...AND *OTHER* FACILITIES.
BUT...
...NO MATTER HOW GIFTED YOU MAY BE...
CHOK
...THE ONLY ONES ALLOWED TO ENTER THE LIGHT OF AKATSUKI...
...ARE THOSE WITH SELECT **HEARTS**.
KREEE
GR
YOU TWO ARE TO BE CONGRATULATED FOR MAKING IT THIS FAR.
YOU MUST HAVE STRONG **HEARTS**.
BUT AS FOR WHETHER YOU QUALIFY FOR AKATSUKI...

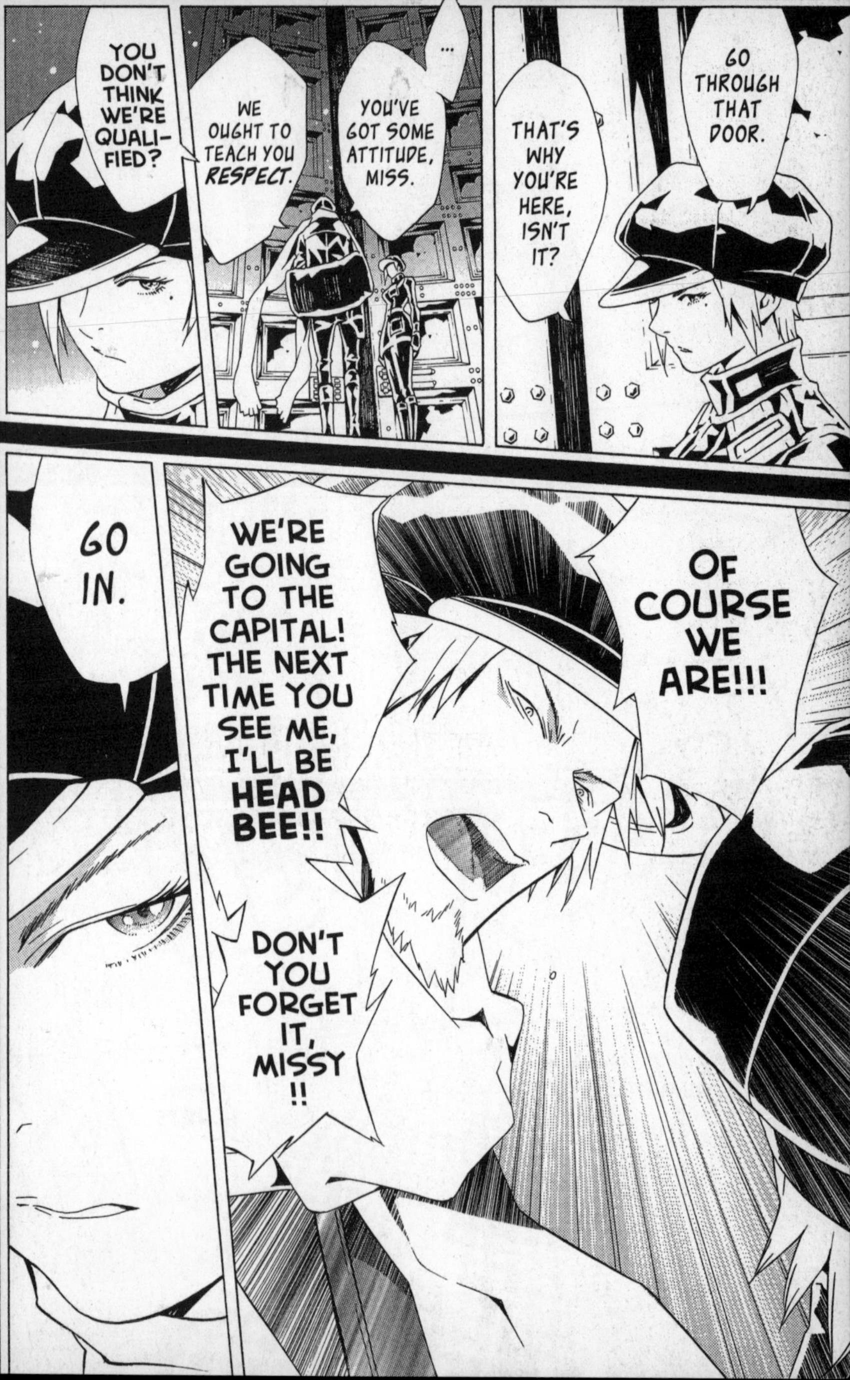
GO THROUGH THAT DOOR.
THAT'S WHY YOU'RE HERE, ISN'T IT?
...
YOU'VE GOT SOME ATTITUDE, MISS.
WE OUGHT TO TEACH YOU *RESPECT*.
YOU DON'T THINK WE'RE QUALIFIED?
OF COURSE WE ARE!!!
WE'RE GOING TO THE CAPITAL! THE NEXT TIME YOU SEE ME, I'LL BE **HEAD BEE!!**
DON'T YOU FORGET IT, MISSY!!
GO IN.

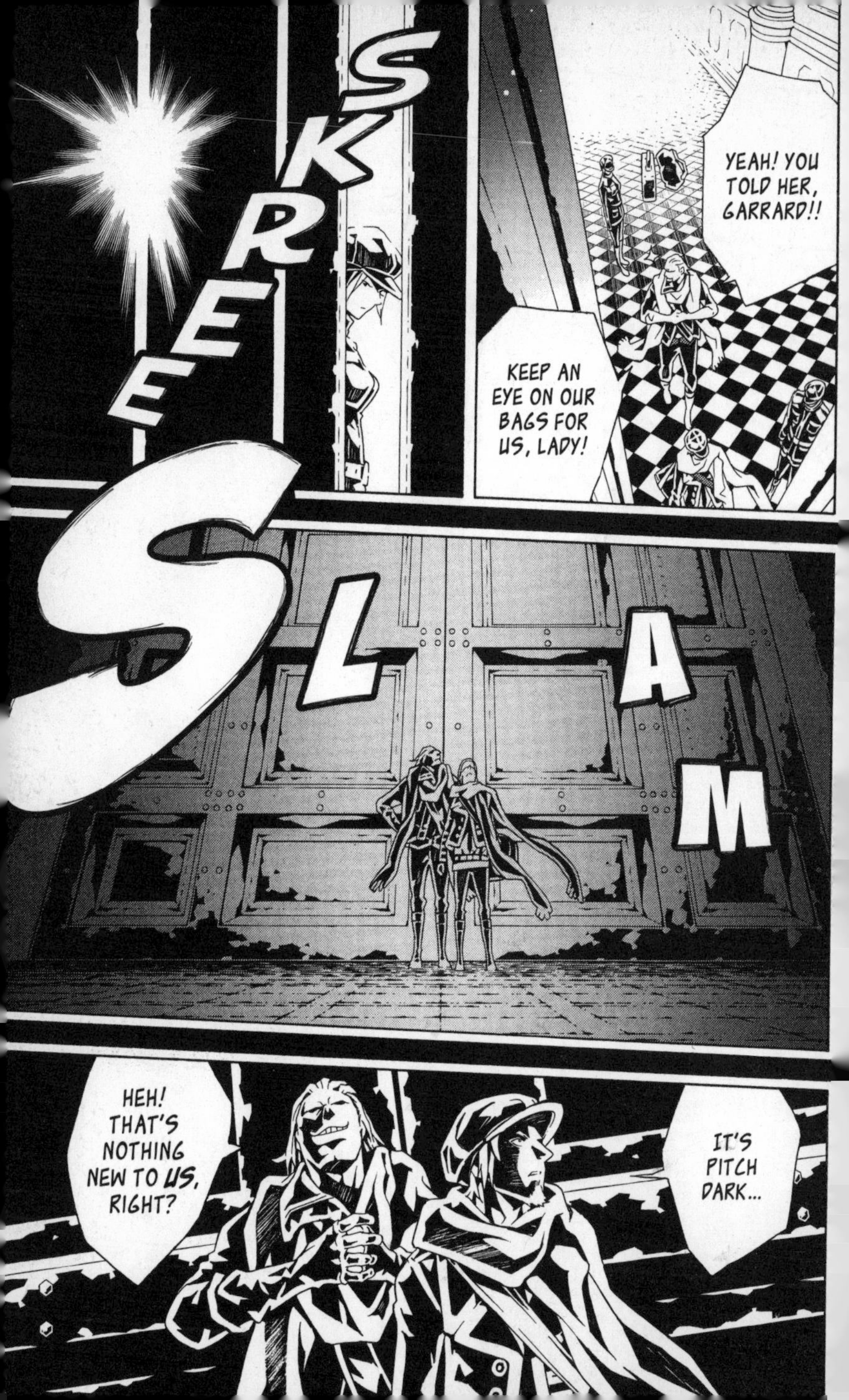
YEAH! YOU TOLD HER, GARRARD!!
KEEP AN EYE ON OUR BAGS FOR US, LADY!
SKREEE
SLAM
IT'S PITCH DARK...
HEH! THAT'S NOTHING NEW TO *US*, RIGHT?

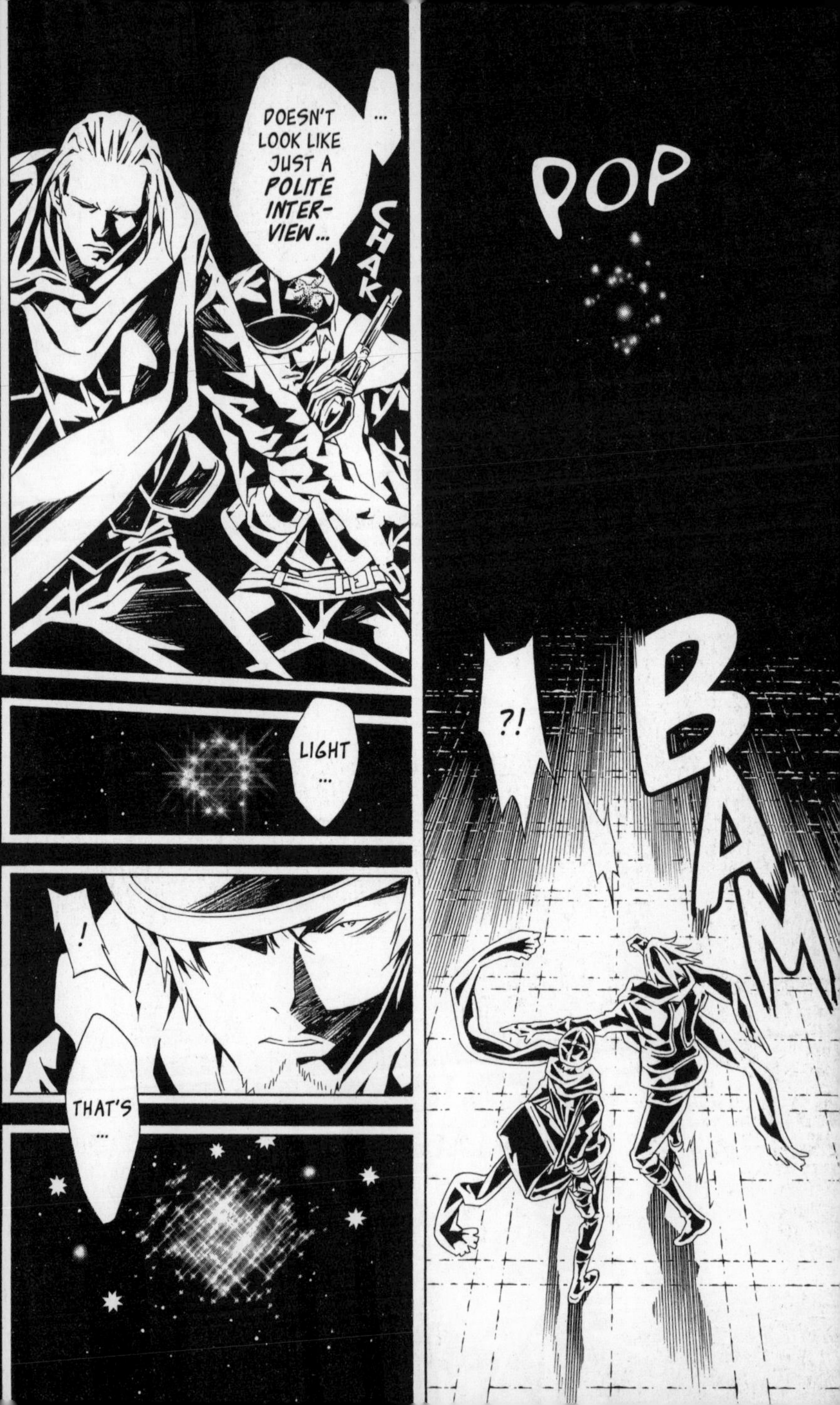
POP
?!
BAM
...
DOESN'T LOOK LIKE JUST A POLITE INTER-VIEW...
CHAK
LIGHT ...
!
THAT'S ...

...SPIRIT AMBER!

THE LIGHT OF THE HEART!

!!

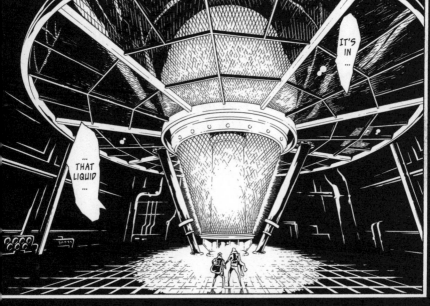

IT'S IN...

...THAT LIQUID...

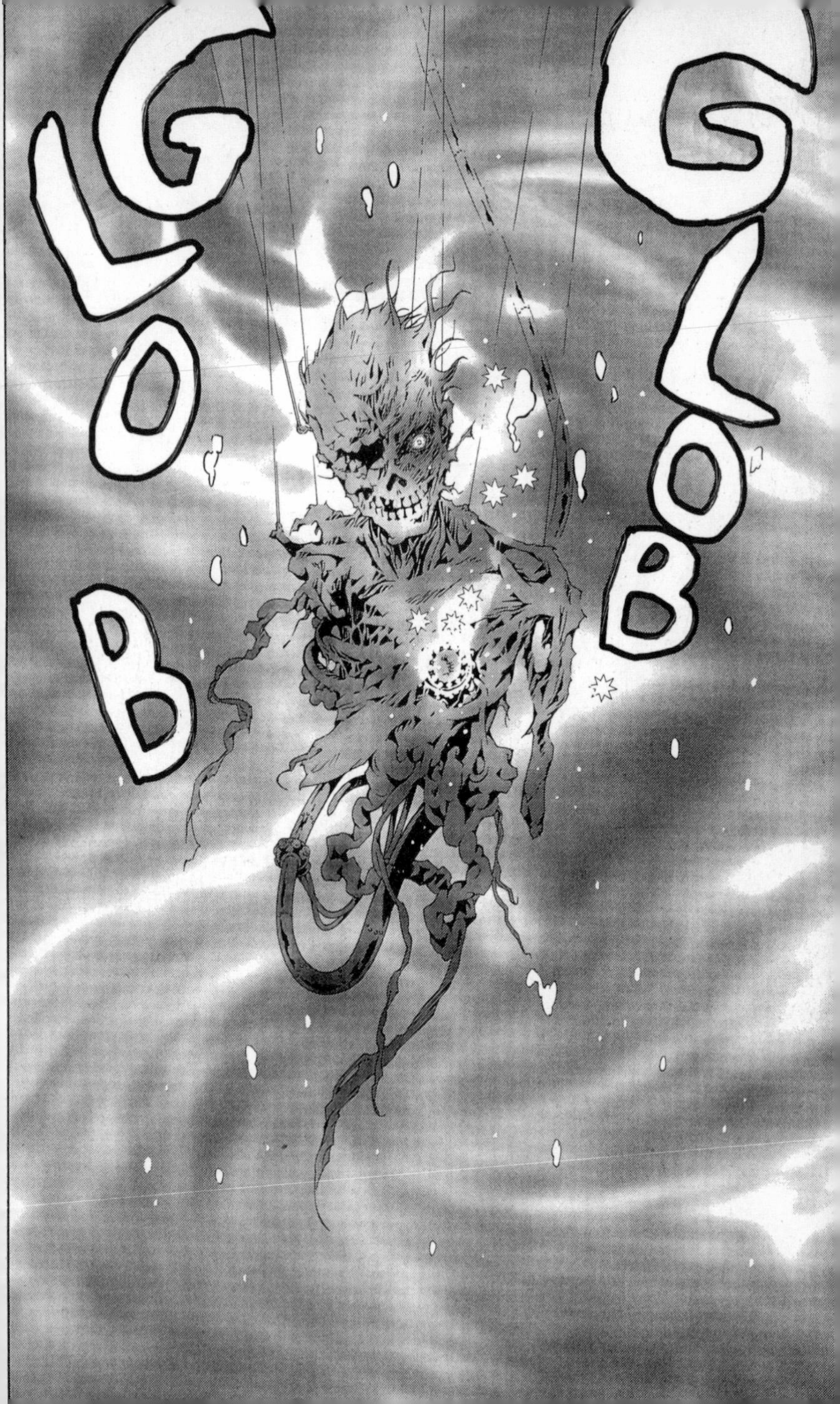
GLOB
GLOB

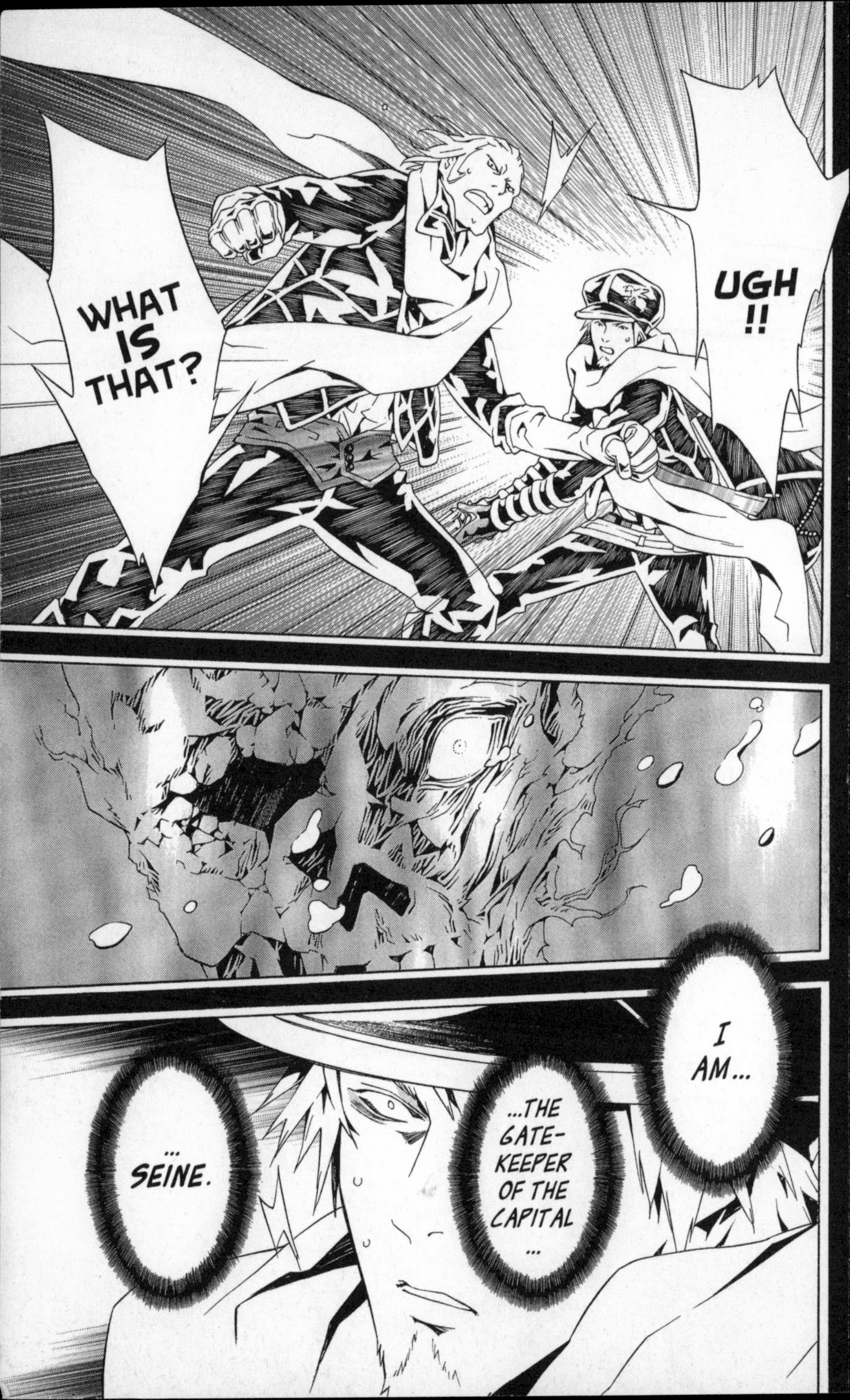
UGH !!
WHAT IS THAT?
I AM...
...THE GATE-KEEPER OF THE CAPITAL ...
... SEINE.

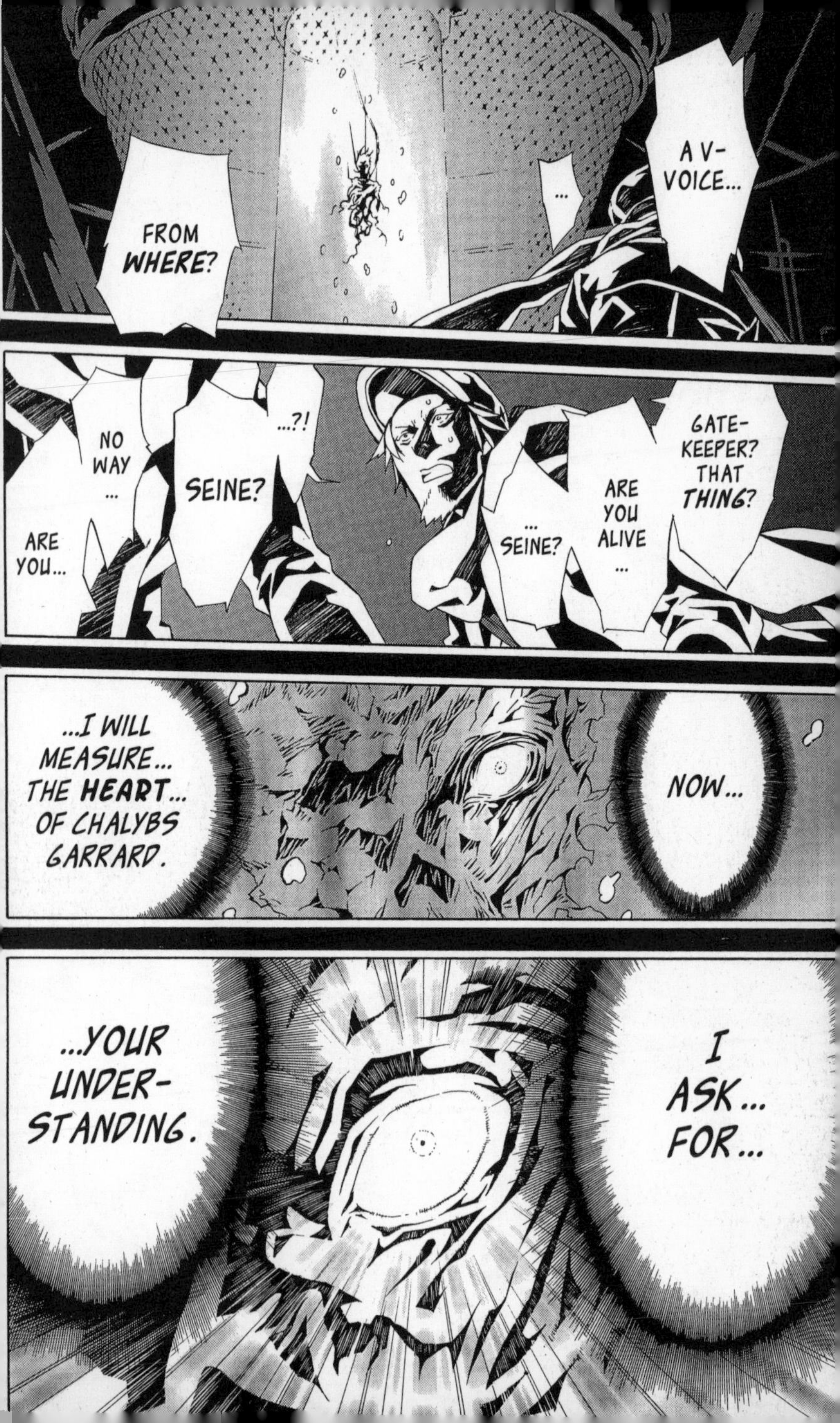
A V-VOICE...
...
FROM WHERE?
GATE-KEEPER? THAT THING?
ARE YOU ALIVE ...
... SEINE?
...?!
SEINE?
NO WAY ...
ARE YOU...
NOW...
...I WILL MEASURE... THE HEART... OF CHALYBS GARRARD.
I ASK... FOR...
...YOUR UNDER-STANDING.

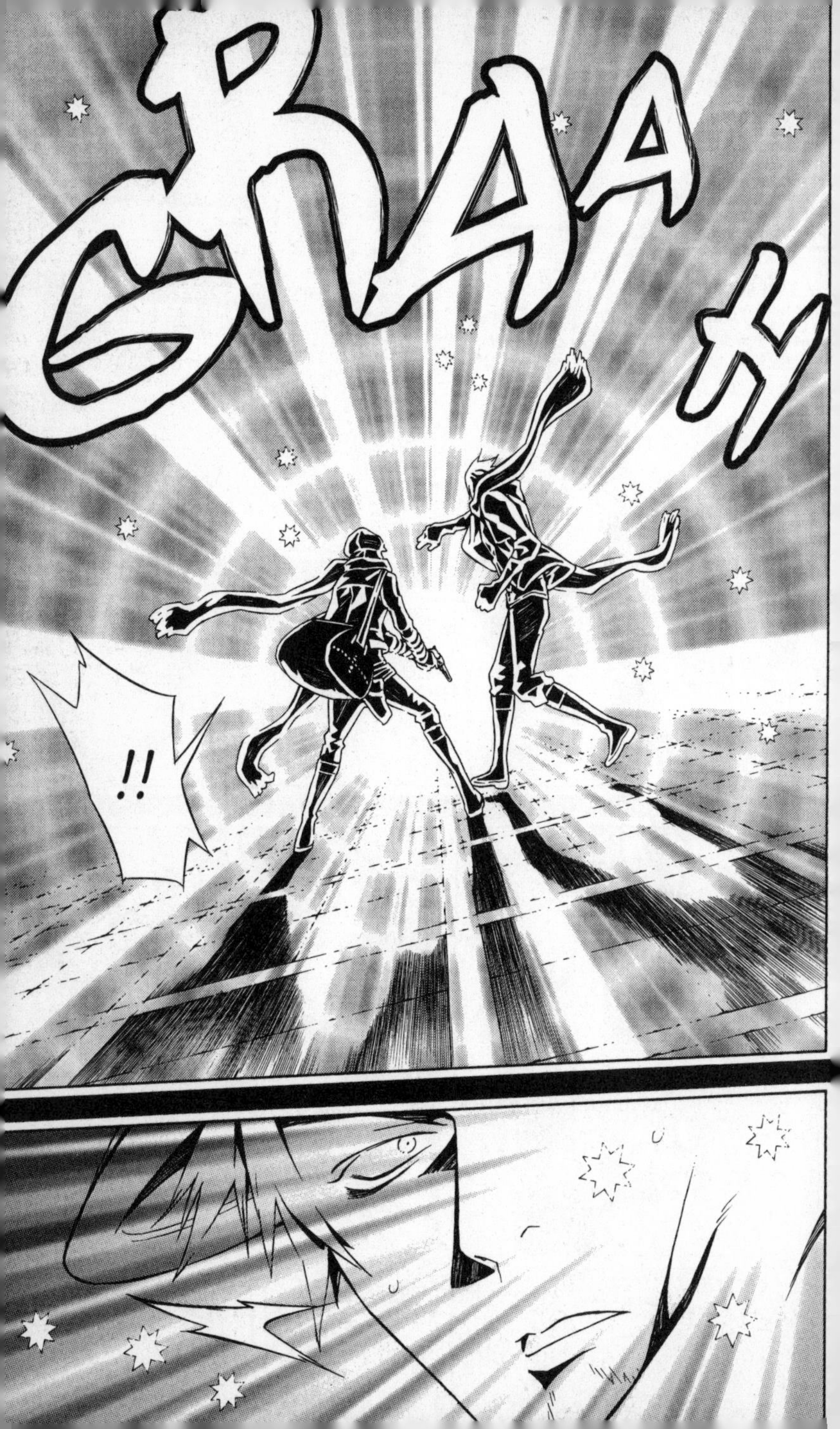
GRAAAH
!!

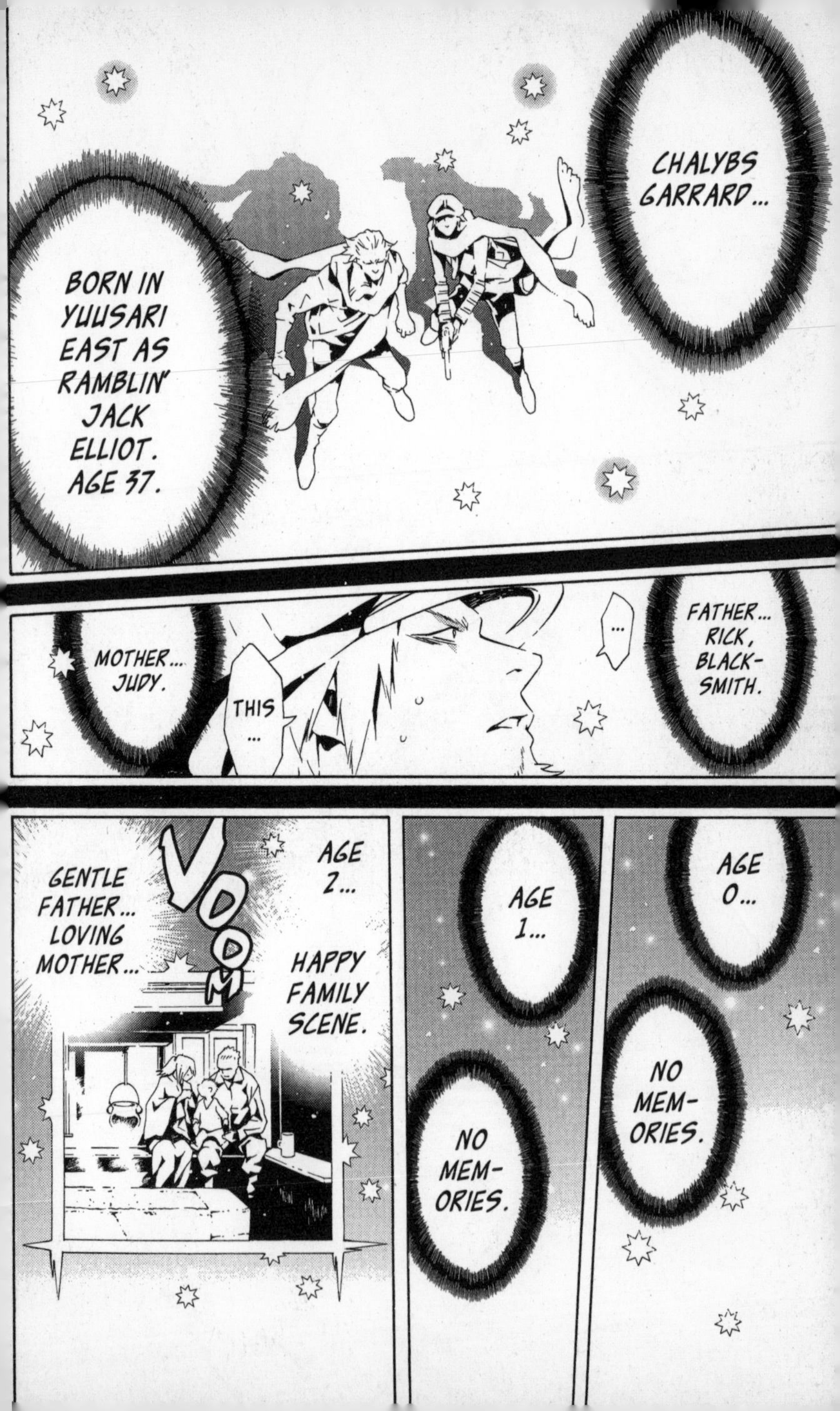
CHALYBS GARRARD...
BORN IN YUUSARI EAST AS RAMBLIN' JACK ELLIOT. AGE 37.
FATHER... RICK, BLACK-SMITH.
...
THIS ...
MOTHER... JUDY.
AGE 0...
NO MEM-ORIES.
AGE 1...
NO MEM-ORIES.
AGE 2...
HAPPY FAMILY SCENE.
VOOM
GENTLE FATHER... LOVING MOTHER...

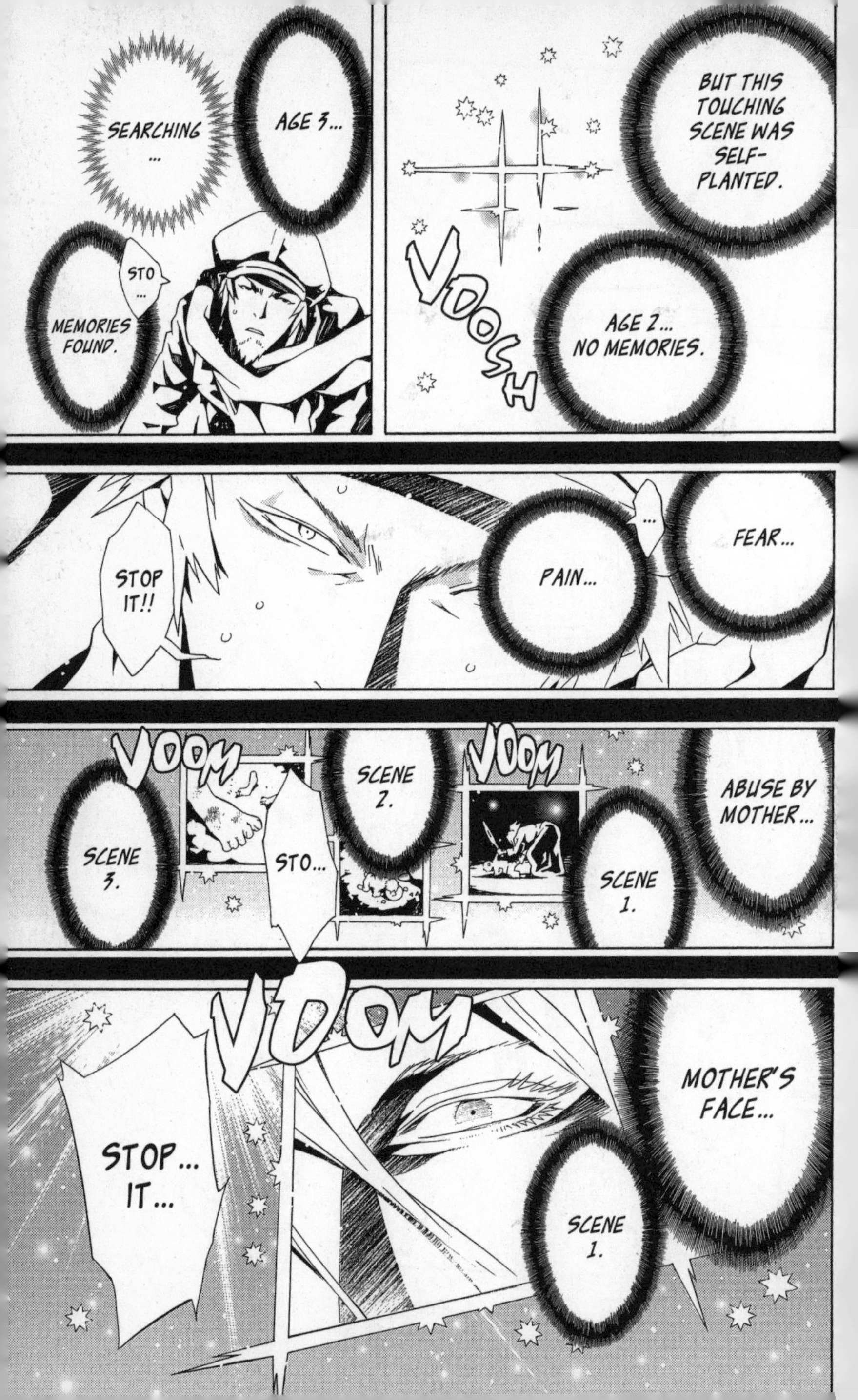
BUT THIS TOUCHING SCENE WAS SELF-PLANTED.
AGE 2... NO MEMORIES.
VOOSH
AGE 3...
SEARCHING ...
STO ...
MEMORIES FOUND.
FEAR...
...
PAIN...
STOP IT!!
ABUSE BY MOTHER...
SCENE 1.
VOOM
SCENE 2.
STO...
VOOM
SCENE 3.
MOTHER'S FACE...
SCENE 1.
VOOM
STOP... IT...

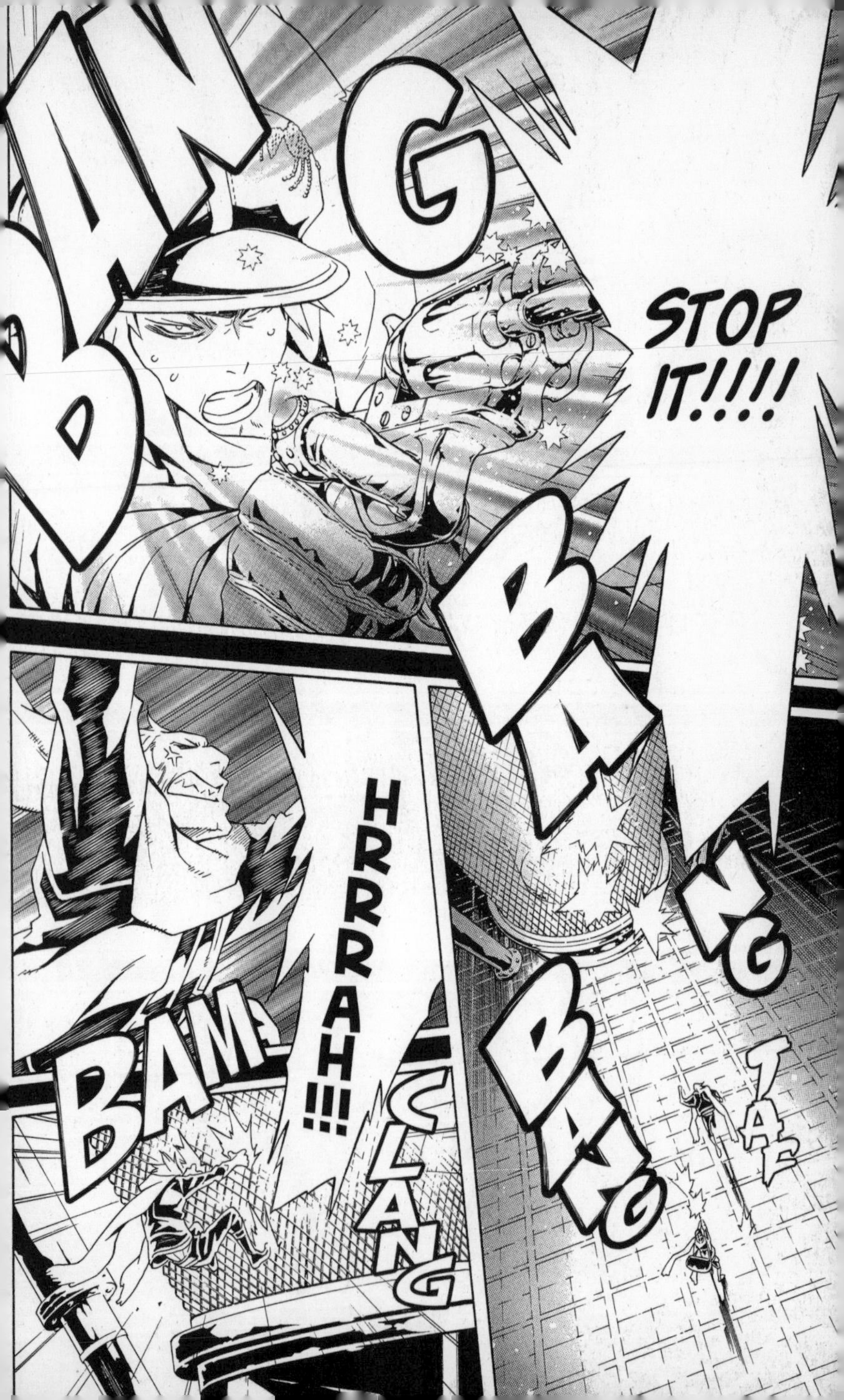
STOP IT!!!!
BANG
BANG
BANG
HRRRAH!!!
BAM
CLANG

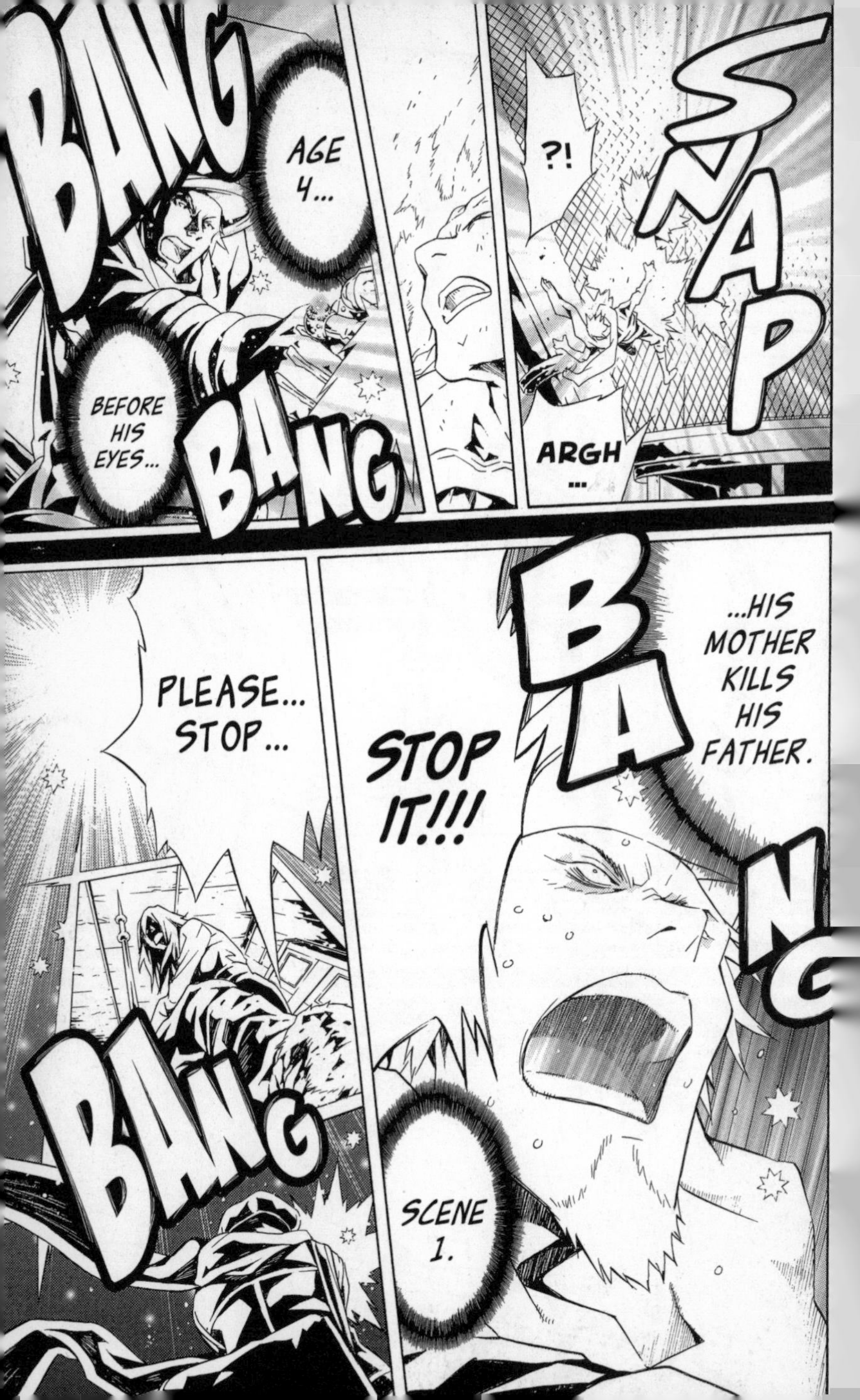
SNAP
?!
ARGH ...
AGE 4...
BANG
BEFORE HIS EYES...
BANG
...HIS MOTHER KILLS HIS FATHER.
BANG
STOP IT!!!
SCENE 1.
PLEASE... STOP...
BANG

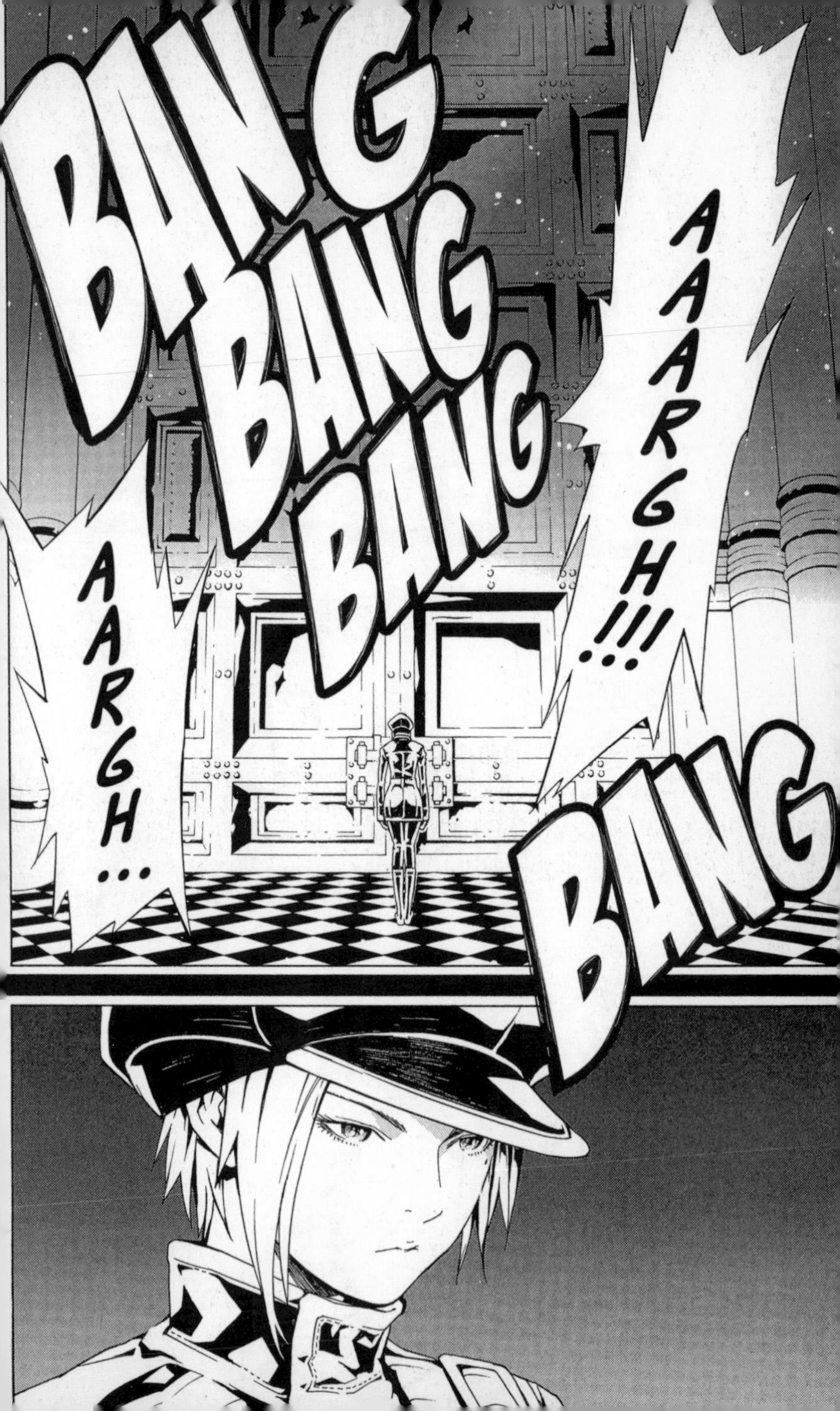
AAARGH!!!
BANG
BANG
BANG
AARGH...
BANG

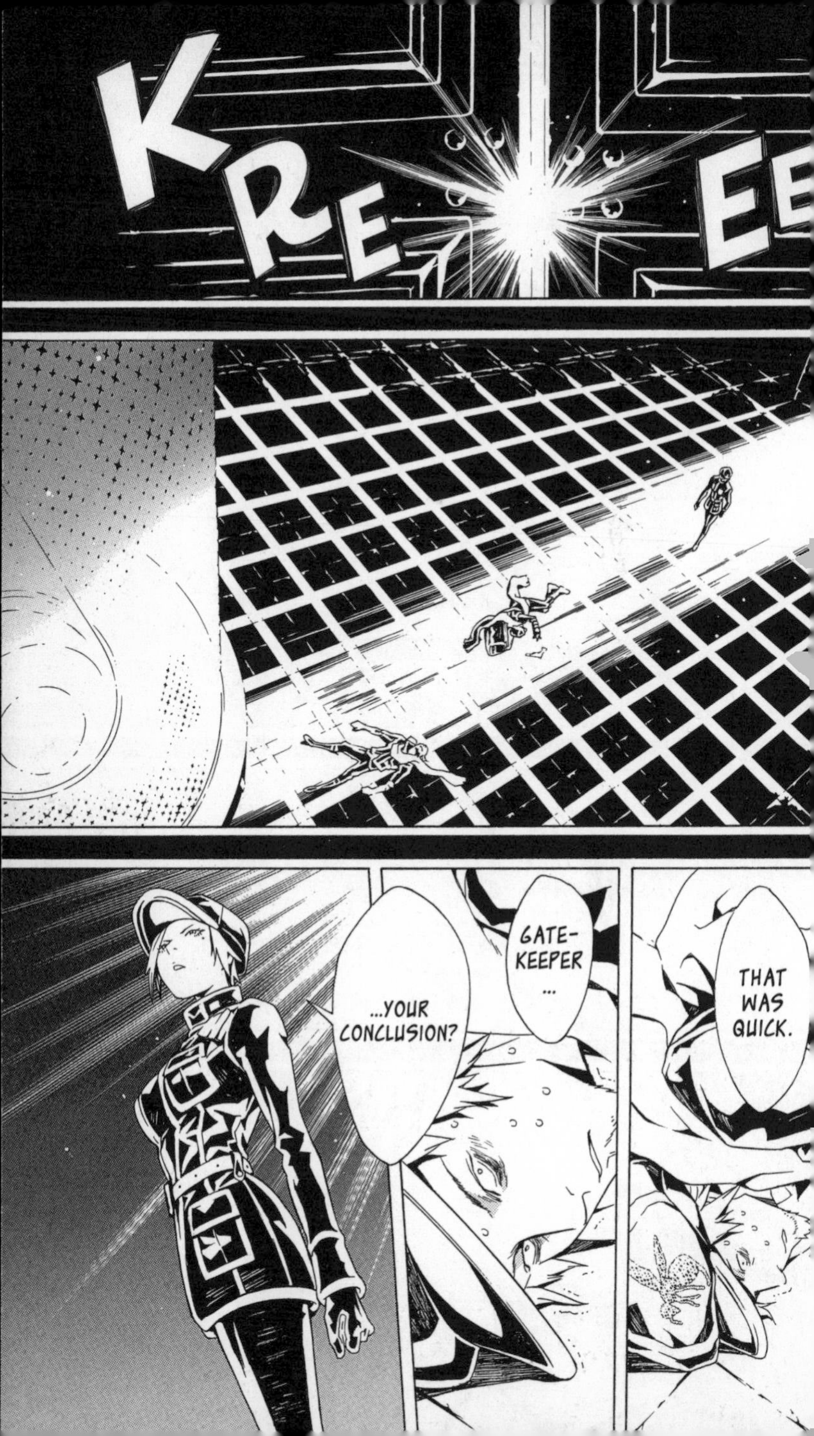
KREEE
THAT WAS QUICK.
GATE-KEEPER ...
...YOUR CONCLUSION?

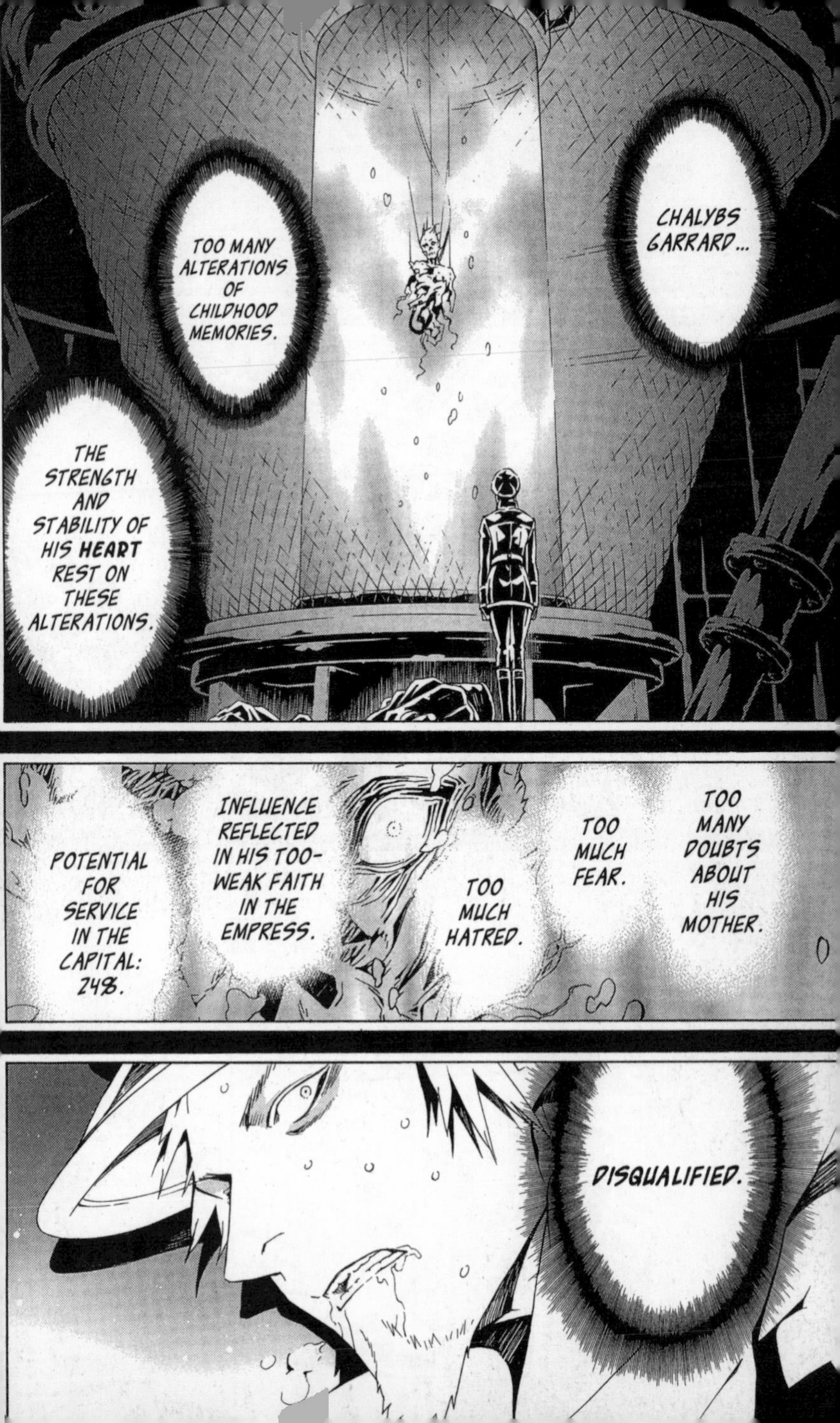
CHALYBS GARRARD...
TOO MANY ALTERATIONS OF CHILDHOOD MEMORIES.
THE STRENGTH AND STABILITY OF HIS **HEART** REST ON THESE ALTERATIONS.
TOO MANY DOUBTS ABOUT HIS MOTHER.
TOO MUCH FEAR.
TOO MUCH HATRED.
INFLUENCE REFLECTED IN HIS TOO-WEAK FAITH IN THE EMPRESS.
POTENTIAL FOR SERVICE IN THE CAPITAL: 24%.
DISQUALIFIED.

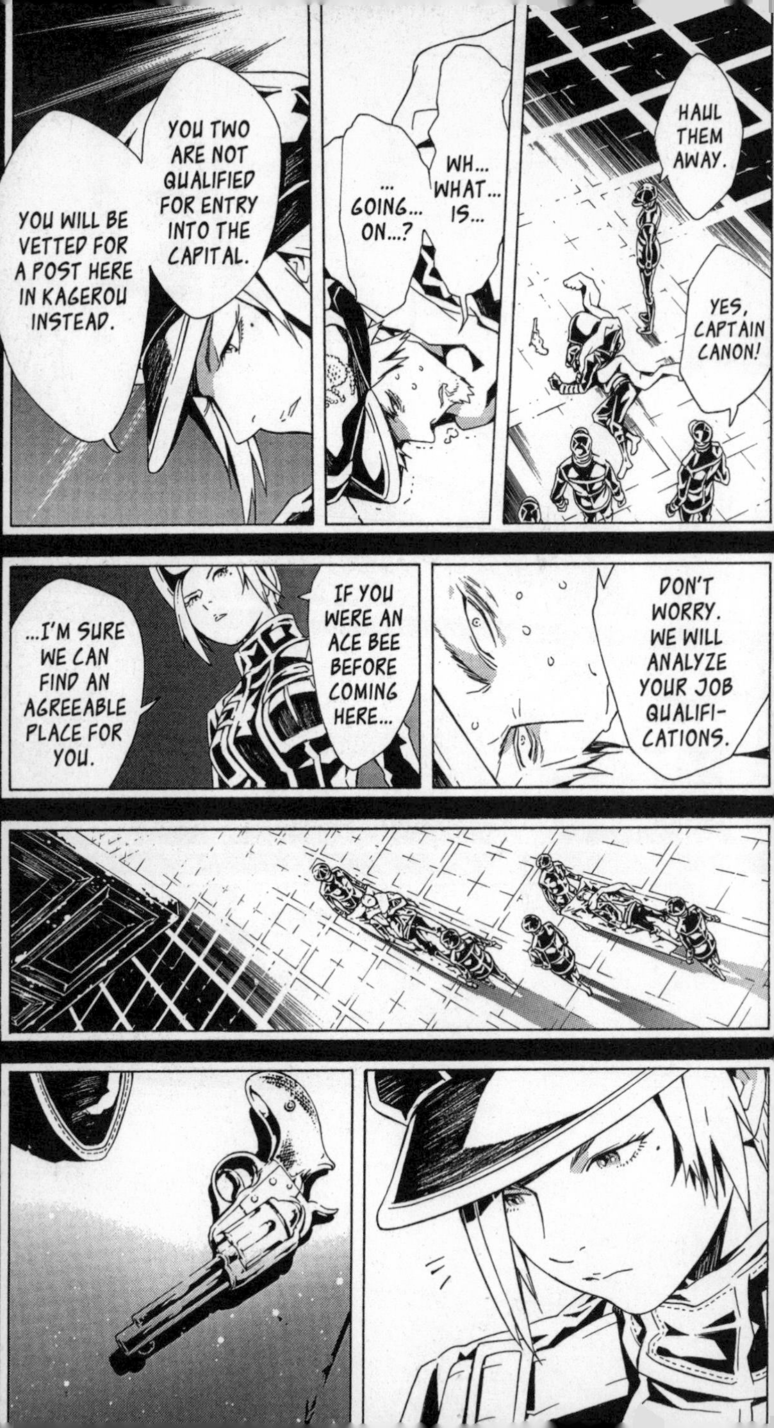
HAUL THEM AWAY.
YES, CAPTAIN CANON!
WH... WHAT... IS...
... GOING... ON...?
YOU TWO ARE NOT QUALIFIED FOR ENTRY INTO THE CAPITAL.
YOU WILL BE VETTED FOR A POST HERE IN KAGEROU INSTEAD.
DON'T WORRY. WE WILL ANALYZE YOUR JOB QUALIFI-CATIONS.
IF YOU WERE AN ACE BEE BEFORE COMING HERE...
...I'M SURE WE CAN FIND AN AGREEABLE PLACE FOR YOU.

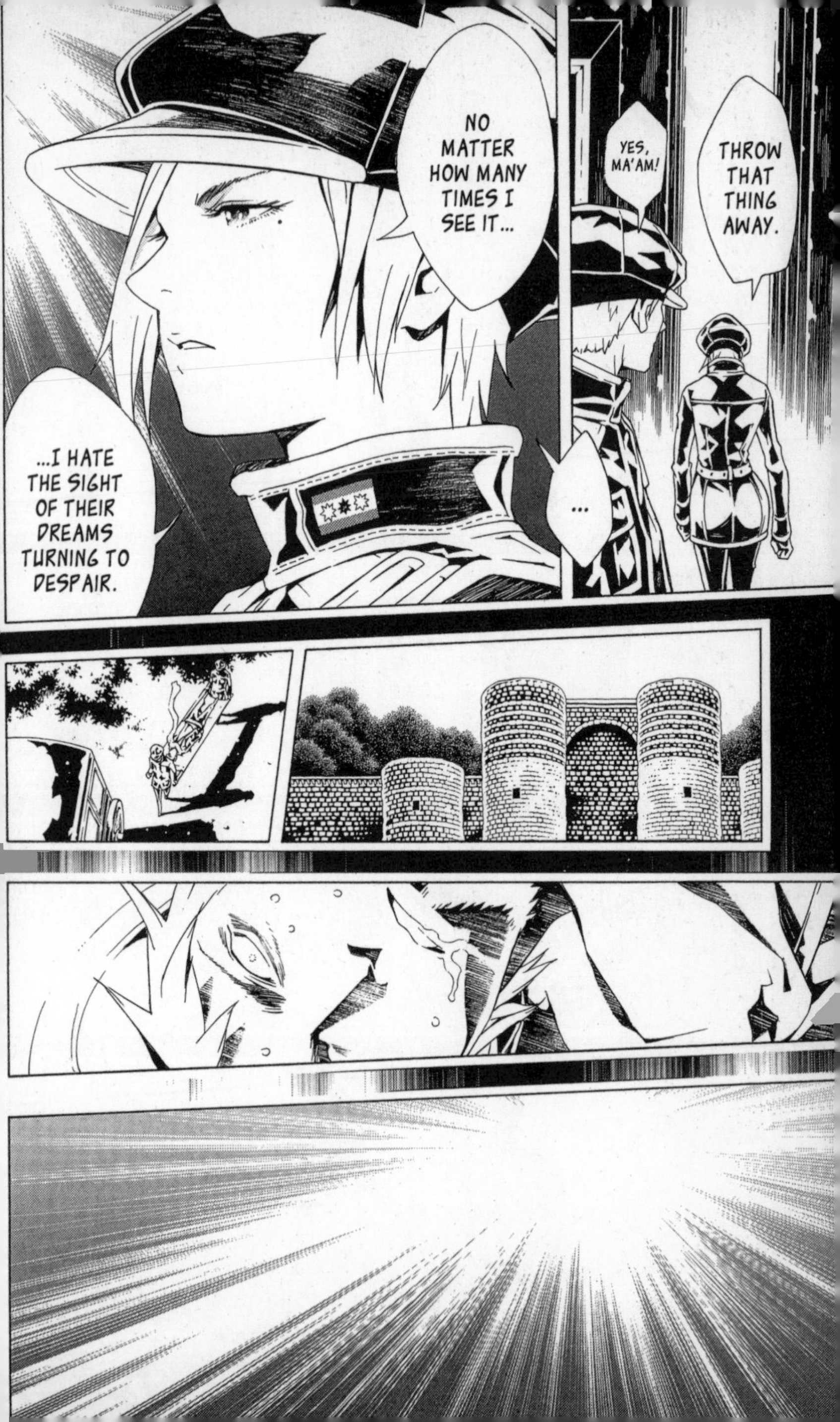
THROW THAT THING AWAY.
YES, MA'AM!
...
NO MATTER HOW MANY TIMES I SEE IT...
...I HATE THE SIGHT OF THEIR DREAMS TURNING TO DESPAIR.

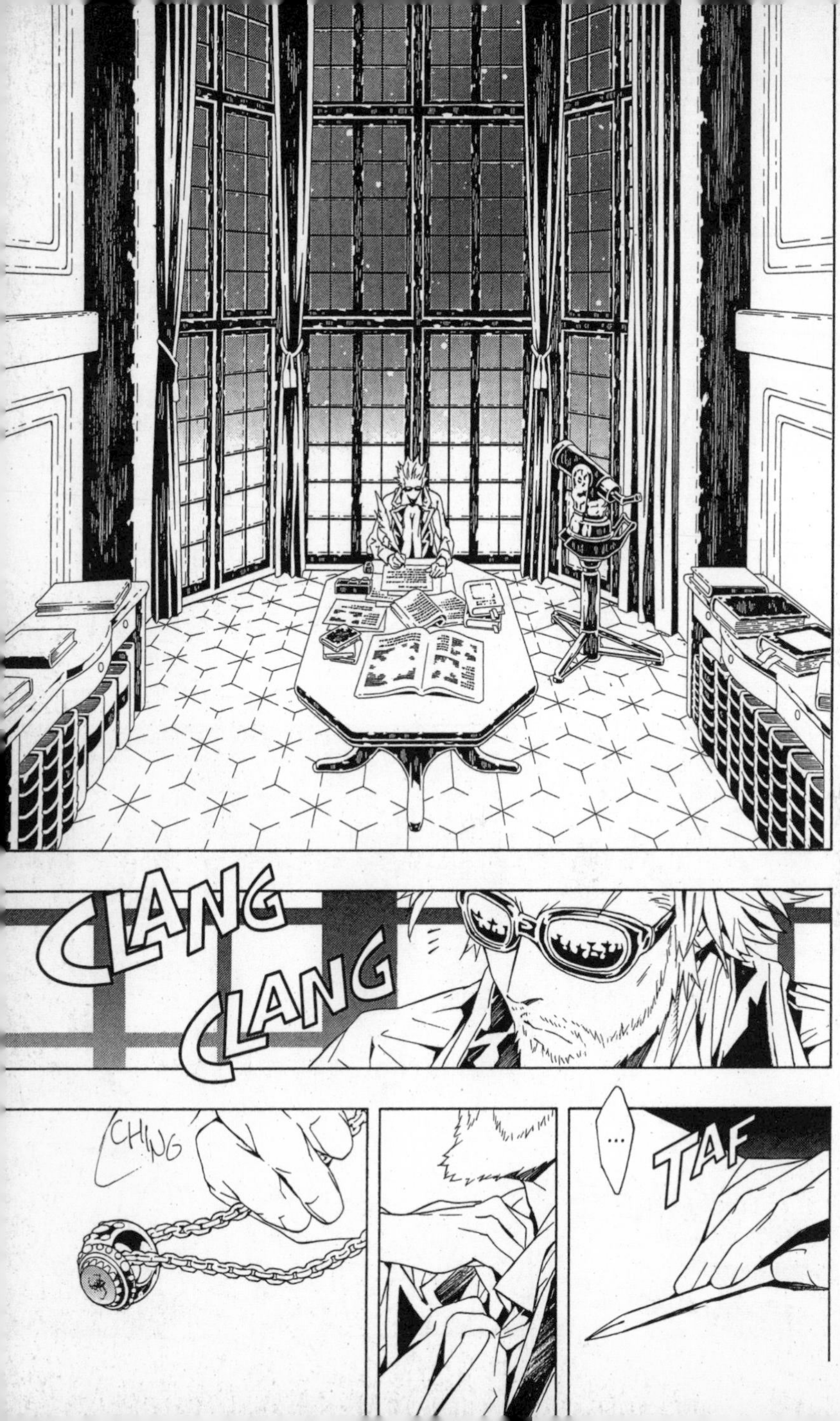
CLANG
CLANG
...
TAF
CHING

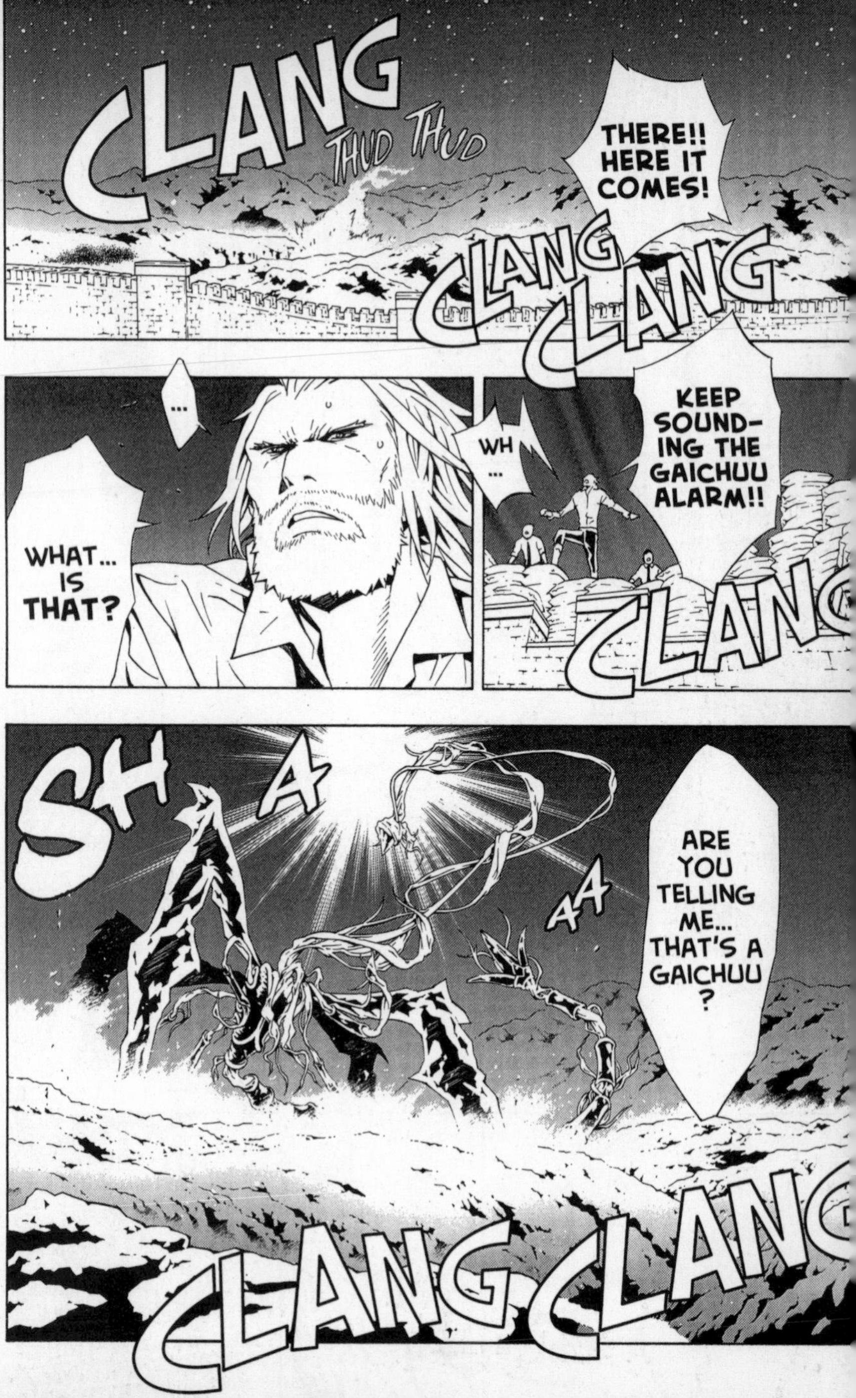
THERE!! HERE IT COMES!
CLANG
THUD THUD
CLANG CLANG
KEEP SOUNDING THE GAICHUU ALARM!!
WH...
CLANG
...
WHAT... IS THAT?
ARE YOU TELLING ME... THAT'S A GAICHUU?
SHAAA
CLANG CLANG

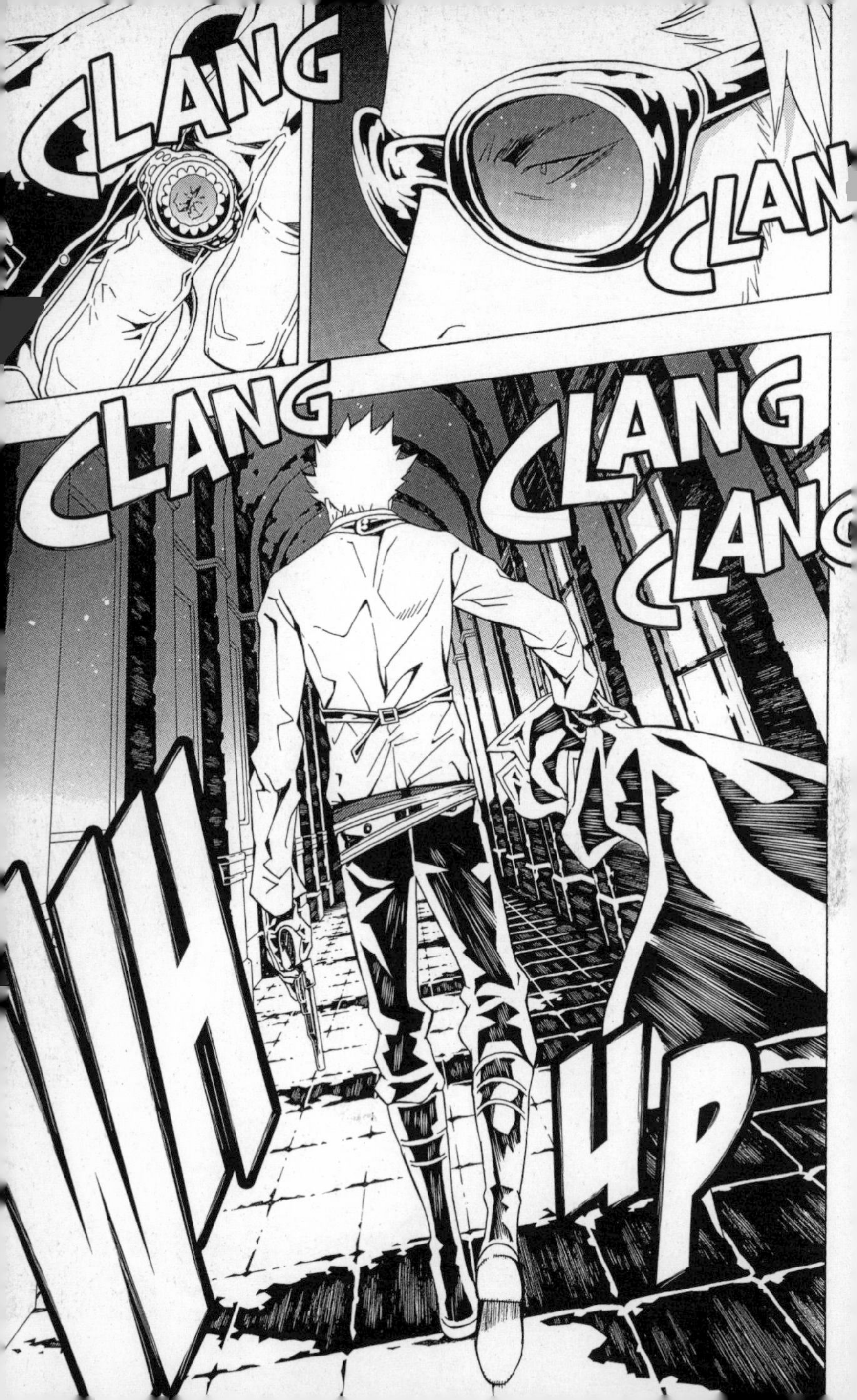
CLAN
CLANG
CLANG
CLAN
CLANG
WHUP

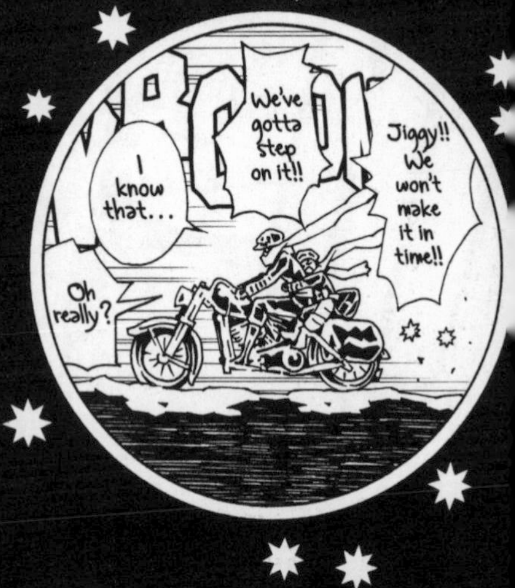
Jiggy!! We won't make it in time!!
We've gotta step on it!!
I know that...
Oh really?

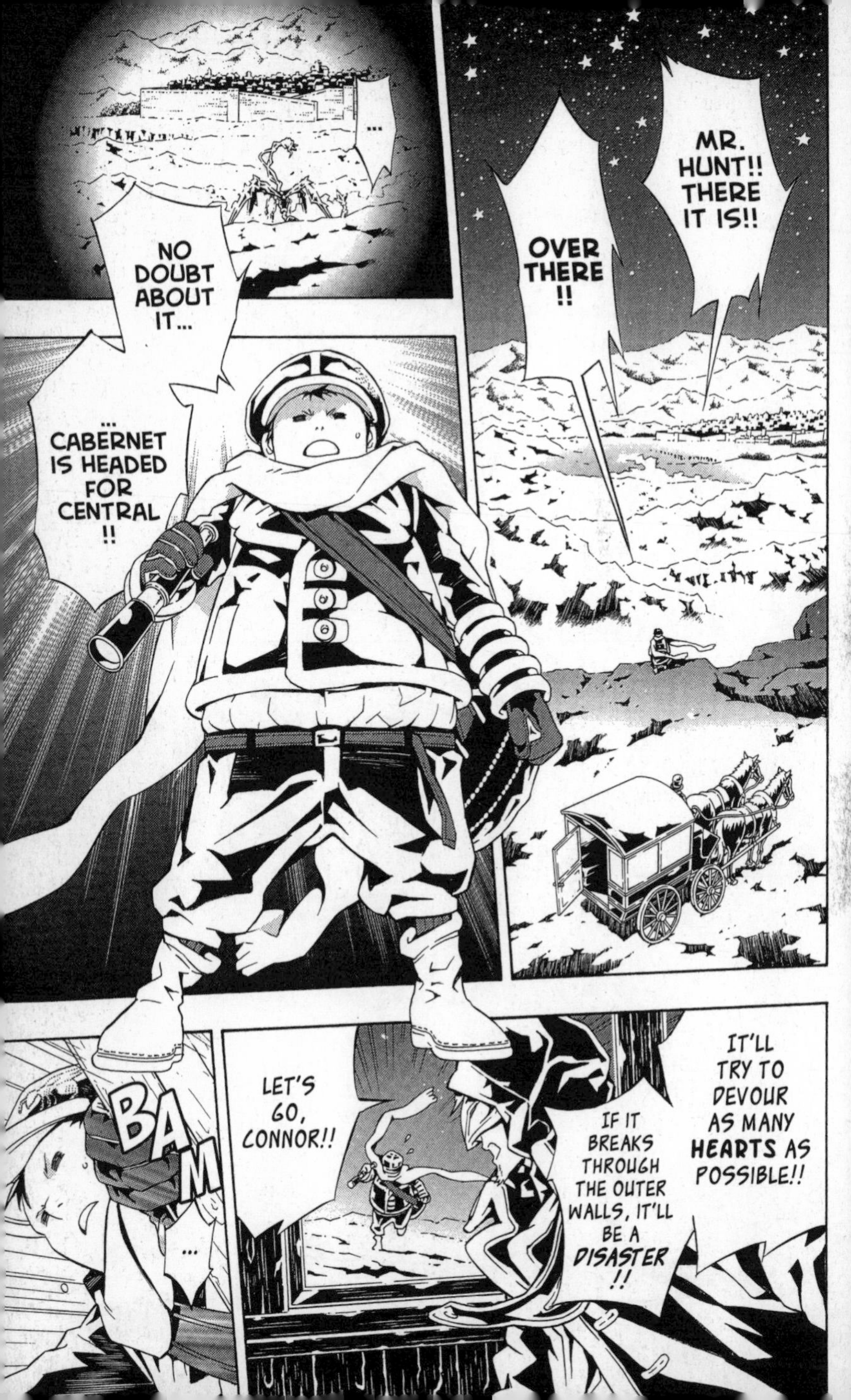
MR. HUNT!! THERE IT IS!!
OVER THERE!!
...
NO DOUBT ABOUT IT...
... CABERNET IS HEADED FOR CENTRAL!!
IT'LL TRY TO DEVOUR AS MANY HEARTS AS POSSIBLE!!
IF IT BREAKS THROUGH THE OUTER WALLS, IT'LL BE A DISASTER!!
LET'S GO, CONNOR!!
BAM
...

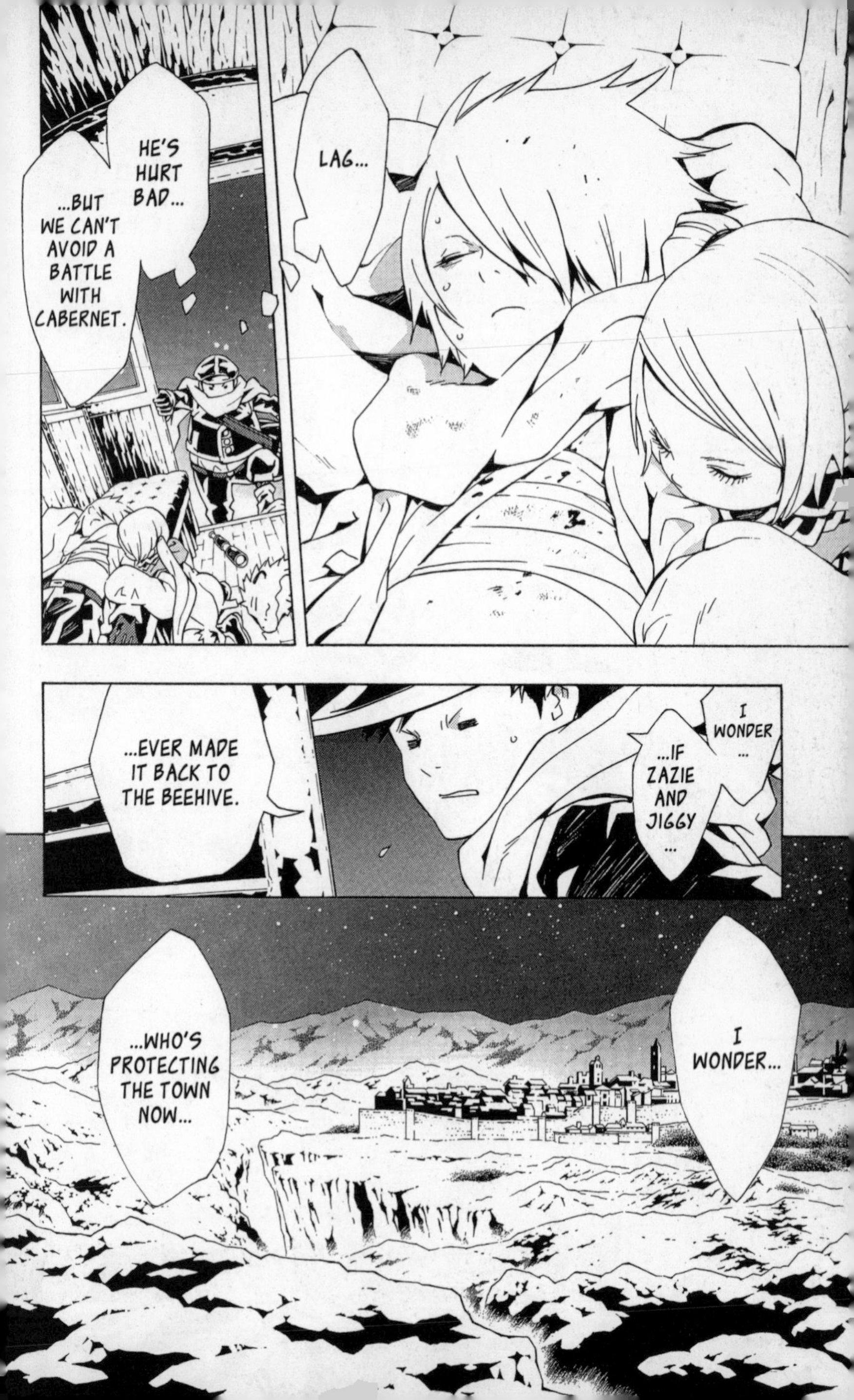
LAG...
HE'S HURT BAD...
...BUT WE CAN'T AVOID A BATTLE WITH CABERNET.
I WONDER...
...IF ZAZIE AND JIGGY...
...EVER MADE IT BACK TO THE BEEHIVE.
I WONDER...
...WHO'S PROTECTING THE TOWN NOW...

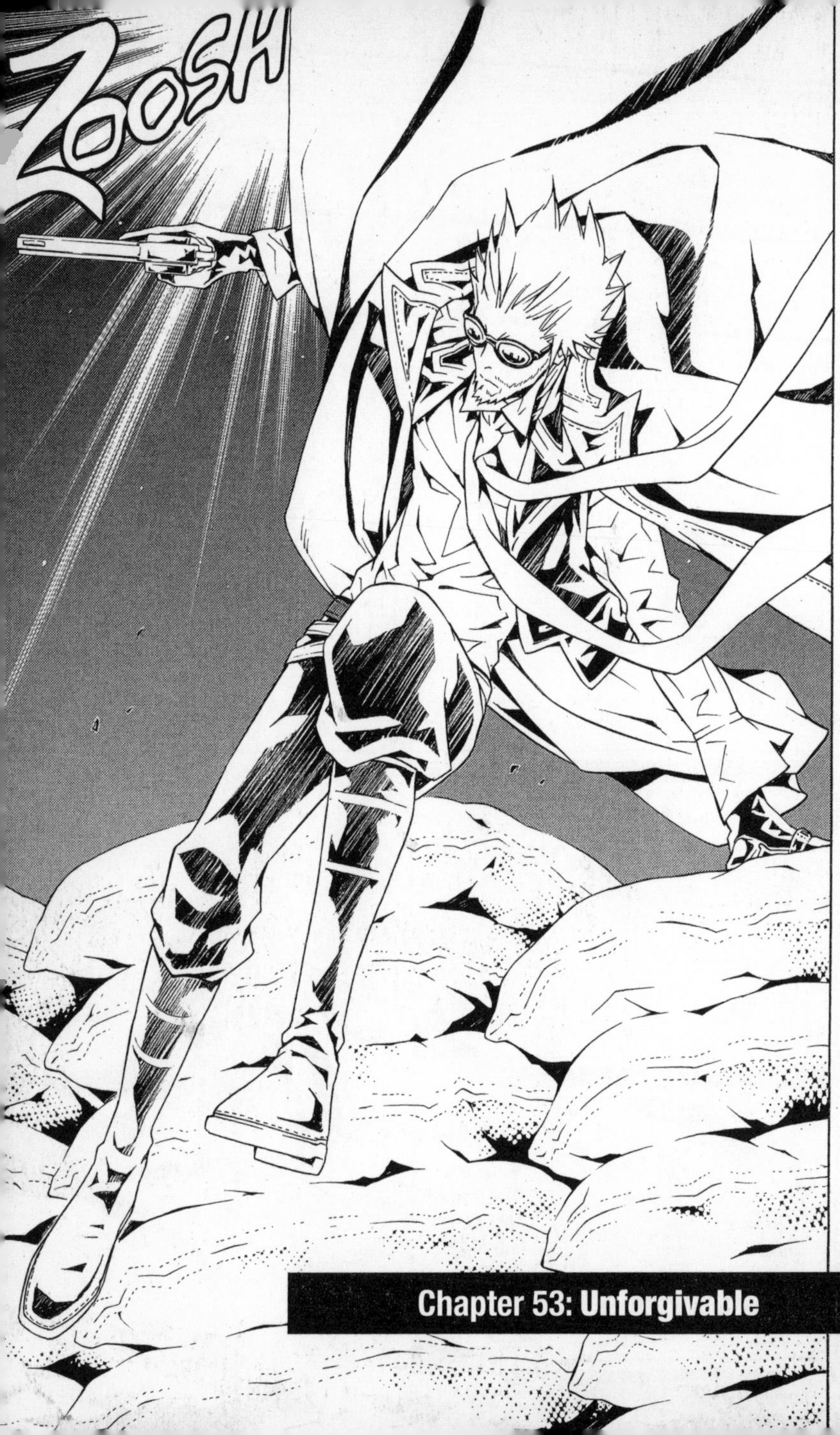
ZOOSH
Chapter 53: Unforgivable

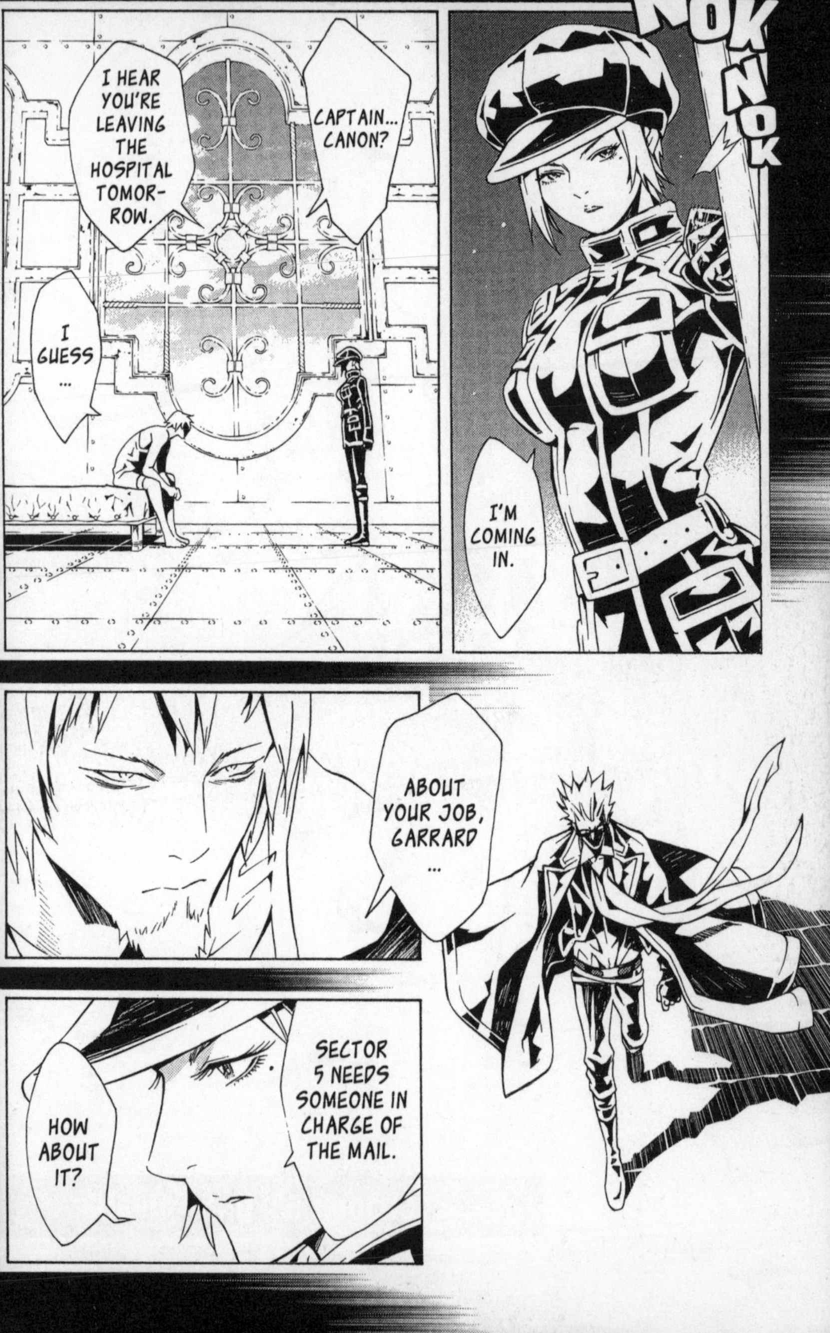
NOK NOK NOK
I'M COMING IN.
CAPTAIN... CANON?
I HEAR YOU'RE LEAVING THE HOSPITAL TOMOR-ROW.
I GUESS...
ABOUT YOUR JOB, GARRARD...
SECTOR 5 NEEDS SOMEONE IN CHARGE OF THE MAIL.
HOW ABOUT IT?

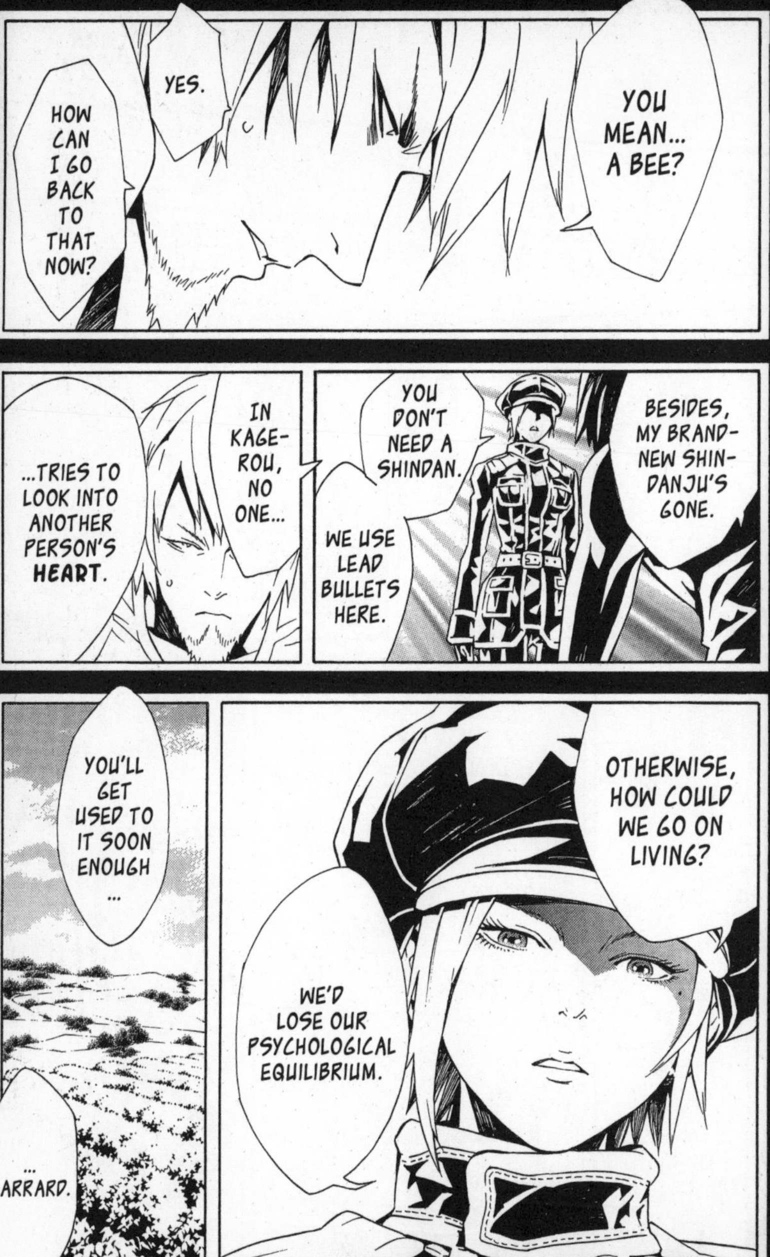
YOU MEAN... A BEE?
YES.
HOW CAN I GO BACK TO THAT NOW?
BESIDES, MY BRAND-NEW SHIN-DANJU'S GONE.
YOU DON'T NEED A SHINDAN.
WE USE LEAD BULLETS HERE.
IN KAGE-ROU, NO ONE...
...TRIES TO LOOK INTO ANOTHER PERSON'S **HEART**.
OTHERWISE, HOW COULD WE GO ON LIVING?
WE'D LOSE OUR PSYCHOLOGICAL EQUILIBRIUM.
YOU'LL GET USED TO IT SOON ENOUGH ...
... GARRARD.

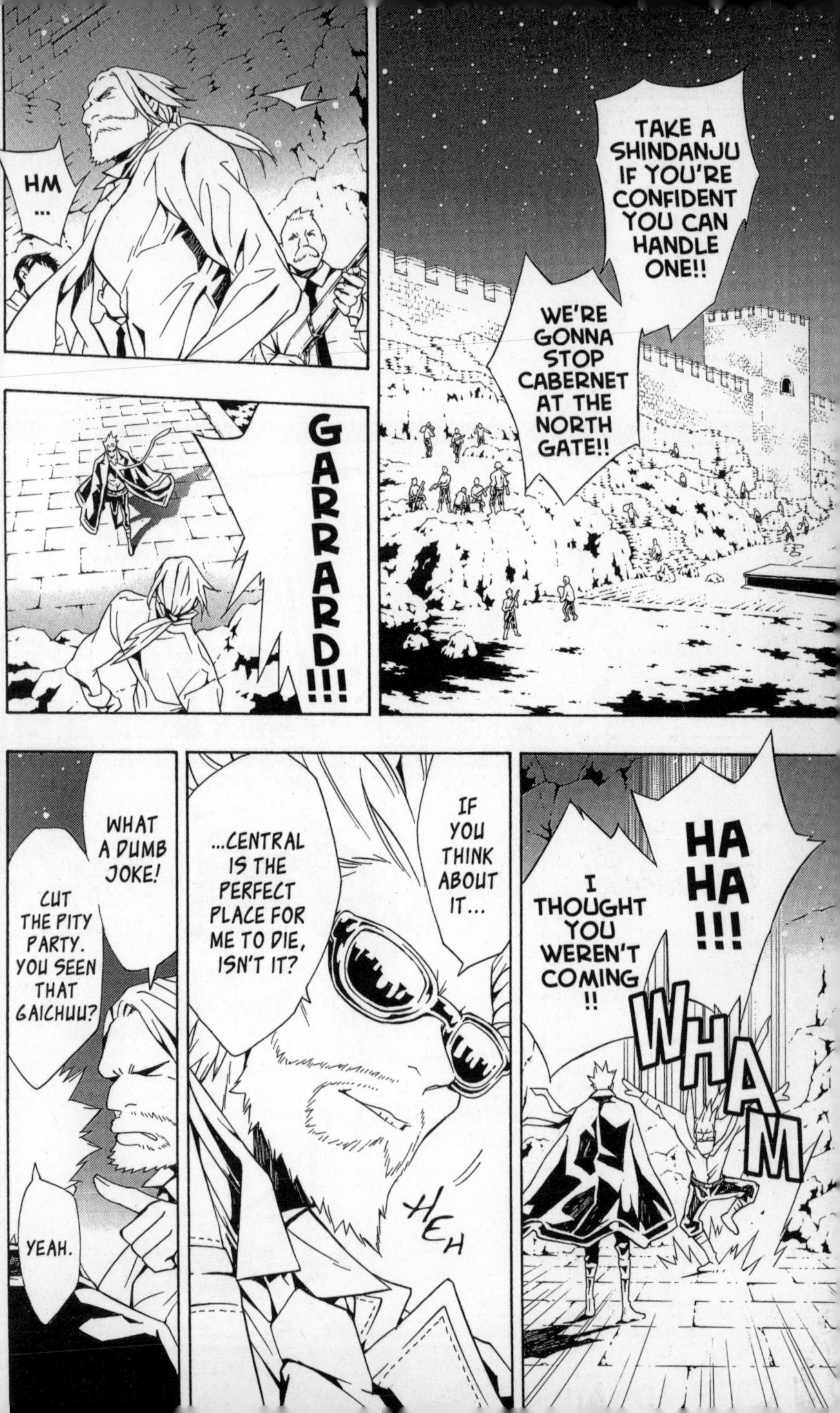
TAKE A SHINDANJU IF YOU'RE CONFIDENT YOU CAN HANDLE ONE!!
WE'RE GONNA STOP CABERNET AT THE NORTH GATE!!
HM ...
GARRARD!!!
HA HA!!!
I THOUGHT YOU WEREN'T COMING!!
WHAM
IF YOU THINK ABOUT IT...
...CENTRAL IS THE PERFECT PLACE FOR ME TO DIE, ISN'T IT?
HEH
WHAT A DUMB JOKE!
CUT THE PITY PARTY. YOU SEEN THAT GAICHUU?
YEAH.

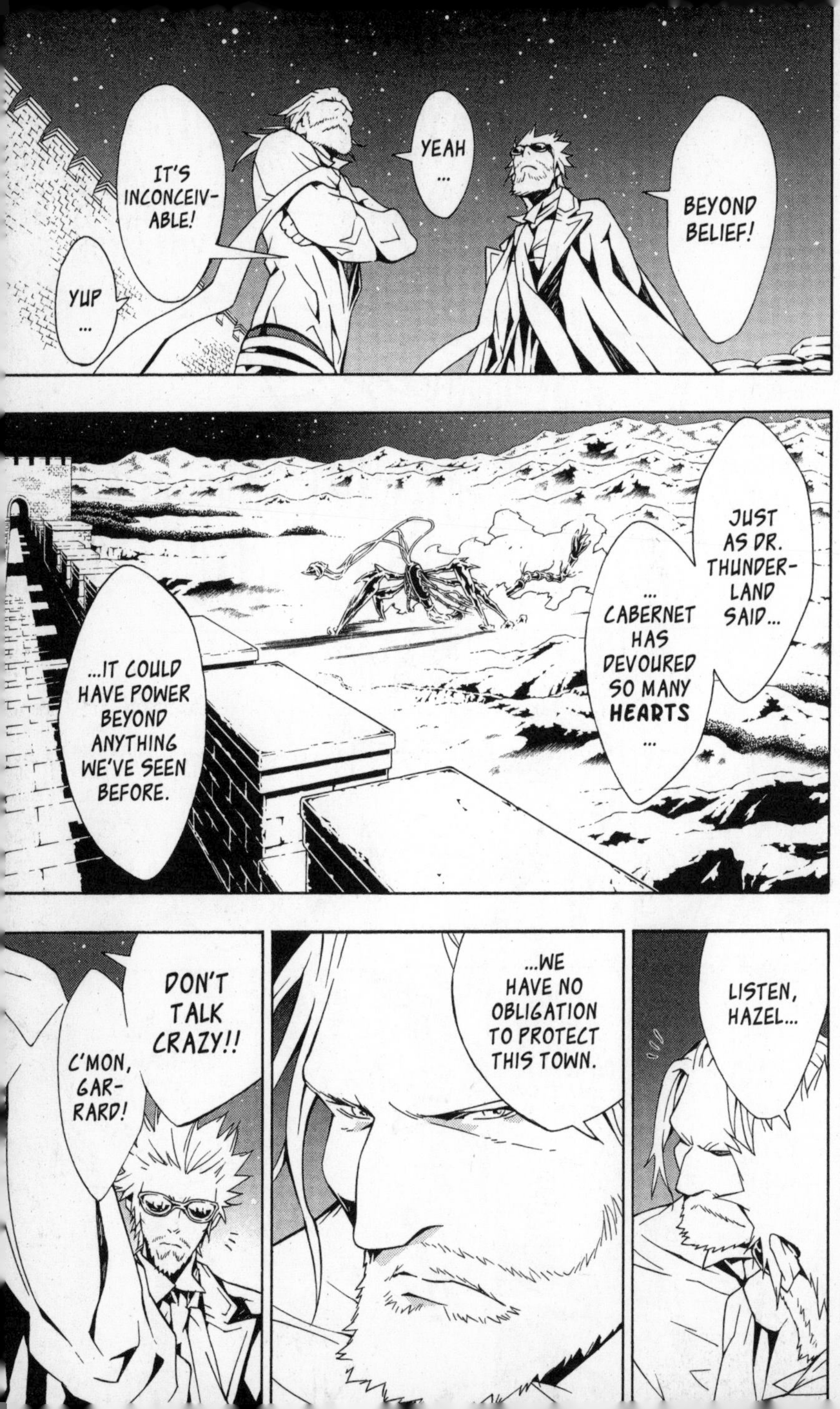
BEYOND BELIEF!
YEAH ...
IT'S INCONCEIVABLE!
YUP ...
JUST AS DR. THUNDERLAND SAID...
... CABERNET HAS DEVOURED SO MANY **HEARTS** ...
...IT COULD HAVE POWER BEYOND ANYTHING WE'VE SEEN BEFORE.
LISTEN, HAZEL...
...WE HAVE NO OBLIGATION TO PROTECT THIS TOWN.
DON'T TALK CRAZY!!
C'MON, GARRARD!

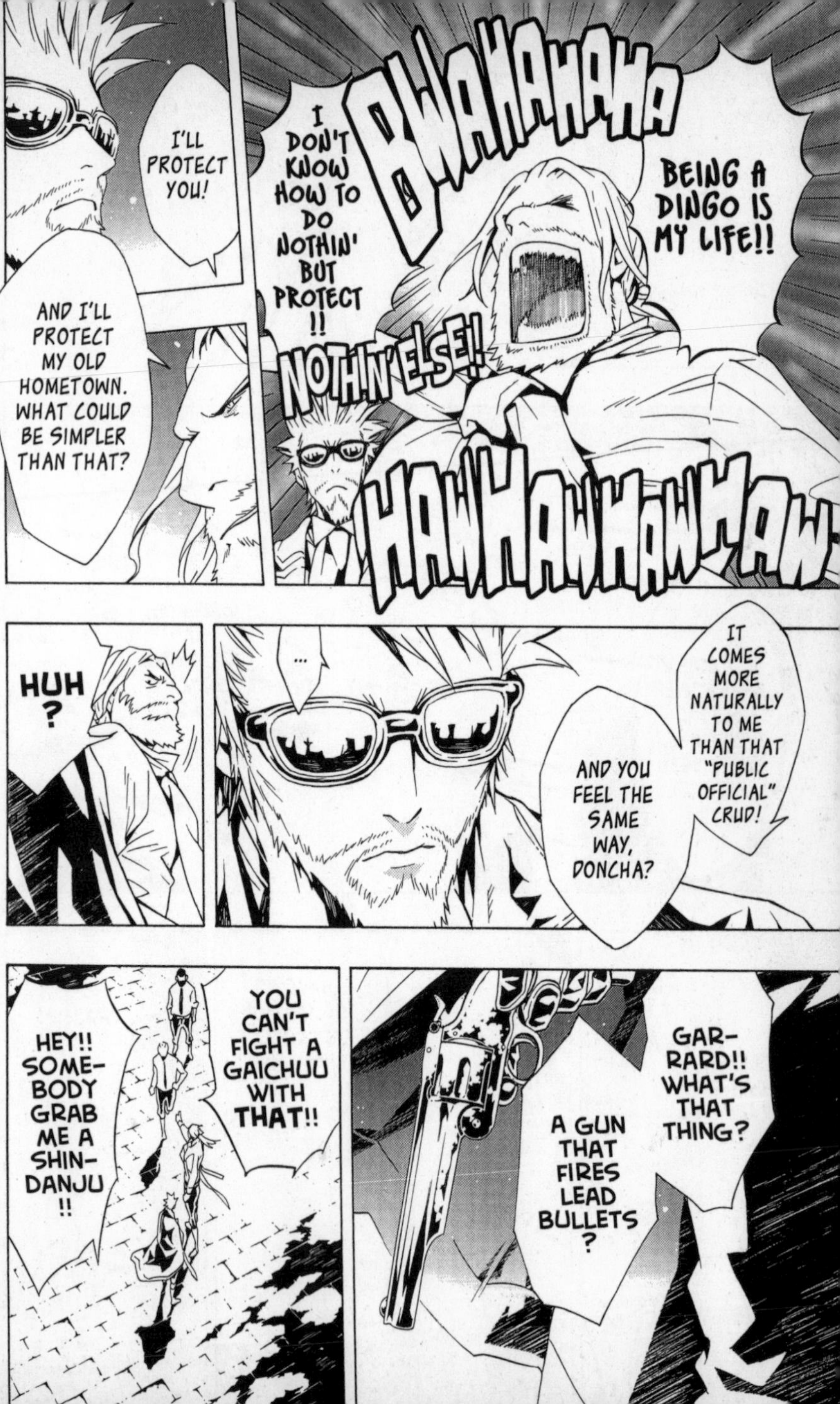
BWAHAHAHAHA
BEING A DINGO IS MY LIFE!!
I DON'T KNOW HOW TO DO NOTHIN' BUT PROTECT!!
NOTHIN' ELSE!!
HAWHAWHAWHAW
I'LL PROTECT YOU!
AND I'LL PROTECT MY OLD HOMETOWN. WHAT COULD BE SIMPLER THAN THAT?
IT COMES MORE NATURALLY TO ME THAN THAT "PUBLIC OFFICIAL" CRUD!
AND YOU FEEL THE SAME WAY, DONCHA?
...
HUH?
GAR-RARD!! WHAT'S THAT THING?
A GUN THAT FIRES LEAD BULLETS?
YOU CAN'T FIGHT A GAICHUU WITH THAT!!
HEY!! SOMEBODY GRAB ME A SHIN-DANJU!!

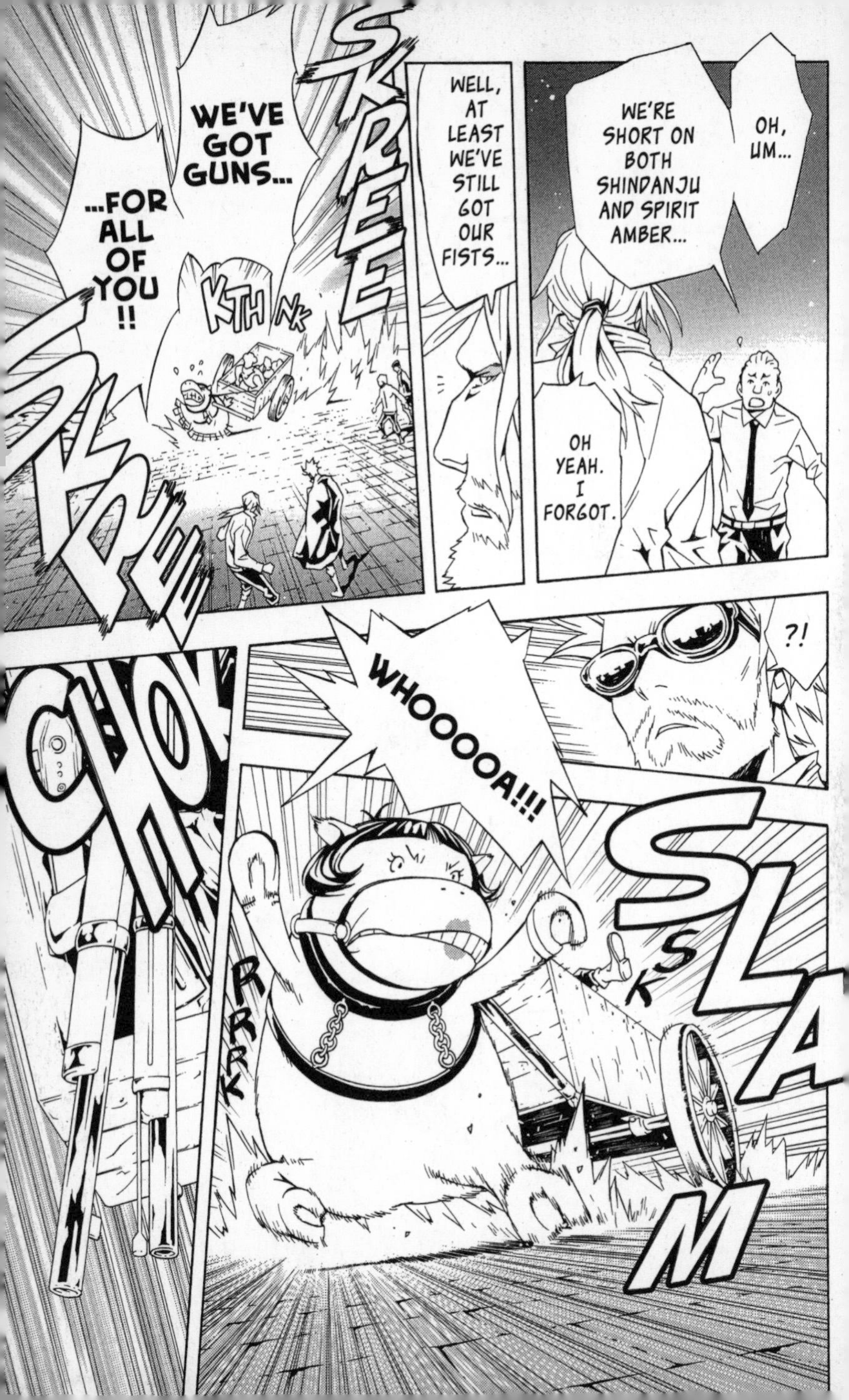
OH, UM...
WE'RE SHORT ON BOTH SHINDANJU AND SPIRIT AMBER...
OH YEAH. I FORGOT.
WELL, AT LEAST WE'VE STILL GOT OUR FISTS...
SKREE
WE'VE GOT GUNS...
...FOR ALL OF YOU!!
KTHNK
?!
WHOOOOOA!!!
SLAM
SKS
RRRK
CHOK

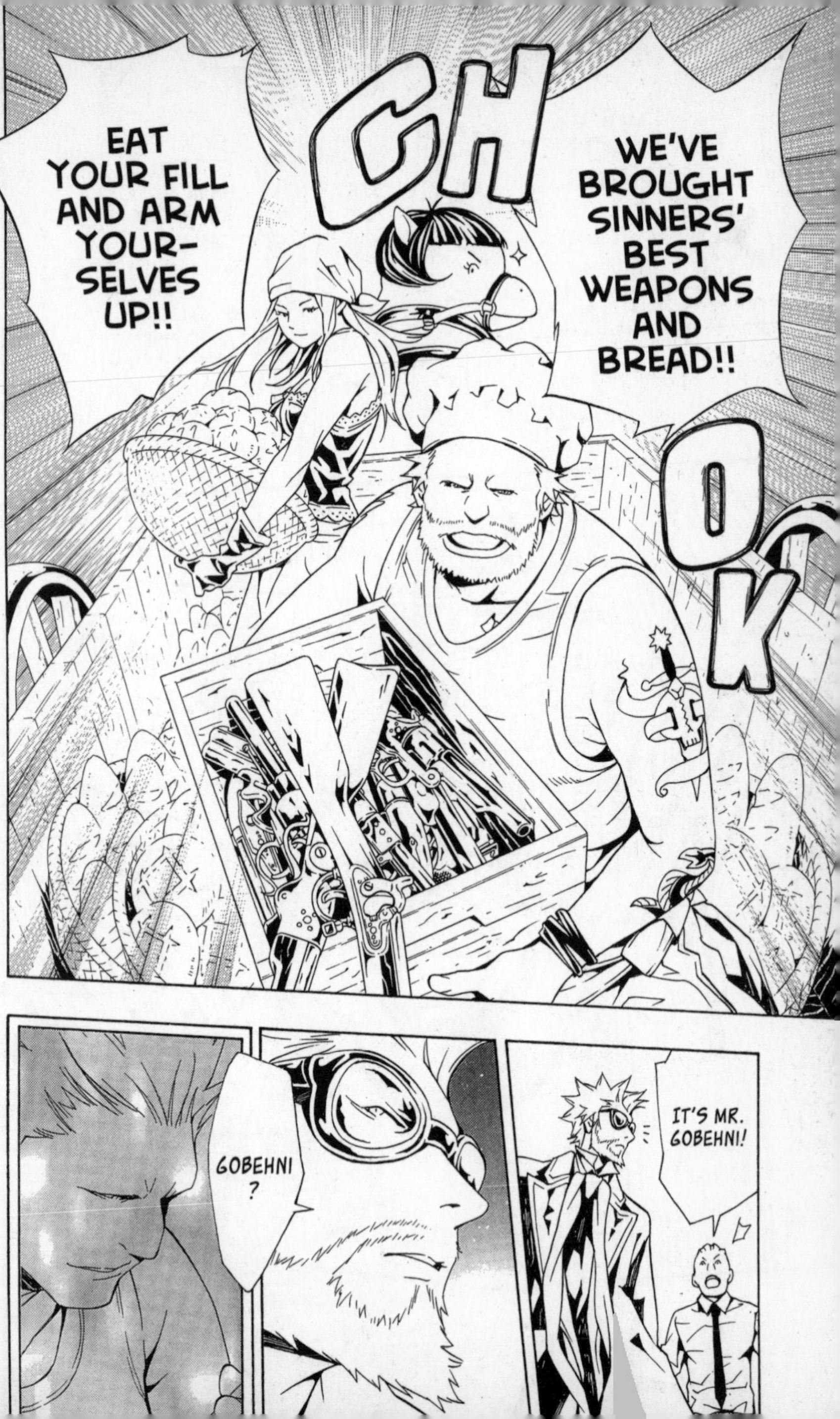
WE'VE BROUGHT SINNERS' BEST WEAPONS AND BREAD!!
CH
OK
EAT YOUR FILL AND ARM YOUR-SELVES UP!!
IT'S MR. GOBEHNI!
GOBEHNI ?

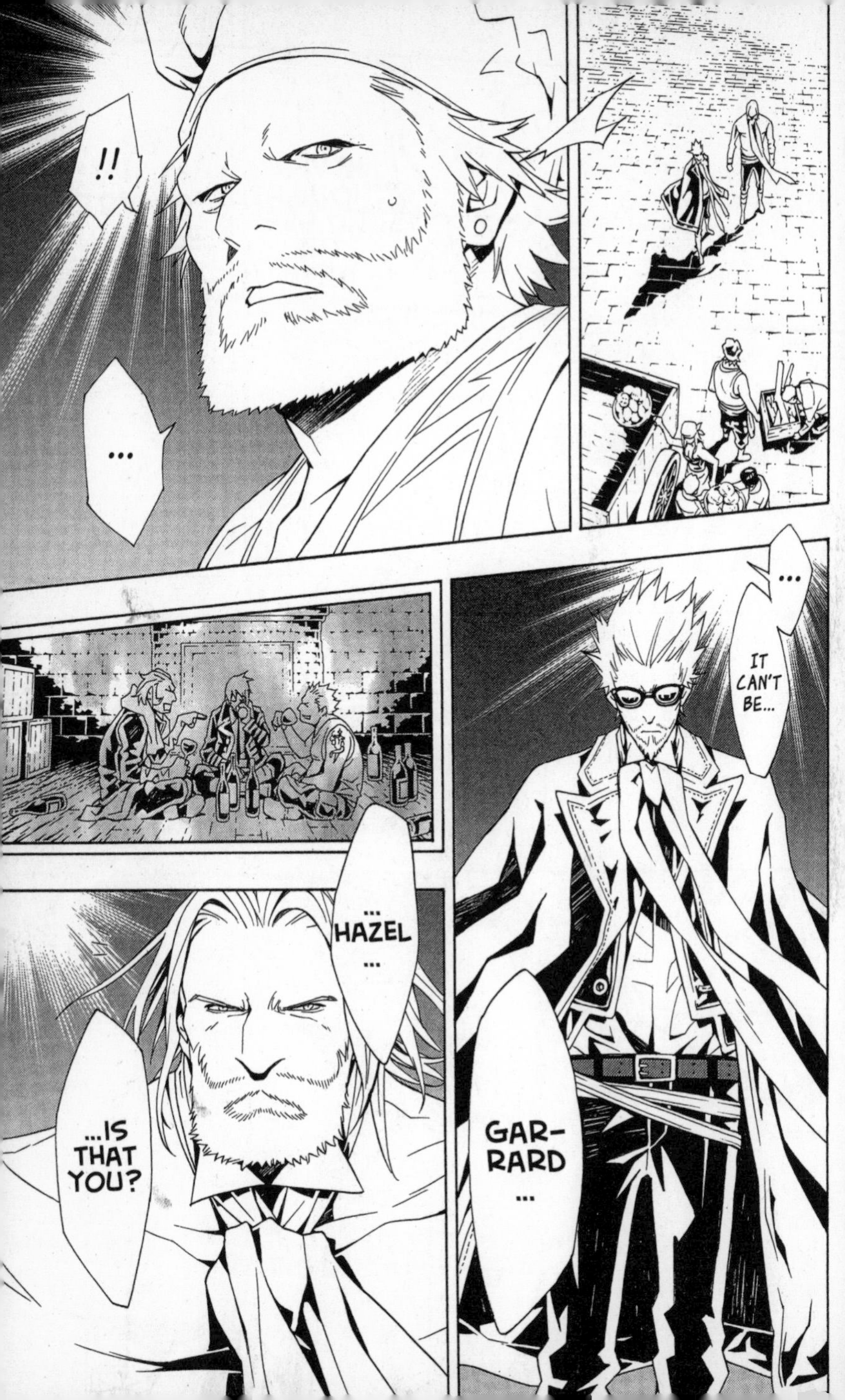
!!
...
...
IT CAN'T BE...
GARRARD...
...HAZEL...
...IS THAT YOU?

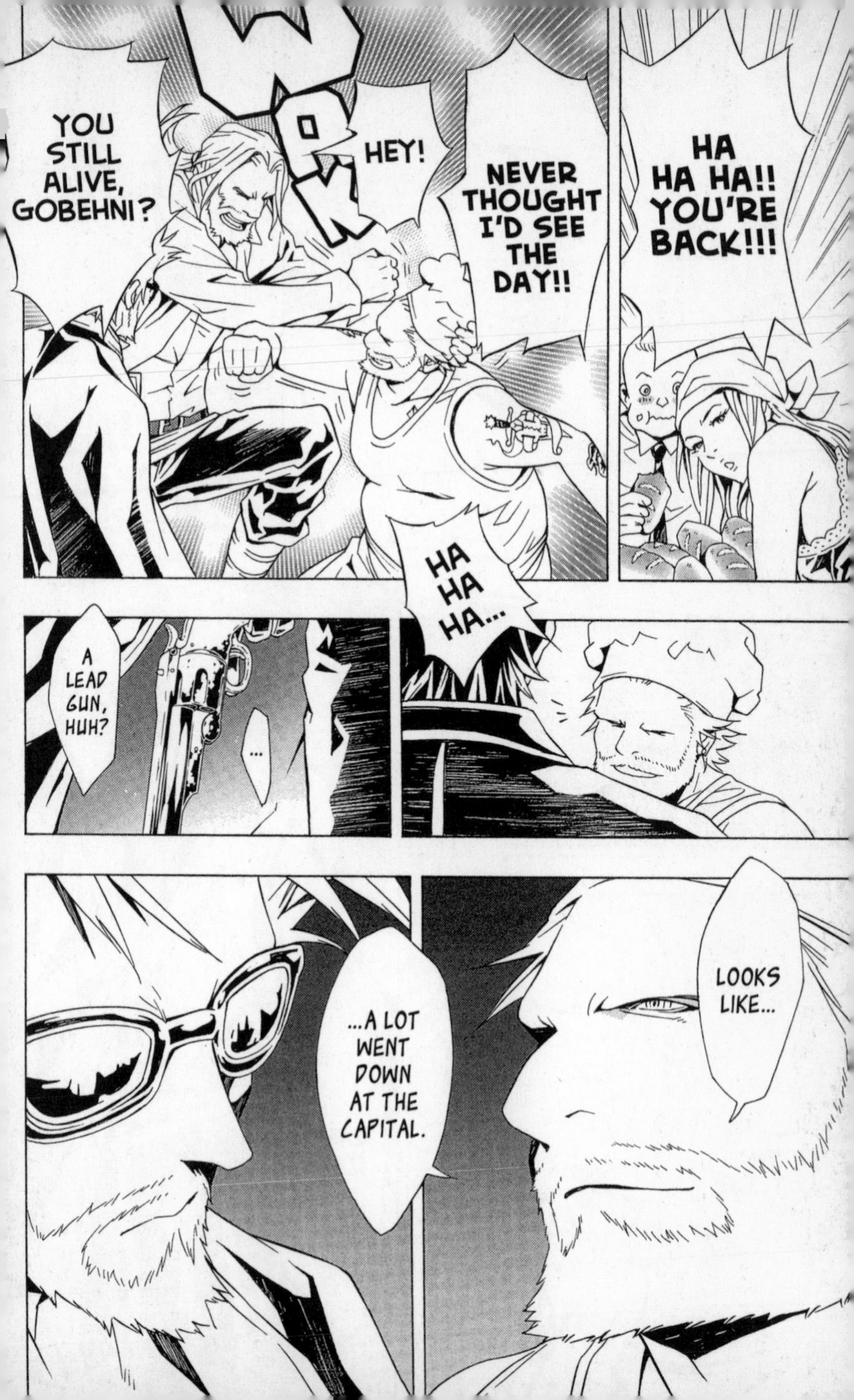
HA HA HA!! YOU'RE BACK!!!
NEVER THOUGHT I'D SEE THE DAY!!
HEY!
YOU STILL ALIVE, GOBEHNI?
HA HA HA...
A LEAD GUN, HUH?
...
LOOKS LIKE...
...A LOT WENT DOWN AT THE CAPITAL.

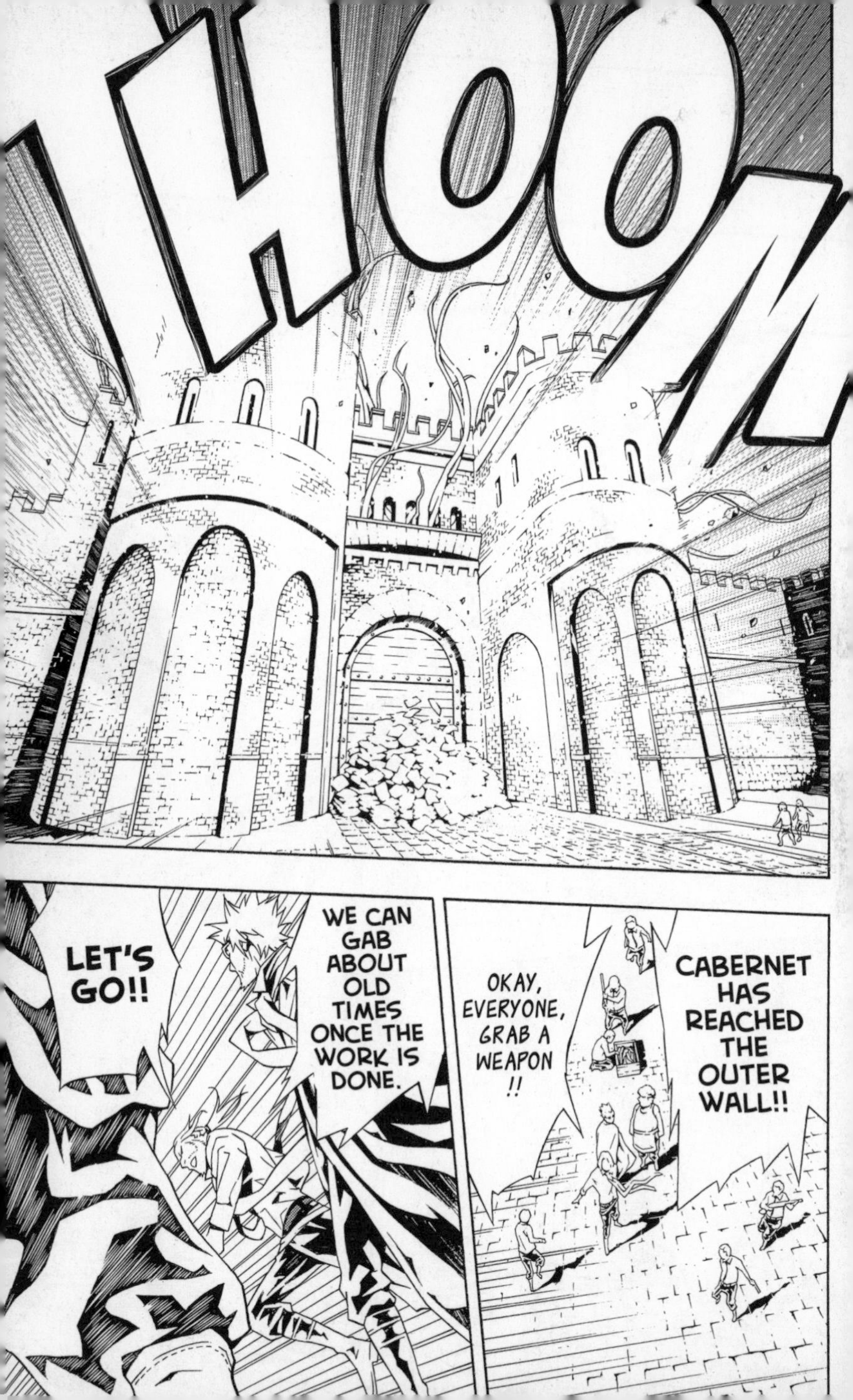
CABERNET HAS REACHED THE OUTER WALL!!
OKAY, EVERYONE, GRAB A WEAPON!!
WE CAN GAB ABOUT OLD TIMES ONCE THE WORK IS DONE.
LET'S GO!!

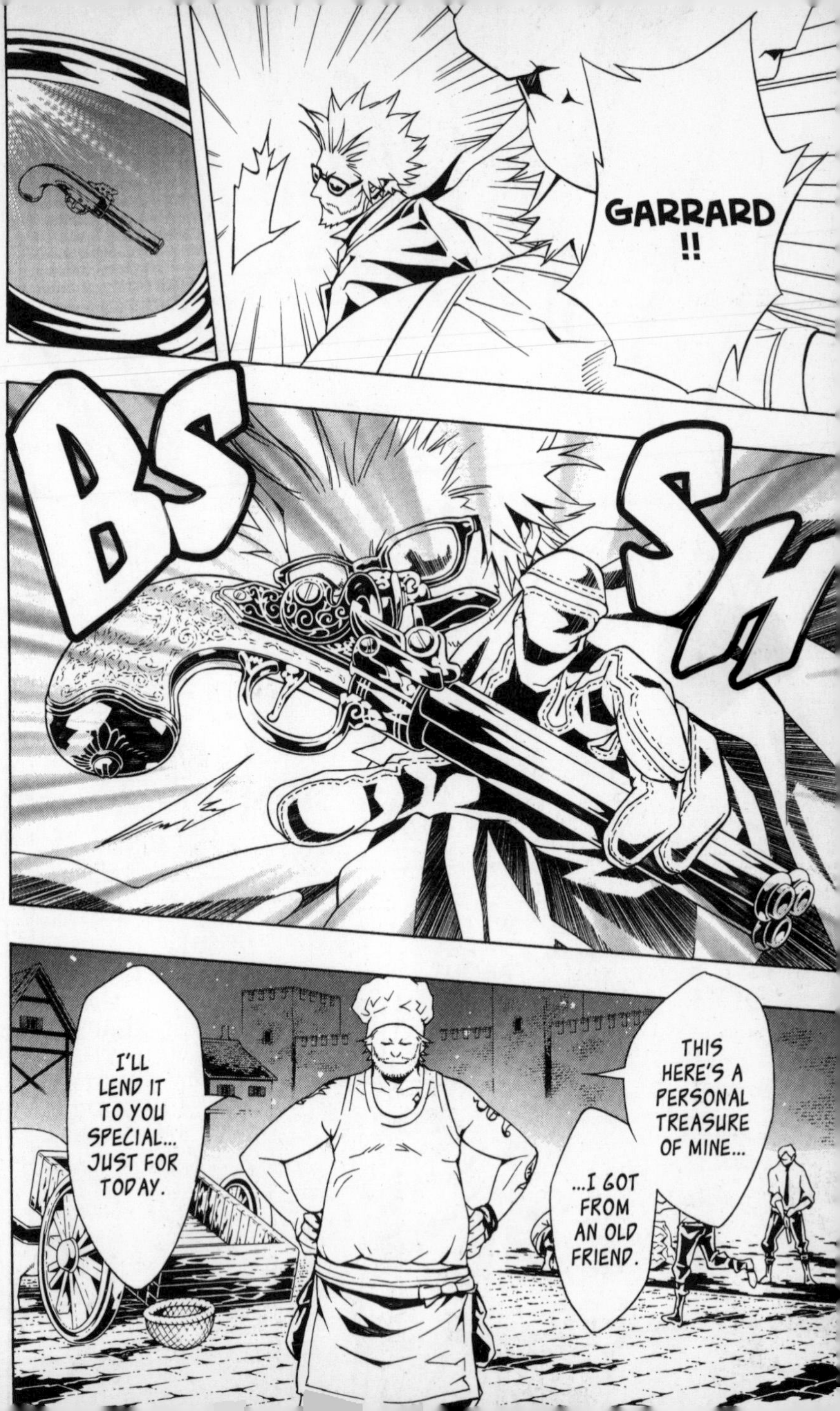
GARRARD !!
BSSH
THIS HERE'S A PERSONAL TREASURE OF MINE...
...I GOT FROM AN OLD FRIEND.
I'LL LEND IT TO YOU SPECIAL... JUST FOR TODAY.

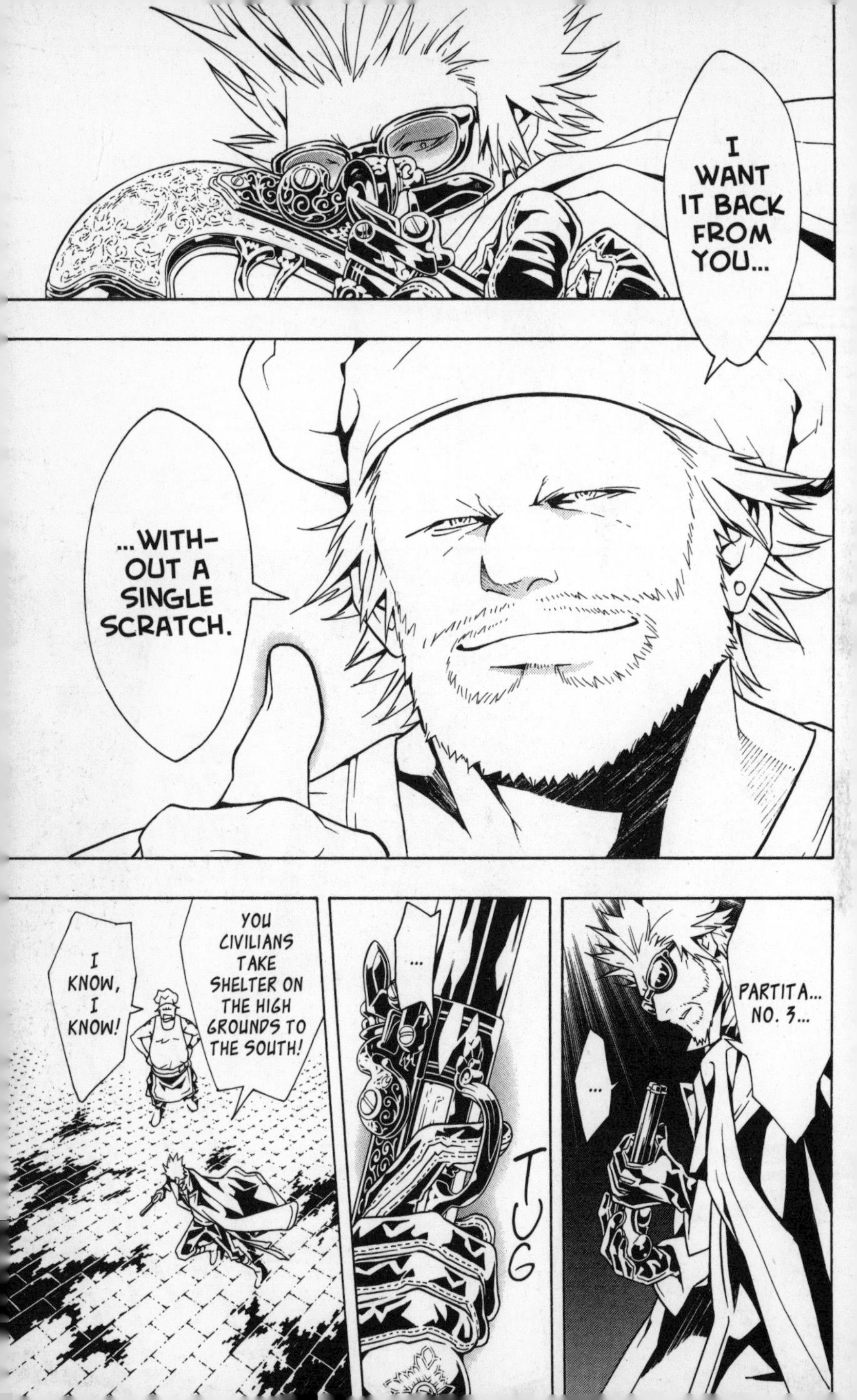
I WANT IT BACK FROM YOU...
...WITH-OUT A SINGLE SCRATCH.
PARTITA... NO. 3...
...
...
TUG
YOU CIVILIANS TAKE SHELTER ON THE HIGH GROUNDS TO THE SOUTH!
I KNOW, I KNOW!

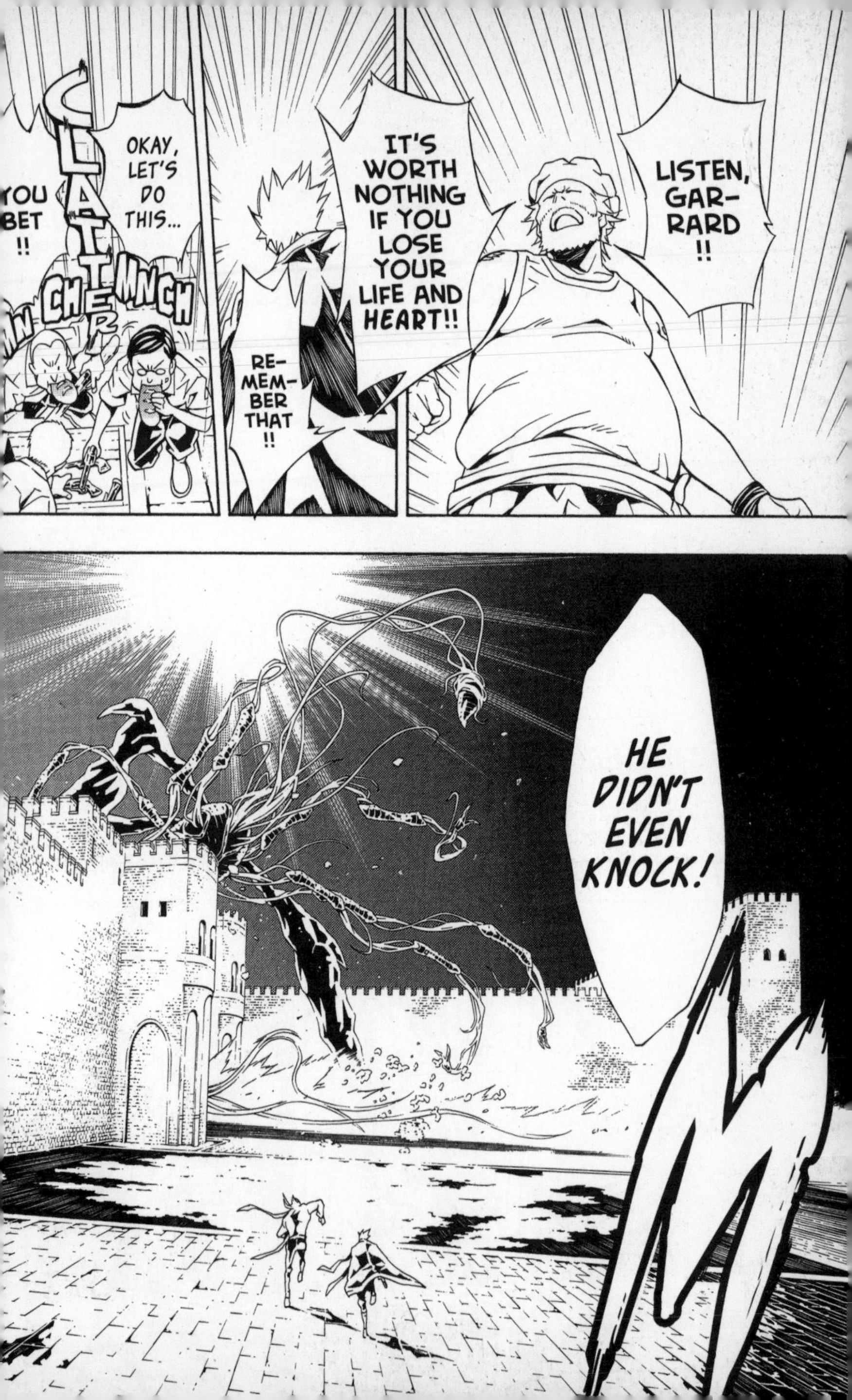
LISTEN, GARRARD!!
IT'S WORTH NOTHING IF YOU LOSE YOUR LIFE AND HEART!!
REMEMBER THAT!!
CLATTER
OKAY, LET'S DO THIS...
MNCH
CHEW
YOU BET!!
HE DIDN'T EVEN KNOCK!

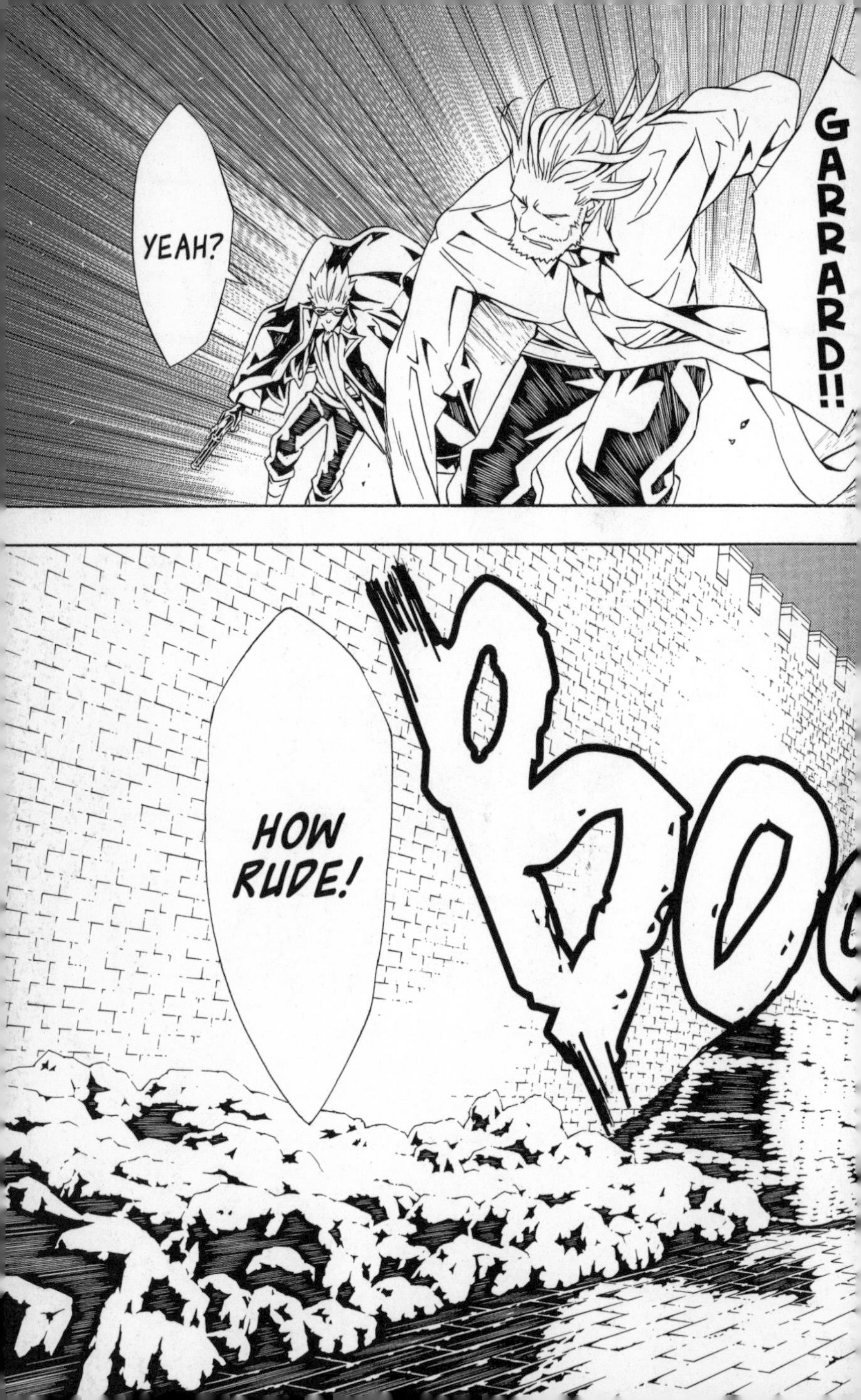
GARRARD!!
YEAH?
HOW RUDE!

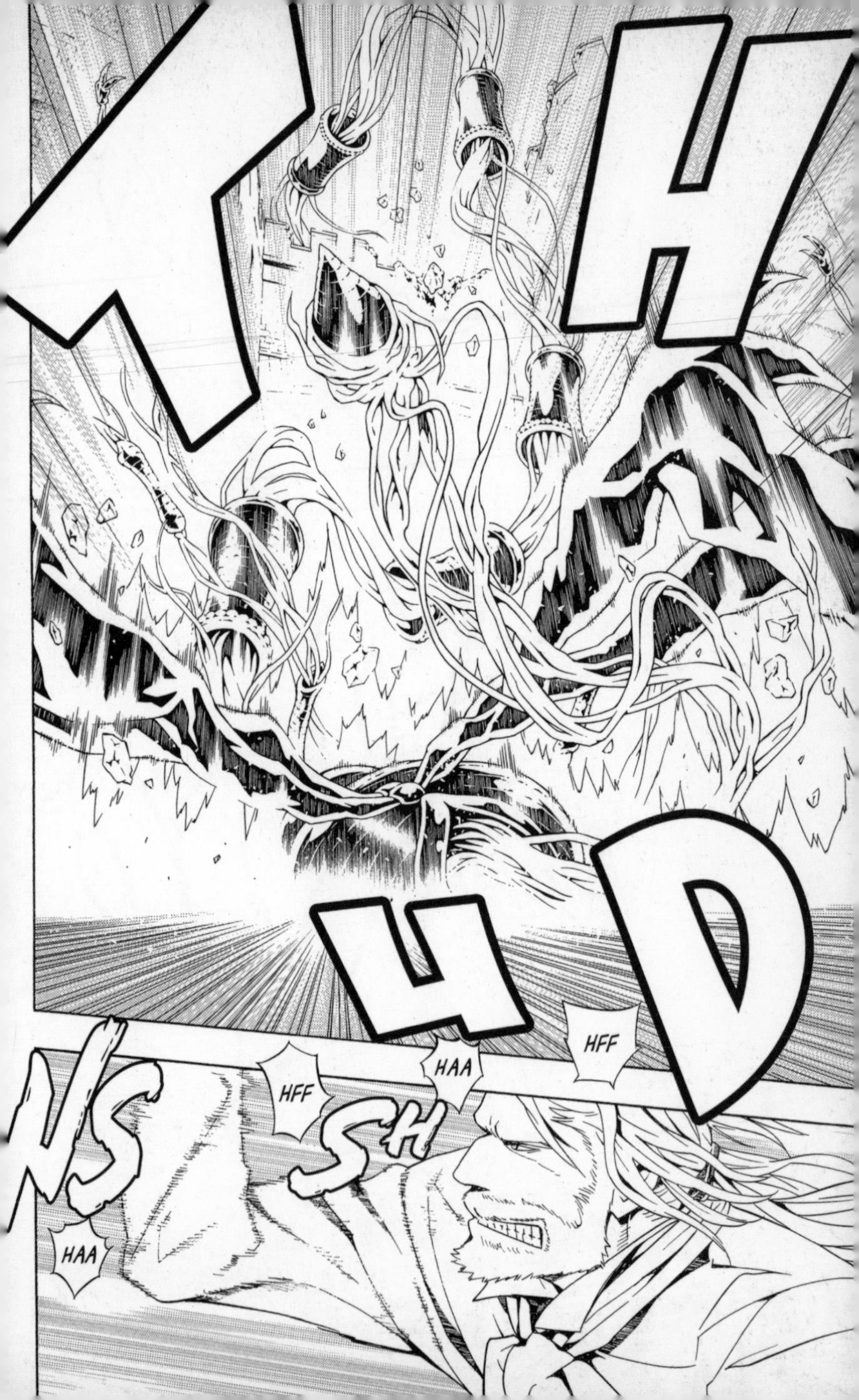
HFF
HAA
HFF
HAA

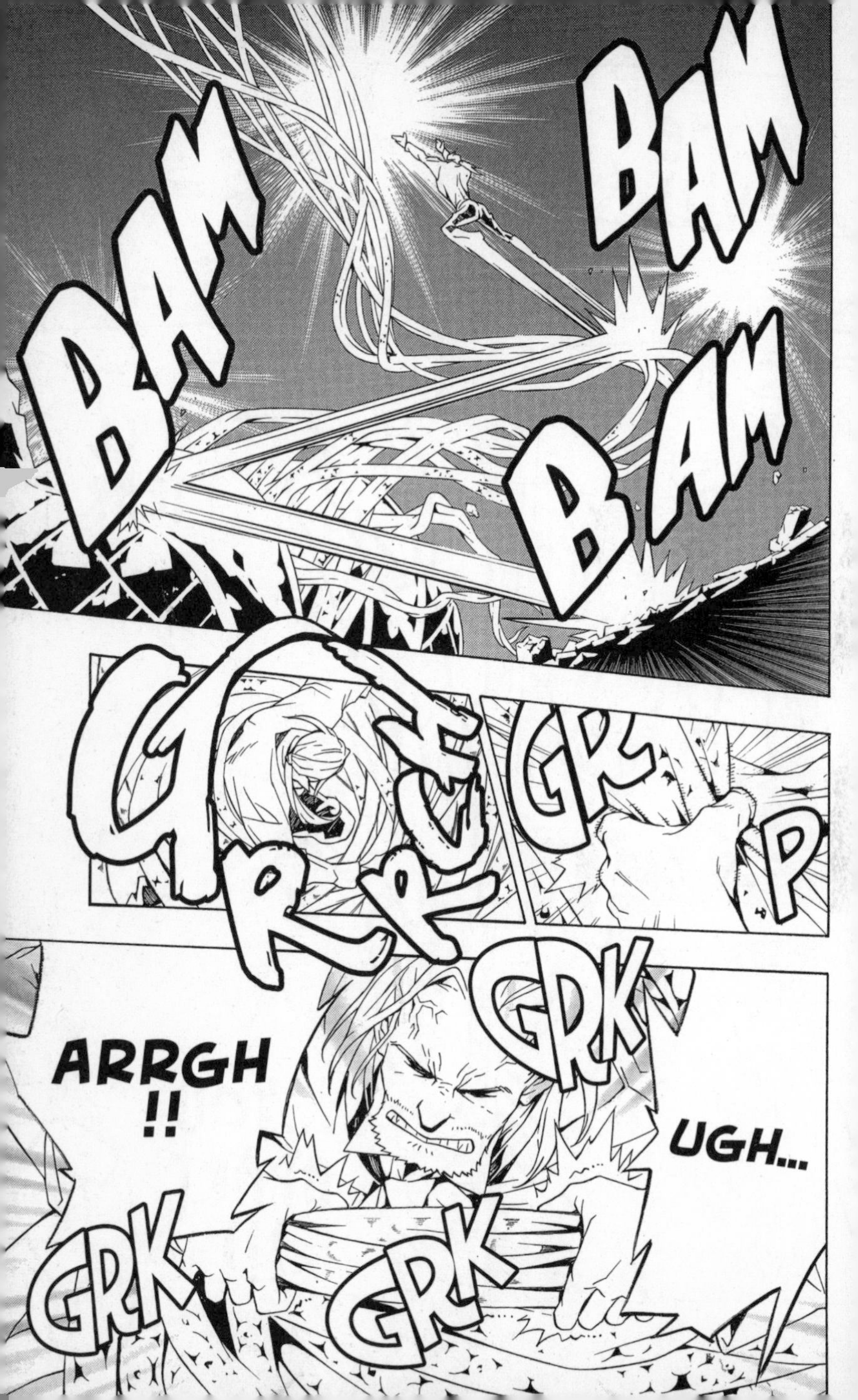

BAM
BAM
BAM
GRP
GRK
UGH...
ARRGH !!
GRK
GRK

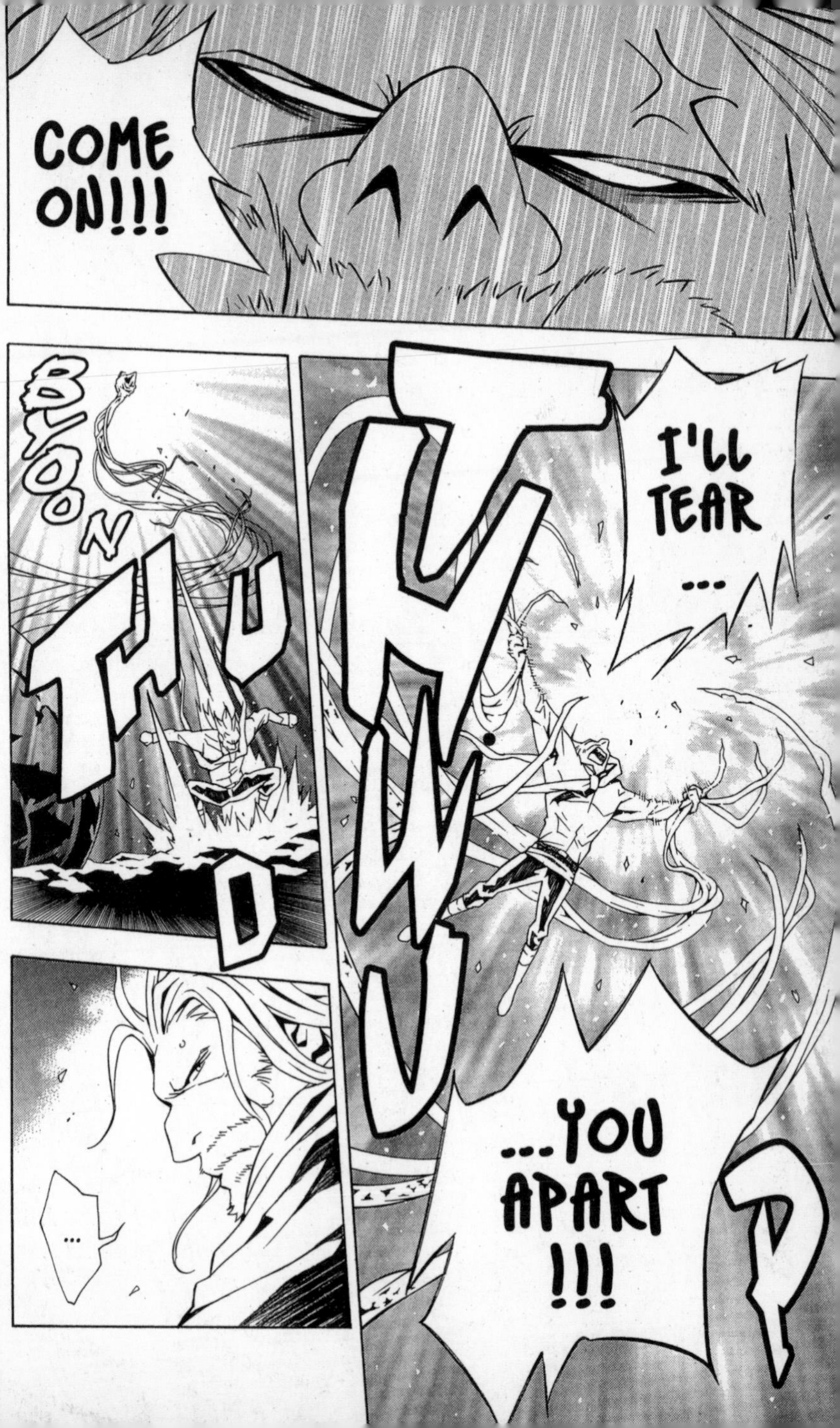
COME ON!!!
I'LL TEAR ...
THWUP
...YOU APART!!!
BYOON
THUD
...

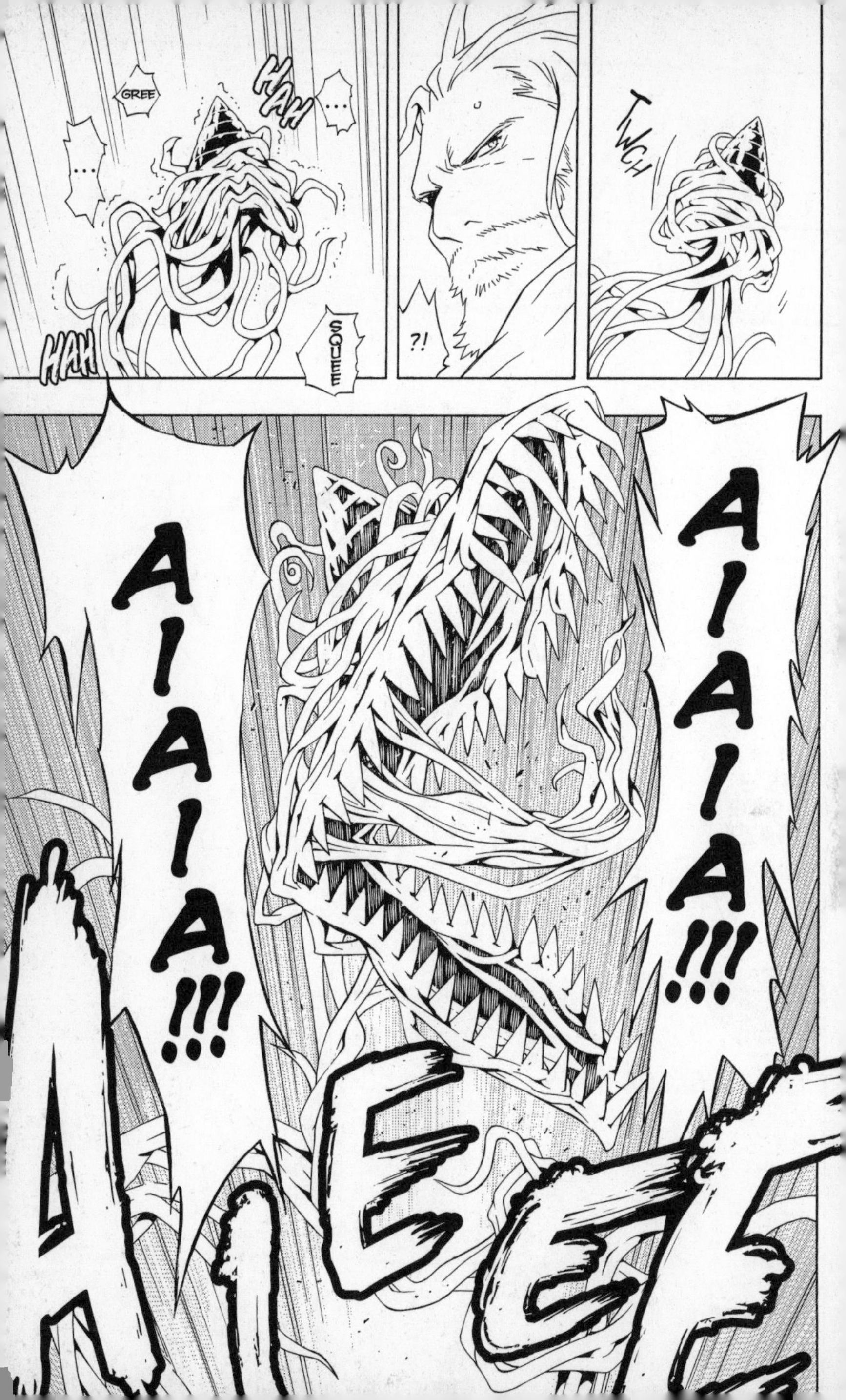

TWCH
?!
...
HAH
GREE
...
SQUEE
HAH
AIAIA!!!
AIAIA!!!

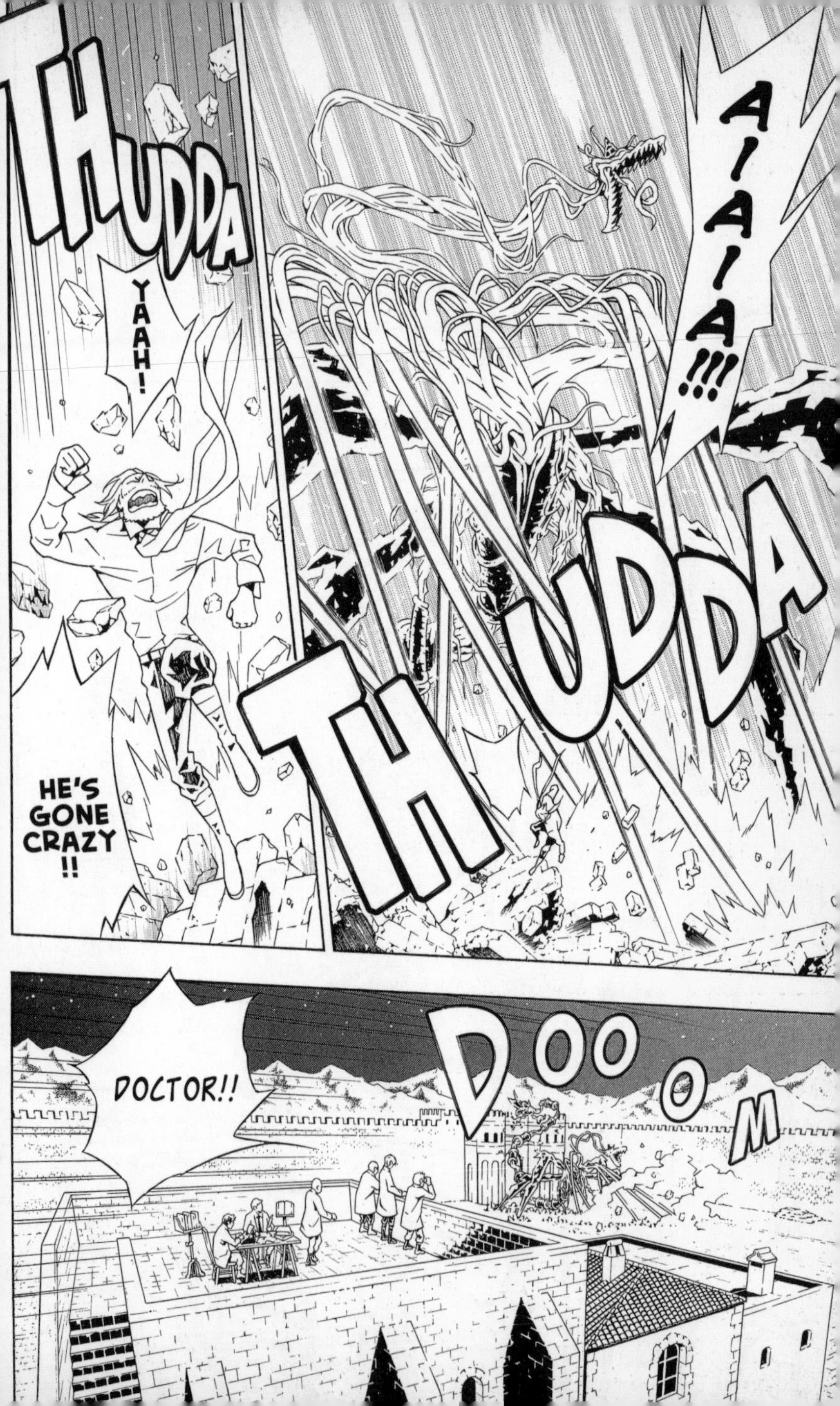
AIAIA!!!
THUDDA
THUDDA
YAAAH!
HE'S GONE CRAZY!!
DOOOOM
DOCTOR!!

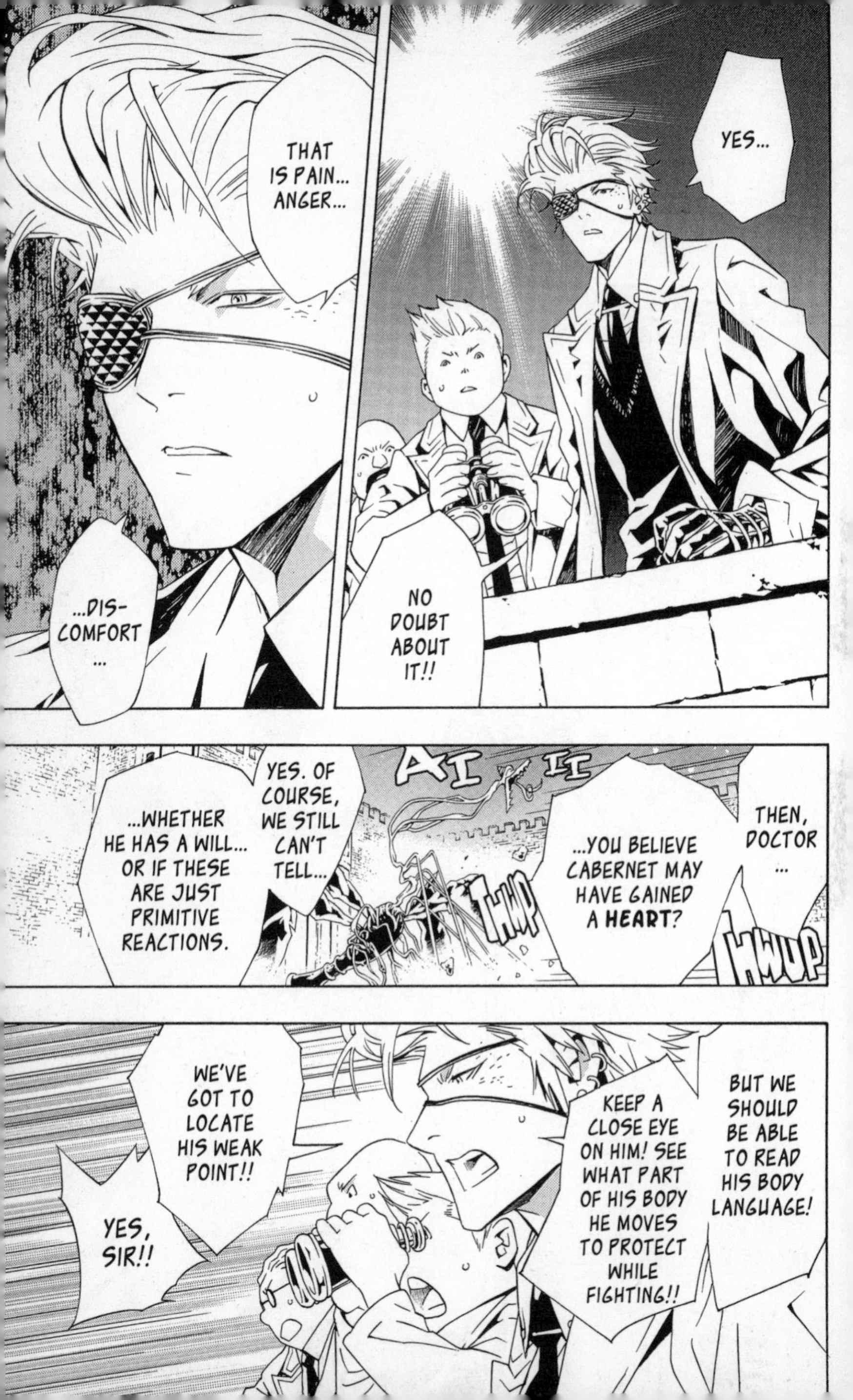
YES...
NO DOUBT ABOUT IT!!
THAT IS PAIN... ANGER...
...DIS-COMFORT ...
THEN, DOCTOR ...
THWUP
...YOU BELIEVE CABERNET MAY HAVE GAINED A **HEART**?
THWP
YES. OF COURSE, WE STILL CAN'T TELL...
...WHETHER HE HAS A WILL... OR IF THESE ARE JUST PRIMITIVE REACTIONS.
BUT WE SHOULD BE ABLE TO READ HIS BODY LANGUAGE!
KEEP A CLOSE EYE ON HIM! SEE WHAT PART OF HIS BODY HE MOVES TO PROTECT WHILE FIGHTING!!
WE'VE GOT TO LOCATE HIS WEAK POINT!!
YES, SIR!!

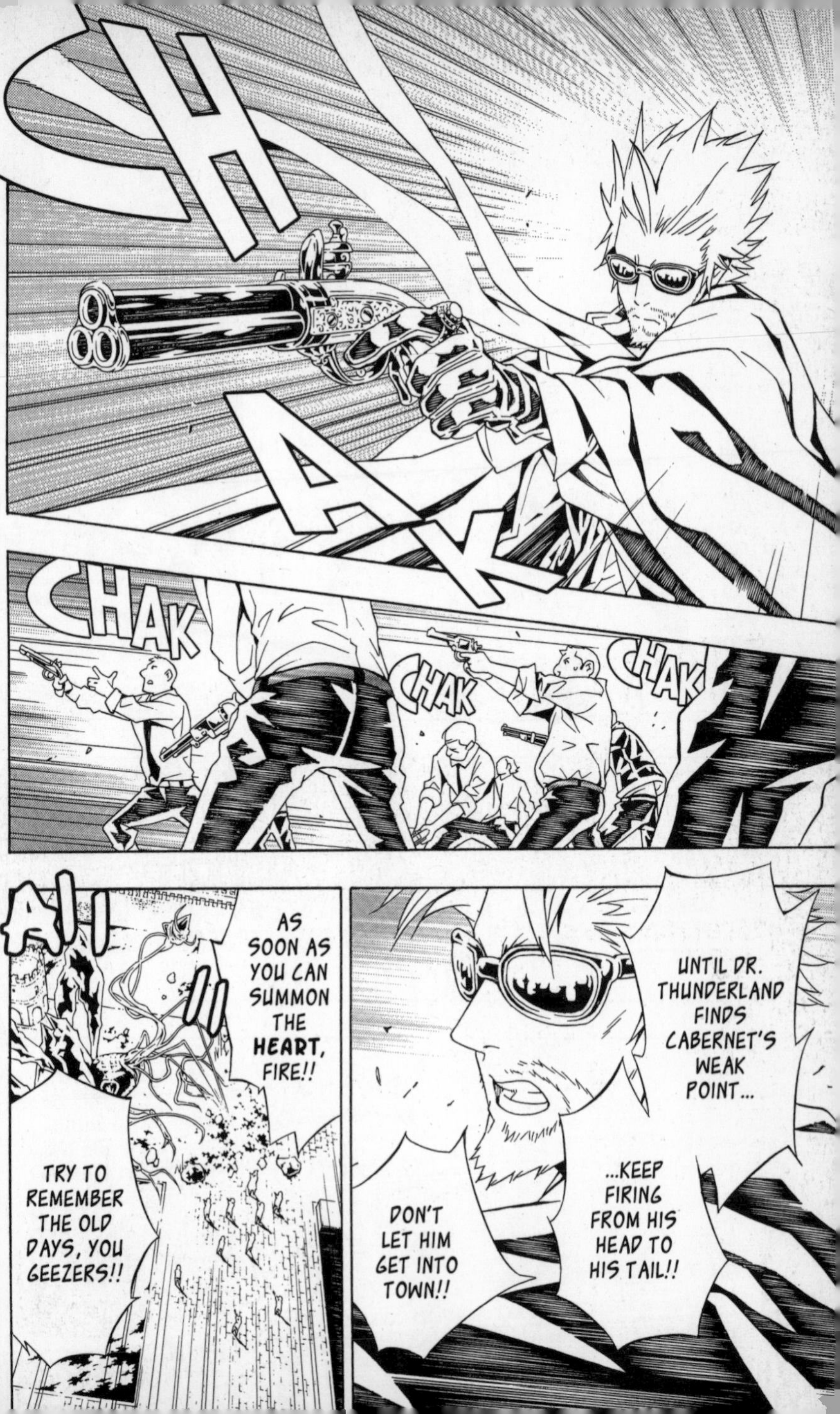
CHAK
CHAK
CHAK
CHAK
UNTIL DR. THUNDERLAND FINDS CABERNET'S WEAK POINT...
...KEEP FIRING FROM HIS HEAD TO HIS TAIL!!
DON'T LET HIM GET INTO TOWN!!
AS SOON AS YOU CAN SUMMON THE **HEART**, FIRE!!
TRY TO REMEMBER THE OLD DAYS, YOU GEEZERS!!
AII

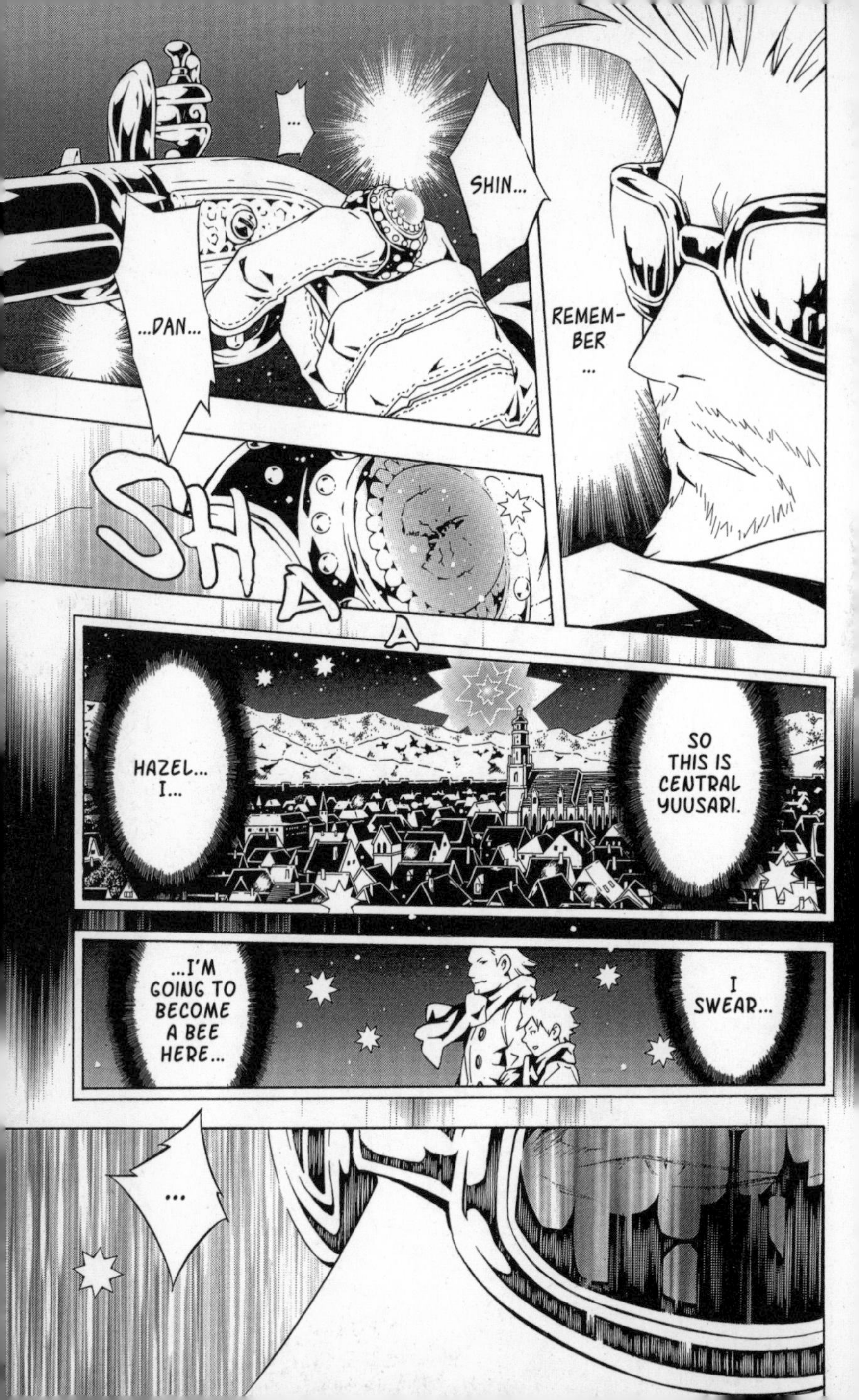
SHIN...
REMEMBER...
...
...DAN...
SHAA
SO THIS IS CENTRAL YUUSARI.
HAZEL... I...
I SWEAR...
...I'M GOING TO BECOME A BEE HERE...
...

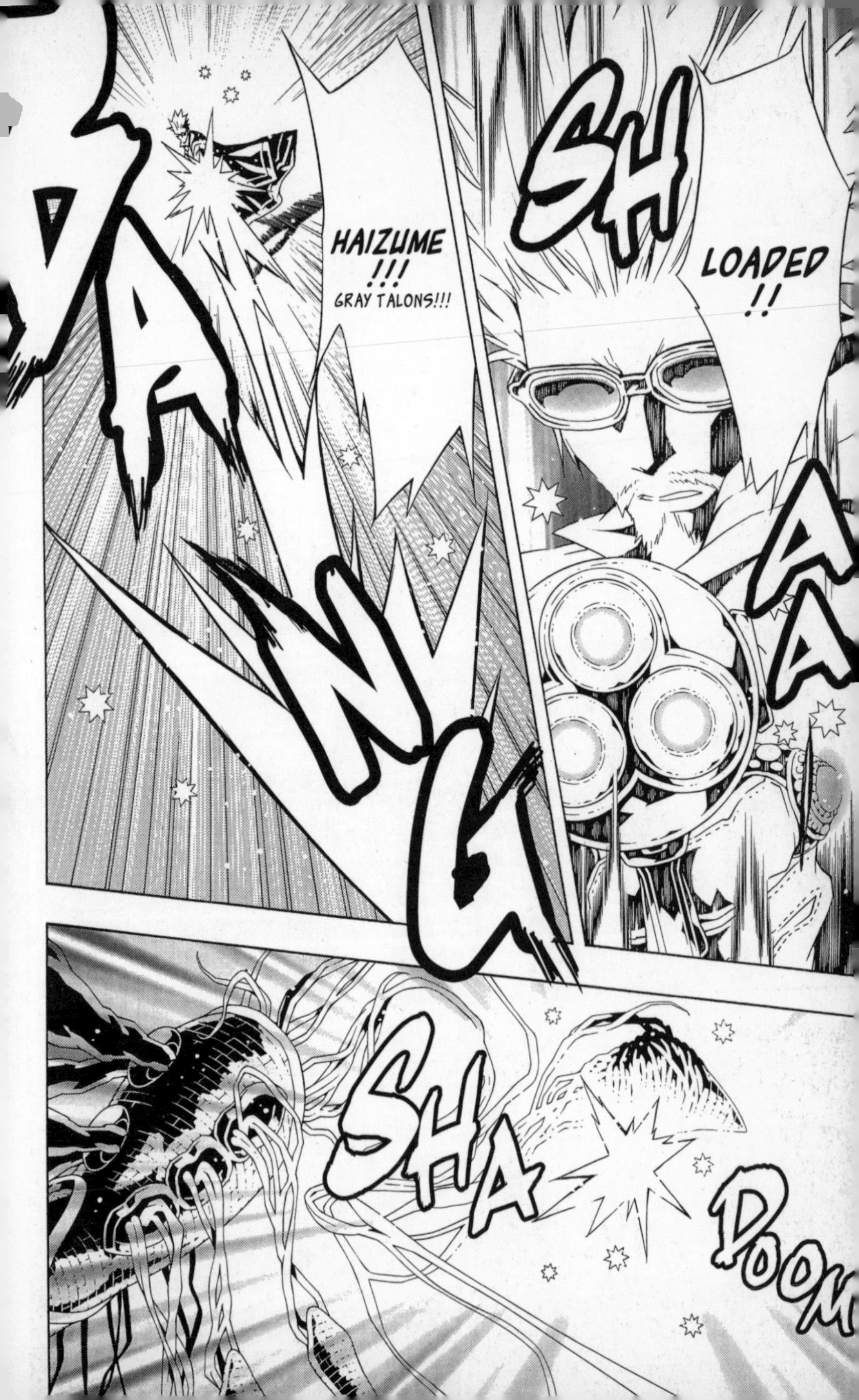
LOADED !!
HAIZUME !!!
GRAY TALONS!!!
SHA
DOOM

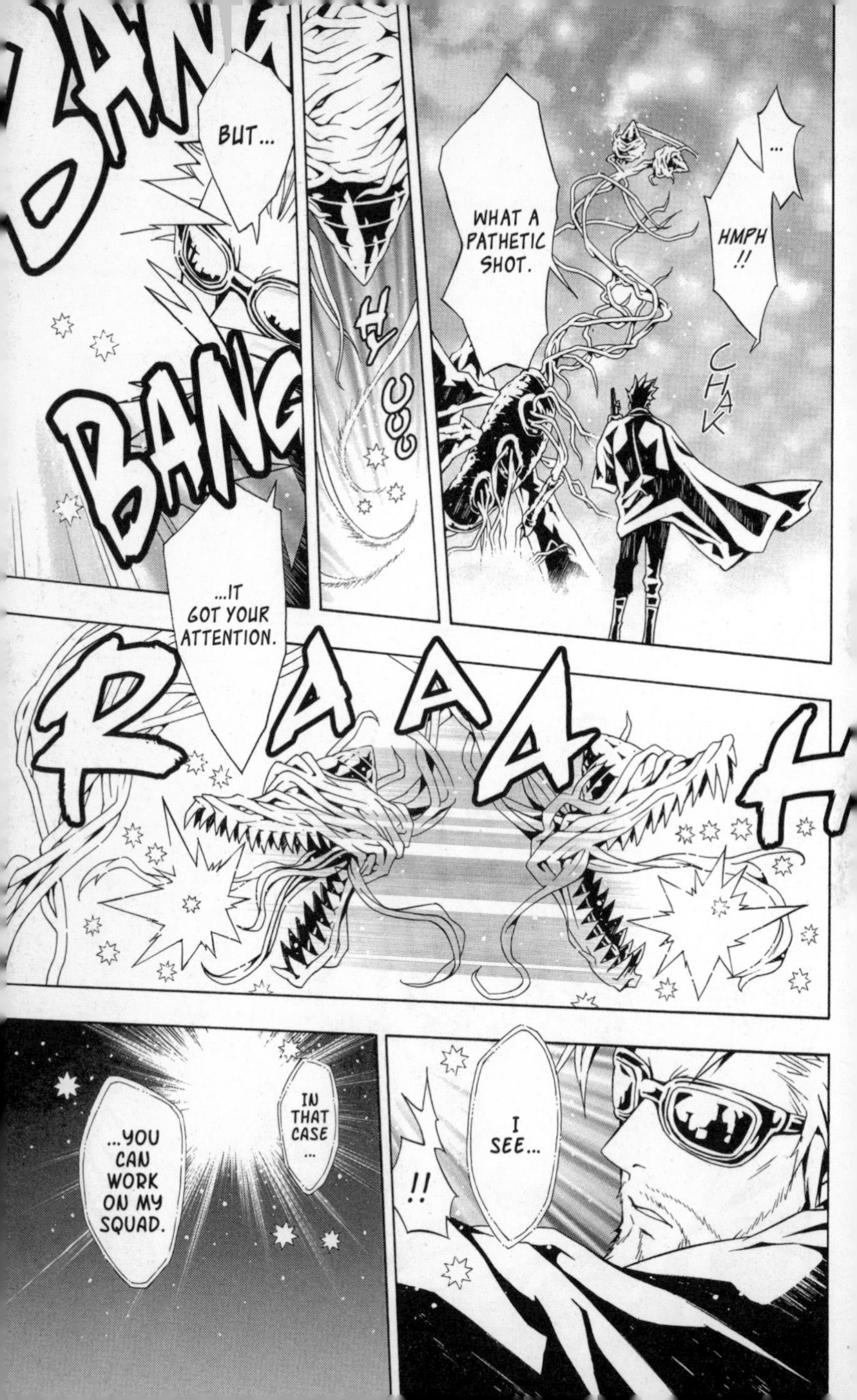
...
HMPH !!
CHAK
WHAT A PATHETIC SHOT.
HYCCC
BANG
BUT...
BANG
...IT GOT YOUR ATTENTION.
RAAAH
I SEE...
!!
IN THAT CASE...
...YOU CAN WORK ON MY SQUAD.

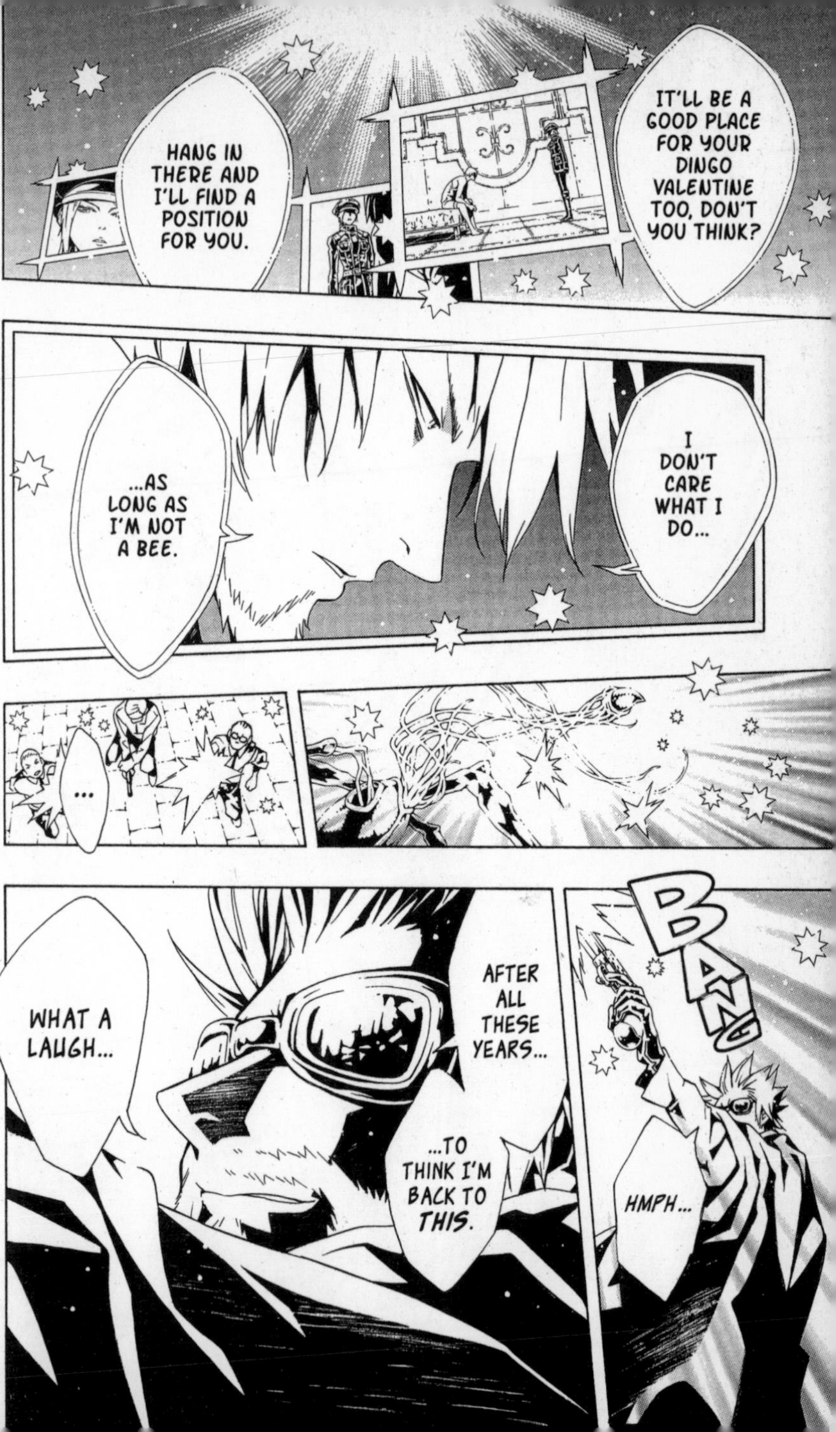
IT'LL BE A GOOD PLACE FOR YOUR DINGO VALENTINE TOO, DON'T YOU THINK?
HANG IN THERE AND I'LL FIND A POSITION FOR YOU.
I DON'T CARE WHAT I DO...
...AS LONG AS I'M NOT A BEE.
...
BANG
HMPH...
AFTER ALL THESE YEARS...
...TO THINK I'M BACK TO *THIS*.
WHAT A LAUGH...

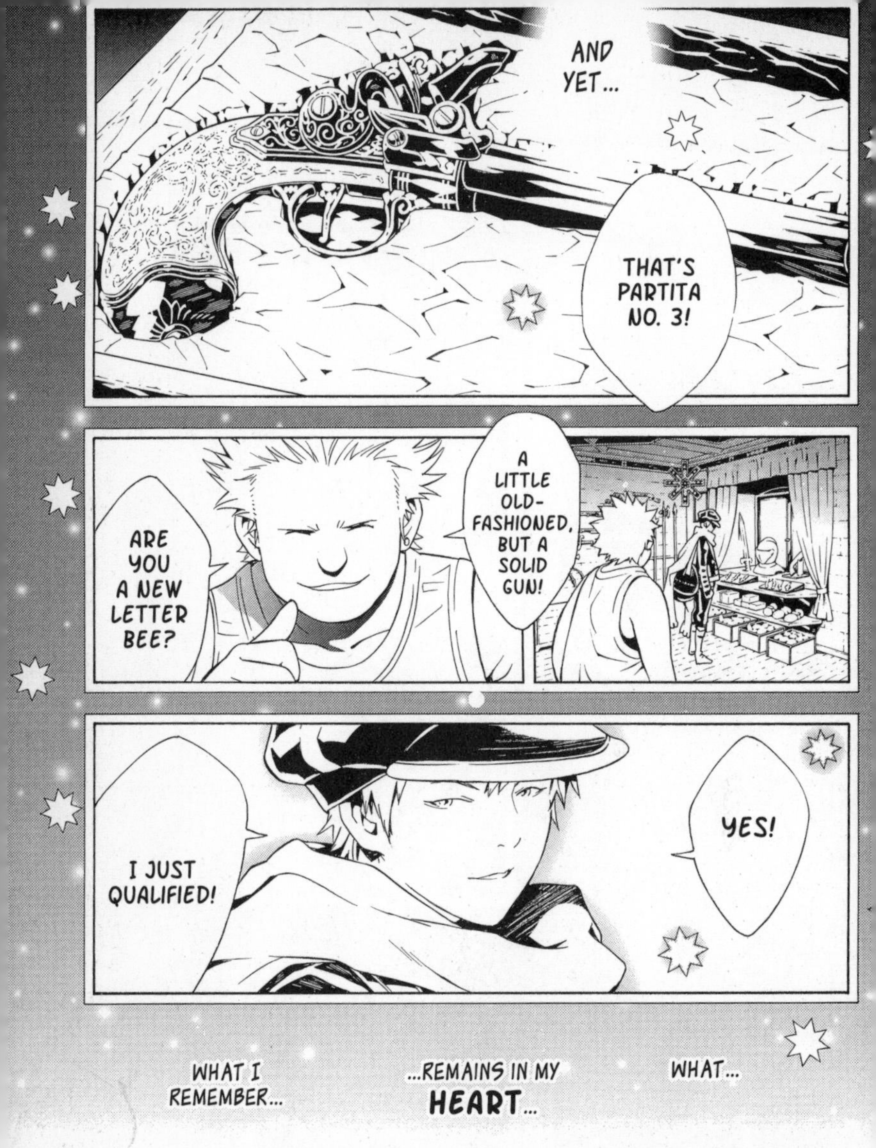
AND YET...
THAT'S PARTITA NO. 3!
A LITTLE OLD-FASHIONED, BUT A SOLID GUN!
ARE YOU A NEW LETTER BEE?
YES!
I JUST QUALIFIED!
WHAT I REMEMBER...
...REMAINS IN MY HEART...
WHAT...

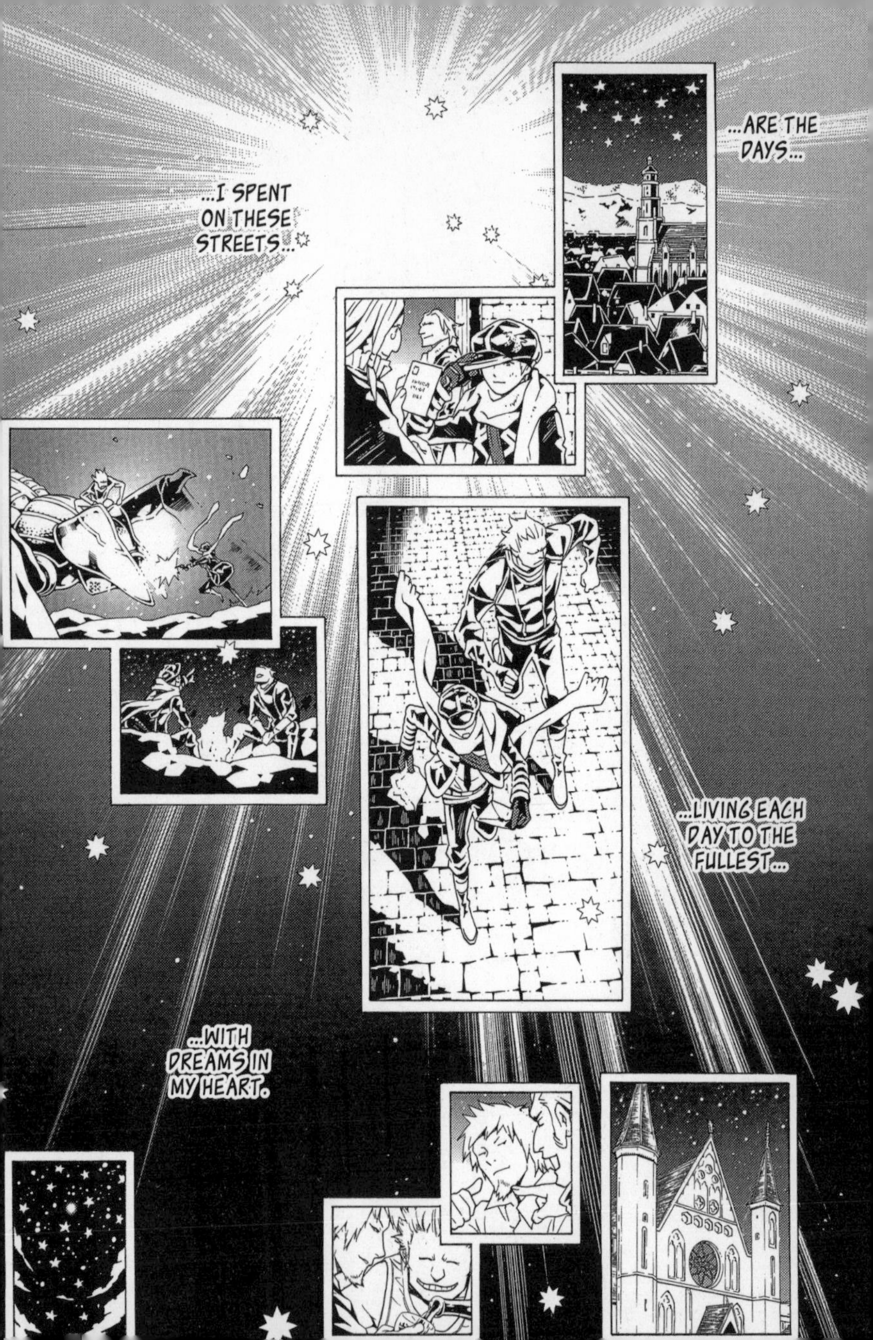
...ARE THE DAYS...
...I SPENT ON THESE STREETS...
...LIVING EACH DAY TO THE FULLEST...
...WITH DREAMS IN MY HEART.

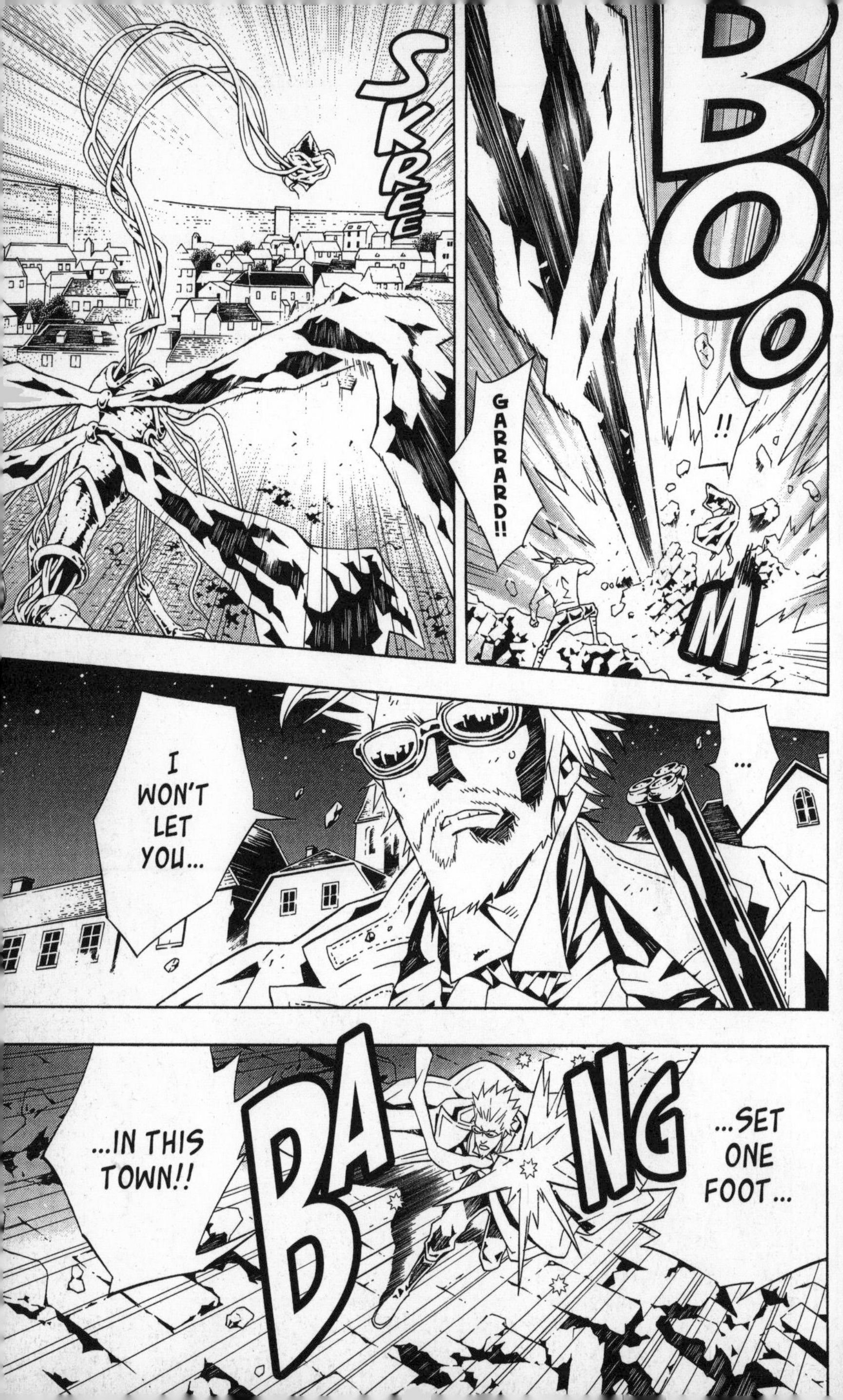

BOOOM
!!
GARRARD!!
SKREE
...
I WON'T LET YOU...
...SET ONE FOOT...
BANG
...IN THIS TOWN!!

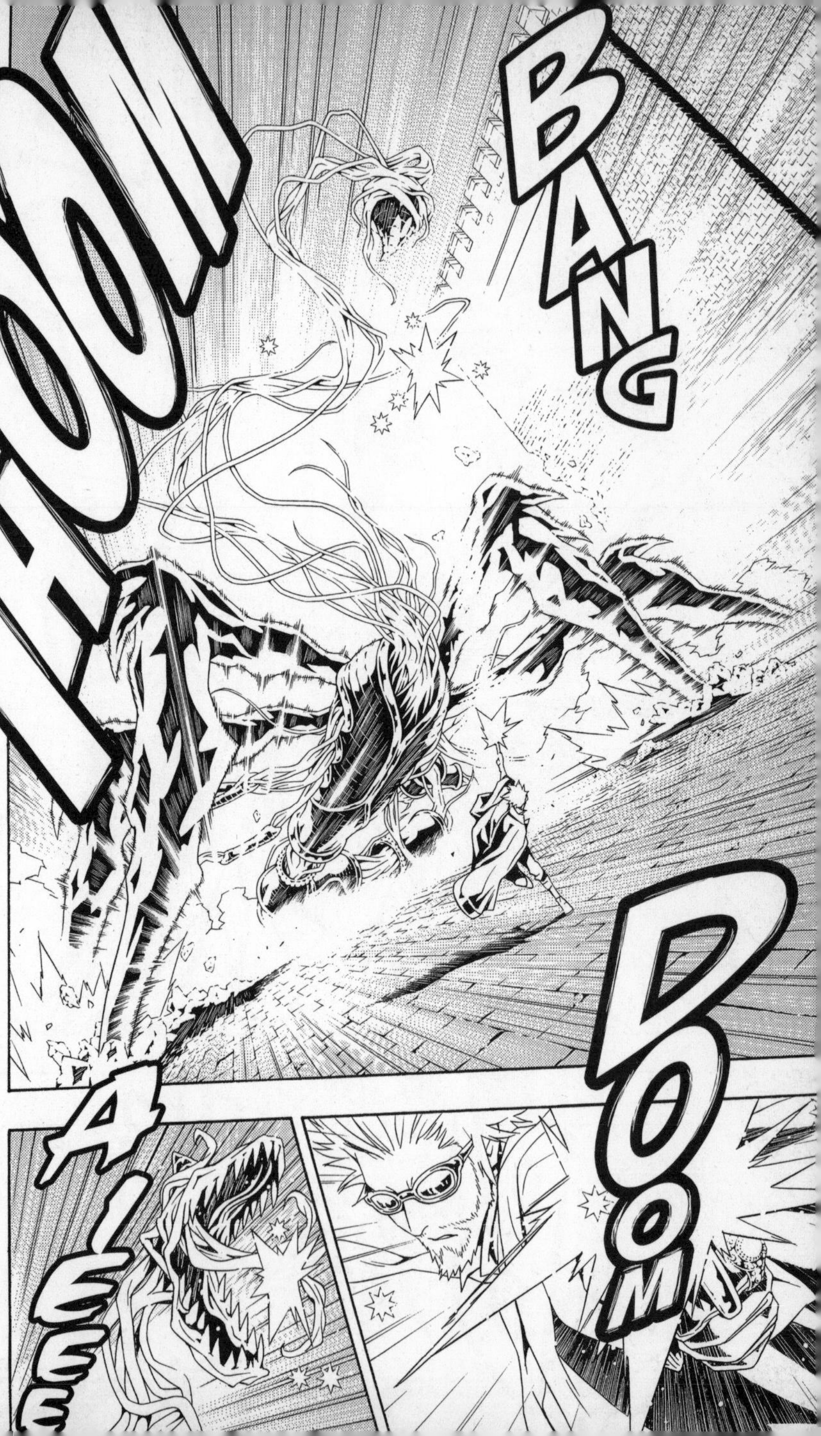
BANG
WHOOM
DOOM
AIEEE

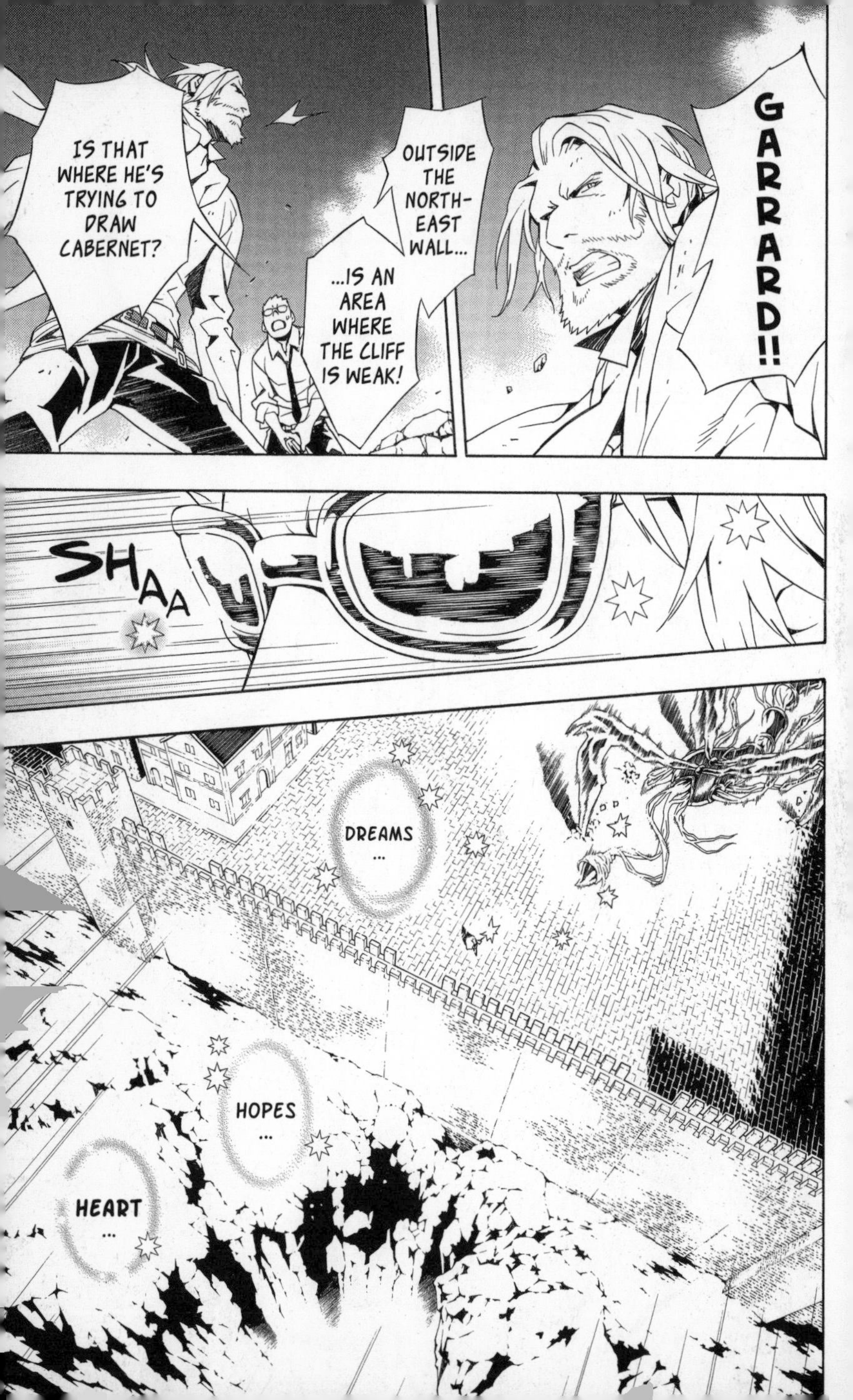
GARRARD!!
OUTSIDE THE NORTH-EAST WALL...
...IS AN AREA WHERE THE CLIFF IS WEAK!
IS THAT WHERE HE'S TRYING TO DRAW CABERNET?
SHAA
DREAMS ...
HOPES ...
HEART ...

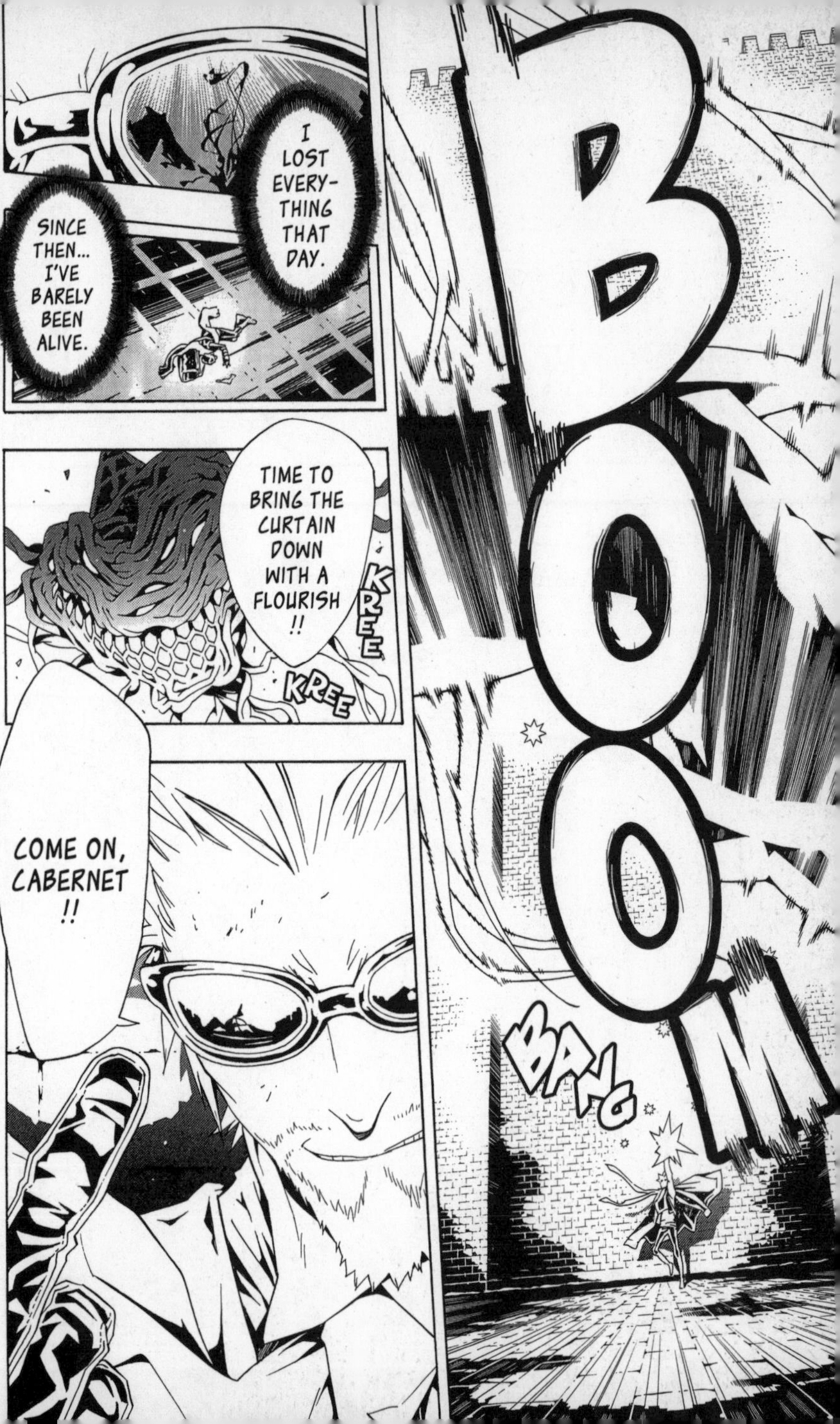
BOOOM
BANG
I LOST EVERYTHING THAT DAY.
SINCE THEN... I'VE BARELY BEEN ALIVE.
TIME TO BRING THE CURTAIN DOWN WITH A FLOURISH!!
KREE
KREE
COME ON, CABERNET!!

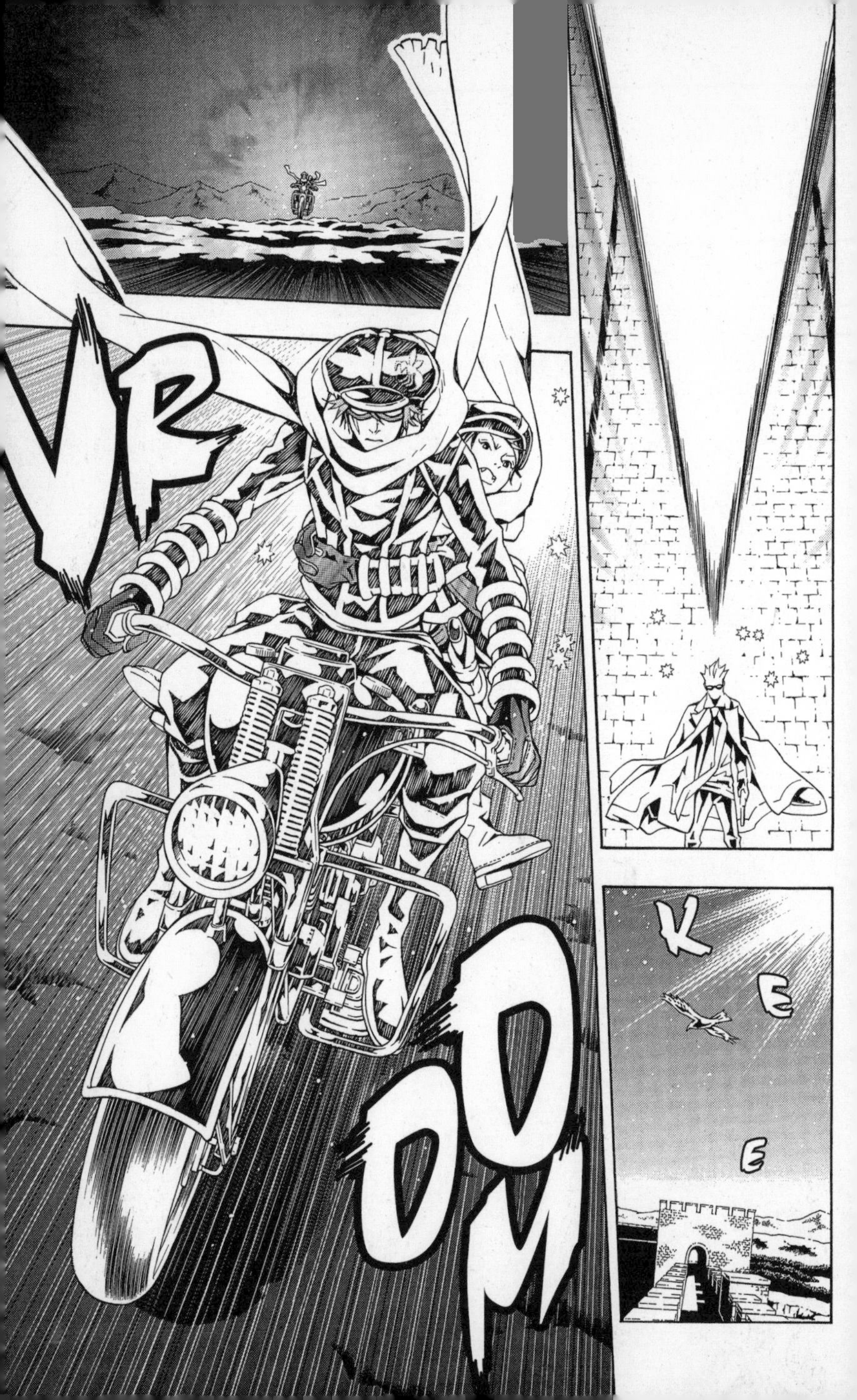
KEE
VR
OOOM

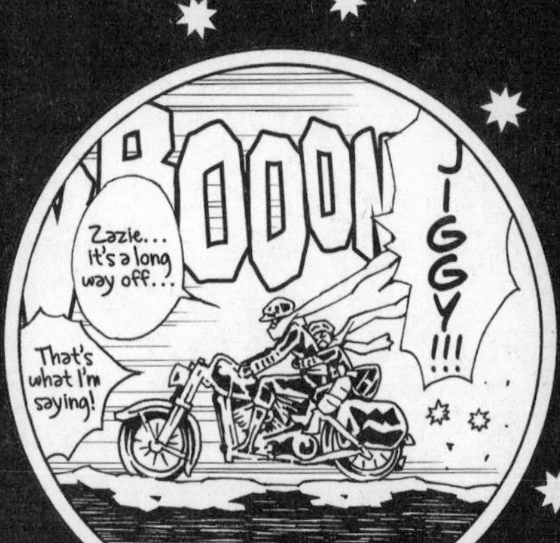
JIGGY!!!
Zazie... it's a long way off...
That's what I'm saying!

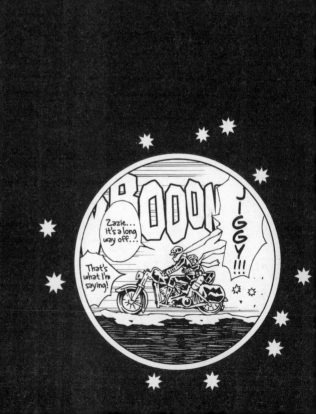

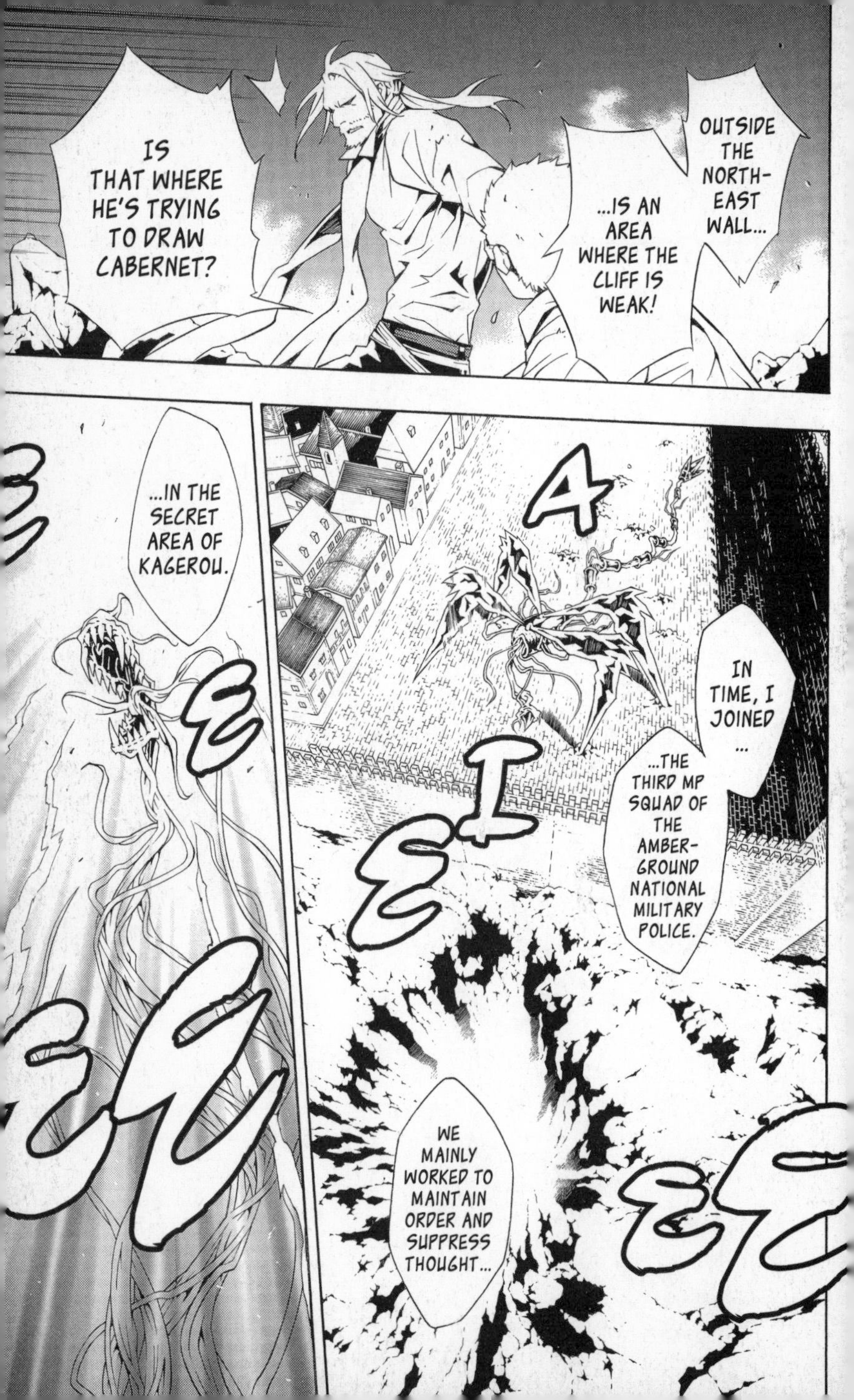
OUTSIDE THE NORTH-EAST WALL...
...IS AN AREA WHERE THE CLIFF IS WEAK!
IS THAT WHERE HE'S TRYING TO DRAW CABERNET?
IN TIME, I JOINED...
...THE THIRD MP SQUAD OF THE AMBER-GROUND NATIONAL MILITARY POLICE.
WE MAINLY WORKED TO MAINTAIN ORDER AND SUPPRESS THOUGHT...
...IN THE SECRET AREA OF KAGEROU.

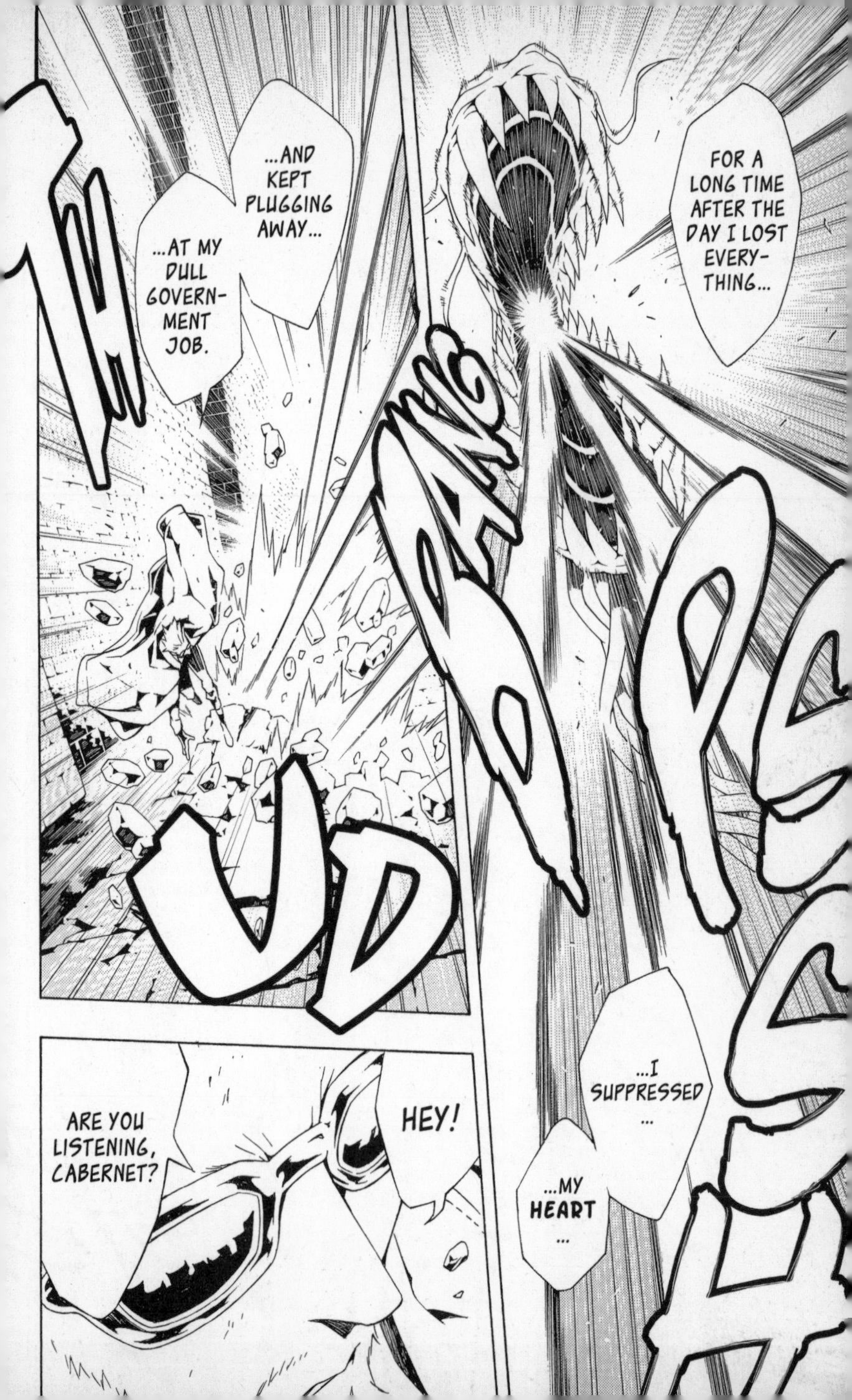
FOR A LONG TIME AFTER THE DAY I LOST EVERY-THING...
BANG
...I SUPPRESSED...
...MY **HEART**...
...AND KEPT PLUGGING AWAY...
...AT MY DULL GOVERN-MENT JOB.
HEY!
ARE YOU LISTENING, CABERNET?

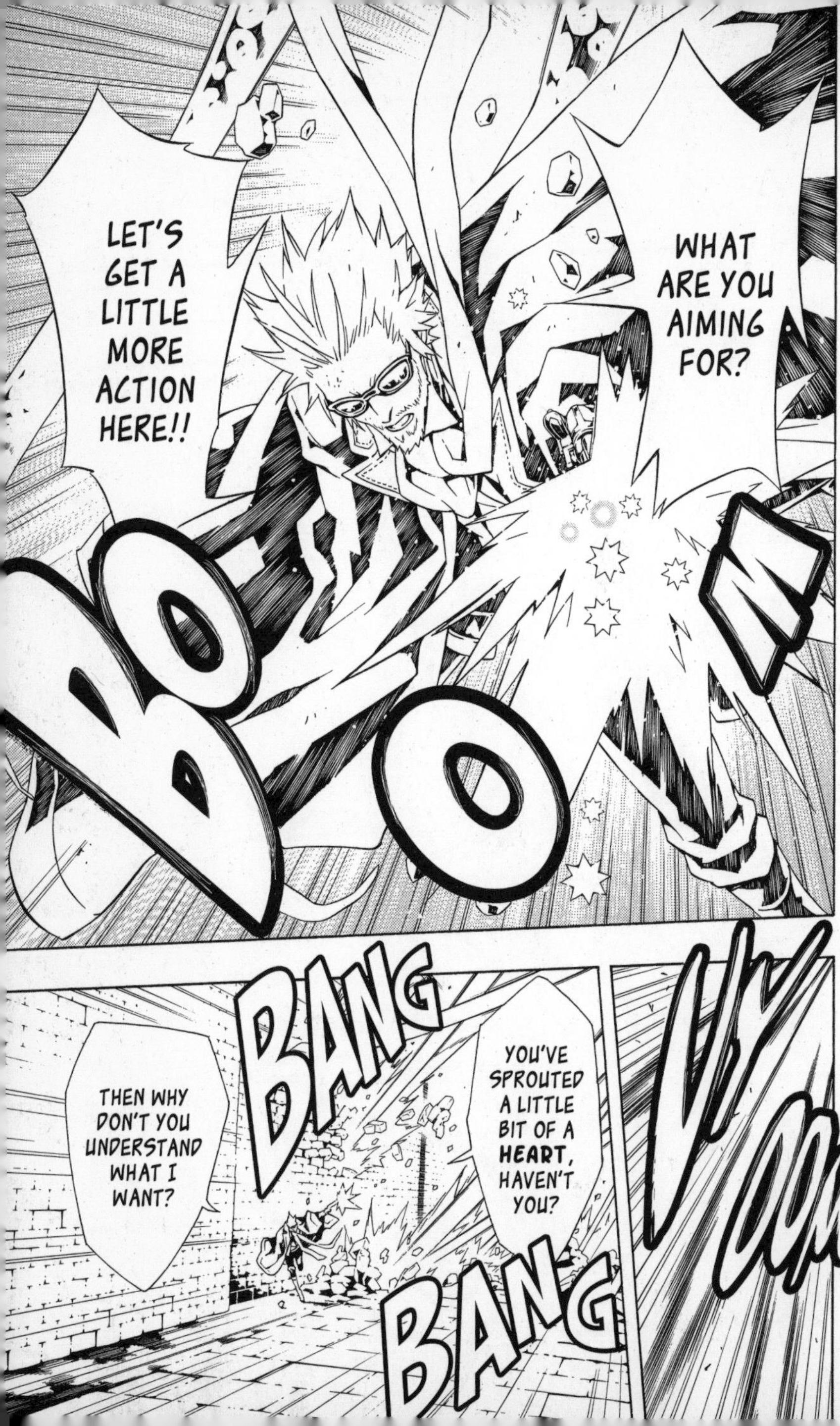
WHAT ARE YOU AIMING FOR?
LET'S GET A LITTLE MORE ACTION HERE!!
BOOM
YOU'VE SPROUTED A LITTLE BIT OF A **HEART**, HAVEN'T YOU?
BANG
BANG
THEN WHY DON'T YOU UNDERSTAND WHAT I WANT?

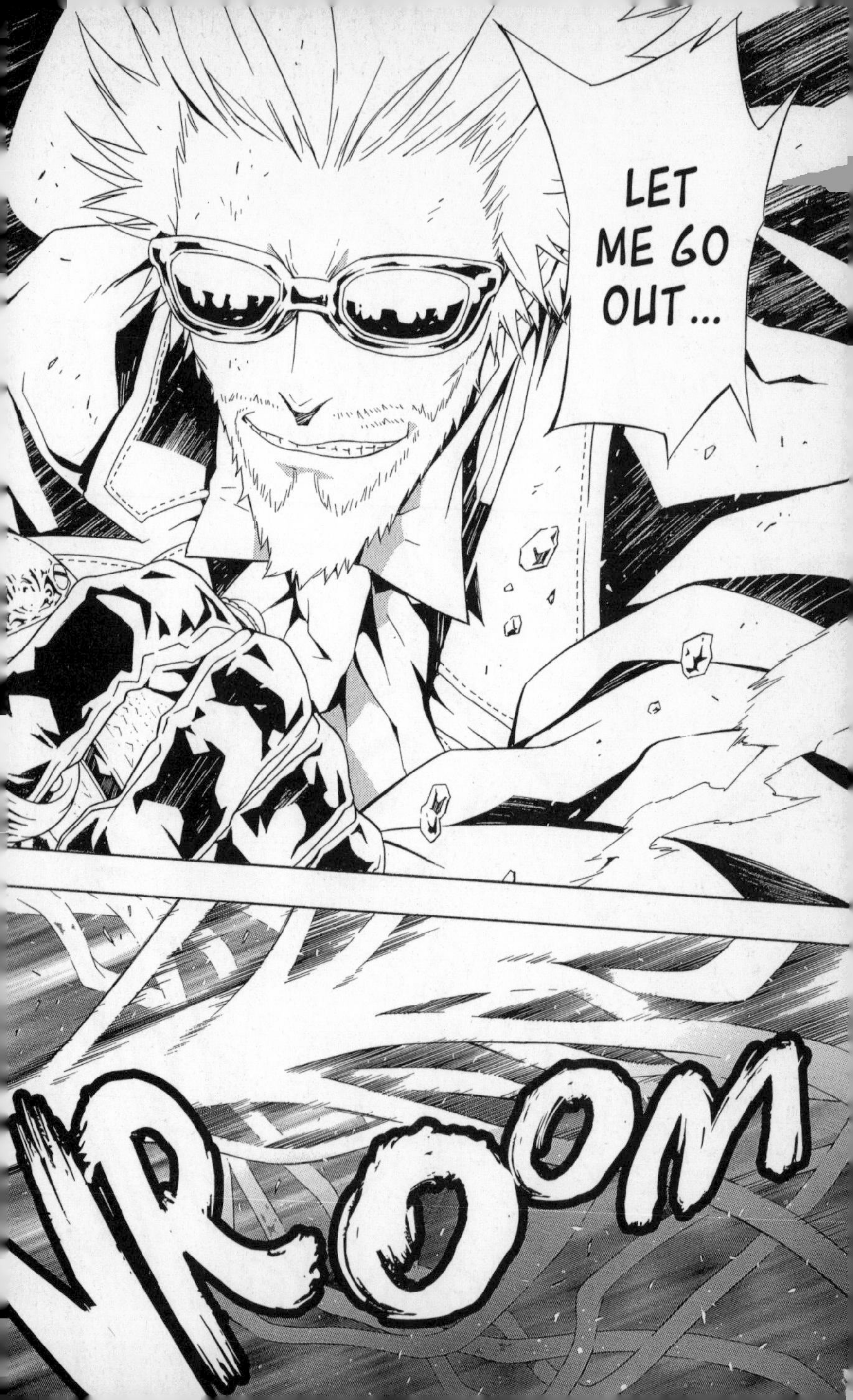
LET ME GO OUT ...
VROOM

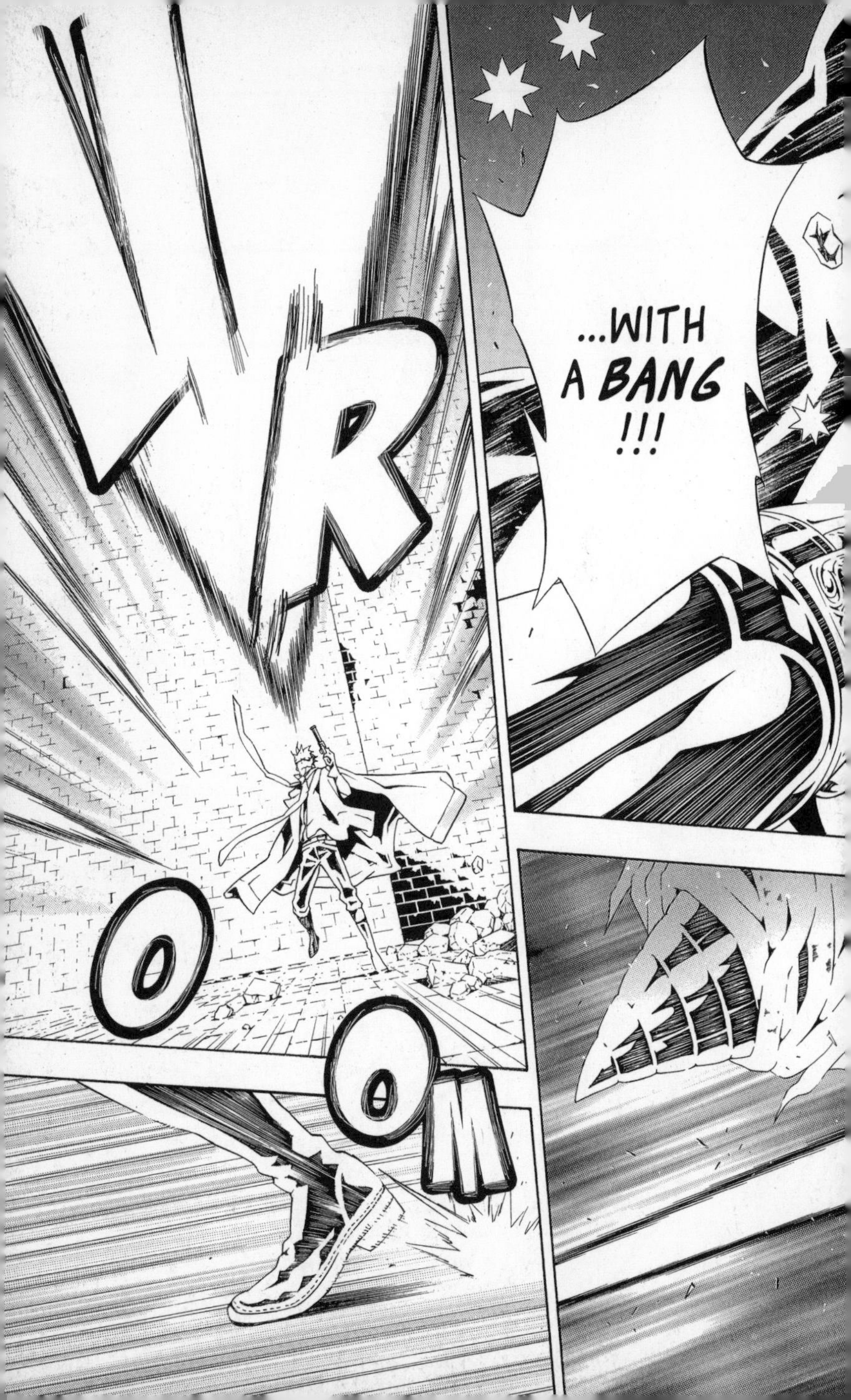
...WITH
A BANG
!!!
VRRR
OOOM

Chapter 54: Smoke Signal

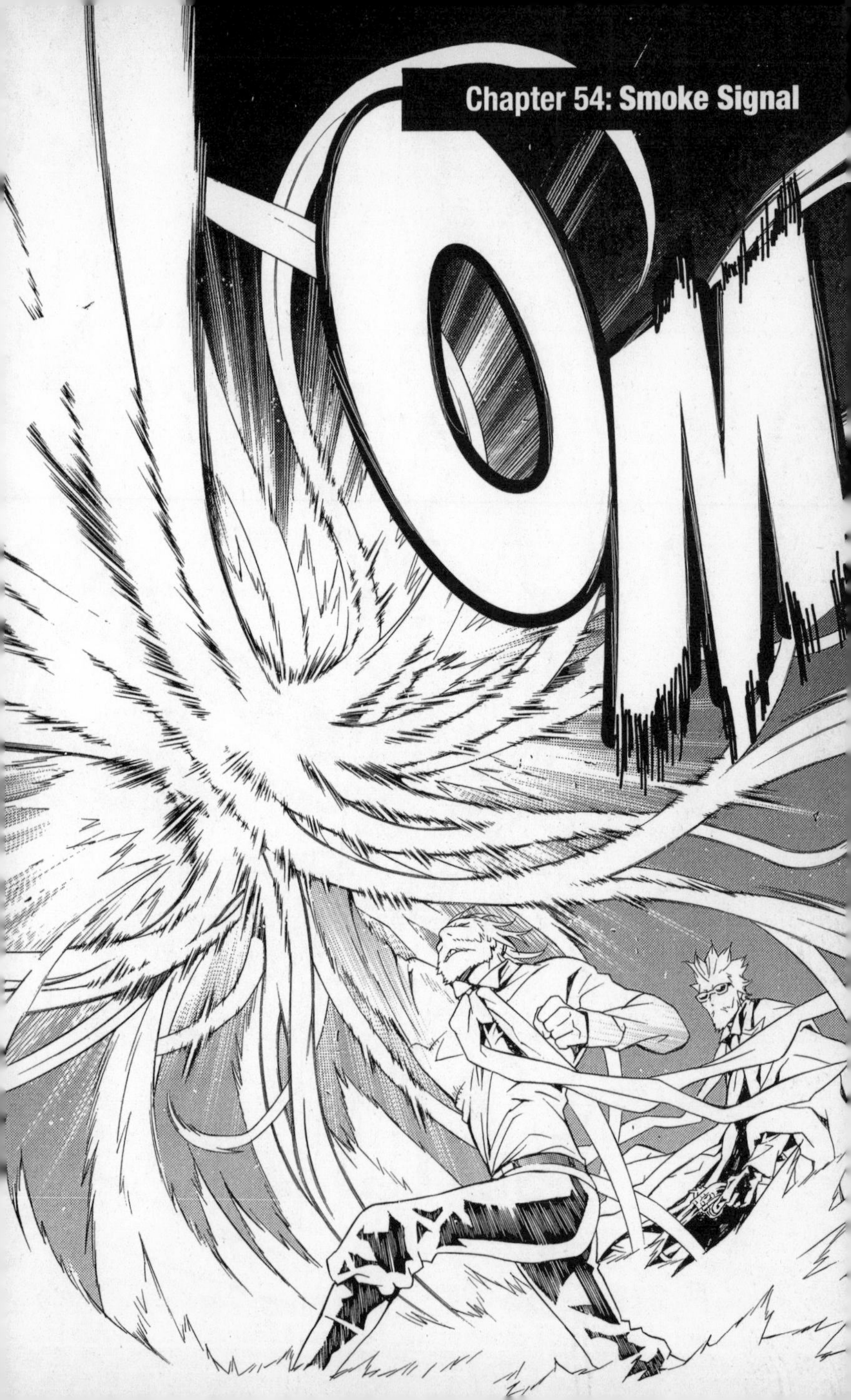

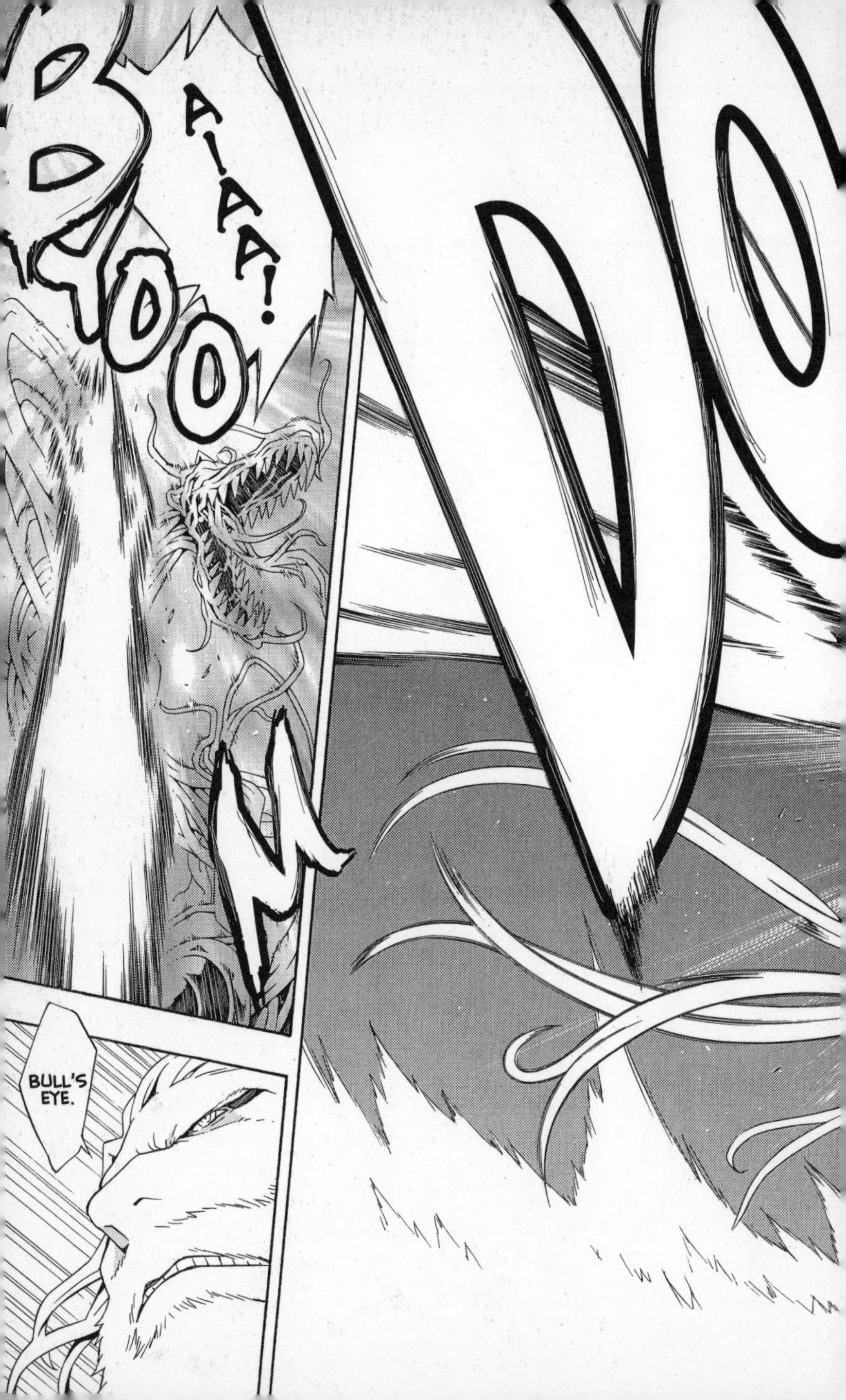
BULL'S EYE.

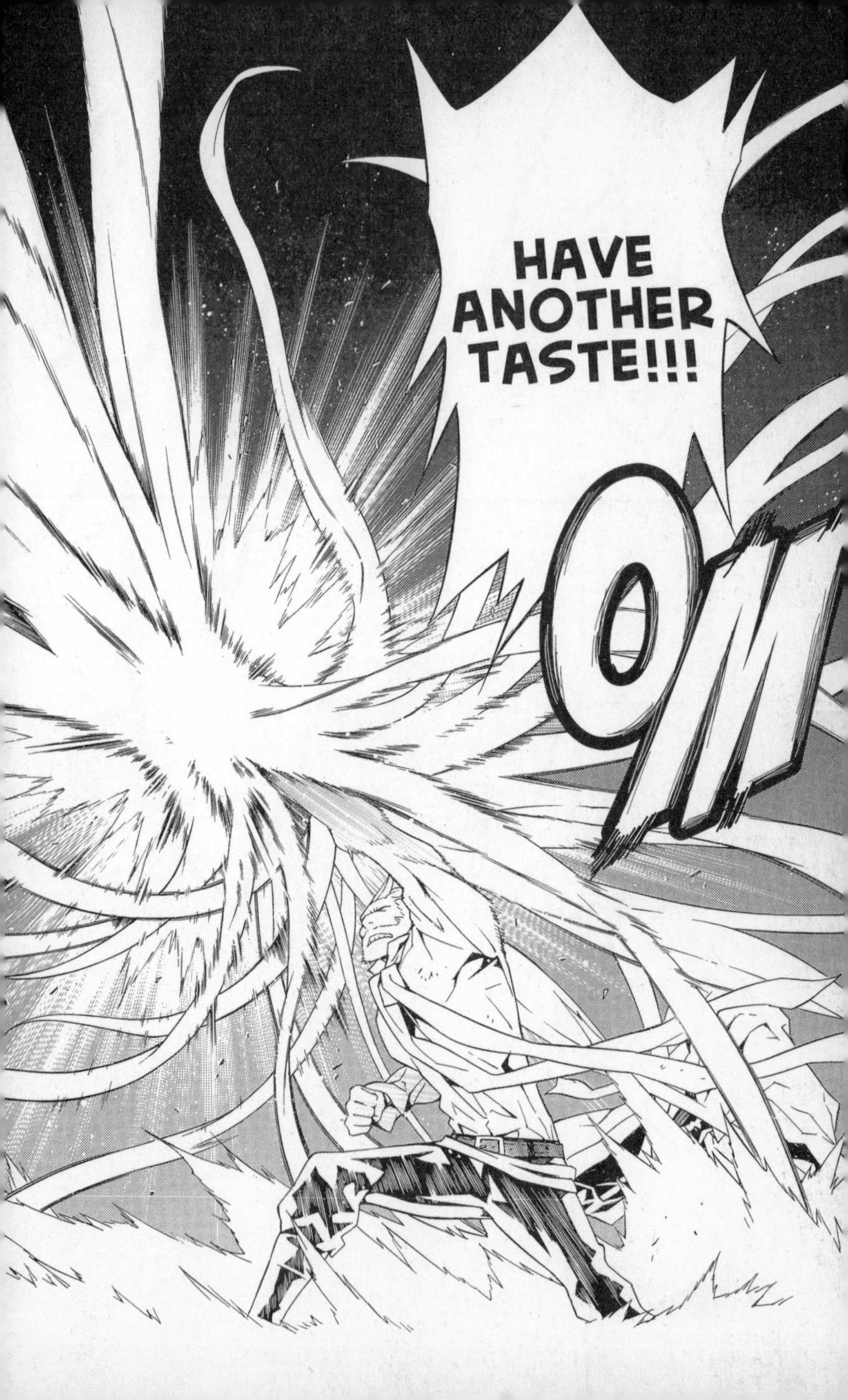
HAVE ANOTHER TASTE!!!

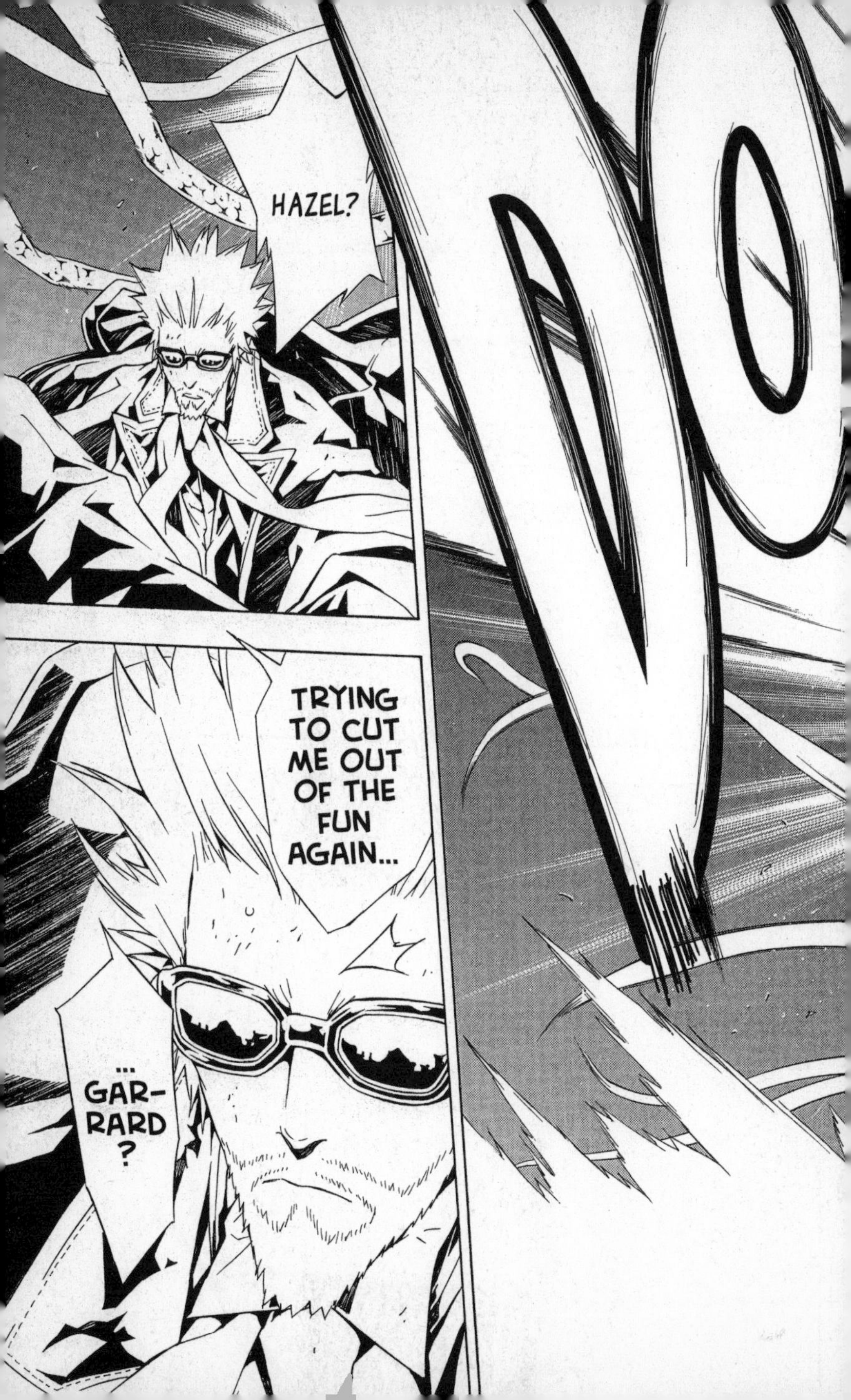
NO
HAZEL?
TRYING TO CUT ME OUT OF THE FUN AGAIN...
...GARRARD?

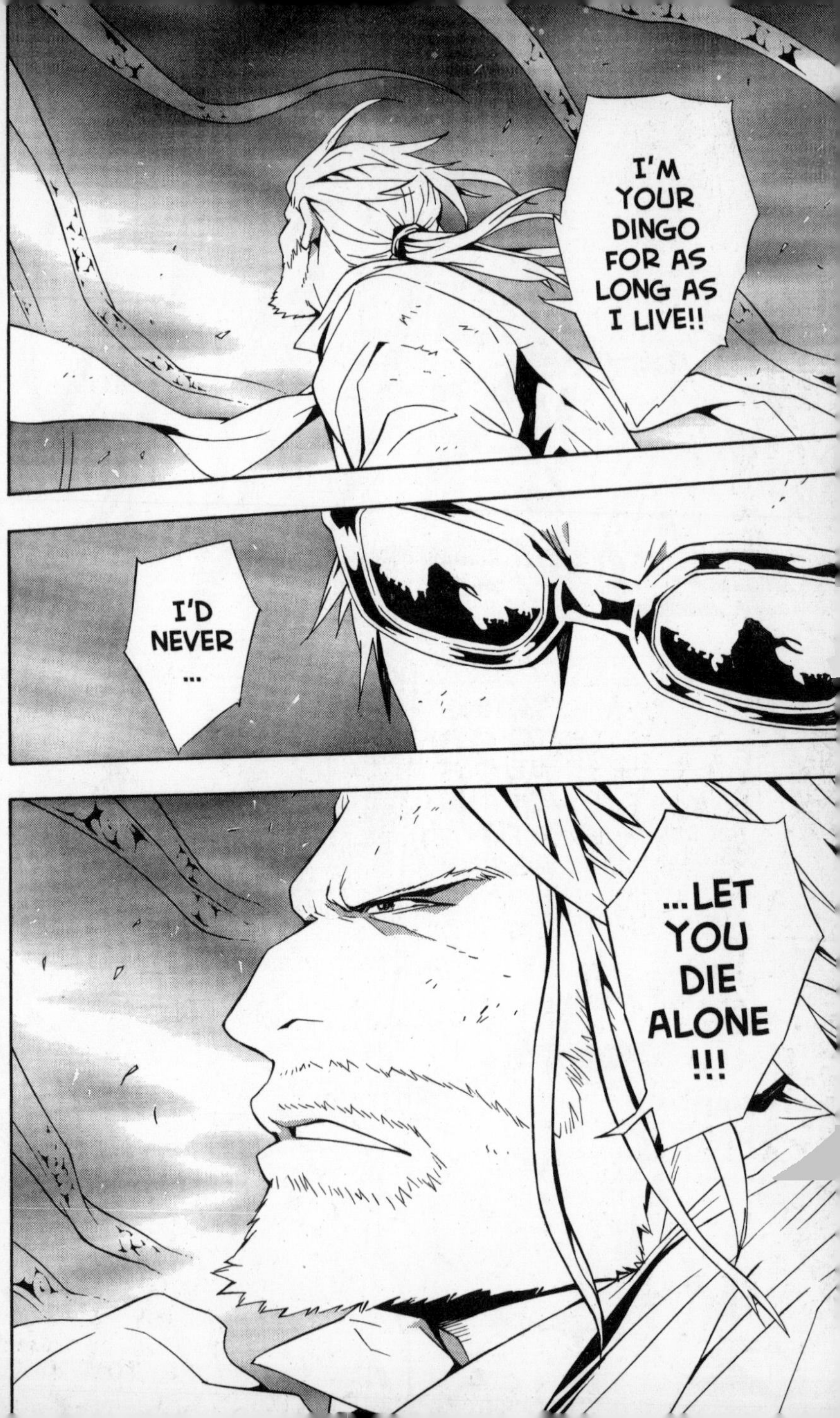
I'M YOUR DINGO FOR AS LONG AS I LIVE!!
I'D NEVER ...
...LET YOU DIE ALONE !!!

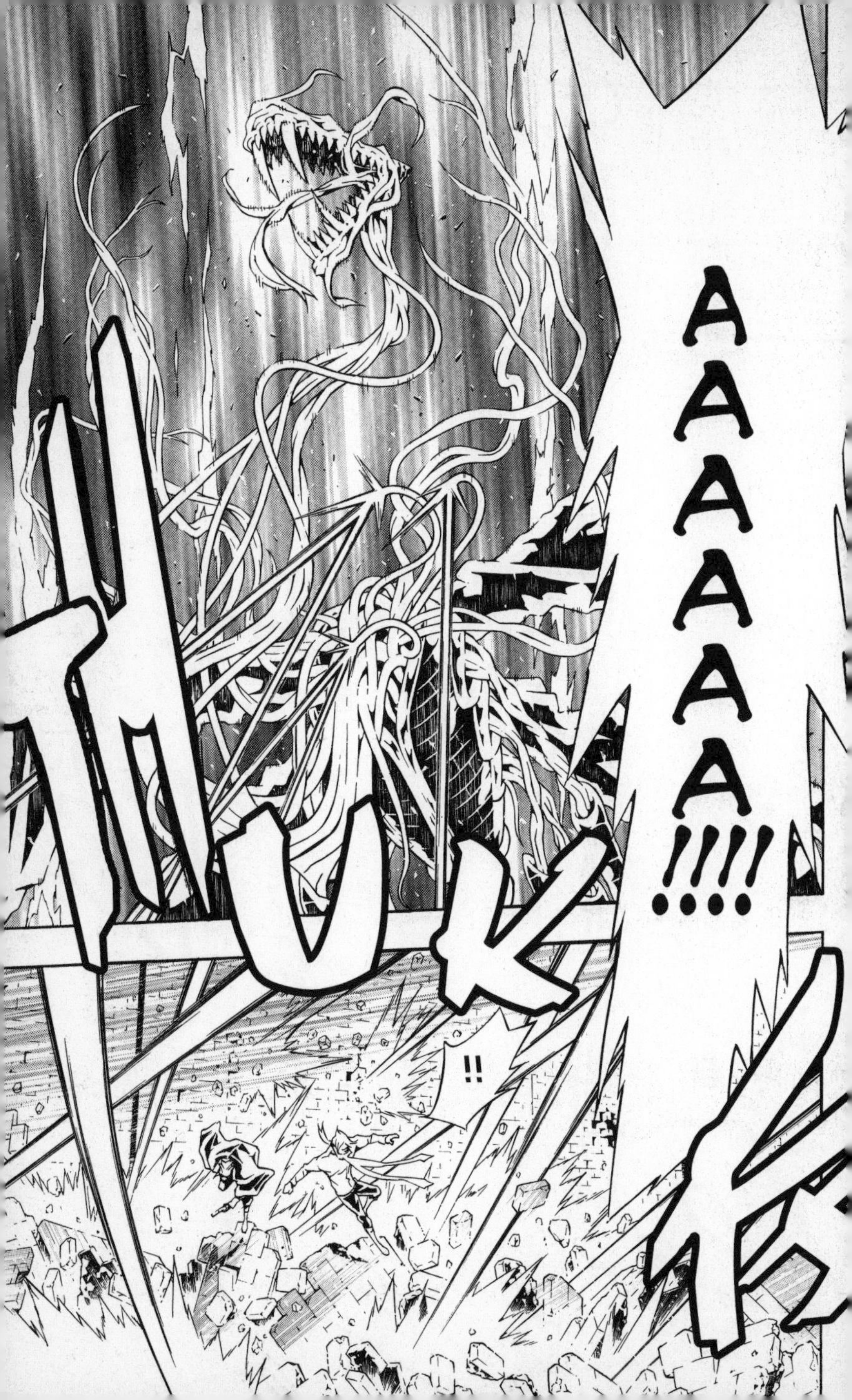
AAAAAAA!!!!
!!
HUK

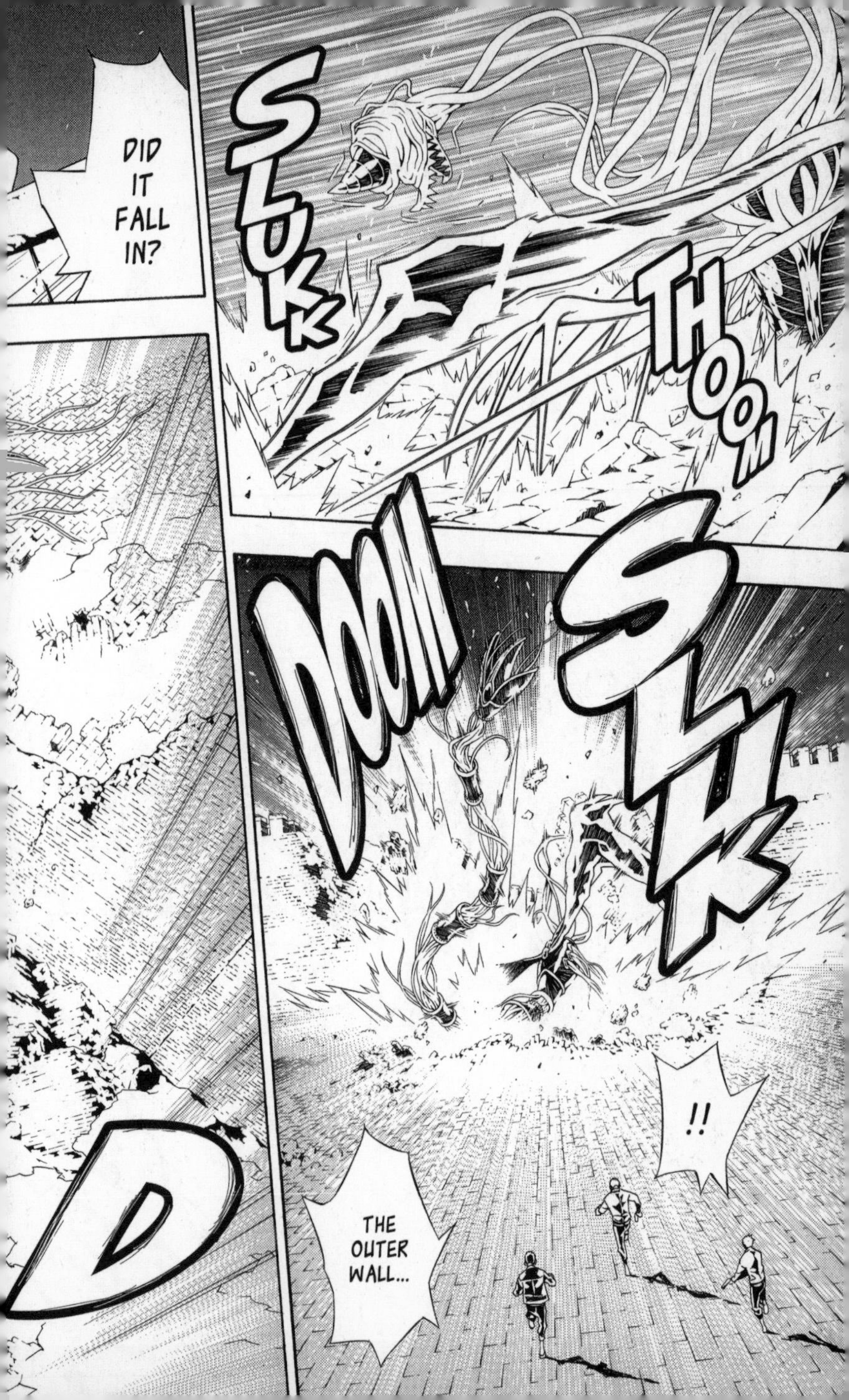
SLUKK
THOOM
DID IT FALL IN?
DOOM
SLUKK
!!
THE OUTER WALL...
D

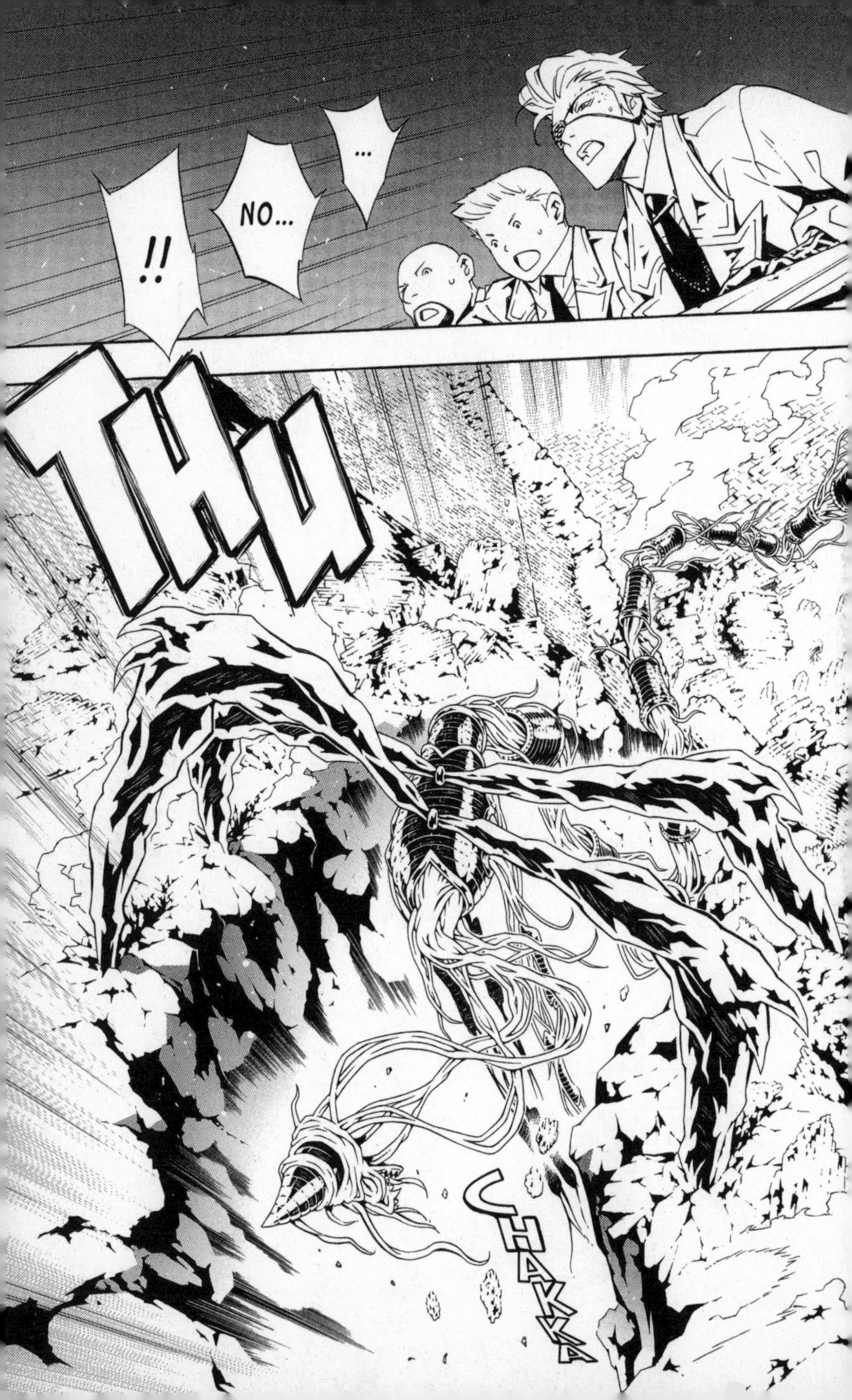
...
NO...
!!
THU
CHAKKA

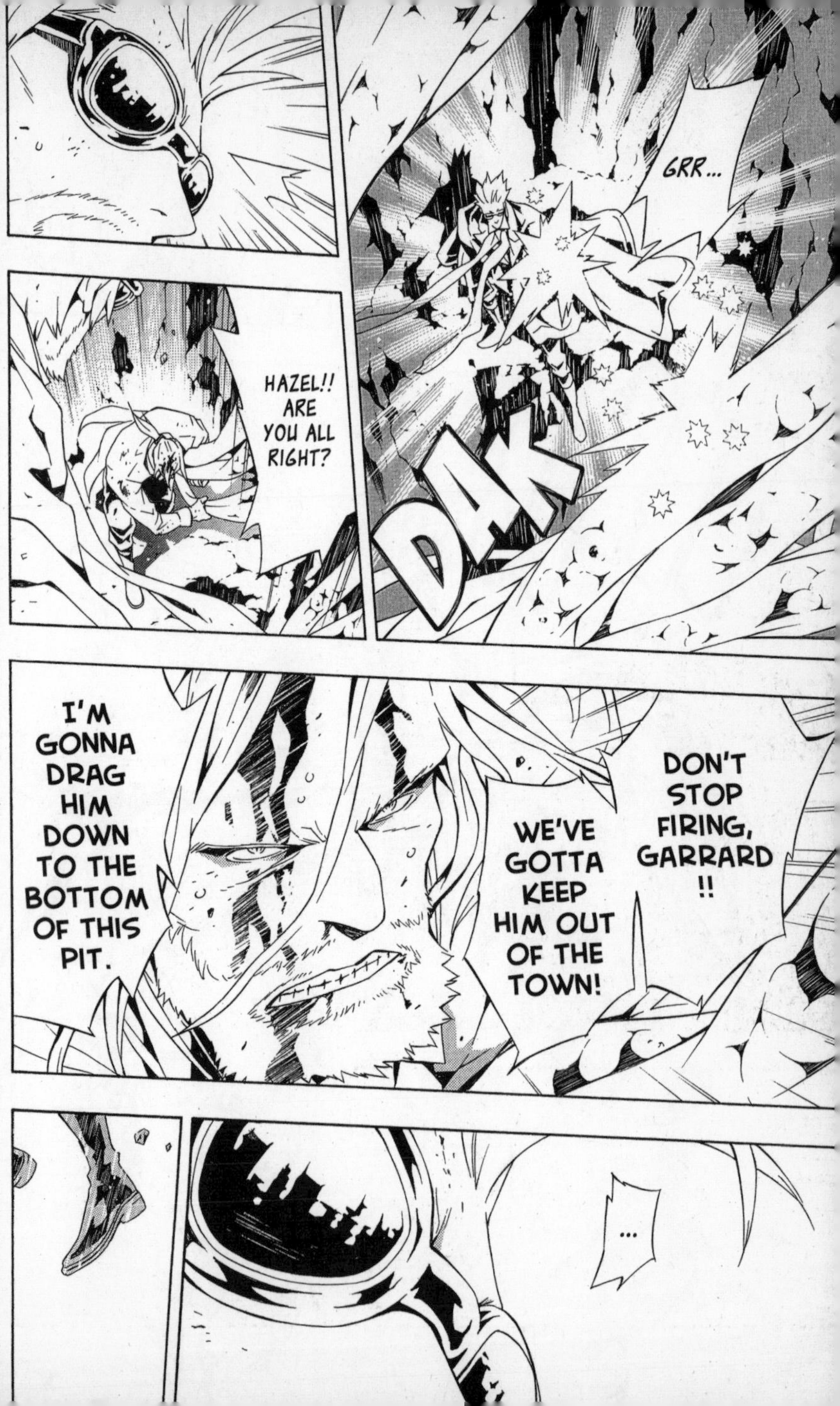
GRR...
DAK
HAZEL!! ARE YOU ALL RIGHT?
DON'T STOP FIRING, GARRARD!!
WE'VE GOTTA KEEP HIM OUT OF THE TOWN!
I'M GONNA DRAG HIM DOWN TO THE BOTTOM OF THIS PIT.
...

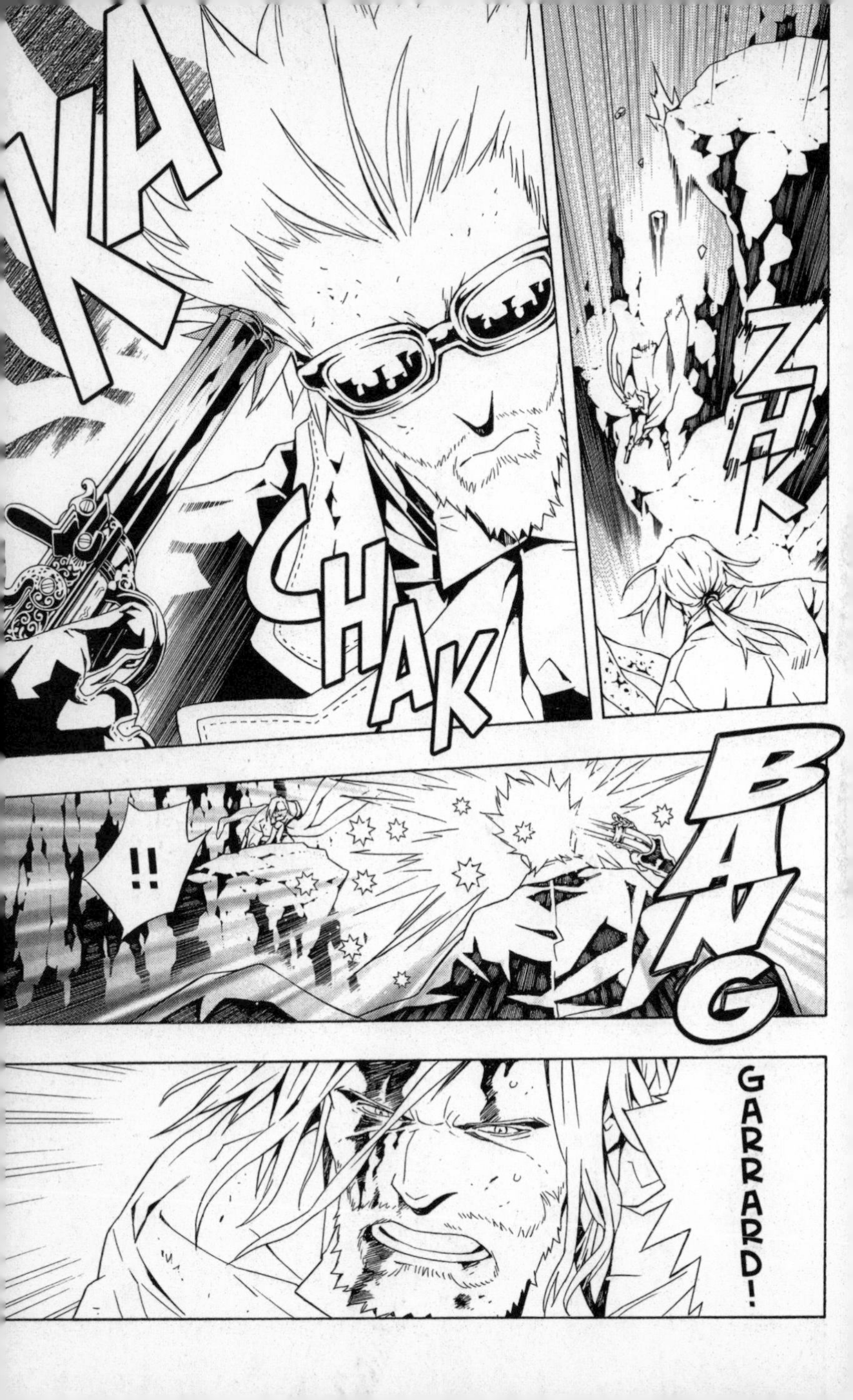
ZHK
KA
CHAK
BANG
!!
GARRARD!

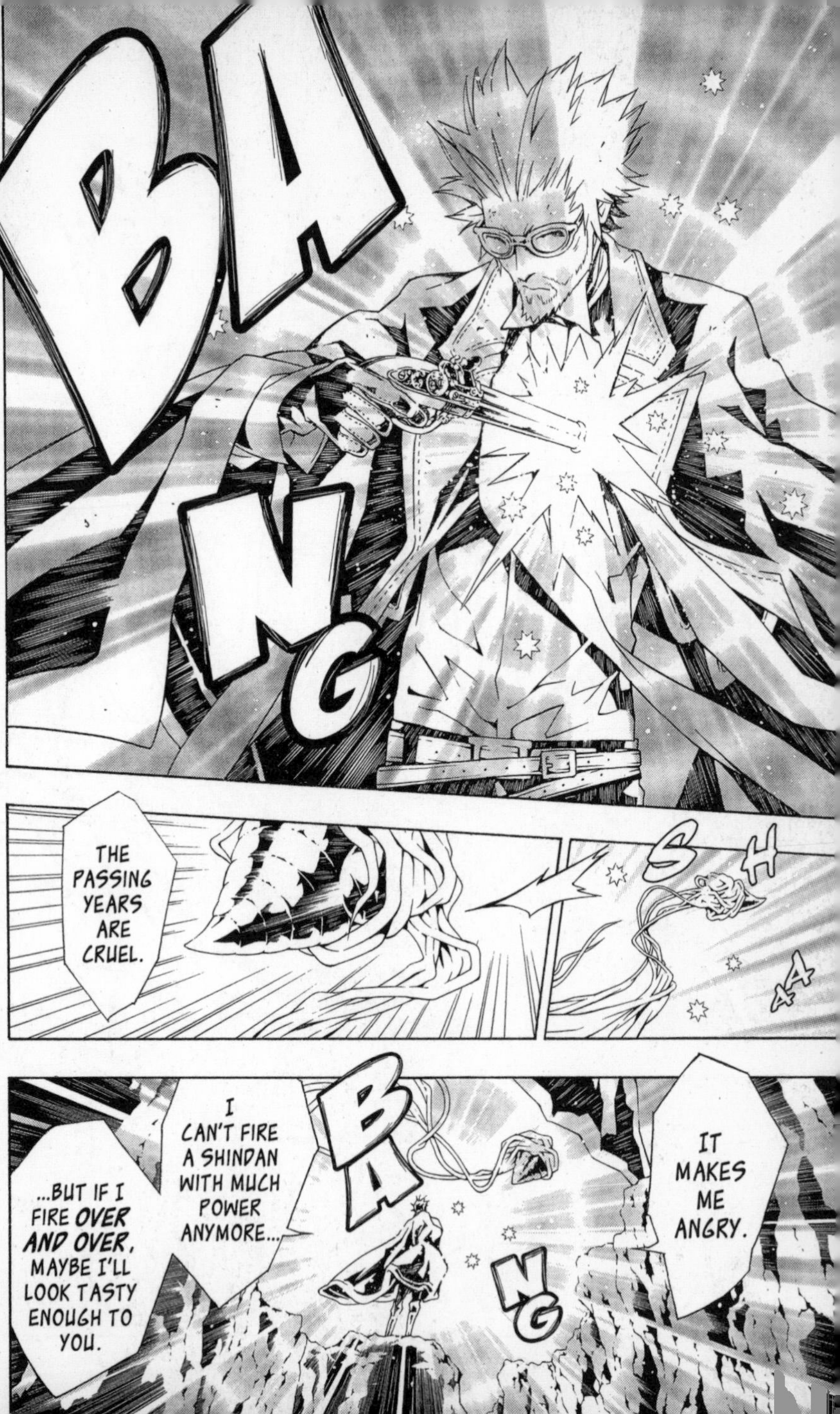
BANG
SHAA
THE PASSING YEARS ARE CRUEL.
IT MAKES ME ANGRY.
BANG
I CAN'T FIRE A SHINDAN WITH MUCH POWER ANYMORE...
...BUT IF I FIRE *OVER AND OVER*, MAYBE I'LL LOOK TASTY ENOUGH TO YOU.

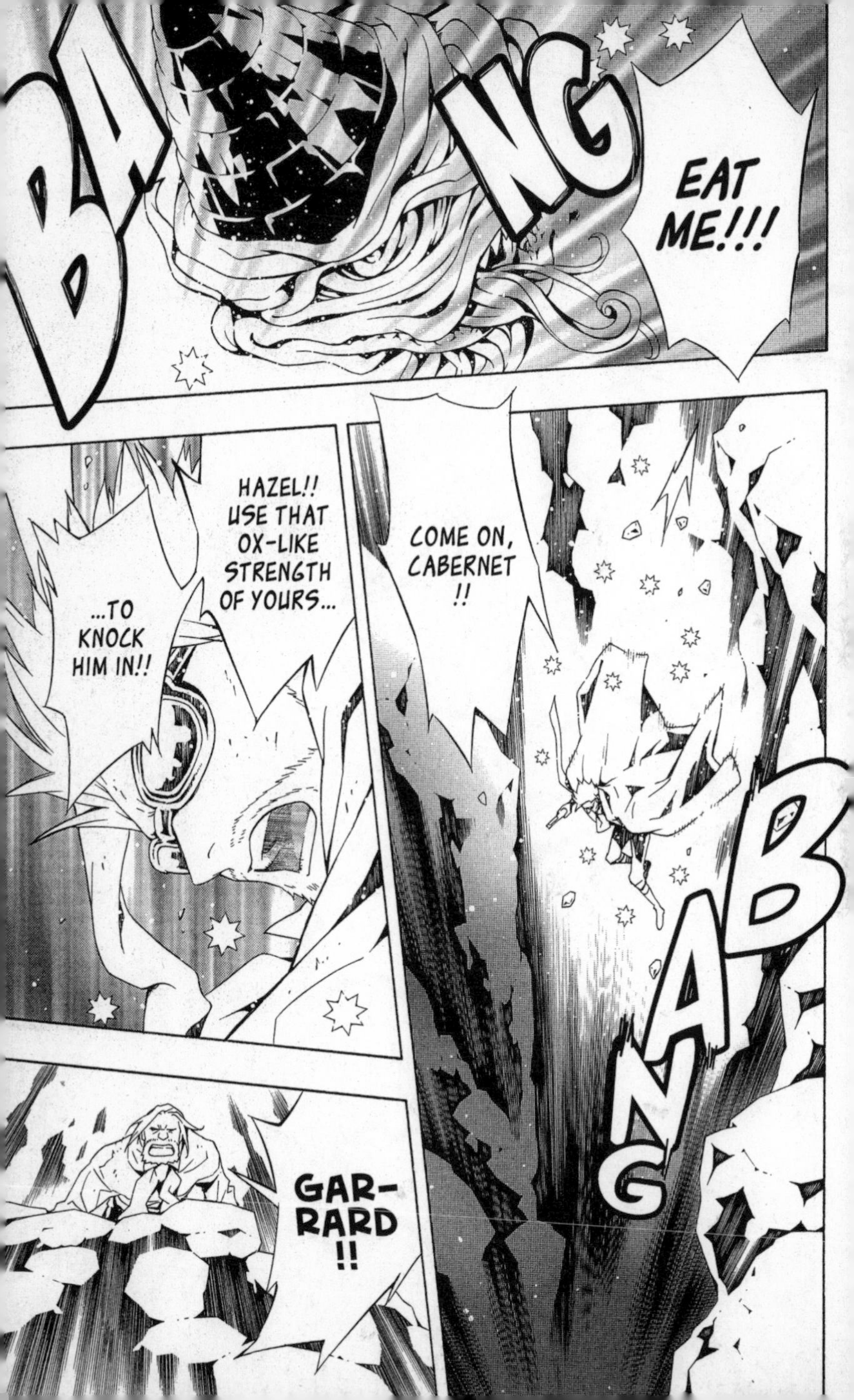
BA
NG
EAT ME!!!
COME ON, CABERNET!!
BANG
HAZEL!! USE THAT OX-LIKE STRENGTH OF YOURS...
...TO KNOCK HIM IN!!
GAR-RARD!!

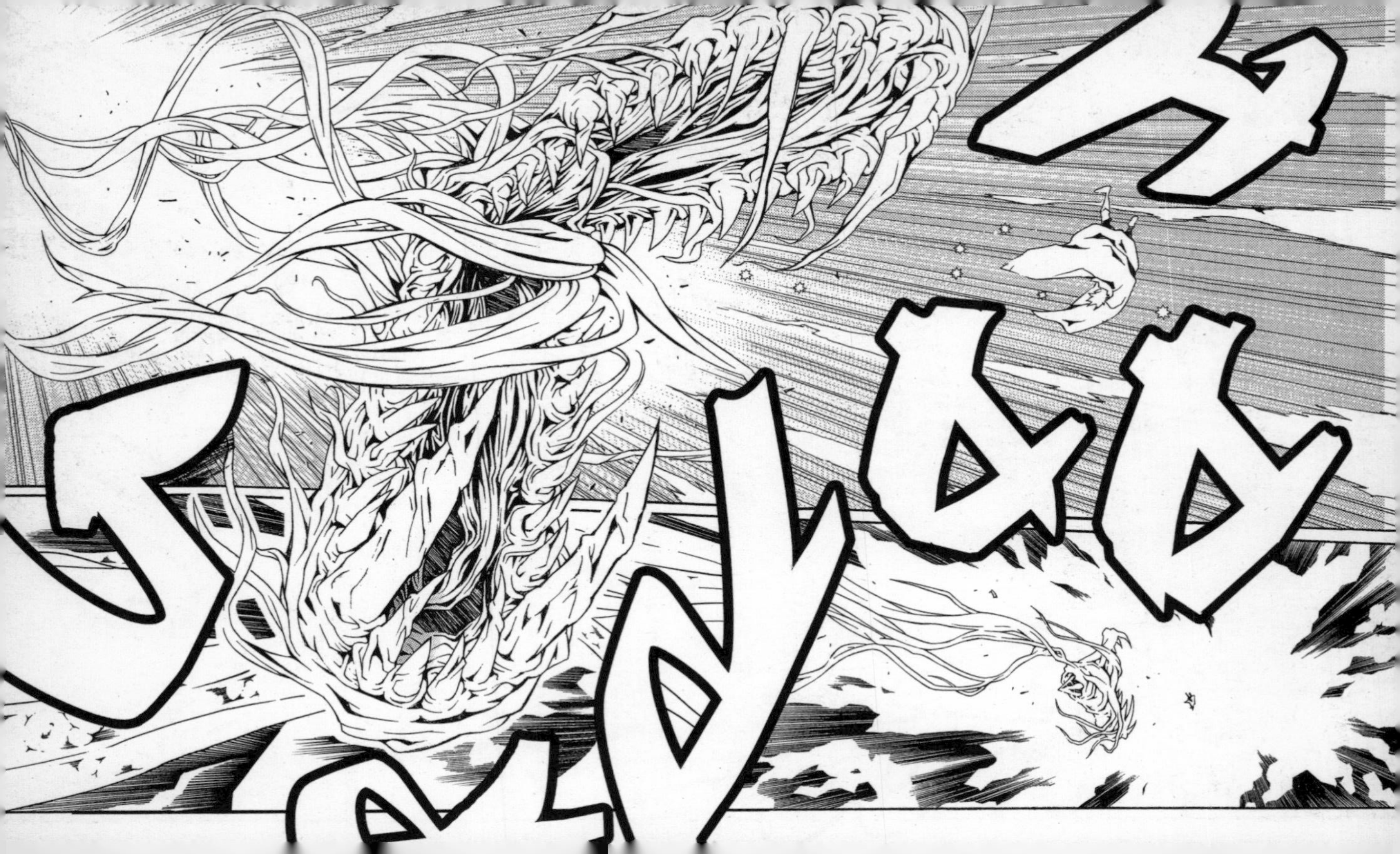

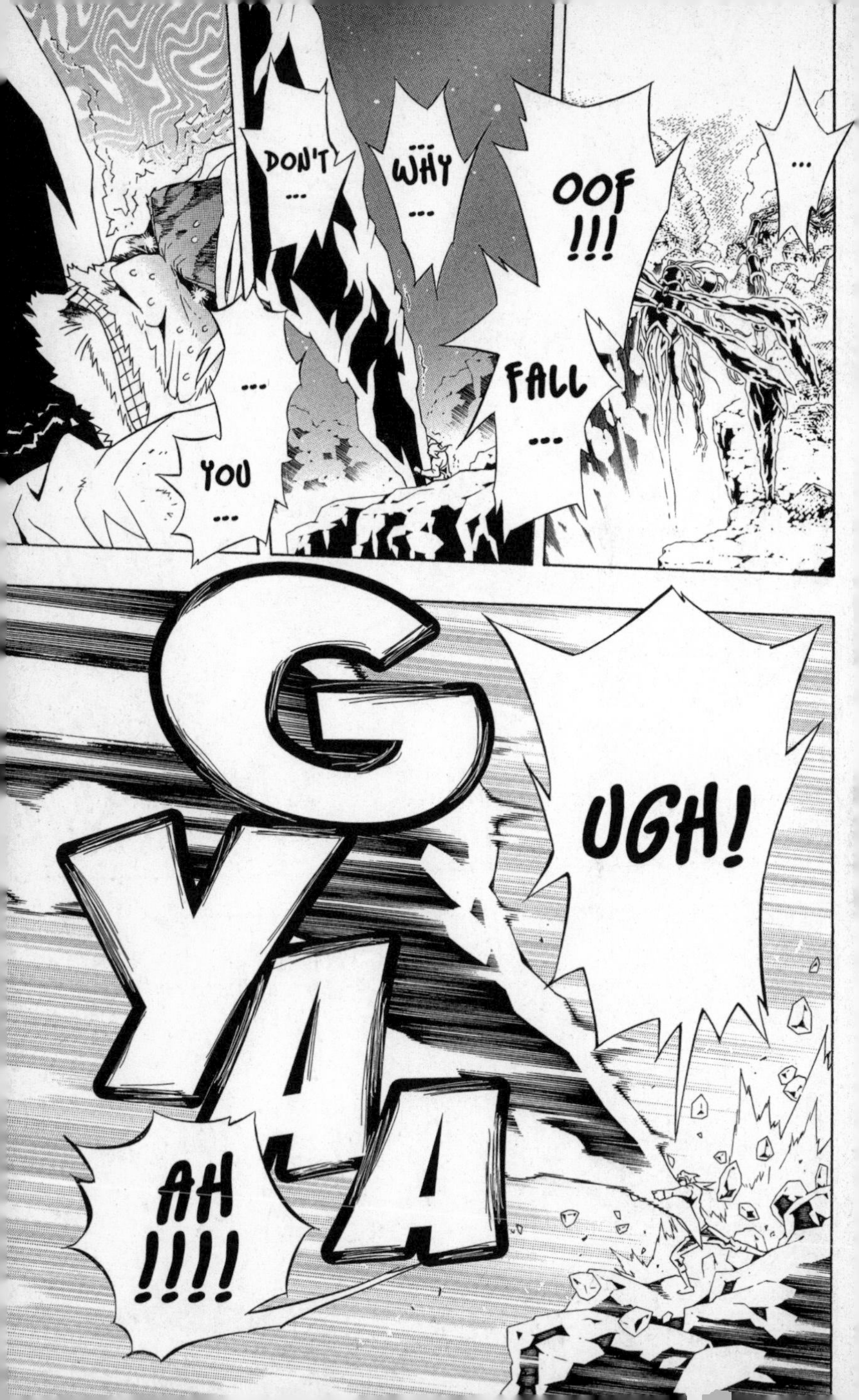
...
OOF !!!
... WHY ...
DON'T ...
FALL ...
... YOU ...
UGH!
GYAA
AH !!!!

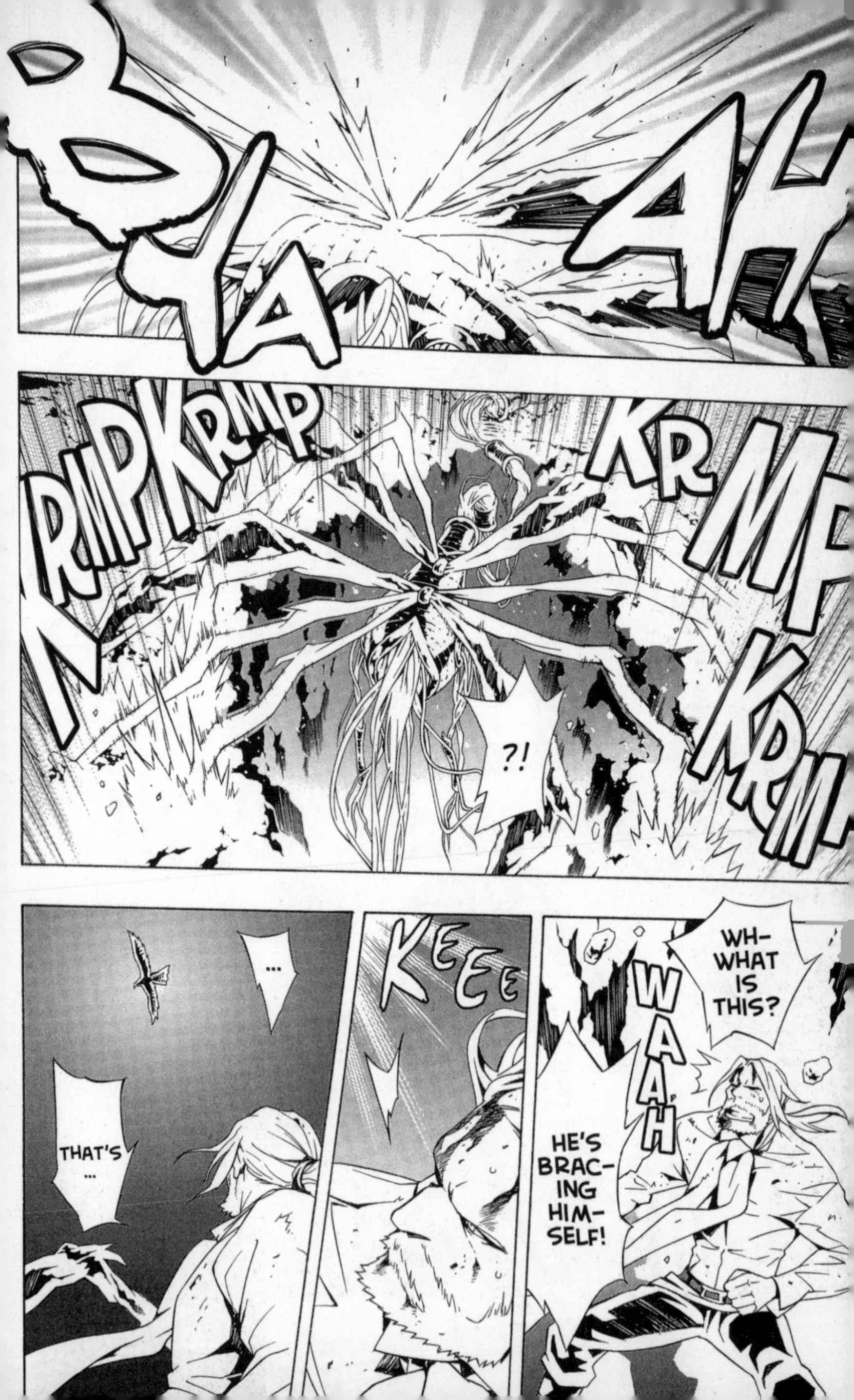
YAAAH
KRMPKRMP
KRMPKRM
?!
WH-WHAT IS THIS?
WAAAH
HE'S BRAC-ING HIM-SELF!
KEEE
...
THAT'S ...

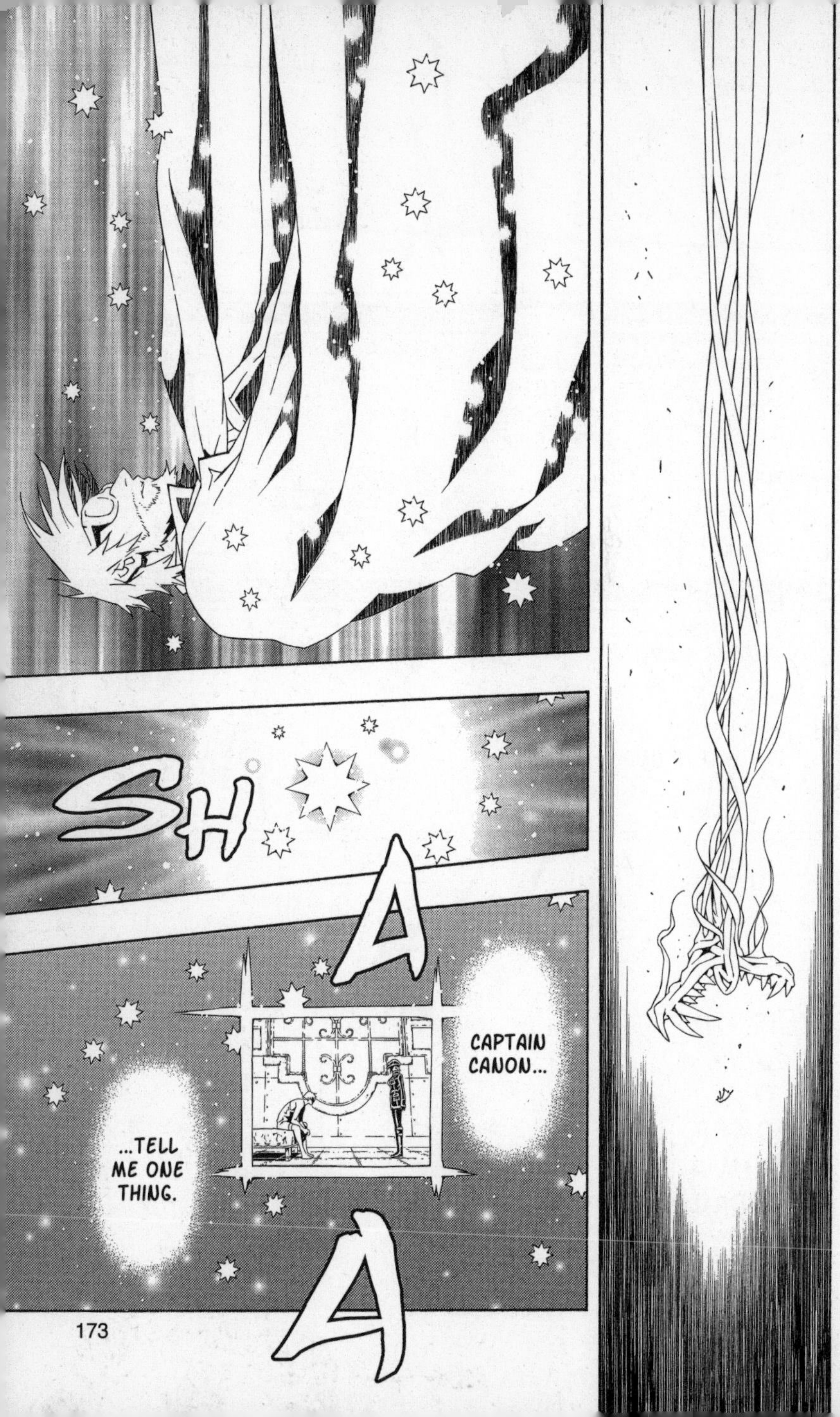
SHAAA
CAPTAIN CANON...
...TELL ME ONE THING.

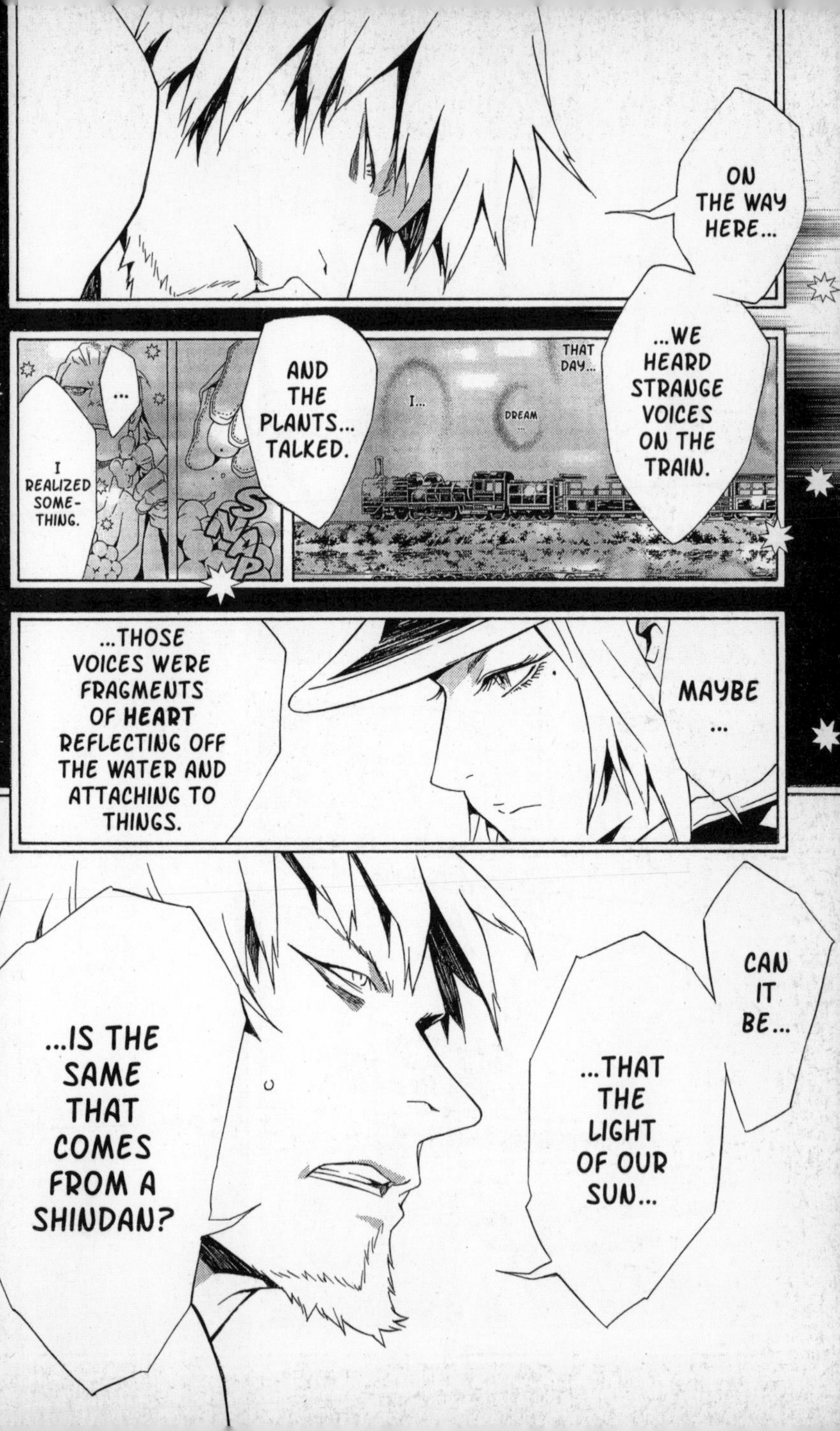
ON THE WAY HERE...
...WE HEARD STRANGE VOICES ON THE TRAIN.
THAT DAY...
DREAM ...
I...
AND THE PLANTS... TALKED.
SNAP
...
I REALIZED SOME-THING.
MAYBE ...
...THOSE VOICES WERE FRAGMENTS OF HEART REFLECTING OFF THE WATER AND ATTACHING TO THINGS.
CAN IT BE...
...THAT THE LIGHT OF OUR SUN...
...IS THE SAME THAT COMES FROM A SHINDAN?

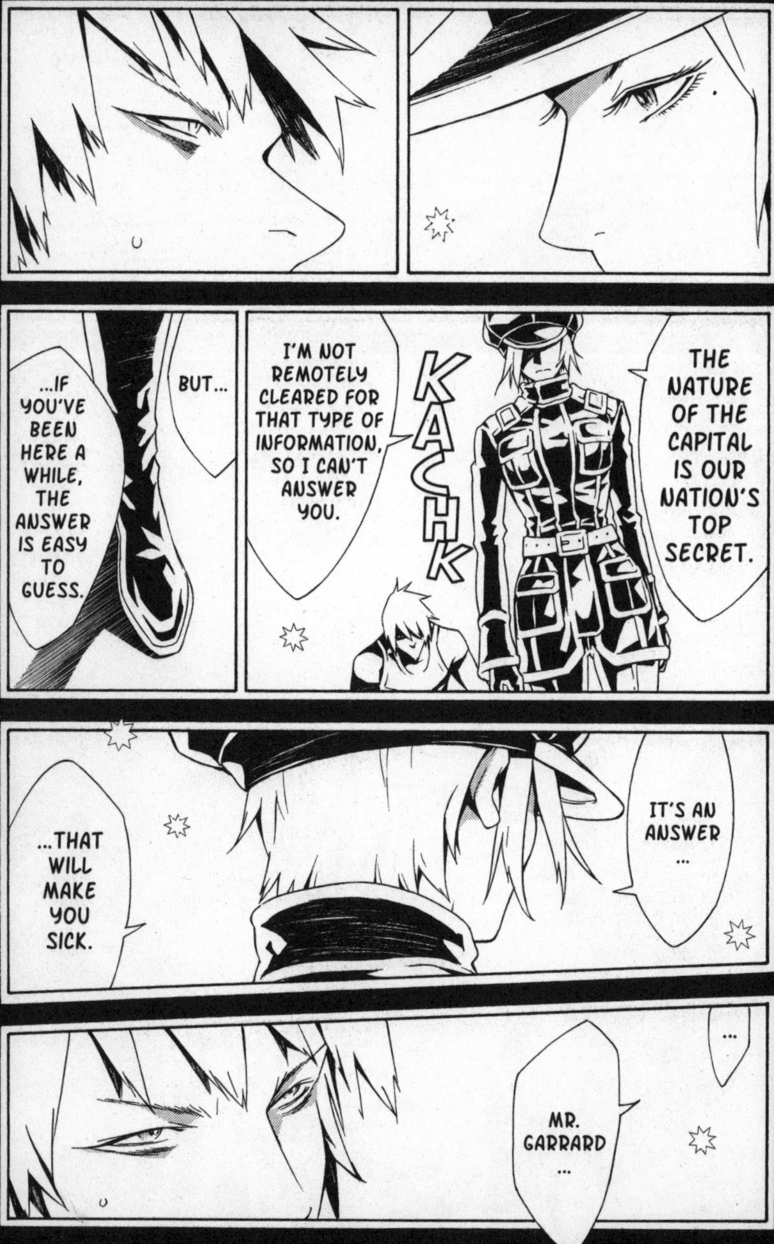
THE NATURE OF THE CAPITAL IS OUR NATION'S TOP SECRET.
KACHK
I'M NOT REMOTELY CLEARED FOR THAT TYPE OF INFORMATION, SO I CAN'T ANSWER YOU.
BUT...
...IF YOU'VE BEEN HERE A WHILE, THE ANSWER IS EASY TO GUESS.
IT'S AN ANSWER ...
...THAT WILL MAKE YOU SICK.
...
MR. GARRARD ...

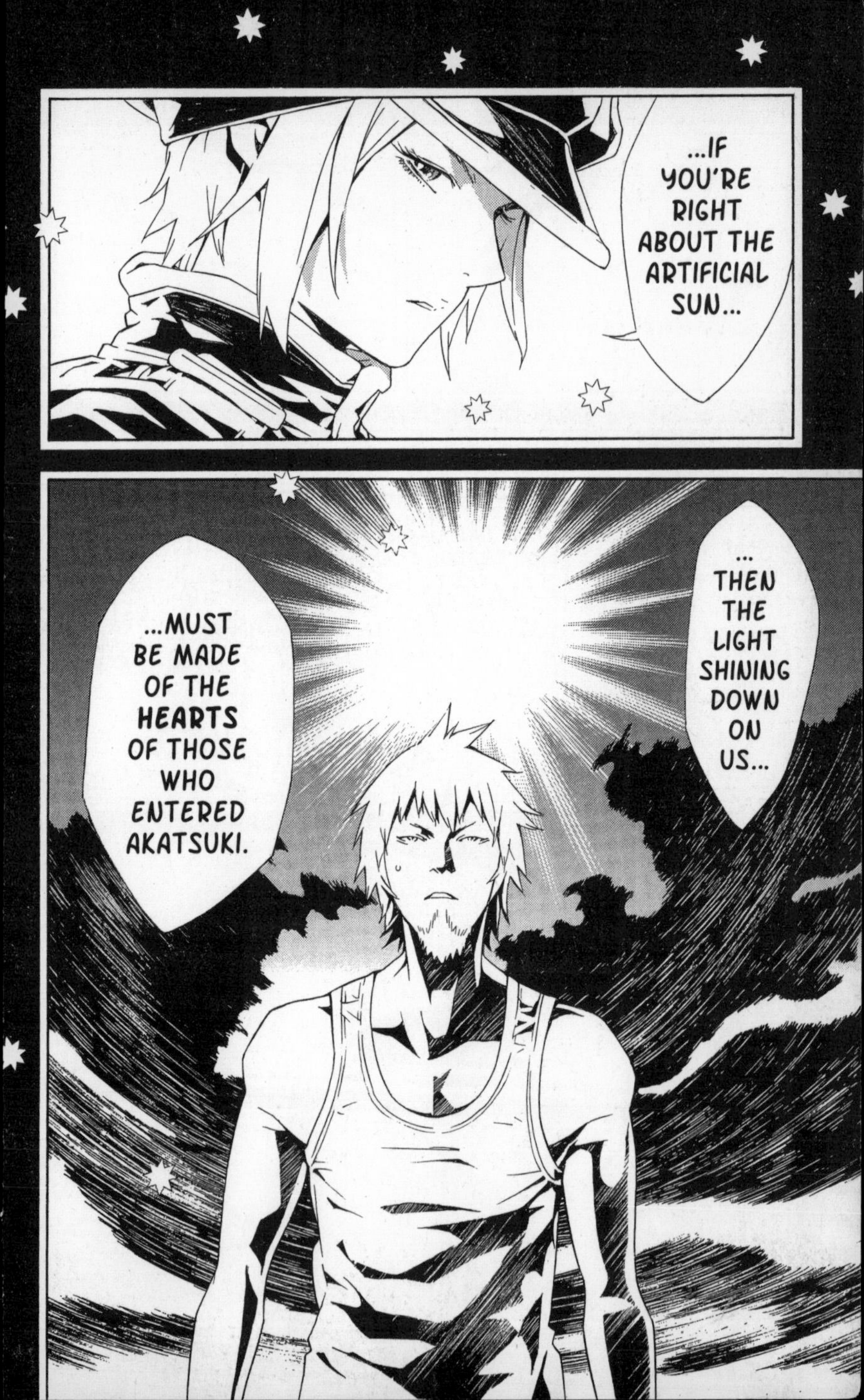
...IF YOU'RE RIGHT ABOUT THE ARTIFICIAL SUN...
... THEN THE LIGHT SHINING DOWN ON US...
...MUST BE MADE OF THE **HEARTS** OF THOSE WHO ENTERED AKATSUKI.

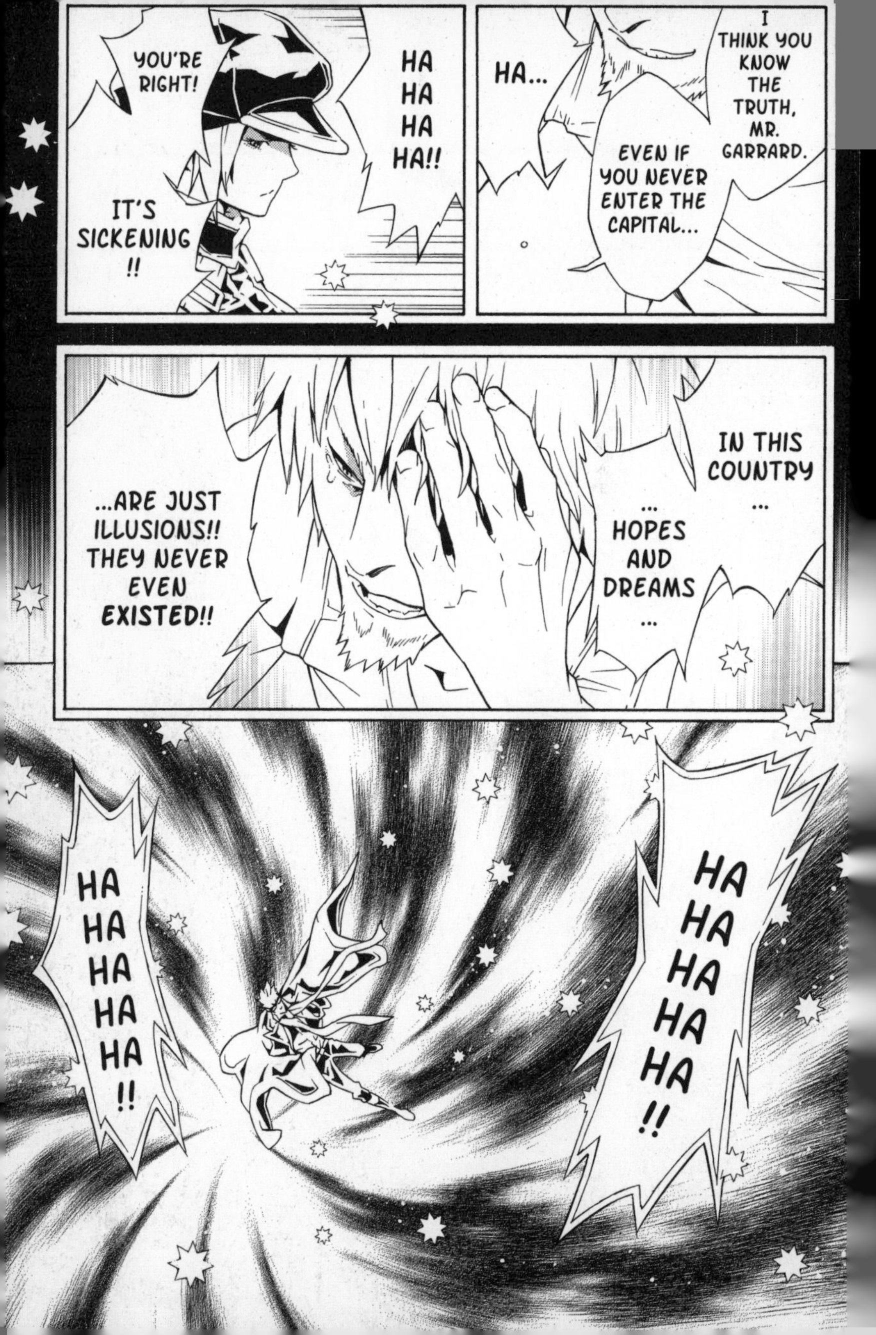
I THINK YOU KNOW THE TRUTH, MR. GARRARD.
EVEN IF YOU NEVER ENTER THE CAPITAL...
HA...
HA HA HA HA!!
YOU'RE RIGHT!
IT'S SICKENING!!
IN THIS COUNTRY...
...HOPES AND DREAMS...
...ARE JUST ILLUSIONS!! THEY NEVER EVEN EXISTED!!
HA HA HA HA HA!!
HA HA HA HA HA!!

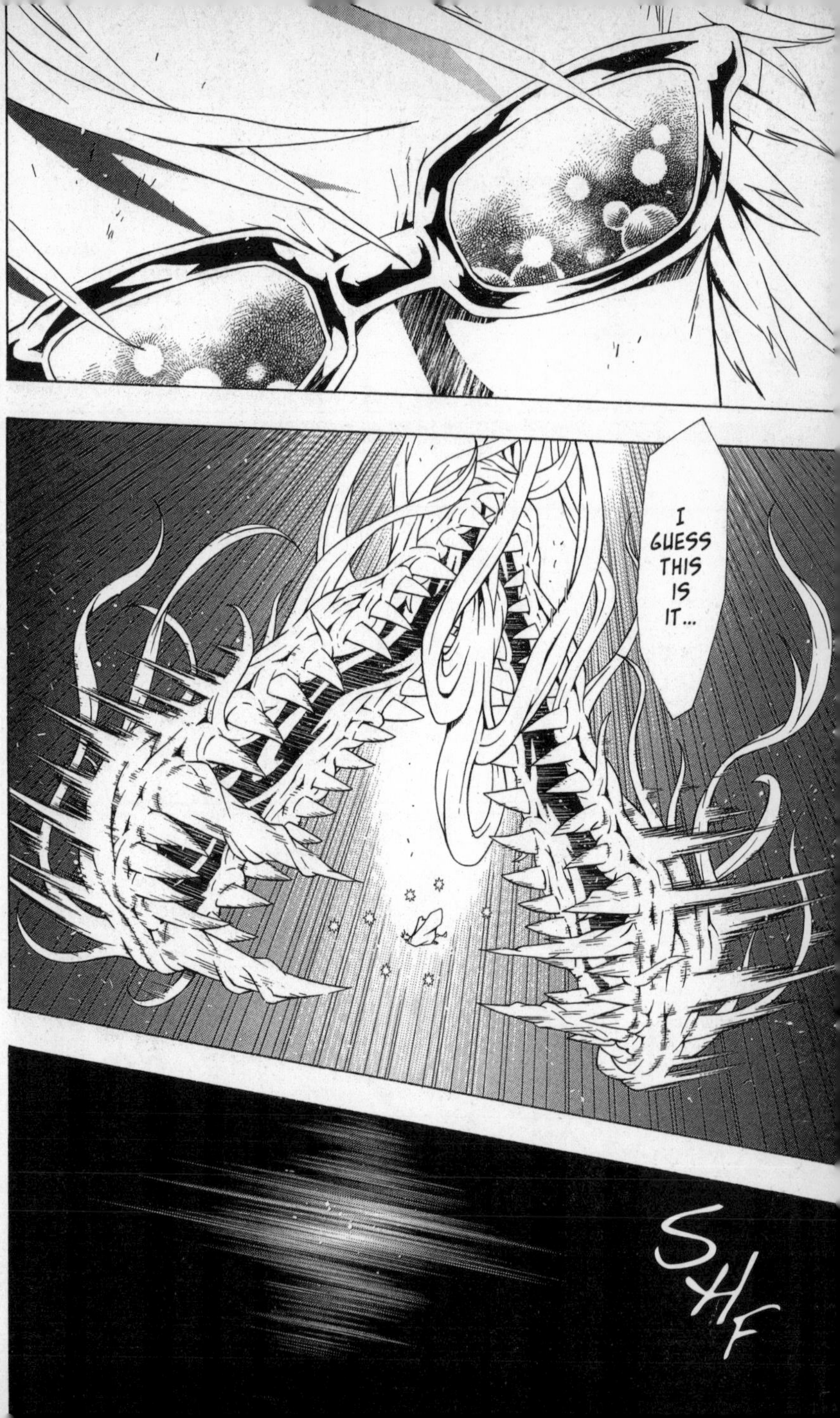
I GUESS THIS IS IT...
SHF

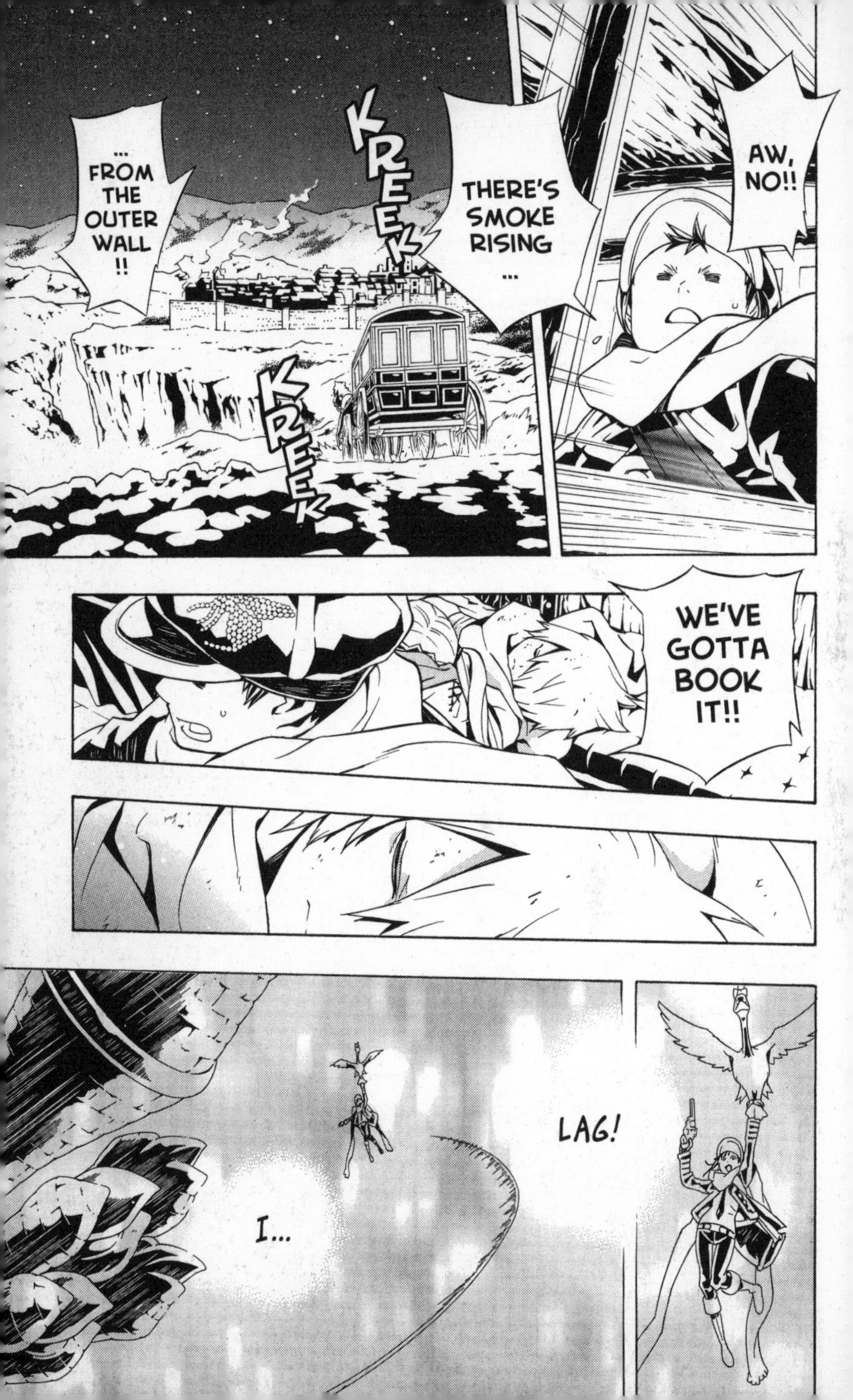
AW, NO!!
THERE'S SMOKE RISING ...
KREEK
KREEK
... FROM THE OUTER WALL !!
WE'VE GOTTA BOOK IT!!
LAG!
I...

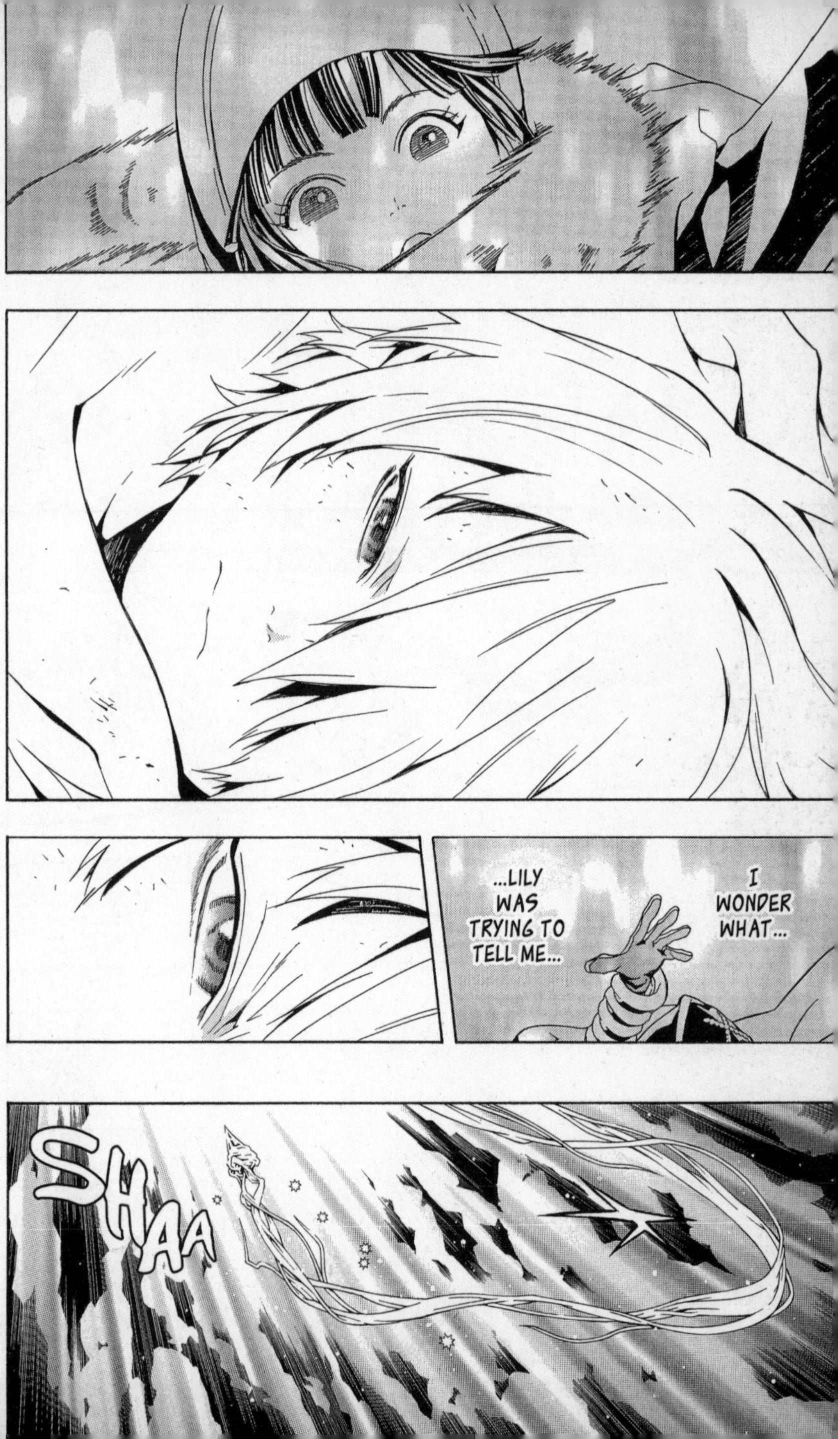
I WONDER WHAT...
...LILY WAS TRYING TO TELL ME...
SHAA

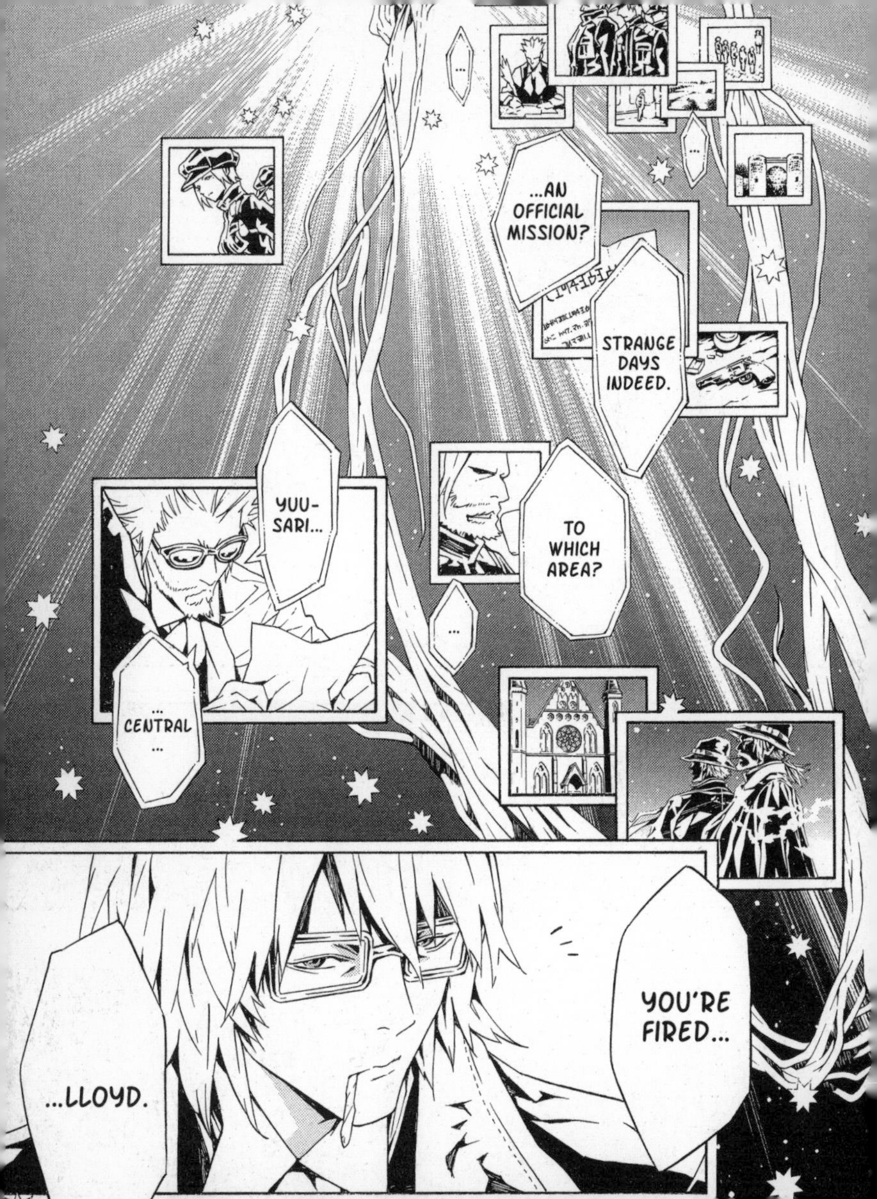
...
...
...AN OFFICIAL MISSION?
STRANGE DAYS INDEED.
TO WHICH AREA?
...
YUU-SARI...
...CENTRAL...
YOU'RE FIRED...
...LLOYD.

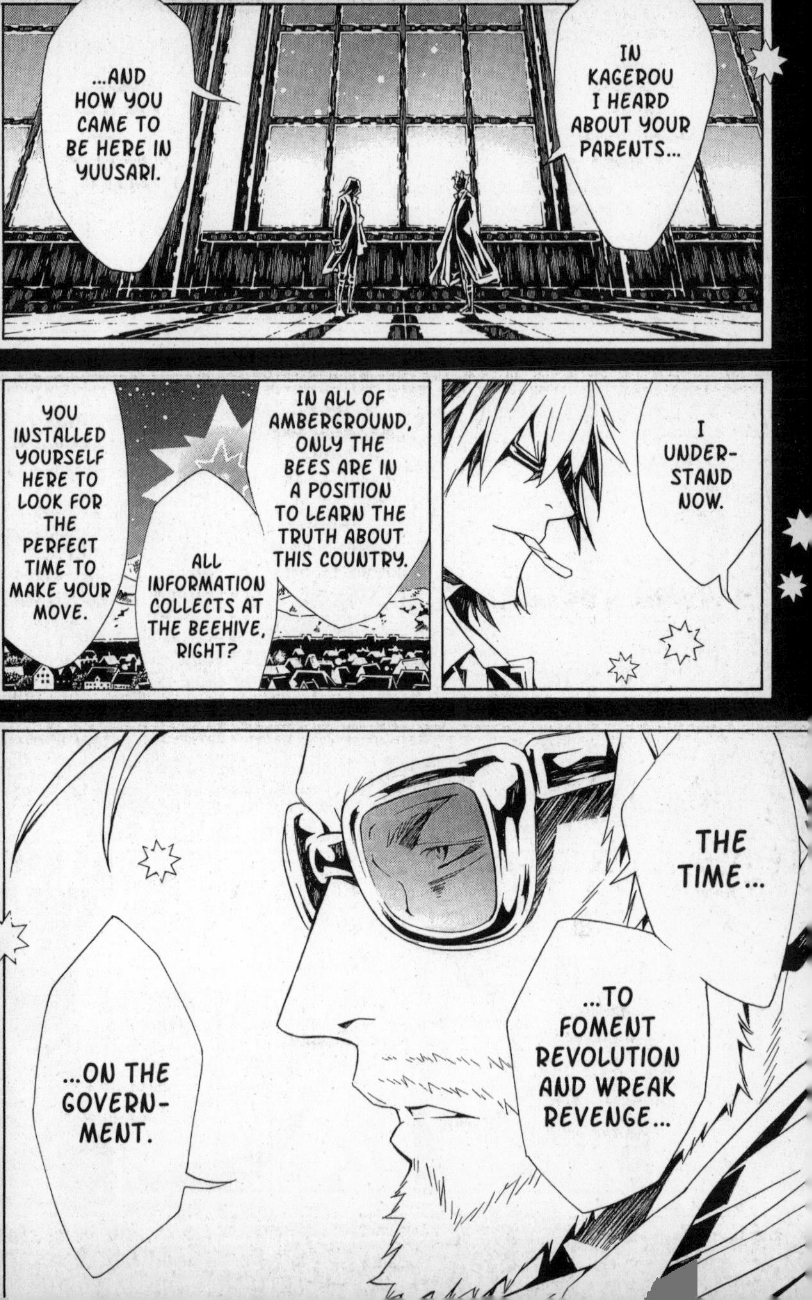
IN KAGEROU I HEARD ABOUT YOUR PARENTS...
...AND HOW YOU CAME TO BE HERE IN YUUSARI.
I UNDER-STAND NOW.
IN ALL OF AMBERGROUND, ONLY THE BEES ARE IN A POSITION TO LEARN THE TRUTH ABOUT THIS COUNTRY.
ALL INFORMATION COLLECTS AT THE BEEHIVE, RIGHT?
YOU INSTALLED YOURSELF HERE TO LOOK FOR THE PERFECT TIME TO MAKE YOUR MOVE.
THE TIME...
...TO FOMENT REVOLUTION AND WREAK REVENGE...
...ON THE GOVERN-MENT.

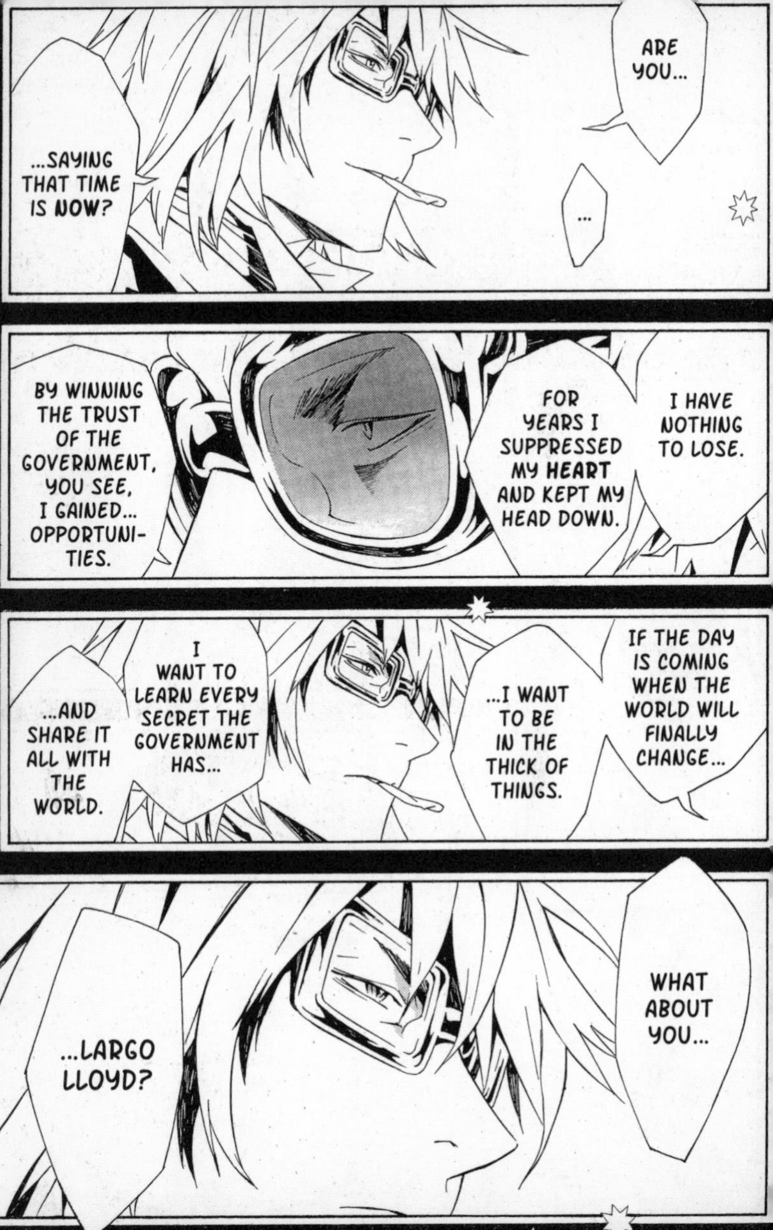
ARE YOU...
...
...SAYING THAT TIME IS NOW?
I HAVE NOTHING TO LOSE.
FOR YEARS I SUPPRESSED MY **HEART** AND KEPT MY HEAD DOWN.
BY WINNING THE TRUST OF THE GOVERNMENT, YOU SEE, I GAINED... OPPORTUNI-TIES.
IF THE DAY IS COMING WHEN THE WORLD WILL FINALLY CHANGE...
...I WANT TO BE IN THE THICK OF THINGS.
I WANT TO LEARN EVERY SECRET THE GOVERNMENT HAS...
...AND SHARE IT ALL WITH THE WORLD.
WHAT ABOUT YOU...
...LARGO LLOYD?

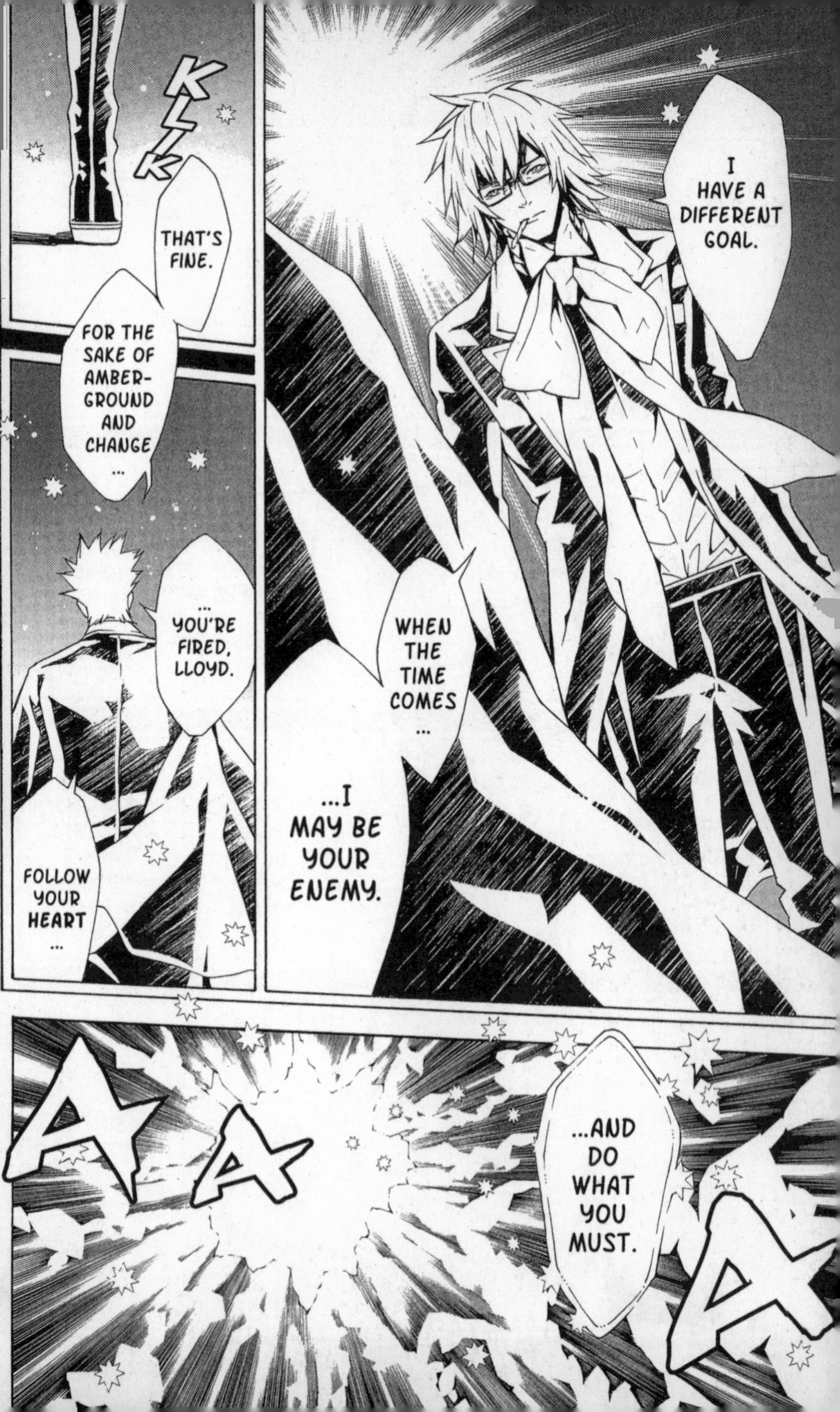
I HAVE A DIFFERENT GOAL.
WHEN THE TIME COMES...
...I MAY BE YOUR ENEMY.
KLIK
THAT'S FINE.
FOR THE SAKE OF AMBER-GROUND AND CHANGE...
...YOU'RE FIRED, LLOYD.
FOLLOW YOUR HEART...
...AND DO WHAT YOU MUST.
AAA

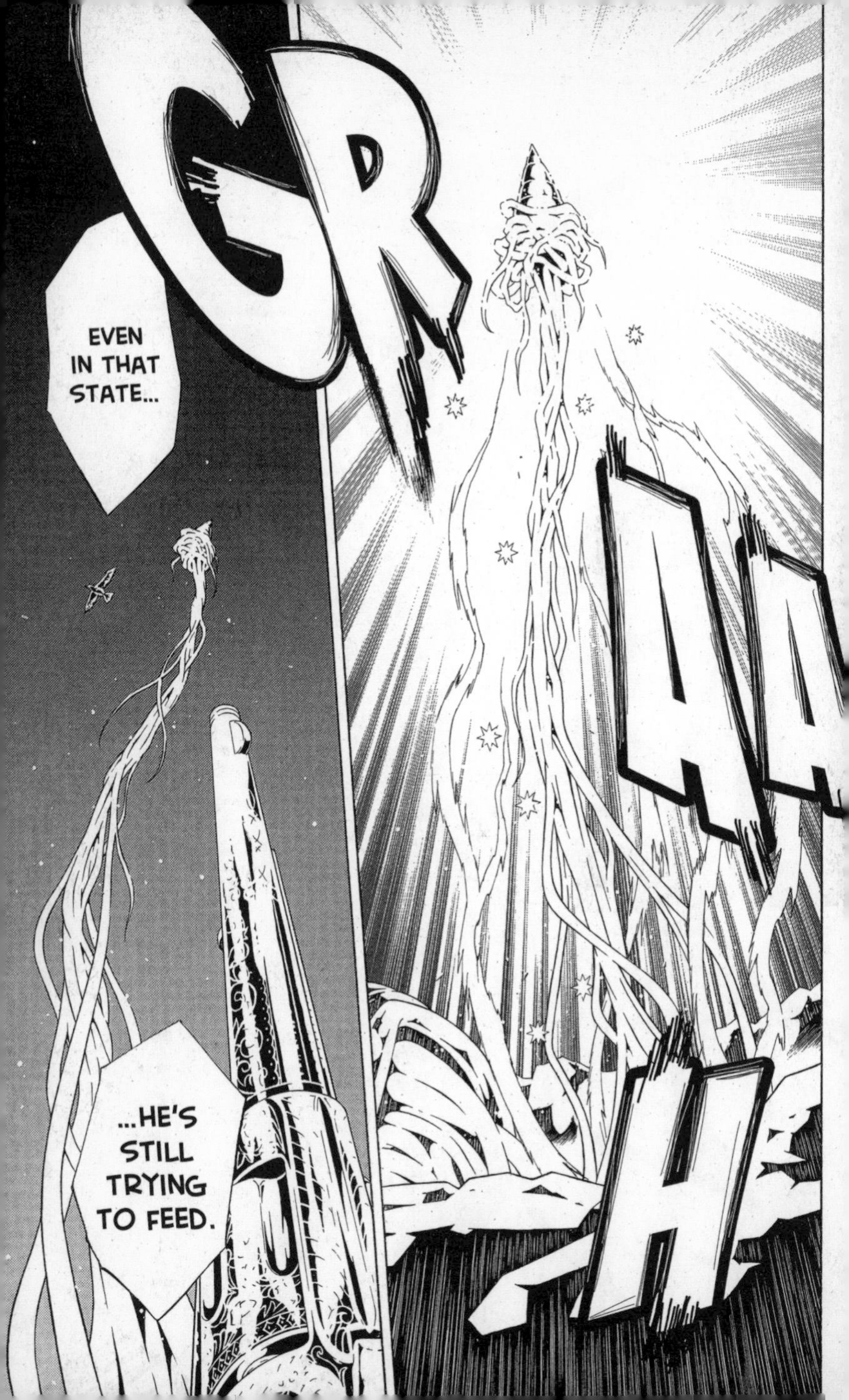
GRAAH
EVEN IN THAT STATE...
...HE'S STILL TRYING TO FEED.

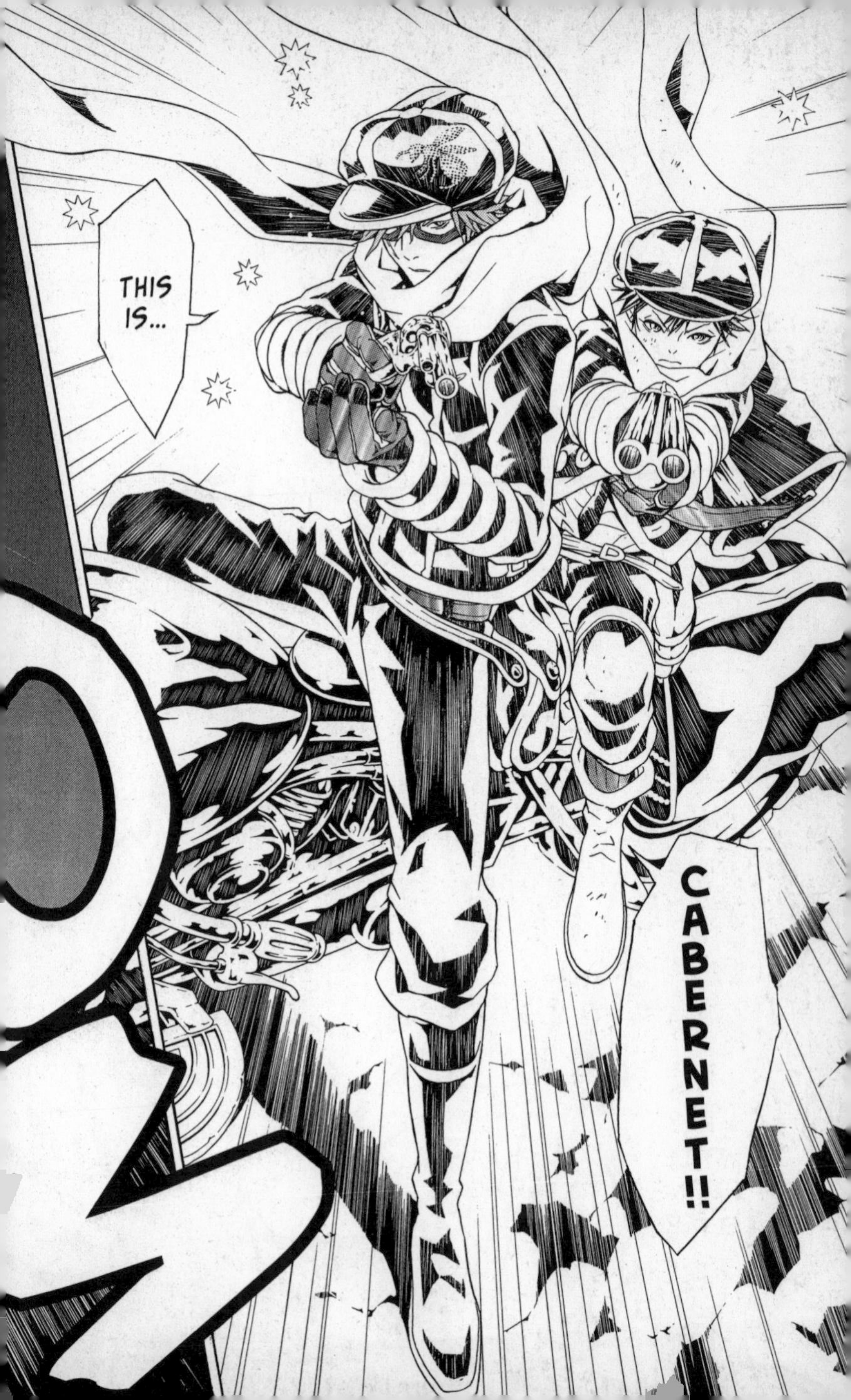
THIS IS...
CABERNET!!

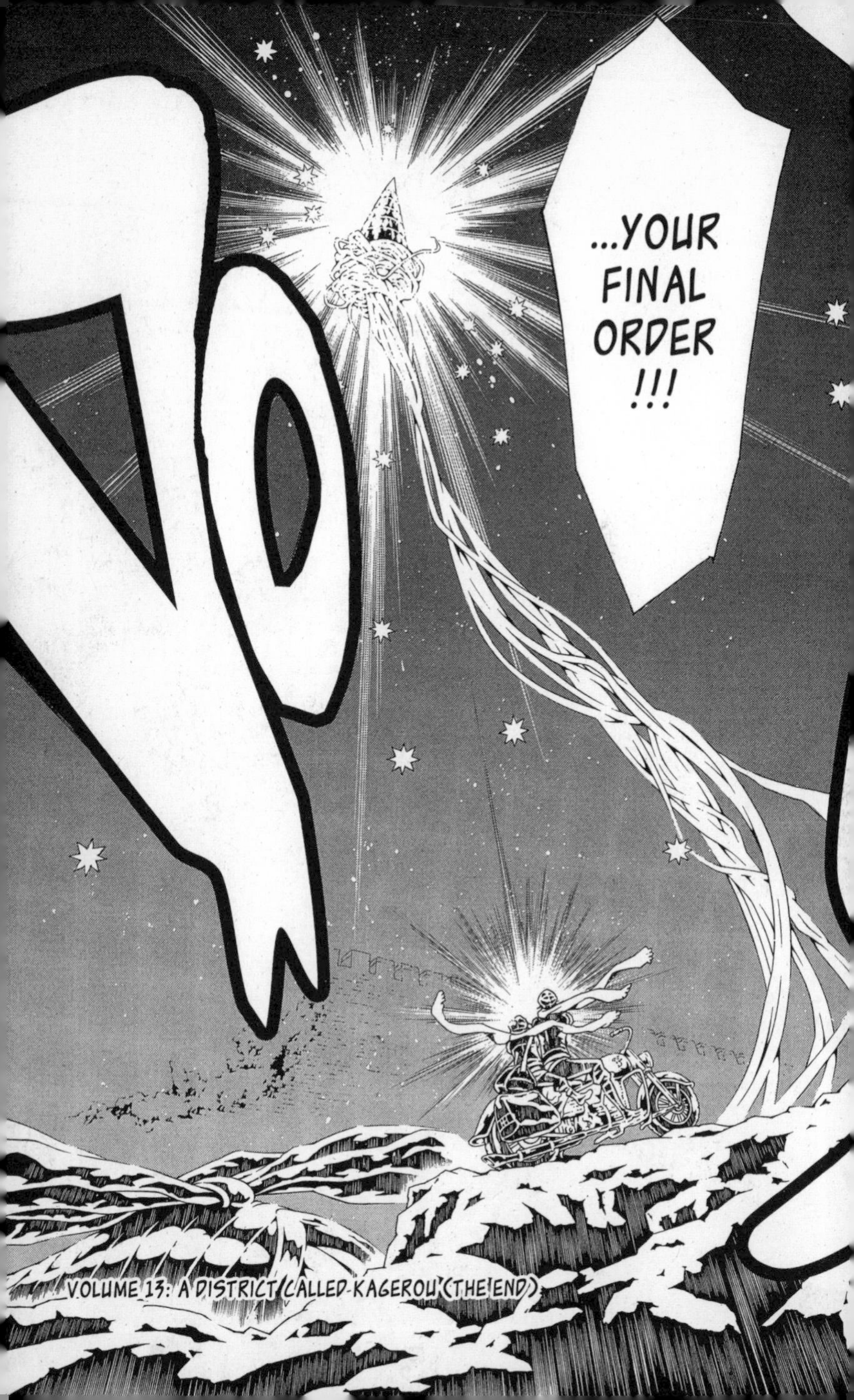
...YOUR FINAL ORDER !!!
VOLUME 13: A DISTRICT CALLED KAGEROU (THE END)

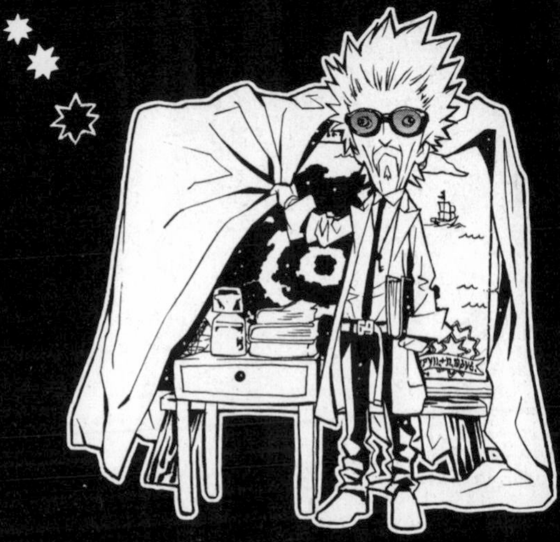

Dr. Thunderland's Reference Desk

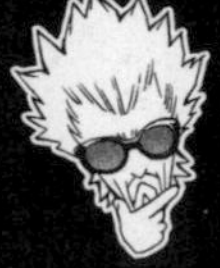

Have you read this volume? What's up with it? Page after page, it's packed with...old guys!! You fresh-faced kiddies buying the series are crying now, aren't you? What's the target audience supposed to be? This volume won't sell, I tell you!!

And yet...the whole book is full of old guys, but *I'm not in it!!*

As always, I work at the Beehive in Yuusari, researching this and that. I'm even kind enough to answer your questions concerning the world depicted in this manga. I'm an old man, but I'm not in this old-man volume! This was a golden opportunity for me to appear. Do I mean nothing?

■ LARGO AND BARROL LLOYD

Sorry for the rant. But soon-to-be-old-man Largo Lloyd made a big confession in this volume! I figured there was something up with him, but to think he was plotting revenge from the Beehive all along...

It seems Largo's father is Barrol, who was on that ill-fated investigative airship! And his mother was used as a guinea pig in Kagerou...as was Largo. Sounds like there are all sorts of complicated issues here. This is deep...

Now Largo has returned to Yuusari. I bet his dad helped him get that job at the Beehive. But no one guessed he would align himself not with the Bees, but with Reverse... Maybe he decided it was impossible to start a revolution from within.

What could be in that book he lifted from the library in Kagerou? I'd like to know...

■ KAGEROU

You can't go directly from Yuusari to Akatsuki, the capital. There's an area in between called Kagerou. It was in the laboratories of Kagerou that Lawrence and the others "who could not become spirit" were created and cast out. And that gatekeeper, Seine, who saw into Garrard's heart...we've seen him before, haven't we? He was one of the triplets in chapter 38 of volume 10!

But destroying Garrard's entire self-worth, after he gambled everything to get that far, was harsh. Garrard said he suppressed his *heart* after that, which is how he was able to return to Yuusari. Perhaps he'll find another reason to live.

But something about that Captain Canon had me... *ahem*...standing at attention! What a formidable young woman! I wonder how she's grown up... Captain, please turn your disdainful stare toward me! I salute you! No, cut me off even *more* cruelly! Yes, Captain! Yes!

nb: Partita for Solo Violin No. 3, Third Movement (*Gavotte en Rondeau*) / Composition by Johann Sebastian Bach known popularly as Bach's Gavotte.

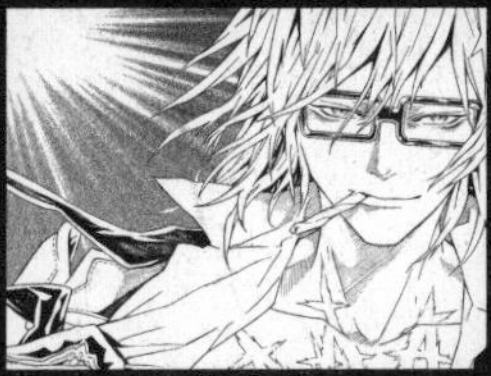
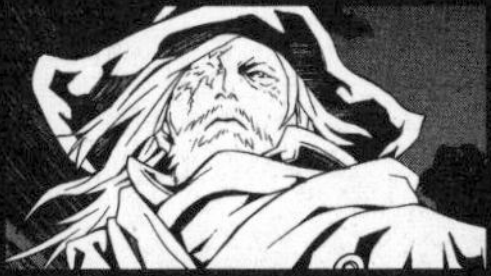
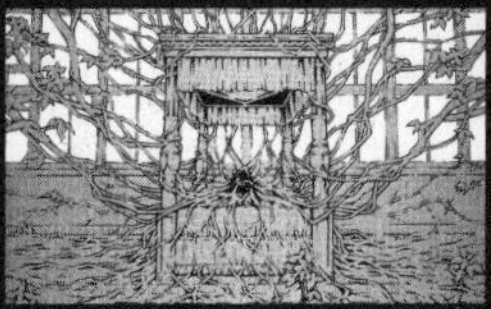
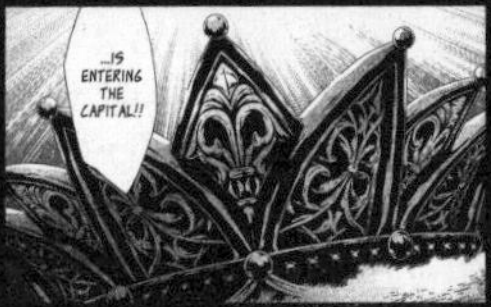
...IS ENTERING THE CAPITAL!!
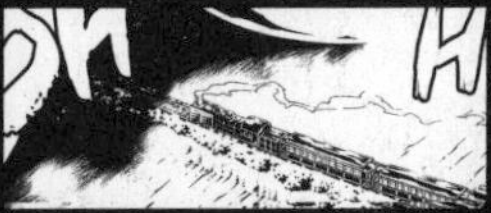
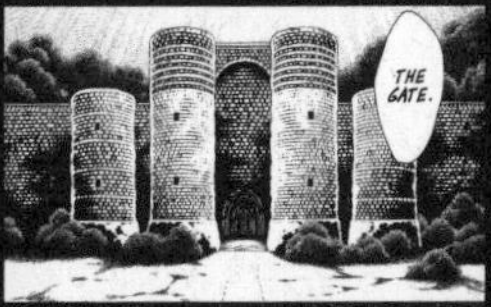
THE GATE.
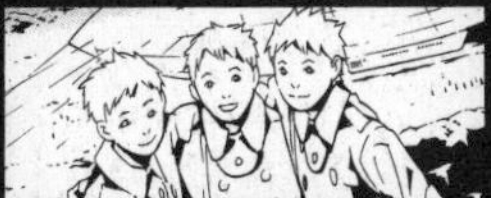
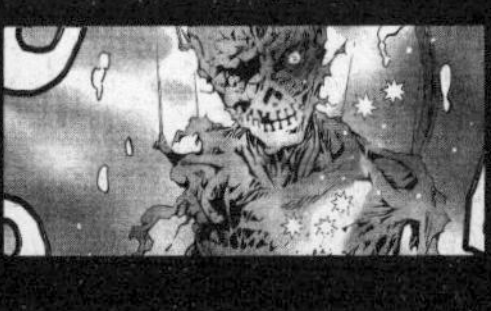

nb: Ramblin' Jack Elliot (1931) / American folk singer of Jewish descent who strongly influenced the young Bob Dylan.

■ LIGHT OF THE ARTIFICIAL SUN
Could it be that terrible sacrifices have been made for our sunlight? No...I can't speculate any further here. Garrard and Hazel...Zazie, Jiggy, Aria, Moc, Connor... and...and...Lag!! I must focus on them and the threat facing them!! They have to defeat Cabernet before anything else! Otherwise Yuusari will be destroyed and the Letter Bees will be annihilated! The story will end! Worst of all, I'll never get my cameo!!

■ THE YUUSARI BELL
Rung in different ways, this signal bell has different meanings. The people of Yodaka and Yuusari, who are constantly threatened by Gaichuu, get reports through the bell and act accordingly. Of course, the urgency level this time is extreme. Run, everyone!

But even in the mass evacuation, I'm nowhere to be seen. Isn't that strange? Why aren't I there? Why, why, why? But I don't mind. In this volume, no one gets to appear except those old guys! Ha! Not Noir, and not even Lag, the main character!!! What a laugh!!

Now all you major characters feel my pain! But we're off and running now. I have a feeling that things are going to get mighty hairy in the next volume. Gather round, Bees! Everyone's joining the fight!! Perhaps even me!! I'd better start building up my muscles!! FLEX!!

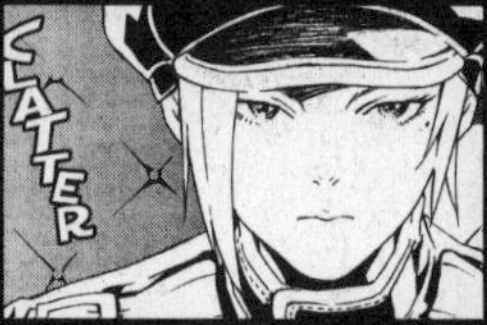
CLATTER

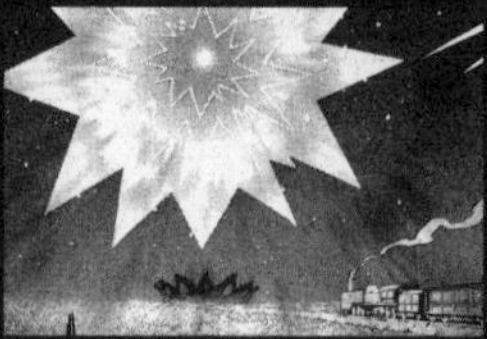

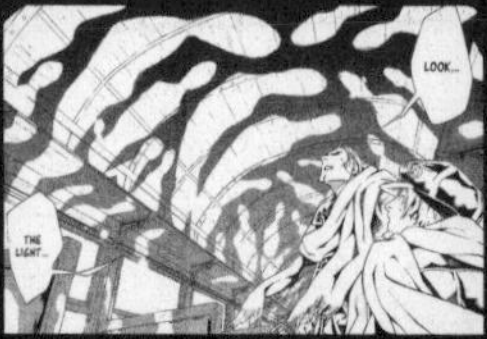
LOOK...
THE LIGHT...

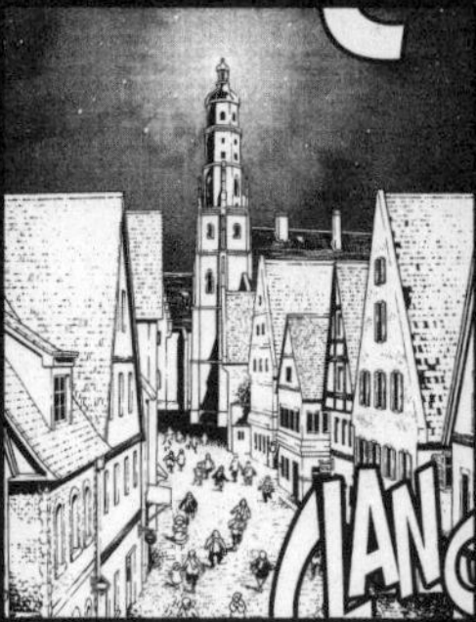

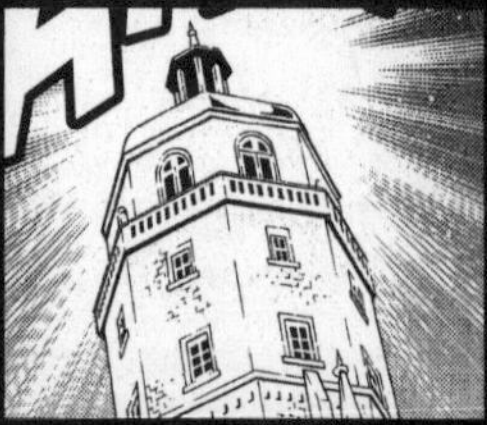

Route Map

Finally, I am including a map, indicating Lag's route and Cabernet's flight path, created at Lonely Goatherd Map Station of Central Yuusari.

A: Akatsuki B: Yuusari C: Yodaka

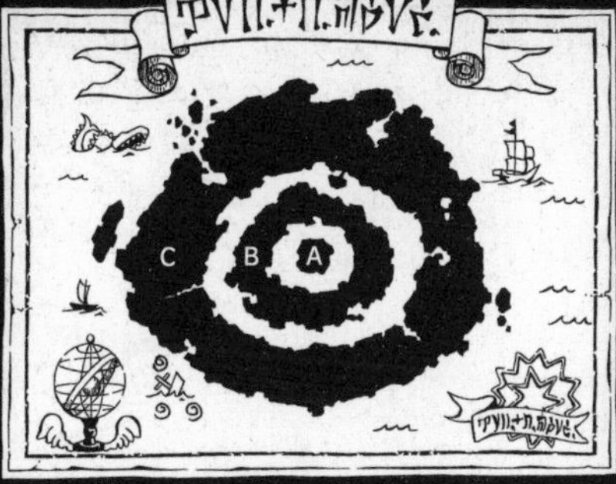
C
B
A

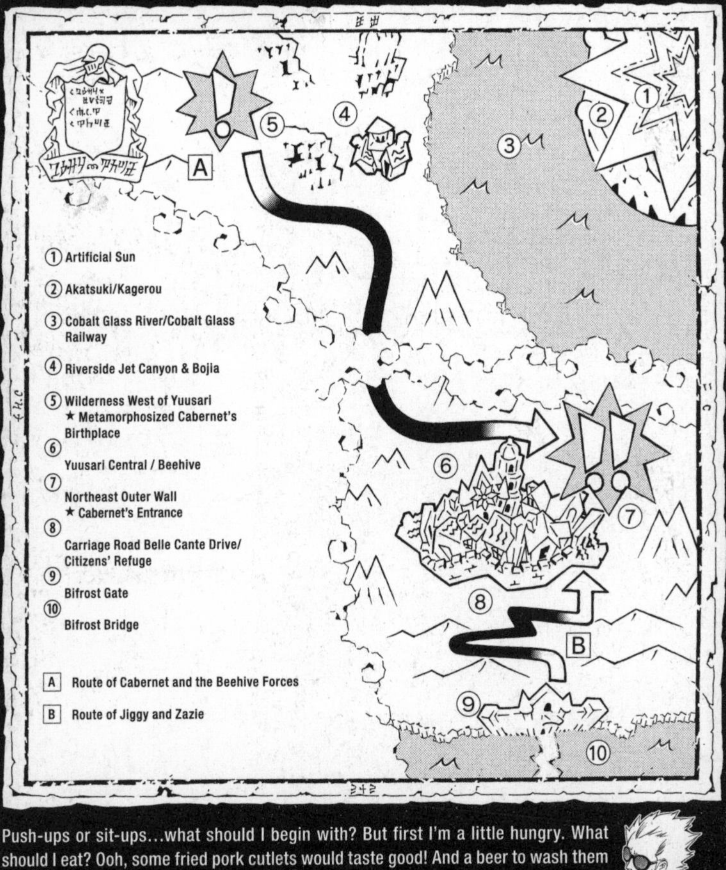
① Artificial Sun
② Akatsuki/Kagerou
③ Cobalt Glass River/Cobalt Glass Railway
④ Riverside Jet Canyon & Bojia
⑤ Wilderness West of Yuusari
★ Metamorphosized Cabernet's Birthplace
⑥ Yuusari Central / Beehive
⑦ Northeast Outer Wall
★ Cabernet's Entrance
⑧ Carriage Road Belle Cante Drive/ Citizens' Refuge
⑨ Bifrost Gate
⑩ Bifrost Bridge
A Route of Cabernet and the Beehive Forces
B Route of Jiggy and Zazie
A
B

Push-ups or sit-ups...what should I begin with? But first I'm a little hungry. What should I eat? Ooh, some fried pork cutlets would taste good! And a beer to wash them down! *Glug glug! Munch munch!* Ahh, this pork is delicious! This is a man's meal! I'm sleepy now...Good night...

In the next volume...

A Letter from Mother

The battle against Cabernet grows desperate, forcing friends and
foes to join forces against the seemingly unstoppable Gaichuu.
Niche undergoes a shocking change. And Lag finds a hidden
message from his long-lost mother...

Available August 2013!